DISCARDED

DICTIONARY

OF

AMERICAN BIOGRAPHY

PUBLISHED UNDER THE AUSPICES OF
THE AMERICAN COUNCIL OF LEARNED SOCIETIES

The American Council of Learned Societies, organized in 1919 for the purpose of advancing the study of the humanities and of the humanistic aspects of the social sciences, is a nonprofit federation comprising forty-three national scholarly groups. The Council represents the humanities in the United States in the International Union of Academies, provides fellowships and grants-in-aid, supports research-and-planning conferences and symposia, and sponsors special projects and scholarly publications.

MEMBER ORGANIZATIONS
AMERICAN PHILOSOPHICAL SOCIETY, 1743
AMERICAN ACADEMY OF ARTS AND SCIENCES, 1780
AMERICAN ANTIQUARIAN SOCIETY, 1812
AMERICAN ORIENTAL SOCIETY, 1842
AMERICAN NUMISMATIC SOCIETY, 1858
AMERICAN PHILOLOGICAL ASSOCIATION, 1869
ARCHAEOLOGICAL INSTITUTE OF AMERICA, 1879
SOCIETY OF BIBLICAL LITERATURE, 1880
MODERN LANGUAGE ASSOCIATION OF AMERICA, 1883
AMERICAN HISTORICAL ASSOCIATION, 1884
AMERICAN ECONOMIC ASSOCIATION, 1885
AMERICAN FOLKLORE SOCIETY, 1888
AMERICAN DIALECT SOCIETY, 1889
AMERICAN PSYCHOLOGICAL ASSOCIATION, 1892
ASSOCIATION OF AMERICAN LAW SCHOOLS, 1900
AMERICAN PHILOSOPHICAL ASSOCIATION, 1901
AMERICAN ANTHROPOLOGICAL ASSOCIATION, 1902
AMERICAN POLITICAL SCIENCE ASSOCIATION, 1903
BIBLIOGRAPHICAL SOCIETY OF AMERICA, 1904
ASSOCIATION OF AMERICAN GEOGRAPHERS, 1904
HISPANIC SOCIETY OF AMERICA, 1904
AMERICAN SOCIOLOGICAL ASSOCIATION, 1905
AMERICAN SOCIETY OF INTERNATIONAL LAW, 1906
ORGANIZATION OF AMERICAN HISTORIANS, 1907
COLLEGE ART ASSOCIATION OF AMERICA, 1912
HISTORY OF SCIENCE SOCIETY, 1924
LINGUISTIC SOCIETY OF AMERICA, 1924
MEDIAEVAL ACADEMY OF AMERICA, 1925
AMERICAN MUSICOLOGICAL SOCIETY, 1934
SOCIETY OF ARCHITECTURAL HISTORIANS, 1940
ECONOMIC HISTORY ASSOCIATION, 1940
ASSOCIATION FOR ASIAN STUDIES, 1941
AMERICAN SOCIETY FOR AESTHETICS, 1942
METAPHYSICAL SOCIETY OF AMERICA, 1950
AMERICAN STUDIES ASSOCIATION, 1950
RENAISSANCE SOCIETY OF AMERICA, 1954
SOCIETY FOR ETHNOMUSICOLOGY, 1955
AMERICAN SOCIETY FOR LEGAL HISTORY, 1956
AMERICAN SOCIETY FOR THEATRE RESEARCH, 1956
SOCIETY FOR THE HISTORY OF TECHNOLOGY, 1958
AMERICAN COMPARATIVE LITERATURE ASSOCIATION, 1960
AMERICAN ACADEMY OF RELIGION, 1963
AMERICAN SOCIETY FOR EIGHTEENTH-CENTURY STUDIES, 1969

DICTIONARY
OF
American Biography

Complete Index Guide

Volumes I–X
Supplements 1–7

Charles Scribner's Sons

NEW YORK

Copyright © 1981 Charles Scribner's Sons

Library of Congress Cataloging in Publication Data

Main entry under title:

Dictionary of American biography.

1. Dictionary of American biography—Indexes.
2. United States—Biography—Indexes. I. American
Council of Learned Societies.
E176.D563 Index   920′.073   81–9216
ISBN 0–684–17152–X   AACR2

1 3 5 7 9 11 13 15 17 19   V/C   20 18 16 14 12 10 8 6 4 2

Printed in the United States of America

Editorial Staff

DICTIONARY

OF

AMERICAN BIOGRAPHY

COMPLETE INDEX GUIDE

The following is a combined complete alphabetical listing of all entries in Volumes I-X and Supplements 1-7 of the *Dictionary of American Biography*. References to volumes in the parent set are in Roman numerals. References to the Supplement are in Arabic numerals.

Name	Vol./Supp	Name	Vol./Supp.
Abbe, Cleveland	I	Abercromby, James	I
Abbett, Leon	I	Abernethy, George	I
Abbey, Edwin Austin	I	Abert, John James	1
Abbey, Henry	I	Aborn, Milton	1
Abbey, Henry Eugene	I	Abrams, Albert	I
Abbot, Benjamin	I	Abt, Isaac Arthur	5
Abbot, Ezra	I	Accau (Accault) Michel	
Abbot, Francis Ellingwood	I	See Aco, Michel	
Abbot, Gorham Dummer	I	Acheson, Edward Goodrich	1
Abbot, Henry Larcom	I	Acker, Charles Ernest	I
Abbot, Joel	I	Aco, Michel	I
Abbot, Willis John	1	Acosta, Bertram Blanchard	
Abbott, Austin	I	("Bert")	5
Abbott, Benjamin	I	Acrelius, Israel	I
Abbott, Benjamin Vaughan	I	Adair, James	I
Abbott, Charles Conrad	I	Adair, John	I
Abbott, Edith	6	Adamic, Louis	5
Abbott, Edward	I	Adams, Abigail	I
Abbott, Eleanor Hallowell	6	Adams, Abijah	I
Abbott, Emma	I	Adams, Alva	I
Abbott, Frank	I	Adams, Alvin	I
Abbott, Frank Frost	I	Adams, Andrew	I
Abbott, Grace	2	Adams, Andy	1
Abbott, Horace	I	Adams, Annette Abbott	6
Abbott, Jacob	I	Adams, Brooks	I
Abbott, John Stevens Cabot	I	Adams, Charles	I
Abbott, Joseph Carter	I	Adams, Charles Baker	I
Abbott, Lyman	I	Adams, Charles Follen	I
Abbott, Robert Sengstacke	2	Adams, Charles Francis	
Abbott, Samuel Warren	I	(d. 1886)	I
Abbott, William Hawkins	I	Adams, Charles Francis	
Abeel, David	I	(d. 1915)	I
Abel, John Jacob	2	Adams, Charles Francis	
Abel-Henderson, Annie Heloise	4	(d. 1954)	5
Abell, Arunah Shepherdson	I	Adams, Charles Kendall	I

1

Complete Index Guide

Name	Vol./Supp.	Name	Vol./Supp.
Adams, Charles R.	I	Adee, Alvey Augustus	I
Adams, Cyrus Cornelius	1	Adgate, Andrew	I
Adams, Daniel	I	Adie, David Craig	3
Adams, Daniel Weissiger	I	Adkins, Homer Burton	4
Adams, Dudley W.	I	Adler, Cyrus	2
Adams, Ebenezer	I	Adler, Elmer	7
Adams, Edward Dean	1	Adler, Felix (d. 1933)	1
Adams, Edwin	I	Adler, Felix (d. 1960)	6
Adams, Eliphalet	I	Adler, George J.	I
Adams, Ephraim Douglass	1	Adler, Polly	7
Adams, Franklin Pierce	6	Adler, Samuel	I
Adams, Frank Ramsay	7	Adler, Sara	5
Adams, Frederick Upham	I	Adlum, John	I
Adams, George Burton	I	Adrain, Robert	I
Adams, Hannah	I	Adrian, Gilbert	6
Adams, Henry Brooks	I	Affleck, Thomas	I
Adams, Henry Carter	I	Agassiz, Alexander	I
Adams, Henry Cullen	I	Agassiz, Elizabeth Cabot	I
Adams, Herbert Baxter	I	Agassiz, Jean Louis Rodo	I
Adams, Herbert Samuel	3	Agate, Alfred T.	I
Adams, Isaac	I	Agate, Frederick Styles	I
Adams, James Hopkins	I	Agee, James Rufus	5
Adams, James Truslow	4	Aggrey, James Emman Kwegyir	1
Adams, Jasper	I	Agnew, Cornelius Rea	I
Adams, John (d. 1826)	I	Agnew, David Hayes	I
Adams, John (d. 1863)	I	Agnew, Eliza	I
Adams, John (d. 1864)	I	Agnus, Felix	I
Adams, John Coleman	I	Agramonte y Simoni, Aristides	1
Adams, John Quincy	I	Aiken, Charles Augustus	I
Adams, Joseph Alexander	I	Aiken, David Wyatt	I
Adams, Joseph Quincy	4	Aiken, George L.	I
Adams, Maude	5	Aiken, William	I
Adams, Nehemiah	I	Aikens, Andrew Jackson	I
Adams, Randolph Greenfield	5	Aime, Valcour	I
Adams, Robert	I	Ainslie, Hew	I
Adams, Samuel	I	Ainslie, Peter	1
Adams, Samuel Hopkins	6	Ainsworth, Frederick Crayton	1
Adams, Thomas Sewall	1	Aitken, Robert	I
Adams, Walter Sydney	6	Aitken, Robert Grant	5
Adams, William	I	Akeley, Carl Ethan	I
Adams, William Lysand	I	Akerman, Amos Tappan	I
Adams, William Taylor	I	Akers, Benjamin Paul	I
Adams, William Wirt	I	Akers, Elizabeth Chase	I
Addams, Jane	1	Akins, Zoë	6
Addicks, John Edward O.	I	Ako, Michel	
Ade, George	3	See Aco, Michel	

Complete Index Guide

Name	Vol./Supp.	Name	Vol./Supp.
Alarcón, Hernando de	I	Alexander, Samuel Davies	I
Albee, Edward Franklin	1	Alexander, Stephen	I
Albee, Ernest	I	Alexander, William	I
Albright, Jacob	I	Alexander, William DeWitt	I
Albro, Lewis Colt	I	Alexander, Will Winton	6
Alcorn, James Lusk	I	Alfonce (Alfonse), Jean	
Alcott, Amos Bronson	I	See Allefonsce, Jean	
Alcott, Louisa May	I	Alford, Leon Pratt	3
Alcott, William Andrus	I	Alger, Cyrus	I
Alden, Cynthia May Westover	1	Alger, Horatio	I
Alden, Ebenezer	I	Alger, Russell Alexander	I
Alden, Henry Mills	I	Alger, William Rounseville	I
Alden, Ichabod	I	Alison, Francis	I
Alden, Isabella Macdonald	1	Allaire, James Peter	I
Alden, James	I	Allan, John	I
Alden, John	I	Allefonsce, Jean	I
Alden, John Ferris	I	Allen, Alexander Viets	
Alden, Joseph	I	Griswold	I
Alden, Raymond MacDonald	I	Allen, Andrew	I
Alden, Timothy	I	Allen, Anthony Benezet	I
Alden, William Livingston	I	Allen, Arthur Augustus	7
Alderman, Edwin Anderson	1	Allen, Charles	I
Aldrich, Bess Genevra Streeter	5	Allen, David Oliver	I
Aldrich, Charles Anderson	4	Allen, Edgar	3
Aldrich, Chester Holmes	2	Allen, Edward Ellis	4
Aldrich, Edgar	I	Allen, Edward Tyson	3
Aldrich, Louis	I	Allen, Elisha Hunt	I
Aldrich, Nelson Wilmarth	I	Allen, Elizabeth Chase Akers	
Aldrich, Richard	2	See Akers, Elizabeth	
Aldrich, Thomas Bailey	I	Chase	
Aldridge, Ira Fredrick	I	Allen, Ethan	I
Alemany, José Sadoc	I	Allen, Fred	6
Alexander, Abraham	I	Allen, Frederic de Forest	I
Alexander, Archibald	I	Allen, Frederick Lewis	5
Alexander, Barton Stone	I	Allen, George	I
Alexander, de Alva Stanwood	I	Allen, Glover Morrill	3
Alexander, Edward Porter	I	Allen, Gracie	7
Alexander, Francis	I	Allen, Harrison	I
Alexander, Franz Gabriel	7	Allen, Henry Justin	4
Alexander, Gross	I	Allen, Henry Tureman	1
Alexander, Grover Cleveland	4	Allen, Henry Watkins	I
Alexander, Hartley Burr	2	Allen, Hervey	4
Alexander, James	I	Allen, Horatio	I
Alexander, John Henry	I	Allen, Ira	I
Alexander, John White	I	Allen, James Lane	I
Alexander, Joseph Addison	I	Allen, Jeremiah Mervin	I

Complete Index Guide

Name	Vol./Supp.	Name	Vol./Supp.
Allen, Joel Asaph	I	Allston, Washington	I
Allen, John	I	Allyn, Robert	I
Allen, John F.	I	Almy, John Jay	I
Allen, John James	I	Aloes (Aloues) Claude Jean	
Allen, Joseph Henry	I	See Allouez, Claude Jean	
Allen, Kelcey	5	Alphonce (Alphonse), Jean	
Allen, Lewis Falley	I	See Allefonsce, Jean	
Allen, Nathan	I	Alphonsa, Mother	I
Allen, Nathan H.	I	Alsop, George	I
Allen, Paul	I	Alsop, Richard	I
Allen, Philip	I	Alston, Joseph	I
Allen, Richard	I	Alston, Theodosia (Burr)	
Allen, Richard Lamb	I	See Burr, Theodosia	
Allen, Robert	I	Alter, David	I
Allen, Thomas	I	Altgeld, John Peter	I
Allen, Thomas M.	I	Altham, John	I
Allen, Timothy Field	I	Altman, Benjamin	I
Allen, Viola	4	Altsheler, Joseph Alexander	I
Allen, William (d. 1780)	I	Alvarado, Juan Bautista	I
Allen, William (d. 1868)	I	Alvey, Richard Henry	I
Allen, William (d. 1879)	I	Alvord, Benjamin	I
Allen, William Francis	I	Alvord, Clarence Walworth	I
Allen, William Frederick	I	Alvord, Corydon Alexis	I
Allen, William Henry (d. 1813)	I	Alvord, Henry Elijah	I
Allen, William Henry (d. 1882)	I	Amadas, Philip	I
Allen, William Joshua	I	Amateis, Louis	I
Allen, William Vincent	I	Ambler, James Markham	
Allen, Young John	I	Marshall	I
Allen, Zachariah	I	Ament, William Scott	I
Allerton, Isaac	I	Ameringer, Oscar	3
Allerton, Samuel Waters	I	Ames, Adelbert	1
Allibone, Samuel Austin	I	Ames, Charles Gordon	I
Alline, Henry	I	Ames, Edward Raymond	I
Allinson, Anne Crosby Emery	1	Ames, Edward Scribner	6
Allinson, Francis Greenleaf	1	Ames, Ezra	I
Allis, Edward Phelps	I	Ames, Fisher	I
Allison, Nathaniel	1	Ames, Frederick Lothrop	I
Allison, Richard	1	Ames, Herman Vandenburg	1
Allison, Samuel King	7	Ames, James Barr	I
Allison, William Boyd	I	Ames, James Tyler	I
Alloez (Alloues), Claude Jean		Ames, Joseph Alexander	I
See Allouez, Claude Jean		Ames, Joseph Sweetman	3
Allouez, Claude Jean	I	Ames, Mary Clemmer	
Allston, Robert Francis		See Clemmer, Mary	
Withers	I	Ames, Nathaniel	I

Complete Index Guide

Name	Vol./Supp.	Name	Vol./Supp.
Ames, Nathan Peabody	I	Andrew, Abram Piatt	2
Ames, Oakes (d. 1873)	I	Andrew, James Osgood	I
Ames, Oakes (d. 1950)	4	Andrew, John Albion	I
Ames, Oliver (d. 1863)	I	Andrew, Samuel	I
Ames, Oliver (d. 1877)	I	Andrews, Alexander Boyd	I
Ames, Oliver (d. 1895)	I	Andrews, Bert	5
Ames, Samuel	I	Andrews, Charles	I
Ames, Winthrop	2	Andrews, Charles Bartlett	I
Amherst, Jeffery	I	Andrews, Charles McLean	3
Amidon, Charles Fremont	2	Andrews, Chauncey Hummason	I
Amman, Othmar Hermann	7	Andrews, Christopher	
Ammen, Daniel	I	Columbus	I
Ammen, Jacob	I	Andrews, Edward Gayer	I
Ammons, Elias Milton	I	Andrews, Elisha Benjamin	I
Amory, Thomas	I	Andrews, Frank Maxwell	3
Anagnos, Michael	I	Andrews, Garnett	I
Anderson, Alexander	I	Andrews, George Leonard	I
Anderson, Benjamin McAlester	4	Andrews, George Pierce	I
Anderson, David Lawrence	I	Andrews, Israel DeWolf	1
Anderson, Edwin Hatfield	4	Andrews, Israel Ward	I
Anderson, Elizabeth Milbank	I	Andrews, John	I
Anderson, Galusha	I	Andrews, John Bertram	3
Anderson, George Thomas	I	Andrews, Joseph	I
Anderson, Henry Tompkins	I	Andrews, Lorin	I
Anderson, James Patton	I	Andrews, Lorrin	I
Anderson, John Alexander	I	Andrews, Roy Chapman	6
Anderson, Joseph	I	Andrews, Samuel James	I
Anderson, Joseph Reid	I	Andrews, Sherlock James	I
Anderson, Martin Brewer	I	Andrews, Sidney	I
Anderson, Mary (d. 1940)	2	Andrews, Stephen Pearl	I
Anderson, Mary (d. 1964)	7	Andrews, William Loring	I
Anderson, Maxwell	6	Andrews, William Watson	I
Anderson, Paul Y.	2	Andros, Sir Edmund	I
Anderson, Richard Clough		Angel, Benjamin Franklin	I
(b. 1750)	I	Angela, Mother	I
Anderson, Richard Clough		Angell, George Thorndike	I
(b. 1788)	I	Angell, Israel	I
Anderson, Richard Heron	I	Angell, James Burrill	I
Anderson, Robert	I	Angell, James Rowland	4
Anderson, Sherwood	3	Angell, Joseph Kinnicutt	I
Anderson, Victor Vance	6	Angell, William Gorham	I
Anderson, William	I	Anglin, Margaret Mary	6
André, Louis	I	Annenberg, Moses Louis	3
Andreis, Andrew James Felix		Anshutz, Thomas Pollock	I
Bartholomew de	I	Anson, Adrian Constantine	I

Complete Index Guide

Name	Vol./Supp.	Name	Vol./Supp.
Antes, Henry	I	Arensberg, Walter Conrad	5
Anthon, Charles	I	Arents, Albert	I
Anthon, Charles Edward	I	Argall, Philip	I
Anthon, John	I	Argall, Sir Samuel	I
Anthony, Andrew Varick Stout	I	Arlen, Michael	6
Anthony, George Tobey	I	Arliss, George	4
Anthony, Henry Bowen	I	Armistead, George	I
Anthony, John Gould	I	Armistead, Lewis Addison	I
Anthony, Katharine Susan	7	Armour, Philip Danforth	I
Anthony, Sister	I	Armsby, Henry Prentiss	I
Anthony, Susan Brownell	I	Armstrong, David Maitland	I
Anthony, William Arnold	1	Armstrong, Edward Cooke	3
Antin, Mary	4	Armstrong, Edwin Howard	5
Antoine, Père	I	Armstrong, Frank C.	I
Anza, Juan Bautista de	I	Armstrong, George Buchanan	I
Apes, William	I	Armstrong, George Dod	I
Appenzeller, Henry Gerhard	I	Armstrong, George Washington	I
Apple, Thomas Gilmore	I	Armstrong, Henry Worthington	
Appleby, John Francis	I	("Harry")	5
Applegate, Jesse	I	Armstrong, John (d. 1795)	I
Appleton, Daniel	I	Armstrong, John (d. 1816)	I
Appleton, James	I	Armstrong, John (d. 1843)	I
Appleton, Jesse	I	Armstrong, Paul	I
Appleton, John (d. 1891)	I	Armstrong, Robert	I
Appleton, John (d. 1864)	I	Armstrong, Samuel Chapman	I
Appleton, Nathan	I	Armstrong, Samuel Turell	I
Appleton, Nathaniel Walker	I	Arnold, Aza	I
Appleton, Samuel	I	Arnold, Benedict	I
Appleton, Thomas Gold	I	Arnold, Edward	6
Appleton, William Henry	I	Arnold, George	I
Appleton, William Sumner	4	Arnold, Harold DeForest	1
Appleton, William Worthen	I	Arnold, Henry Hartley	4
Apthorp, William Foster	I	Arnold, Isaac Newton	I
Arbuckle, John	I	Arnold, Jonathan	I
Archbold, John Dustin	I	Arnold, Lauren Briggs	I
Archdale, John	I	Arnold, Leslie Philip	7
Archer, Branch Tanner	I	Arnold, Lewis Golding	I
Archer, Frederic	I	Arnold, Richard	I
Archer, James J.	I	Arnold, Richard Dennis	I
Archer, John	I	Arnold, Samuel	
Archer, Samuel	I	See Booth, John Wilkes	
Archer, Stevenson	I	Arnold, Samuel Greene	I
Archer, William Segar	I	Arrington, Alfred W.	I
Archipenko, Alexander	7	Arthur, Chester Alan	I
Arden, Edwin Hunter		Arthur, Joseph Charles	3
Pendleton	I	Arthur, Peter M.	I

Complete Index Guide

Name	Vol./Supp.	Name	Vol./Supp.
Arthur, Timothy Shay	I	Atkinson, John	I
Arthur, William	I	Atkinson, Thomas	I
Artzybasheff, Boris	7	Atkinson, William Biddle	I
Arvin, Newton	7	Atkinson, William Yates	I
Asboth, Alexander Sandor	I	Atkinson, Wilmer	I
Asbury, Francis	I	Atlee, John Light	I
Asbury, Herbert	7	Atlee, Washington Lemuel	I
Asch, Morris Joseph	I	Atterbury, Grosvenor	6
Ashburner, Charles Albert	I	Atterbury, William Wallace	1
Ashby, Turner	I	Attucks, Crispus	I
Ashe, John	I	Atwater, Caleb	I
Ashe, John Baptista	I	Atwater, Lyman Hotchkiss	I
Ashe, Samuel	I	Atwater, Wilbur Olin	I
Ashe, Thomas Samuel	I	Atwood, Charles B.	I
Ashe, William Shepperd	I	Atwood, David	I
Asher, Joseph Mayor	I	Atwood, Lewis John	I
Ashford, Bailey Kelly	1	Atwood, Wallace Walter	4
Ashhurst, John	I	Atzerodt, George A.	
Ashley, James Mitchell	I	See Booth, John Wilkes	
Ashley, William Henry	I	Auchmuty, Richard Tylden	I
Ashmead, Isaac	I	Auchmuty, Robert (d. 1750)	I
Ashmead, William Harris	I	Auchmuty, Robert (d. 1788)	I
Ashmore, William	I	Auchmuty, Samuel	I
Ashmun, George	I	Audsley, George Ashdown	I
Ashmun, Jehudi	I	Audubon, John James	I
Ashurst, Henry Fountain	7	Auer, John	4
Aspinwall, William	I	Augur, Christopher Columbus	I
Aspinwall, William Henry	I	Augur, Hezekiah	I
Astor, John Jacob (d. 1848)	I	Augustus, John	I
Astor, John Jacob (d. 1890)	I	Austell, Alfred	I
Astor, John Jacob (d. 1912)	I	Austen, (Elizabeth) Alice	5
Astor, William Backhouse	I	Austen, Peter Townsend	I
Astor, William Vincent	6	Austin, Benjamin	I
Astor, William Waldorf	I	Austin, David	I
Atchison, David Rice	I	Austin, Henry	I
Atherton, Charles Gordon	I	Austin, James Trecothick	I
Atherton, George Washington	I	Austin, Jane Goodwin	I
Atherton, Gertrude	4	Austin, Jonathan Loring	I
Atherton, Joshua	I	Austin, Mary	1
Atkins, Jearum	I	Austin, Moses	I
Atkinson, Edward	I	Austin, Samuel	I
Atkinson, George Francis	I	Austin, Stephen Fuller	I
Atkinson, George Henry	I	Austin, Warren Robinson	7
Atkinson, George Wesley	I	Austin, William	I
Atkinson, Henry	I	Averell, William Woods	I
Atkinson, Henry Avery	6	Avery, Benjamin Parke	I

Complete Index Guide

Name	Vol./Supp.	Name	Vol./Supp.
Avery, Isaac Wheeler	I	Bacheller, Irving	4
Avery, John	I	Bacher, Otto Henry	I
Avery, Milton Clark	7	Bachman, John	I
Avery, Oswald Theodore	5	Bachmann, Werner Emmanuel	5
Avery, Samuel Putnam	I	Bachrach, Louis Fabian	7
Avery, Sewell Lee	6	Backus, Azel	I
Avery, William Waigstill	I	Backus, Isaac	I
Awl, William Maclay	I	Backus, Truman Jay	I
Axtell, Samuel Beach	I	Bacon, Alice Mabel	I
Ayala, Juan Manuel de	I	Bacon, Augustus Octavius	I
Aycock, Charles Brantley	I	Bacon, Benjamin Wisner	1
Aydelotte, Frank	6	Bacon, David	I
Ayer, Edward Everett	I	Bacon, Delia Salter	I
Ayer, Francis Wayland	I	Bacon, Edward Payson	I
Ayer, James Cook	I	Bacon, Edwin Munroe	I
Ayllon, Lucas Vasquez de	I	Bacon, Frank	I
Aylwin, John Cushing	I	Bacon, Henry	I
Ayres, Anne	I	Bacon, John	I
Ayres, Brown	I	Bacon, Leonard (d. 1881)	I
Ayres, Leonard Porter	4	Bacon, Leonard (d. 1954)	5
Ayres, Romeyn Beck	I	Bacon, Leonard Woolsey	I
Ayres, William Augustus	5	Bacon, Nathaniel	I
Azarias, Brother	I	Bacon, Robert	I
		Bacon, Thomas	I
Baade, Wilhelm Heinrich		Badè, William Frederic	2
Walter	6	Badeau, Adam	I
Babbitt, Benjamin Talbot	I	Badger, Charles Johnston	1
Babbitt, Irving	1	Badger, George Edmund	I
Babbitt, Isaac	I	Badger, Joseph (d. 1765)	I
Babcock, George Herman	I	Badger, Joseph (d. 1846)	I
Babcock, Howard Edward	4	Badger, Oscar Charles	I
Babcock, James Francis	I	Badin, Stephen Theodore	I
Babcock, James Woods	I	Baekeland, Leo Hendrik	3
Babcock, Joseph Weeks	I	Baer, George Frederick	I
Babcock, Maltbie Davenport	I	Baer, William Stevenson	1
Babcock, Orville E.	I	Baermann, Carl	I
Babcock, Stephen Moulton	1	Baetjer, Frederick Henry	1
Babcock, Washington Irving	I	Bagby, Arthur Pendleton	I
Bache, Alexander Dallas	I	Bagby, George William	I
Bache, Benjamin Franklin	I	Bagley, William Chandler	4
Bache, Franklin	I	Bailey, Ann	I
Bache, Jules Semon	3	Bailey, Anna Warner	I
Bache, Richard	I	Bailey, Ebenezer	I
Bache, Theophylact	I	Bailey, Florence	4
Bachelder, John	I	Bailey, Francis	I

Complete Index Guide

Name	Vol./Supp.	Name	Vol./Supp.
Bailey, Frank Harvey	I	Baker, Marcus	I
Bailey, Gamaliel	I	Baker, Newton Diehl	2
Bailey, (Irene) Temple	5	Baker, Oliver Edwin	4
Bailey, Jacob	I	Baker, Osmon Cleander	I
Bailey, Jacob Whitman	I	Baker, Peter Carpenter	I
Bailey, James Anthony	I	Baker, Ray Stannard	4
Bailey, James Montgomery	I	Baker, Remember	I
Bailey, Joseph	I	Baker, Sara Josephine	3
Bailey, Joseph Weldon	1	Baker, Walter Ransom Gail	6
Bailey, Josiah William	4	Baker, William Mumford	I
Bailey, Liberty Hyde	5	Balbach, Edward	I
Bailey, Lydia R.	I	Balch, Emily Greene	7
Bailey, Mildred	5	Balch, George Beall	I
Bailey, Rufus William	I	Balch, Thomas Willing	I
Bailey, Solon Irving	1	Baldwin, Abraham	I
Bailey, Theodorus	I	Baldwin, Edward Robinson	4
Bailly, Joseph Alexis	I	Baldwin, Elihu Whittlesey	I
Bain, George Luke Scobie	I	Baldwin, Evelyn Briggs	1
Bainbridge, William	I	Baldwin, Frank Stephen	I
Baird, Absalom	I	Baldwin, Henry	I
Baird, Charles Washington	I	Baldwin, Henry Perrine	1
Baird, Henry Carey	I	Baldwin, Henry Porter	I
Baird, Henry Martyn	I	Baldwin, James Mark	1
Baird, Matthew	I	Baldwin, John	I
Baird, Robert	I	Baldwin, John Brown	I
Baird, Samuel John	I	Baldwin, John Denison	I
Baird, Spencer Fullerton	I	Baldwin, Joseph	I
Baker, Benjamin A.	I	Baldwin, Joseph Glover	I
Baker, Benjamin Franklin	I	Baldwin, Loammi (d. 1807)	I
Baker, Daniel	I	Baldwin, Loammi (d. 1838)	I
Baker, Edward Dickinson	I	Baldwin, Matthias William	I
Baker, Frank	I	Baldwin, Roger Sherman	I
Baker, George Augustus	I	Baldwin, Simeon	I
Baker, George Fisher	1	Baldwin, Simeon Eben	I
Baker, George Pierce	1	Baldwin, Theron	I
Baker, Harvey Humphrey	I	Baldwin, William	I
Baker, Hugh Potter	4	Baldwin, William Henry	I
Baker, James	I	Balestier, Charles Wolcott	I
Baker, James Heaton	I	Ball, Albert	I
Baker, James Hutchins	I	Ball, Ephraim	I
Baker, Jehu	1	Ball, Frank Clayton	3
Baker, John Franklin	7	Ball, George Alexander	5
Baker, La Fayette Curry	I	Ball, Thomas	I
Baker, Laurence Simmons	I	Ballantine, Arthur Atwood	6
Baker, Lorenzo Dow	I	Ballard, Bland Williams	I

Complete Index Guide

Name	Vol./Supp.	Name	Vol./Supp.
Ballinger, Richard Achilles	I	Barber, Donn	I
Ballou, Adin	I	Barber, Edwin Atlee	I
Ballou, Hosea (d. 1852)	I	Barber, Francis	I
Ballou, Hosea (d. 1861)	I	Barber, John Warner	I
Ballou, Maturin Murray	I	Barber, Ohio Columbus	I
Baltimore, Charles Calvert,		Barbour, Clarence Augustus	2
Third Lord		Barbour, Henry Gray	3
See Calvert, Charles		Barbour, James	I
Baltimore, George Calvert,		Barbour, John Strode, Jr.	I
First Lord		Barbour, Oliver Lorenzo	I
See Calvert, George		Barbour, Philip Pendleton	I
Bamberger, Louis	3	Barbour, Thomas	4
Bancroft, Aaron	I	Barclay, Thomas	I
Bancroft, Cecil Franklin Patch	I	Bard, John	I
Bancroft, Edgar Addison	I	Bard, Samuel	I
Bancroft, Edward	I	Bard, William	I
Bancroft, Frederic	3	Bardeen, Charles William	I
Bancroft, George	I	Barker, Albert Smith	I
Bancroft, Hubert Howe	I	Barker, Benjamin Fordyce	I
Bancroft, Wilder Dwight	5	Barker, George Frederick	I
Bandelier, Adolph Francis		Barker, Jacob	I
Alphonse	I	Barker, James Nelson	I
Bangs, Francis Nehemiah	I	Barker, James William	I
Bangs, Frank C.	I	Barker, Jeremiah	I
Bangs, John Kendrick	I	Barker, Josiah	I
Bangs, Nathan	I	Barker, Wharton	I
Banister, John (d. 1692)	I	Barkley, Alben William	6
Banister, John (d. 1788)	I	Barksdale, William	I
Banister, Zilpah Polly Grant	I	Barlow, Francis Channing	I
Bankhead, John Hollis		Barlow, Joel	I
(d. 1920)	I	Barlow, John Whitney	I
Bankhead, John Hollis		Barlow, Samuel Latham	
(d. 1946)	4	Mitchill	I
Bankhead, William Brockman	2	Barlowe, Arthur	
Banks, Charles Edward	1	See Amadas, Philip	
Banks, Nathaniel Prentiss	I	Barnabee, Henry Clay	I
Banner, Peter	I	Barnard, Charles	I
Bannister, Nathaniel		Barnard, Charles Francis	I
Harrington	I	Barnard, Chester Irving	7
Banvard, John	I	Barnard, Daniel Dewey	I
Banvard, Joseph	I	Barnard, Edward Emerson	I
Bapst, John	I	Barnard, Frederick Augustus	
Bara, Theda	5	Porter	I
Baraga, Frederic	I	Barnard, George Grey	2
Baranov, Alexander Andreevich	I	Barnard, Henry	I
Barber, Amzi Lorenzo	I	Barnard, John	I

Complete Index Guide

Name	Vol./Supp.	Name	Vol./Supp.
Barnard, John Gross	I	Barry, John Stewart	I
Barnes, Albert	I	Barry, Patrick	I
Barnes, Albert Coombs	5	Barry, Philip	4
Barnes, Charles Reid	I	Barry, William Farquhar	I
Barnes, Charlotte Mary Sanford	I	Barry, William Taylor	I
Barnes, James	I	Barry, William Taylor Sullivan	I
Barnes, Joseph K.	I	Barrymore, Ethel	6
Barnes, Julius Howland	6	Barrymore, Georgiana Emma	
Barnes, Mary Downing Sheldon	I	Drew	I
Barnett, George Ernest	2	Barrymore, John	3
Barney, Joshua	I	Barrymore, Lionel	5
Barnum, Frances Courtenay		Barrymore, Maurice	I
Baylor		Barsotti, Charles	I
See Baylor, Frances		Barstow, William Augustus	I
Courtenay		Barth, Carl Georg Lange	2
Barnum, Henry A.	I	Barthelmess, Richard	7
Barnum, Phineas Taylor	I	Bartholdt, Richard	1
Barnum, Zenus	I	Bartholomew, Edward Sheffield	I
Barnwell, John	I	Bartholow, Roberts	I
Barnwell, Robert Woodward	I	Bartlet, William	I
Barr, Amelia Edith Huddleston	I	Bartlett, Elisha	I
Barr, Charles	I	Bartlett, Francis Alonzo	7
Barradall, Edward	I	Bartlett, Homer Newton	I
Barrell, Joseph	I	Bartlett, Ichabod	I
Barrère, Georges	3	Bartlett, John	I
Barrett, Albert Moore	2	Bartlett, John Russell	I
Barrett, Benjamin Fiske	I	Bartlett, John Sherren	I
Barrett, Charles Simon	1	Bartlett, Joseph	I
Barrett, Frank Aloysius	7	Bartlett, Josiah	I
Barrett, George Horton	I	Bartlett, Paul Wayland	I
Barrett, Janie Porter	4	Bartlett, Samuel Colcord	I
Barrett, John	2	Bartlett, William Holmes	
Barrett, Kate Waller	I	Chambers	1
Barrett, Lawrence	I	Bartley, Mordecai	I
Barringer, Daniel Moreau	I	Bartol, Cyrus Augustus	I
Barringer, Rufus	I	Barton, Benjamin Smith	I
Barron, Clarence Walker	1	Barton, Clara	I
Barron, James	I	Barton, David	1
Barron, Samuel	I	Barton, George Aaron	3
Barrow, Edward Grant	5	Barton, James Edward	7
Barrow, Washington	I	Barton, James Levi	2
Barrows, Alice Prentice	5	Barton, John Rhea	I
Barrows, David Prescott	5	Barton, Robert Thomas	I
Barrows, John Henry	I	Barton, Seth Maxwell	I
Barrows, Samuel June	I	Barton, Thomas Pennant	I
Barry, John	I	Barton, William	I

Complete Index Guide

Name	Vol./Supp.	Name	Vol./Supp.
Barton, William Eleazar	1	Bates, Onward	2
Barton, William Paul Crillon	I	Bates, Samuel Penniman	I
Bartram, John	I	Bates, Walter	I
Bartram, William	I	Batterson, James Goodwin	I
Baruch, Bernard Mannes	7	Battey, Robert	I
Baruch, Simon	I	Battle, Burrell Bunn	I
Barus, Carl	1	Battle, Cullen Andrews	I
Barzyński, Vincent	I	Battle, Kemp Plummer	I
Bascom, Florence	3	Battle, William Horn	I
Bascom, Henry Bidleman	I	Batts, Robert Lynn	1
Bascom, John	I	Bauer, Harold Victor	5
Bashford, Coles	I	Bauer, Louis Agricola	1
Bashford, James Whitford	I	Baugher, Henry Louis	I
Baskerville, Charles	I	Baum, Hedwig ("Vicki")	6
Bass, Edward	I	Baum, Lyman Frank	I
Bass, Sam	I	Bausch, Edward	3
Bass, William Capers	I	Bausman, Benjamin	I
Basse, Jeremiah	I	Baxley, Henry Willis	I
Bassett, Edward Murray	4	Baxter, Elisha	I
Bassett, James	I	Baxter, Henry	I
Bassett, John Spencer	I	Baxter, John	I
Bassett, Richard	I	Baxter, William	I
Bassett, William Hastings	1	Bayard, James Ash(e)ton	
Basso, Hamilton	7	(d. 1815)	I
Batchelder, John Putnam	I	Bayard, James Asheton	
Batchelder, Samuel	I	(d. 1880)	I
Batcheller, George Sherman	I	Bayard, John Bubenheim	I
Batchelor, George	I	Bayard, Nicholas	I
Bate, William Brimage	I	Bayard, Richard Henry	I
Bateman, Harry	4	Bayard, Samuel	I
Bateman, Kate Josephine	I	Bayard, Thomas Francis	I
Bateman, Newton	I	Bayard, William	I
Bateman, Sidney Frances		Bayles, James Copper	I
Cowell	I	Bayley, James Roosevelt	I
Bates, Arlo	I	Bayley, Richard	I
Bates, Barnabas	I	Baylies, Francis	I
Bates, Blanche	3	Baylor, Frances Courtenay	I
Bates, Daniel Moore	I	Baylor, George	I
Bates, Edward	I	Baylor, Robert Emmet Bledsoe	I
Bates, Frederick	I	Bayly, Thomas Henry	I
Bates, George Handy	I	Bayma, Joseph	I
Bates, James	I	Baynham, William	I
Bates, John Coalter	I	Bazett, Henry Cuthbert	4
Bates, Joshua	I	Baziotes, William	7
Bates, Katharine Lee	1	Beach, Alfred Ely	I

Complete Index Guide

Name	Vol./Supp.	Name	Vol./Supp.
Beach, Amy Marcy Cheney	3	Beatty, Willard Walcott	7
Beach, Frederick Converse	I	Beatty, William Henry	I
Beach, Harlan Page	1	Beaty, Amos Leonidas	2
Beach, Moses Sperry	I	Beauchamp, William	I
Beach, Moses Yale	I	Beauchamp, William Martin	I
Beach, Mrs. H. H. A.		Beaumont, John Colt	I
See Beach, Amy Marcy		Beaumont, William	I
Cheney		Beaupré, Arthur Matthias	I
Beach, Rex	4	Beauregard, Pierre Gustave	
Beach, Sylvia Woodbridge	7	Toutant	I
Beach, William Augustus	I	Beaux, Cecilia	3
Beach, Wooster	I	Beaver, James Addams	I
Beadle, Erastus Flavel	1	Beavers, Louise	7
Beadle, William Henry		Bechet, Sidney	6
Harrison	I	Beck, Carl	I
Beal, William James	I	Beck, Charles	I
Beale, Edward Fitzgerald	I	Beck, James Montgomery	2
Beale, Joseph Henry	3	Beck, Johann Heinrich	I
Beale, Richard Lee Turberville	I	Beck, John Brodhead	I
Beall, John Yates	I	Beck, Lewis Caleb	I
Beall, Samuel Wootton	I	Beck, Martin	2
Beals, Ralph Albert	5	Beck, Theodric Romeyn	I
Beaman, Charles Cotesworth	I	Becker, Carl Lotus	3
Bean, Tarleton Hoffman	I	Becker, George Ferdinand	I
Beard, Charles Austin	4	Becket, Frederick Mark	3
Beard, Daniel Carter	3	Becknell, William	I
Beard, George Miller	I	Beckwith, Clarence Augustine	1
Beard, James Carter	I	Beckwith, James Carroll	I
Beard, James Henry	I	Beckwourth, James P.	I
Beard, Mary	4	Bedaux, Charles Eugene	3
Beard, Mary Ritter	6	Bedford, Gunning (d. 1797)	I
Beard, Richard	I	Bedford, Gunning (d. 1812)	I
Beard, Thomas Francis	I	Bedinger, George Michael	I
Beard, William Holbrook	I	Bee, Barnard Elliott	I
Beardshear, William Miller	I	Bee, Hamilton Prioleau	I
Beardsley, Eben Edwards	I	Beebe, (Charles) William	7
Beardsley, Samuel	I	Beecher, Catharine Esther	I
Beasley, Frederick	I	Beecher, Charles	I
Beasley, Mercer	I	Beecher, Charles Emerson	I
Beattie, Francis Robert	I	Beecher, Edward	I
Beatty, Adam	I	Beecher, Henry Ward	I
Beatty, Charles Clinton	I	Beecher, Lyman	I
Beatty, Clyde Raymond	7	Beecher, Thomas Kinnicut	I
Beatty, John (d. 1826)	I	Beer, George Louis	I
Beatty, John (d. 1914)	I	Beer, Thomas	2

Complete Index Guide

Name	Vol./Supp.	Name	Vol./Supp.
Beer, William	I	Bellamy, Joseph	I
Beers, Clifford Whittingham	3	Bellanca, Dorothy Jacobs	4
Beers, Ethel Lynn	I	Bellanca, Giuseppe Mario	6
Beers, Henry Augustin	I	Bellew, Frank Henry Temple	I
Beery, Wallace	4	Bellingham, Richard	I
Beeson, Charles Henry	4	Bellomont, Earl of	
Behan, William James	I	See Coote, Richard	
Behn, Sosthenes	6	Bellows, Albert Fitch	I
Behrend, Bernard Arthur	1	Bellows, George Wesley	I
Behrends, Adolphus Julius		Bellows, Henry Whitney	I
Frederick	I	Belmont, Alva Ertskin Smith	
Behrendt, Walter Curt	3	Vanderbilt	1
Behrens, Henry	I	Belmont, August	I
Beissel, Johann Conrad	I	Belo, Alfred Horatio	I
Belasco, David	1	Beman, Nathan Sidney Smith	I
Belcher, Jonathan	I	Bemelmans, Ludwig	7
Belcourt, George Antoine	I	Bement, Caleb N.	I
Belden, Josiah	I	Bement, Clarence Sweet	I
Belknap, George Eugene	I	Bemis, George	I
Belknap, Jeremy	I	Bemis, Harold Edward	1
Belknap, William Worth	I	Benavides, Alonzo de	I
Bell, Alexander Graham	I	Benbridge, Henry	I
Bell, Alexander Melville	I	Benchley, Robert Charles	3
Bell, Bernard Iddings	6	Bender, Charles Albert	
Bell, Charles Henry	I	("Chief")	5
Bell, Clark	I	Bender, George Harrison	7
Bell, De Benneville ("Bert")	6	Bendix, Vincent	3
Bell, Eric Temple	6	Benedict, David	I
Bell, Frederic Somers	2	Benedict, Erastus Cornelius	I
Bell, Henry Haywood	I	Benedict, Ruth	4
Bell, Isaac	I	Benedict, Stanley Rossiter	2
Bell, Jacob	I	Benét, Stephen Vincent	3
Bell, James Ford	7	Benét, William Rose	4
Bell, James Franklin	1	Benezet, Anthony	I
Bell, James Madison	I	Benham, Henry Washington	I
Bell, James Stroud	I	Benjamin, Asher	I
Bell, John	I	Benjamin, George Hillard	I
Bell, Lawrence Dale	6	Benjamin, Judah Philip	I
Bell, Louis	I	Benjamin, Nathan	I
Bell, Luther Vose	I	Benjamin, Park (d. 1864)	I
Bell, Peter Hansborough	I	Benjamin, Park (d. 1922)	I
Bell, Robert	I	Benjamin, Samuel Greene	
Bell, Samuel	I	Wheeler	I
Bellamy, Edward	I	Benner, Philip	I
Bellamy, Elizabeth Whitfield		Bennet, Sanford Fillmore	I
Croom	I	Bennett, Caleb Prew	I

Complete Index Guide

Name	Vol./Supp.	Name	Vol./Supp.
Bennett, Charles Edwin	I	Bergmann, Carl	I
Bennett, Constance Campbell	7	Bergmann, Max	3
Bennett, de Robigne Mortimer	I	Berkeley, John	I
Bennett, Edmund Hatch	I	Berkeley, Norborne	
Bennett, Emerson	I	See Botetourt, Norborne	
Bennett, Floyd	I	Berkeley, Baron de	
Bennett, Henry Garland	5	Berkeley, Sir William	I
Bennett, Hugh Hammond	6	Berkenmeyer, Wilhelm	
Bennett, James Gordon		Christoph	I
(d. 1872)	I	Berkman, Alexander	2
Bennett, James Gordon		Berkowitz, Henry	I
(d. 1918)	I	Berliner, Emile	1
Bennett, Nathaniel	I	Bermudez, Edouard Edmond	I
Bennett, Richard	3	Bernard, Bayle	
Benning, Henry Lewis	I	See Bernard, William Bayle	
Bensley, Robert Russell	6	Bernard, Sir Francis	I
Benson, Egbert	I	Bernard, John	I
Benson, Eugene	I	Bernard, Simon	I
Benson, Frank Weston	5	Bernard, William Bayle	I
Benson, Oscar Herman	5	Bernays, Augustus Charles	I
Benson, William Shepherd	1	Bernet, John Joseph	1
Bent, Charles	I	Bernstein, Aline	5
Bent, Josiah	I	Bernstein, Herman	1
Bent, Silas (d. 1887)	I	Berrien, John Macpherson	I
Bent, Silas (d. 1945)	3	Berry, Edward Wilber	3
Bent, William	I	Berry, George Leonard	4
Bentley, Arthur Fisher	6	Berry, Hiram Gregory	I
Bentley, Elizabeth Terrill	7	Berry, James Henderson	I
Bentley, William	I	Berry, Martha McChesney	3
Bentley, Wilson Alwyn	1	Berry, Nathaniel Springer	I
Benton, Allen Richardson	I	Berryman, Clifford Kennedy	4
Benton, James Gilchrist	I	Bertram, John	I
Benton, Joel	I	Berwind, Edward Julius	2
Benton, Josiah Henry	I	Besse, Arthur Lyman	5
Benton, Thomas Hart		Bessey, Charles Edwin	I
(d. 1858)	I	Bestor, Arthur Eugene	3
Benton, Thomas Hart		Bethune, George Washington	I
(d. 1879)	I	Bethune, Mary McLeod	5
Berenson, Bernard	6	Bettendorf, William Peter	I
Berenson, Senda	5	Bettman, Alfred	3
Berg, Joseph Frederic	I	Betts, Samuel Rossiter	I
Berger, Daniel	I	Bevan, Arthur Dean	3
Berger, Meyer	6	Beveridge, Albert Jeremiah	I
Berger, Victor Louis	1	Beverley, Robert	I
Bergh, Christian	I	Bevier, Isabel	3
Bergh, Henry	I	Bewley, Anthony	I

Complete Index Guide

Name	Vol./Supp.	Name	Vol./Supp.
Biard, Pierre	I	Billings, John Shaw	I
Bibb, George Mortimer	I	Billings, Josh	
Bibb, William Wyatt	I	See Shaw, Henry Wheeler	
Bickel, Luke Washington	I	Billings, William	I
Bickerdyke, Mary Ann Ball	I	Billy the Kid	I
Bickett, Thomas Walter	I	Bimeler, Joseph Michael	I
Bickmore, Albert Smith	I	Binga, Jesse	4
Bidaga		Bingay, Malcolm Wallace	5
See Son of Many Beads		Bingham, Amelia	I
Biddle, Anthony Joseph Drexel,		Bingham, Anne Willing	I
Jr.	7	Bingham, Caleb	I
Biddle, Clement	I	Bingham, George Caleb	I
Biddle, Horace P.	I	Bingham, Harry	I
Biddle, James	I	Bingham, Hiram (d. 1869)	I
Biddle, Nicholas (d. 1778)	I	Bingham, Hiram (d. 1908)	I
Biddle, Nicholas (d. 1844)	I	Bingham, Hiram (d. 1956)	6
Bidlack, Benjamin Alden	I	Bingham, John Armor	I
Bidwell, Barnabas	I	Bingham, Robert Worth	2
Bidwell, John	I	Bingham, Walter Van Dyke	5
Bidwell, Marshall Spring	I	Bingham, William (d. 1804)	I
Bidwell, Walter Hilliard	I	Bingham, William (d. 1873)	I
Bien, Julius	I	Binkley, Robert Cedric	2
Bienville, Jean Baptiste Le		Binkley, Wilfred Ellsworth	7
Moyne, Sieur de	I	Binney, Amos	I
Bierce, Ambrose Gwinett	I	Binney, Horace	I
Bierstadt, Albert	I	Binns, John	I
Bigelow, Erastus Brigham	I	Binns, John Alexander	I
Bigelow, Frank Hagar	I	Birch, Reginald Bathurst	3
Bigelow, Harry Augustus	4	Birch, Thomas	I
Bigelow, Henry Jacob	I	Birch, William Russell	I
Bigelow, Jacob	I	Birchall, Frederick Thomas	5
Bigelow, John	I	Bird, Arthur	I
Bigelow, Melville Madison	I	Bird, Frederic Mayer	I
Bigelow, William Sturgis	I	Bird, Robert Montgomery	I
Biggers, Earl Derr	1	Birdseye, Clarence	6
Biggs, Asa	I	Bird Woman	
Biggs, Hermann Michael	I	See Sacagawea	
Bigler, John	I	Birge, Edward Asahel	4
Bigler, William	I	Birge, Henry Warner	I
Bilbo, Theodore Gilmore	4	Birkbeck, Morris	I
Billikopf, Jacob	4	Birkhoff, George David	3
Billings, Asa White Kenney	4	Birney, David Bell	I
Billings, Charles Ethan	I	Birney, James	I
Billings, Frank	1	Birney, James Gillespie	I
Billings, Frederick	I	Birney, William	I

Complete Index Guide

Name	Vol./Supp.	Name	Vol./Supp.
Bishop, Abraham	I	Blackwell, Lucy Stone	
Bishop, Charles Reed	1	See Stone, Lucy	
Bishop, Joel Prentiss	I	Bladen, William	I
Bishop, John Peale	3	Blaikie, William	I
Bishop, Nathan	I	Blaine, Anita (Eugenie)	
Bishop, Robert Hamilton	1	McCormick	5
Bishop, Robert Roberts	I	Blaine, James Gillespie	I
Bishop, Seth Scott	I	Blaine, John James	1
Bishop, William Darius	I	Blair, Austin	I
Bispham, David Scull	I	Blair, Emily Newell	5
Bissell, Edwin Cone	I	Blair, Francis Preston (b. 1791)	I
Bissell, George Edwin	I	Blair, Francis Preston (b. 1821)	I
Bissell, George Henry	I	Blair, Henry William	I
Bissell, William Henry	I	Blair, James	I
Bissell, Wilson Shannon	I	Blair, John (d. 1771)	I
Bitter, Karl Theodore Francis	I	Blair, John (d. 1800)	I
Bitzer, George William	3	Blair, John Insley	I
Bixby, Horace Ezra	I	Blair, Montgomery	I
Bixby, James Thompson	I	Blair, Samuel	I
Bjerregaard, Carl Henrik		Blair, William Richards	7
Andreas	I	Blake, Eli Whitney	I
Black, Eugene Robert	1	Blake, Francis	I
Black, Frank Sweet	I	Blake, Francis Gilman	5
Black, Greene Vardiman	I	Blake, Homer Crane	I
Black, James	I	Blake, John Lauris	I
Black, Jeremiah Sullivan	I	Blake, Lillie Devereux	I
Black, John Charles	I	Blake, Lyman Reed	I
Black, William Murray	1	Blake, Mary Elizabeth	
Blackburn, Gideon	I	McGrath	I
Blackburn, Joseph	I	Blake, William Phipps	I
Blackburn, Joseph Clay Styles	I	Blake, William Rufus	I
Blackburn, Luke Pryor	I	Blakeley, George Henry	3
Blackburn, William Maxwell	I	Blakelock, Ralph Albert	I
Blackfan, Kenneth Daniel	3	Blakely, Johnston	I
Blackford, Charles Minor	I	Blakeslee, Erastus	I
Black Hawk	I	Blakeslee, Howard Walter	5
Blackmur, Richard Palmer	7	Blalock, Alfred	7
Blackstone, Harry	7	Blalock, Nelson Gales	I
Blackstone, William	I	Blanc, Antoine	I
Blackton, James Stuart	3	Blanchard, Jonathan	I
Blackwell, Alice Stone	4	Blanchard, Newton Crain	I
Blackwell, Antoinette Louisa		Blanchard, Thomas	I
Brown	I	Blanchet, François Norbert	I
Blackwell, Elizabeth	I	Bland, Richard	I
Blackwell, Henry Brown	I	Bland, Richard Parks	I

Complete Index Guide

Name	Vol./Supp.	Name	Vol./Supp.
Bland, Theodorick	I	Block, Adriaen	I
Bland, Thomas	I	Block, Paul	3
Blandy, William Henry Purnell	5	Blodget, Lorin	I
Blankenburg, Rudolph	I	Blodget, Samuel (*d. 1807*)	I
Blasdel, Henry Goode	I	Blodget, Samuel (*d. 1814*)	I
Blashfield, Edwin Howland	2	Blodgett, Benjamin Colman	I
Blatch, Harriot Eaton Stanton	2	Blodgett, Henry Williams	I
Blatchford, Richard Milford	I	Blodgett, John Wood	5
Blatchford, Samuel	I	Bloede, Gertrude	I
Blaustein, David	I	Blood, Benjamin Paul	I
Blavatsky, Helena Petrovna		Bloodgood, Joseph Colt	1
Hahn	I	Bloodworth, Timothy	I
Blease, Coleman Livingston	3	Bloom, Sol	4
Bleckley, Logan Edwin	I	Bloomer, Amelia Jenks	I
Bledsoe, Albert Taylor	I	Bloomfield, Joseph	I
Bleecker, Ann Eliza	I	Bloomfield, Leonard	4
Blenk, James Hubert	I	Bloomfield, Maurice	I
Blennerhassett, Harman	I	Bloomfield, Meyer	2
Bleyer, Willard Grosvenor	1	Bloomfield-Zeisler, Fannie	
Blichfeldt, Hans Frederik	3	See Zeisler, Fannie	
Blinn, Holbrook	I	Bloomfield	
Bliss, Aaron Thomas	I	Bloomgarden, Solomon	I
Bliss, Cornelius Newton		Bloor, Ella Reeve	5
(*d. 1911*)	I	Blount, James Henderson	I
Bliss, Cornelius Newton		Blount, Thomas	I
(*d. 1949*)	4	Blount, William	I
Bliss, Daniel	I	Blount, Willie	I
Bliss, Edwin Elisha	I	Blow, Henry Taylor	I
Bliss, Edwin Munsell	I	Blow, Susan Elizabeth	I
Bliss, Eliphalet Williams	I	Blowers, Sampson Salter	I
Bliss, Frederick Jones	2	Bloxham, William Dunnington	I
Bliss, George (*b. 1816*)	I	Blue, Gerald Montgomery	
Bliss, George (*b. 1830*)	I	("Monte")	7
Bliss, Gilbert Ames	5	Blue, Victor	I
Bliss, Howard Sweetser	I	Bluemner, Oscar Florians	2
Bliss, Jonathan	I	Blum, Robert Frederick	I
Bliss, Philemon	I	Blunt, Edmund March	I
Bliss, Philip Paul	I	Blunt, George William	I
Bliss, Porter Cornelius	I	Blunt, James Gillpatrick	I
Bliss, Robert Woods	7	Blythe, Herbert	
Bliss, Tasker Howard	1	See Barrymore, Maurice	
Bliss, William Dwight Porter	I	Boardman, Mabel Thorp	4
Blitz, Antonio	I	Boardman, Thomas Danforth	I
Blitzstein, Marc	7	Boas, Emil Leopold	I
Bloch, Ernest	6	Boas, Franz	3

Complete Index Guide

Name	Vol./Supp.	Name	Vol./Supp.
Bôcher, Maxime	I	Bomford, George	I
Bocock, Thomas Stanley	I	Bonaparte, Charles Joseph	I
Bodanzky, Artur	2	Bonaparte, Elizabeth Patterson	I
Bode, Boyd Henry	5	Bonaparte, Jerome Napoleon	I
Bodenheim, Maxwell	5	Bonard, Louis	I
Boehler, Peter	I	Bond, Carrie Jacobs	4
Boehm, Henry	I	Bond, Elizabeth Powell	I
Boehm, John Philip	I	Bond, George Phillips	I
Boehm, Martin	I	Bond, Hugh Lennox	I
Boeing, William Edward	6	Bond, Shadrach	I
Boelen, Jacob	I	Bond, Thomas	I
Bogardus, Everardus	I	Bond, William Cranch	I
Bogardus, James	I	Boner, John Henry	I
Bogart, Humphrey DeForest	6	Bonfils, Frederick Gilmer	1
Bogart, John	I	Bonham, Milledge Luke	I
Boggs, Charles Stuart	I	Bonner, John	I
Boggs, Lillburn W.	I	Bonner, Robert	I
Bogue, Virgil Gay	I	Bonneville, Benjamin Louis	
Bogy, Lewis Vital	I	Eulalie de	I
Bohm, Max	I	Bonney, Charles Carroll	I
Bohune, Lawrence	I	Bonney, William H.	
Boies, Henry Martyn	I	See Billy the Kid	
Boies, Horace	I	Bonsal, Stephen	5
Boise, Reuben Patrick	I	Bonstelle, Jessie	1
Boisen, Anton Theophilus	7	Bonwill, William Gibson	
Boissevain, Inez Milholland	I	Arlington	I
Bok, Edward William	1	Bonzano, Adolphus	I
Boker, George Henry	I	Boole, Ella Alexander	5
Boldt, George C.	I	Boone, Daniel	I
Boll, Jacob	I	Boorman, James	I
Boller, Alfred Pancoast	I	Booth, Agnes	I
Bolles, Frank	I	Booth, Albert James, Jr.	
Bollman, Justus Erich	I	("Albie")	6
Bollman, William	I	Booth, Ballington	2
Bolm, Adolph Rudolphovitch	5	Booth, Edwin Thomas	I
Bolton, Henry Carrington	I	Booth, Evangeline	4
Bolton, Herbert Eugene	5	Booth, James Curtis	I
Bolton, Sarah Knowles	I	Booth, John Wilkes	I
Bolton, Sarah Tittle Barrett	I	Booth, Junius Brutus	I
Boltwood, Bertram Borden	I	Booth, Mary Louise	I
Boltzius, Johann Martin	I	Booth, Newton	I
Bolza, Oskar	3	Booth-Tucker, Emma Moss	I
Bomberger, John Henry		Boott, Kirk	I
Augustus	I	Borah, William Edgar	2
		Borchard, Edwin Montefiore	5

Complete Index Guide

Name	Vol./Supp.	Name	Vol./Supp.
Borden, Gail	I	Bourke, John Gregory	I
Borden, Lizzie Andrew	1	Bourne, Benjamin	I
Borden, Richard	I	Bourne, Edward Gaylord	I
Borden, Simeon	I	Bourne, George	I
Bordley, John Beale	I	Bourne, Jonathan	2
Boré, Jean Étienne	I	Bourne, Nehemiah	I
Boreman, Arthur Ingram	I	Bourne, Randolph Silliman	I
Borg, George William	6	Boutell, Henry Sherman	I
Borglum, John Gutzon de la		Boutelle, Charles Addison	I
Mothe	3	Bouton, John Bell	I
Bori, Lucrezia	6	Bouton, Nathaniel	I
Borie, Adolphe	1	Boutwell, George Sewall	I
Borie, Adolph Edward	I	Bouvet, Marie Marguerite	I
Boring, William Alciphron	2	Bouvier, John	I
Borland, Solon	I	Bovard, Oliver Kirby	3
Borzage, Frank	7	Bovie, William T.	6
Boss, Lewis	I	Bow, Clara Gordon	7
Boston, Charles Anderson	1	Bowden, John	I
Bostwick, Arthur Elmore	3	Bowditch, Charles Pickering	I
Bosworth, Edward Increase	I	Bowditch, Henry Ingersoll	I
Bosworth, Francke Huntington	I	Bowditch, Henry Pickering	I
Boteler, Alexander Robinson	I	Bowditch, Nathaniel	I
Botetourt, Norborne Berkeley	I	Bowdoin, James (d. 1790)	I
Botsford, George Willis	I	Bowdoin, James (d. 1811)	I
Botta, Anne Charlotte Lynch	I	Bowen, Abel	I
Botta, Vincenzo	I	Bowen, Francis	I
Bottineau, Pierre	I	Bowen, George	I
Bottome, Margaret McDonald	I	Bowen, Henry Chandler	I
Botts, Charles Tyler	I	Bowen, Herbert Wolcott	I
Botts, John Minor	I	Bowen, Louise De Koven	5
Bouché, René Robert	7	Bowen, Norman Levi	6
Boucher, Horace Edward	1	Bowen, Thomas Meade	I
Boucher, Jonathan	I	Bowers, Claude Gernade	6
Boucicault, Dion	I	Bowers, Elizabeth Crocker	I
Bouck, William C.	I	Bowers, Lloyd Wheaton	I
Boudin, Louis Boudinoff	5	Bowers, Theodore Shelton	I
Boudinot, Elias (d. 1821)	I	Bowes, Edward J.	4
Boudinot, Elias (d. 1839)	I	Bowie, James	I
Boudinot, Elias Cornelius	I	Bowie, Oden	I
Bouligny, Dominique	I	Bowie, Richard Johns	I
Bounetheau, Henry Brintnell	I	Bowie, Robert	I
Bouquet, Henry	I	Bowie, William	2
Bouquillon, Thomas Joseph	I	Bowker, Richard Rogers	1
Bourgmont, Étienne Venyard,		Bowler, Metcalf	I
Sieur de	I	Bowles, Samuel (d. 1851)	I

Complete Index Guide

Name	Vol./Supp.	Name	Vol./Supp.
Bowles, Samuel (d. 1878)	I	Brackenridge, William D.	I
Bowles, Samuel (d. 1915)	I	Brackett, Anna Callender	I
Bowles, William Augustus	I	Brackett, Edward Augustus	I
Bowman, Isaiah	4	Brackett, Jeffrey Richardson	4
Bowman, John Bryan	I	Bradbury, James Ware	I
Bowman, Thomas	I	Bradbury, Theophilus	I
Bowne, Borden Parker	I	Bradbury, William Batchelder	I
Bowne, John	I	Braddock, Edward	I
Boyce, James Petigru	I	Bradford, Alden	I
Boyd, Belle	I	Bradford, Alexander Warfield	I
Boyd, David French	I	Bradford, Amory Howe	I
Boyd, Harriet Ann		Bradford, Andrew	I
See Hawes, Harriet Ann		Bradford, Augustus Williamson	I
Boyd		Bradford, Edward Green	I
Boyd, James	3	Bradford, Edward Hickling	I
Boyd, John Parker	I	Bradford, Gamaliel (d. 1911)	I
Boyd, Lynn	I	Bradford, Gamaliel (d. 1932)	1
Boyd, Richard Henry	I	Bradford, John	I
Boyd, Thomas Alexander	1	Bradford, Joseph	I
Boyd, Thomas Duckett	1	Bradford, Roark	4
Boyd, William Kenneth	2	Bradford, Thomas	I
Boyden, Roland William	1	Bradford, William (d. 1657)	I
Boyden, Seth	I	Bradford, William (d. 1752)	I
Boyden, Uriah Atherton	I	Bradford, William (d. 1791)	I
Boyé, Martin Hans	I	Bradford, William (d. 1795)	I
Boyesen, Hjalmar Hjorth	I	Bradford, William (d. 1892)	I
Boyle, Jeremiah Tilford	I	Bradish, Luther	I
Boyle, John	I	Bradley, Charles Henry	I
Boyle, John J.	I	Bradley, Charles William	I
Boyle, Michael J.	6	Bradley, Denis Mary	I
Boyle, Thomas	I	Bradley, Frank Howe	I
Boylston, Zabdiel	I	Bradley, Frederick Worthen	1
Boynton, Charles Brandon	I	Bradley, John Edwin	I
Boynton, Edward Carlisle	I	Bradley, Joseph P.	I
Bozeman, John M.	I	Bradley, Lydia Moss	I
Bozeman, Nathan	I	Bradley, Milton	I
Bozman, John Leeds	I	Bradley, Stephen Row	I
Brace, Charles Loring (d. 1890)	I	Bradley, William Czar	I
Brace, Charles Loring (d. 1938)	2	Bradley, William O'Connell	I
Brace, Dewitt Bristol	I	Bradstreet, Anne	I
Brace, Donald Clifford	5	Bradstreet, John	I
Brace, John Pierce	I	Bradstreet, Simon	I
Brachvogel, Udo	I	Bradwell, James Bolesworth	I
Brackenridge, Henry Marie	I	Bradwell, Myra	I
Brackenridge, Hugh Henry	I	Brady, Alice	2

Complete Index Guide

Name	Vol./Supp.	Name	Vol./Supp.
Brady, Anthony Nicholas	I	Bray, Thomas	I
Brady, Cyrus Townsend	I	Brayman, Mason	I
Brady, James Topham	I	Brayton, Charles Ray	I
Brady, John Green	1	Brazer, John	I
Brady, Mathew B.	I	Brearly, David	II
Brady, Mildred Alice Edie	7	Breasted, James Henry	1
Brady, William Aloysius	4	Breaux, Joseph Arsenne	II
Bragdon, Claude Fayette	4	Breck, George William	II
Bragg, Braxton	I	Breck, James Lloyd	II
Bragg, Edward Stuyvesant	I	Breck, Samuel	II
Bragg, Thomas	I	Breckenridge, James	II
Brainard, Daniel	I	Breckinridge, Aida de Acosta	7
Brainard, John Gardiner		Breckinridge, Desha	1
Calkins	I	Breckinridge, Henry Skillman	6
Brainerd, David	I	Breckinridge, John (d. 1806)	II
Brainerd, Erastus	I	Breckinridge, John (d. 1841)	II
Brainerd, Ezra	I	Breckinridge, John Cabell	II
Brainerd, John	I	Breckinridge, Robert Jefferson	II
Brainerd, Lawrence	I	Breckinridge, Sophonisba	
Brainerd, Thomas	I	Preston	4
Bramlette, Thomas E.	I	Breckinridge, William	
Branch, John	I	Campbell Preston	II
Branch, Lawrence O'Bryan	I	Breed, Ebenezer	II
Brand, Max		Breen, Joseph Ignatius	7
See Faust, Frederick		Breen, Patrick	II
Shiller		Breese, Kidder Randolph	II
Brandegee, Frank Bosworth	I	Breese, Sidney	II
Brandegee, Townshend Stith	I	Brennan, Alfred Laurens	II
Brandeis, Louis Dembitz	3	Brennemann, Joseph	3
Brandon, Gerard Chittocque	I	Brenner, Victor David	II
Braniff, Thomas Elmer	5	Brenon, Herbert	6
Brann, William Cowper	1	Brent, Charles Henry	1
Brannan, John Milton	I	Brent, Margaret	II
Brannan, Samuel	I	Brentano, Lorenz	II
Branner, John Casper	I	Brereton, John	
Brannon, Henry	I	See Brierton, John	
Brant, Joseph	I	Brett, George Platt	2
Brantley, Theodore	I	Brett, William Howard	II
Brashear, John Alfred	I	Brevoort, James Renwick	II
Braslau, Sophie	1	Brewer, Charles	II
Brattle, Thomas	I	Brewer, David Josiah	II
Brattle, William	I	Brewer, Mark Spencer	II
Bratton, John	I	Brewer, Thomas Mayo	II
Brawley, William Hiram	I	Brewer, William Henry	II
Braxton, Carter	I	Brewster, Benjamin Harris	II

Complete Index Guide

Name	Vol./Supp.	Name	Vol./Supp.
Brewster, Frederick Carroll	II	Brinton, Daniel Garrison	II
Brewster, James	II	Brinton, John Hill	II
Brewster, Osmyn	II	Brisbane, Albert	II
Brewster, Ralph Owen	7	Brisbane, Arthur	2
Brewster, William (d. 1644)	II	Bristed, Charles Astor	II
Brewster, William (d. 1919)	II	Bristed, John	II
Brice, Calvin Stewart	II	Bristol, John Bunyan	II
Brice, Fanny	5	Bristol, Mark Lambert	2
Brickell, Henry Herschel	5	Bristol, William Henry	1
Brickell, Robert Coman	II	Bristow, Benjamin Helm	II
Bridger, James	II	Bristow, George Frederick	II
Bridgers, Robert Rufus	II	Bristow, Joseph Little	3
Bridges, Calvin Blackman	2	Britton, Nathaniel Lord	1
Bridges, (Henry) Styles	7	Broadhead, Garland Carr	II
Bridges, Robert (d. 1656)	II	Broadhead, James Overton	II
Bridges, Robert (d. 1882)	II	Broadus, John Albert	II
Bridgman, Elijah Coleman	II	Brockett, Linus Pierpont	II
Bridgman, Frederic Arthur	II	Brockmeyer, Henry C.	
Bridgman, Herbert Lawrence	II	See Brokmeyer, Henry C.	
Bridgman, Laura Dewey	II	Brockway, Zebulon Reed	II
Bridgman, Percy Williams	7	Brödel, Max	3
Brierton, John	II	Broderick, David Colbreth	II
Briggs, Charles Augustus	II	Brodhead, Daniel	II
Briggs, Charles Frederick	II	Brodhead, John Romeyn	II
Briggs, Clare A.	1	Brokenshire, Norman Ernest	7
Briggs, George Nixon	II	Brokmeyer, Henry C.	II
Briggs, LeBaron Russell	1	Bromfield, John	II
Briggs, Lloyd Vernon	3	Bromfield, Louis	6
Briggs, Lyman James	7	Bromley, Isaac Hill	II
Brigham, Albert Perry	1	Brondel, John Baptist	II
Brigham, Amariah	II	Bronson, Henry	II
Brigham, Joseph Henry	II	Bronson, Walter Cochrane	II
Brigham, Mary Ann	II	Brooke, Charles Frederick	
Bright, Edward	II	Tucker	4
Bright, James Wilson	II	Brooke, Francis Taliaferro	II
Bright, Jesse David	II	Brooke, John Mercer	II
Bright Eyes	II	Brooke, John Rutter	II
Brightly, Frederick Charles	II	Brooker, Charles Frederick	II
Brightman, Edgar Sheffield	5	Brookhart, Smith Wildman	3
Brill, Abraham Arden	4	Brookings, Robert Somers	1
Brill, Nathan Edwin	II	Brooks, Alfred Hulse	II
Brincklé, William Draper	II	Brooks, Byron Alden	II
Brinkerhoff, Jacob	II	Brooks, Charles	II
Brinkerhoff, Roeliff	II	Brooks, Charles Timothy	II
Brinkley, John Richard	3	Brooks, Elbridge Streeter	II

Complete Index Guide

Name	Vol./Supp.	Name	Vol./Supp.
Brooks, Erastus	II	Brown, Charles Rufus	II
Brooks, George Washington	II	Brown, Charlotte Emerson	II
Brooks, James	II	Brown, Charlotte Hawkins	7
Brooks, James Gordon	II	Brown, Clarence James	7
Brooks, John	II	Brown, David Paul	II
Brooks, John Graham	2	Brown, Ebenezer	II
Brooks, Maria Gowen	II	Brown, Elmer Ellsworth	1
Brooks, Mary Elizabeth Aiken		Brown, Ernest William	2
See Brooks, James Gordon		Brown, Ethan Allen	II
Brooks, Noah	II	Brown, Fayette	II
Brooks, Overton	7	Brown, Francis (d. 1820)	II
Brooks, Peter Chardon	II	Brown, Francis (d. 1916)	II
Brooks, Phillips	II	Brown, Frederic Tilden	II
Brooks, Preston Smith	II	Brown, George (d. 1859)	II
Brooks, Richard Edwin	II	Brown, George (d. 1892)	II
Brooks, Thomas Benton	II	Brown, George Pliny	II
Brooks, Van Wyck	7	Brown, George William	II
Brooks, William Keith	II	Brown, Gertrude Foster	6
Brooks, William Robert	II	Brown, Goold	II
Brooks, William Thomas		Brown, Henry Billings	II
Harbaugh	II	Brown, Henry Cordis	II
Brophy, John	7	Brown, Henry Kirke	II
Brophy, Truman William	II	Brown, Isaac Van Arsdale	II
Bross, William	II	Brown, Jacob Jennings	II
Brough, Charles Hillman	1	Brown, James (d. 1835)	II
Brough, John	II	Brown, James (d. 1877)	II
Brougham, John	II	Brown, James (d. 1855)	II
Broun, Heywood Campbell	2	Brown, James Salisbury	II
Broward, Napoleon Bonaparte	II	Brown, John (b. 1736)	II
Brower, Jacob Vradenberg	II	Brown, John (b. 1744)	II
Browere, John Henri Isaac	II	Brown, John (b. 1757)	II
Brown, Aaron Venable	II	Brown, John (b. 1800)	II
Brown, Addison	II	Brown, John A.	II
Brown, Albert Gallatin	II	Brown, John Appleton	II
Brown, Alexander (d. 1834)	II	Brown, John Calvin	II
Brown, Alexander (d. 1906)	II	Brown, John Carter	II
Brown, Alexander Ephraim	II	Brown, John George	II
Brown, Antoinette		Brown, John Mifflin	II
See Blackwell, Antoinette		Brown, John Newton	II
Louisa Brown		Brown, John Porter	II
Brown, Bedford	II	Brown, John Young	II
Brown, Benjamin Gratz	II	Brown, Joseph	II
Brown, Carleton	3	Brown, Joseph Emerson	II
Brown, Charles Brockden	II	Brown, Joseph Rogers	II
Brown, Charles Reynolds	4	Brown, Lawrason	2

Complete Index Guide

Name	Vol./Supp.	Name	Vol./Supp.
Brown, Margaret Wise	5	Browning, Orville Hickman	II
Brown, Mather	II	Browning, Tod	7
Brown, Morris	II	Brownlee, James Forbis	6
Brown, Moses (d. 1836)	II	Brownlee, William Craig	II
Brown, Moses (d. 1827)	II	Brownlow, William Gannaway	II
Brown, Neill Smith	II	Brownson, Orestes Augustus	II
Brown, Nicholas (d. 1791)	II	Brownson, Willard Herbert	1
Brown, Nicholas (d. 1841)	II	Bruce, Andrew Alexander	1
Brown, Obadiah	II	Bruce, Archibald	II
Brown, Olympia	II	Bruce, Blanche K.	II
Brown, Percy	4	Bruce, Edward Bright	3
Brown, Phoebe Hinsdale	II	Bruce, George	II
Brown, Ralph Hall	4	Bruce, Philip Alexander	1
Brown, Samuel	II	Bruce, Robert	II
Brown, Samuel Gilman	II	Bruce, William Cabell	4
Brown, Samuel Robbins	II	Brühl, Gustav	II
Brown, Simon	II	Brulé, Étienne	II
Brown, Solyman	II	Brumby, Richard Trapier	II
Brown, Sylvanus	II	Brumidi, Constantino	II
Brown, Walter Folger	7	Brunner, Arnold William	II
Brown, William	II	Brunswick, Ruth Mack	4
Brown, William Adams	3	Brunton, David William	II
Brown, William Carlos	II	Brush, Charles Francis	1
Brown, William Garrott	II	Brush, Edward Nathaniel	1
Brown, William Henry	II	Brush, George de Forest	3
Brown, William Hill	1	Brush, George Jarvis	II
Brown, William Hughey	II	Bruté de Rémur, Simon	
Brown, William Wells	II	William Gabriel	II
Browne, Benjamin Frederick	II	Bryan, Charles Wayland	3
Browne, Charles Albert	4	Bryan, George	II
Browne, Charles Farrar	II	Bryan, John Stewart	3
Browne, Daniel Jay	II	Bryan, Kirk	4
Browne, Francis Fisher	II	Bryan, Mary Edwards	II
Browne, Herbert	4	Bryan, Thomas Barbour	II
Browne, Irving	II	Bryan, William Jennings	II
Browne, John	II	Bryant, Gridley	II
Browne, John Ross	II	Bryant, John Howard	II
Browne, Junius Henri	II	Bryant, Joseph Decatur	II
Browne, Thomas	II	Bryant, Louise Frances Stevens	6
Browne, William	II	Bryant, Ralph Clement	2
Browne, William Hand	II	Bryant, William Cullen	II
Brownell, Henry Howard	II	Bryce, Lloyd Stephens	II
Brownell, Thomas Church	II	Bryson, Lyman Lloyd	6
Brownell, William Crary	II	Buchanan, Franklin	II
Browning, John Moses	II	Buchanan, James	II

Complete Index Guide

Name	Vol./Supp.	Name	Vol./Supp.
Buchanan, John	II	Buford, Abraham (d. 1884)	II
Buchanan, Joseph	II	Buford, John	II
Buchanan, Joseph Ray	II	Buford, Napoleon Bonaparte	II
Buchanan, Joseph Rodes	II	Bulfinch, Charles	II
Buchanan, Robert Christie	II	Bulfinch, Thomas	II
Buchanan, Thomas	II	Bulkeley, Morgan Gardner	II
Buchanan, William Insco	II	Bulkeley, Peter	II
Bucher, John Conrad	II	Bulkley, John Williams	II
Buchman, Frank Nathan		Bulkley, Lucius Duncan	II
Daniel	7	Bull, Ephraim Wales	II
Buchtel, John Richards	II	Bull, William (d. 1755)	II
Buck, Albert Henry	II	Bull, William (d. 1791)	II
Buck, Daniel	II	Bull, William Tillinghast	II
Buck, Dudley	II	Bullard, Henry Adams	II
Buck, Frank	4	Bullard, Robert Lee	4
Buck, Gurdon	II	Bullard, William Hannum	
Buck, Leffert Lefferts	II	Grubb	II
Buck, Philo Melvin	II	Bullitt, Alexander Scott	II
Buckalew, Charles Rollin	II	Bullitt, Henry Massie	II
Buckhout, Isaac Craig	II	Bulloch, Archibald	II
Buckingham, Joseph Tinker	II	Bulloch, James Dunwody	II
Buckingham, William Alfred	II	Bullock, Rufus Brown	II
Buckland, Cyrus	II	Bullock, William A.	II
Buckland, Ralph Pomeroy	II	Bumstead, Freeman Josiah	II
Buckler, Thomas Hepburn	II	Bumstead, Henry Andrews	II
Buckley, James Monroe	II	Bumstead, Horace	II
Buckley, Oliver Ellsworth	6	Bunce, Oliver Bell	II
Buckley, Samuel Botsford	II	Bunce, William Gedney	II
Buckminster, Joseph Stevens	II	Bundy, Harvey Hollister	7
Bucknell, William	II	Bundy, Jonas Mills	II
Buckner, Emory Roy	3	Bunker, Arthur Hugh	7
Buckner, Simon Bolivar	II	Bunner, Henry Cuyler	II
Buckner, Simon Bolivar	3	Burbank, Luther	II
Budd, Edward Gowen	4	Burbridge, Stephen Gano	II
Budd, Joseph Lancaster	II	Burchard, Samuel Dickinson	II
Budd, Ralph	7	Burdeck, Francis Marion	II
Buehler, Huber Gray	II	Burden, Henry	II
Buel, Jesse	II	Burdette, Robert Jones	II
Buell, Abel	II	Burdick, Eugene Leonard	7
Buell, Don Carlos	II	Burdick, Usher Lloyd	6
Buffalo Bill		Burgess, Alexander	II
See Cody, William		Burgess, Edward	II
Frederick		Burgess, Frank Gelett	5
Buffum, Arnold	II	Burgess, George	II
Buford, Abraham (d. 1833)	II	Burgess, George Kimball	1

Complete Index Guide

Name	Vol./Supp.	Name	Vol./Supp.
Burgess, John William	1	Burns, Anthony	II
Burgess, Neil	II	Burns, Bob	6
Burgess, Thornton Waldo	7	Burns, Otway	II
Burgess, William Starling	4	Burns, William John	1
Burgevine, Henry Andrea	II	Burnside, Ambrose Everett	II
Burgis, William	II	Burr, Aaron (d. 1757)	II
Burk, Frederic Lister	II	Burr, Aaron (d. 1836)	II
Burk, John Daly	II	Burr, Alfred Edmund	II
Burke, Aedanus	II	Burr, Enoch Fitch	II
Burke, Charles St. Thomas	II	Burr, George Lincoln	2
Burke, John G.		Burr, Theodosia	II
See Bourke, John Gregory		Burr, William Hubert	1
Burke, John Joseph	2	Burrage, Henry Sweetser	II
Burke, Stevenson	II	Burrage, Walter Lincoln	1
Burke, Thomas (d. 1783)	II	Burrall, William Porter	II
Burke, Thomas (d. 1925)	II	Burrell, David James	II
Burleigh, Charles Calistus	II	Burrill, Alexander Mansfield	II
Burleigh, George Shepard	II	Burrill, James	II
Burleigh, Henry Thacker	4	Burrill, Thomas Jonathan	II
Burleigh, William Henry	II	Burrington, George	II
Burleson, Albert Sidney	2	Burritt, Elihu	II
Burleson, Edward	II	Burroughs, Bryson	1
Burleson, Hugh Latimer	1	Burroughs, Edgar Rice	4
Burleson, Rufus Clarence	II	Burroughs, John	II
Burlin, Natalie Curtis	II	Burroughs, John Curtis	II
Burlingame, Anson	II	Burroughs, William Seward	1
Burlingame, Edward Livermore	II	Burrow, Trigant	4
Burlingham, Charles Culp	6	Burrowes, Edward Thomas	II
Burnam, John Miller	II	Burrowes, Thomas Henry	II
Burnap, George Washington	II	Burrows, Julius Caesar	II
Burnet, David Gouverneur	II	Burrows, William	II
Burnet, Jacob	II	Burson, William Worth	II
Burnet, William (d. 1729)	II	Burt, John	II
Burnet, William (d. 1791)	II	Burt, Mary Elizabeth	II
Burnett, Charles Henry	II	Burt, William Austin	II
Burnett, Frances Eliza Hodgson	II	Burton, Asa	II
Burnett, Henry Lawrence	II	Burton, Clarence Monroe	1
Burnett, Joseph	II	Burton, Ernest De Witt	II
Burnett, Peter Hardeman	II	Burton, Frederick Russell	II
Burnett, Swan Moses	II	Burton, Harold Hitz	7
Burnham, Clara Louise Root	II	Burton, Hutchins Gordon	II
Burnham, Daniel Hudson	II	Burton, Marion Le Roy	II
Burnham, Frederick Russell	4	Burton, Nathaniel Judson	II
Burnham, Sherburne Wesley	II	Burton, Richard Eugene	2
Burnham, William Henry	3	Burton, Theodore Elijah	1

Complete Index Guide

Name	Vol./Supp.	Name	Vol./Supp.
Burton, Warren	II	Buttrick, Wallace	II
Burton, William	II	Butts, Isaac	II
Burton, William Evans	II	Buttz, Henry Anson	II
Busch, Adolphus	1	Byerly, William Elwood	1
Bush, George	II	Byford, William Heath	II
Bush, Lincoln	2	Byington, Cyrus	II
Bush-Brown, Henry Kirke	1	Byles, Mather	II
Bushnell, Asa Smith	II	Bynum, William Preston	II
Bushnell, David	II	Byoir, Carl Robert	6
Bushnell, George Ensign	II	Byrd, Richard Evelyn	6
Bushnell, Horace	II	Byrd, William (d. 1704)	II
Bussey, Cyrus	II	Byrd, William (d. 1744)	II
Butler, Andrew Pickens	II	Byrne, Andrew	II
Butler, Benjamin Franklin		Byrne, Donn	
(d. 1858)	II	See Donn-Byrne, Brian	
Butler, Benjamin Franklin		Oswald	
(d. 1893)	II	Byrne, John	II
Butler, Burridge Davenal	4	Byrnes, Thomas F.	II
Butler, Charles	II	Byrns, Joseph Wellington	2
Butler, Ezra	II		
Butler, Howard Crosby	II	Cabell, James Branch	6
Butler, John	II	Cabell, James Lawrence	II
Butler, John Wesley	II	Cabell, Joseph Carrington	II
Butler, Marion	2	Cabell, Nathaniel Francis	II
Butler, Matthew Calbraith	II	Cabell, Samuel Jordan	II
Butler, Nicholas Murray	4	Cabell, William	II
Butler, Pierce (d. 1822)	II	Cabell, William H.	II
Butler, Pierce (d. 1939)	2	Cabell, William Lewis	II
Butler, Pierce Mason	II	Cabet, Étienne	II
Butler, Richard	II	Cable, Frank Taylor	3
Butler, Simeon	II	Cable, George Washington	II
Butler, Smedley Darlington	2	Cabot, Arthur Tracy	II
Butler, Thomas Belden	II	Cabot, Edward Clarke	II
Butler, Walter N.	II	Cabot, George	II
Butler, William (d. 1821)	II	Cabot, Godfrey Lowell	7
Butler, William (d. 1899)	II	Cabot, Hugh	3
Butler, William Allen	II	Cabot, Richard Clarke	2
Butler, William Orlando	II	Cabrillo, Juan Rodriguez	II
Butler, Zebulon	II	Cabrini, Frances Xavier	1
Butterfield, Daniel	II	Cadillac, Antoine de la Mothe,	
Butterfield, John	II	Sieur	II
Butterfield, Kenyon Leech	1	Cadman, Charles Wakefield	4
Butterick, Ebenezer	II	Cadman, Samuel Parkes	2
Butterworth, Benjamin	II	Cadwalader, John (d. 1786)	II
Butterworth, Hezekiah	II	Cadwalader, John (d. 1879)	II

Complete Index Guide

Name	Vol./Supp.	Name	Vol./Supp.
Cadwalader, Lambert	II	Callender, John	II
Cadwalader, Thomas	II	Callimachos, Panos Demetrios	7
Cady, Daniel	II	Calverley, Charles	II
Cady, Sarah Louise Ensign	II	Calvert, Charles	II
Caffery, Donelson	II	Calvert, Charles Benedict	II
Caffin, Charles Henry	II	Calvert, George	II
Cahan, Abraham	5	Calvert, George Henry	II
Cahill, Holger	6	Calvert, Leonard	II
Cahn, Edmond Nathaniel	7	Calverton, Victor Francis	2
Cain, Richard Harvey	II	Calvin, Samuel	II
Cain, William	1	Cambreleng, Churchill Caldom	II
Caines, George	II	Camden, Johnson Newlon	II
Cajori, Florian	1	Cameron, Andrew Carr	II
Calder, Alexander Stirling	3	Cameron, Archibald	II
Caldwell, Alexander	II	Cameron, James Donald	II
Caldwell, Charles	II	Cameron, Robert Alexander	II
Caldwell, Charles Henry		Cameron, Simon	II
Bromedge	II	Cameron, William Evelyn	II
Caldwell, David	II	Camm, John	II
Caldwell, Eugene Wilson	II	Cammerhoff, John Christopher	
Caldwell, Henry Clay	II	Frederick	II
Caldwell, James	II	Camp, David Nelson	II
Caldwell, Joseph	II	Camp, Hiram	II
Caldwell, Otis William	4	Camp, John Lafayette	
Calef, Robert	II	(d. 1891)	II
Calhoun, John	II	Camp, John Lafayette	
Calhoun, John Caldwell	II	(d. 1918)	II
Calhoun, Patrick	3	Camp, Walter Chauncey	II
Calhoun, William Barron	II	Campanius, John	II
Calhoun, William James	II	Campau, Joseph	II
California Joe	II	Campbell, Alexander	II
Calkins, Earnest Elmo	7	Campbell, Allen	II
Calkins, Gary Nathan	3	Campbell, Andrew	II
Calkins, Mary Whiton	1	Campbell, Bartley	II
Calkins, Norman Allison	II	Campbell, Charles	II
Calkins, Phineas Wolcott	II	Campbell, Charles Macfie	3
Calkins, Wolcott		Campbell, Douglas Houghton	5
See Calkins, Phineas		Campbell, Francis Joseph	II
Wolcott		Campbell, George Washington	
Call, Richard Keith	II	(b. 1769)	II
Callahan, Patrick Henry	2	Campbell, George Washington	
Callaway, Morgan	2	(b. 1817)	II
Callaway, Samuel Rodger	II	Campbell, Henry Fraser	II
Callender, Guy Stevens	II	Campbell, James	II
Callender, James Thomson	II	Campbell, James Hepburn	II

Complete Index Guide

Name	Vol./Supp.	Name	Vol./Supp.
Campbell, James Valentine	II	Canonchet	II
Campbell, John (d. 1727/8)	II	Canonge, Louis Placide	II
Campbell, John (d. 1782)		Canonicus	II
See Loudoun, John		Cantor, Eddie	7
Campbell, Fourth Earl of		Capen, Elmer Hewitt	II
Campbell, John Archibald	II	Capen, Nahum	II
Campbell, John Wilson	II	Capen, Samuel Billings	II
Campbell, Josiah A. Patterson	II	Capen, Samuel Paul	6
Campbell, Lewis Davis	II	Capers, Ellison	II
Campbell, Marius Robinson	2	Capers, William	II
Campbell, Prince Lucien	II	Capone, Alphonse	4
Campbell, Robert	II	Capper, Arthur	5
Campbell, Thomas	II	Capps, Edward	4
Campbell, Thomas Joseph	II	Capps, Washington Lee	1
Campbell, Lord William	II	Capron, Horace	II
Campbell, William (d. 1781)	II	Captain Jack	II
Campbell, William (d. 1936)	2	Caraway, Hattie	4
Campbell, William Bowen	II	Caraway, Thaddeus Horatius	1
Campbell, William Edward		Carbutt, John	II
March	5	Cárdenas, García Lópéz de	II
Campbell, William Henry	II	Cardozo, Benjamin Nathan	2
Campbell, William W.	II	Cardozo, Jacob Newton	II
Campbell, William Wallace	2	Carey, Henry Charles	II
Canaga, Alfred Bruce	II	Carey, Joseph Maull	II
Canby, Edward Richard Sprigg	II	Carey, Mathew	II
Canby, Henry Seidel	7	Carleton, Henry	II
Candee, Leverett	II	Carleton, Henry Guy	II
Candler, Allen Daniel	II	Carleton, Will	II
Candler, Asa Griggs	II	Carlile, John Snyder	II
Candler, Warren Akin	3	Carlisle, Floyd Leslie	3
Canfield, James Hulme	II	Carlisle, James Mandeville	II
Canfield, Richard A.	II	Carlisle, John Griffin	II
Cannon, Annie Jump	3	Carll, John Franklin	II
Cannon, Charles James	II	Carlson, Anton Julius	6
Cannon, Clarence	7	Carlson, Evans Fordyce	4
Cannon, George Quayle	II	Carmack, Edward Ward	II
Cannon, Harriet Starr	II	Carmichael, William	II
Cannon, Ida Maud	6	Carnahan, James	II
Cannon, James	3	Carnegie, Andrew	II
Cannon, James Graham	II	Carnegie, Dale	5
Cannon, Joseph Gurney	II	Carnegie, Hattie	6
Cannon, Newton	II	Carnegie, Mary Crowninshield	
Cannon, Walter Bradford	3	Endicott Chamberlain	6
Cannon, William	II	Carney, Thomas	II

Complete Index Guide

Name	Vol./Supp.	Name	Vol./Supp.
Carnochan, John Murray	II	Carruth, Fred Hayden	1
Carondelet, Francisco Luis		Carryl, Guy Wetmore	II
Hector, Baron de	II	Carson, Christopher	II
Carothers, Wallace Hume	2	Carson, Hampton Lawrence	1
Carpenter, Cyrus Clay	II	Carson, Jack	7
Carpenter, Edmund Janes	II	Carson, John Renshaw	2
Carpenter, Francis Bicknell	II	Carson, Joseph	II
Carpenter, Frank George	II	Carson, Rachel Louise	7
Carpenter, Franklin Reuben	II	Carson, Simeon Lewis	5
Carpenter, George Rice	II	Carter, Boake	3
Carpenter, John Alden	5	Carter, Caroline Louise Dudley	2
Carpenter, Matthew Hale	II	Carter, Elias	II
Carpenter, Stephen Cullen	II	Carter, Franklin	II
Carpenter, Stephen Haskins	II	Carter, Henry Alpheus Peirce	II
Carr, Benjamin	II	Carter, Henry Rose	II
Carr, Charlotte Elizabeth	6	Carter, James Coolidge	II
Carr, Dabney	II	Carter, James Gordon	II
Carr, Dabney Smith	II	Carter, Jesse Benedict	II
Carr, Elias	II	Carter, John (d. 1781)	II
Carr, Eugene Asa	II	Carter, John (d. 1814)	II
Carr, Joseph Bradford	II	Carter, Landon	II
Carr, Matthew		Carter, Mrs. Leslie	
See Carr, Thomas		See Carter, Caroline	
Matthew		Louise Dudley	
Carr, Thomas Matthew	II	Carter, Robert (d. 1732)	II
Carr, Wilbur John	3	Carter, Robert (d. 1879)	II
Carrel, Alexis	3	Carter, Samuel Powhatan	II
Carrère, John Merven	II	Carter, Thomas Henry	II
Carrick, Samuel	II	Carter, William Samuel	II
Carrier, Willis Haviland	4	Carteret, Philip	II
Carrington, Elaine Stern	6	Cartwright, Peter	II
Carrington, Henry Beebee	II	Carty, John Joseph	1
Carrington, Paul	II	Carus, Paul	II
Carroll, Charles	II	Caruso, Enrico	II
Carroll, Daniel	II	Caruthers, William Alexander	II
Carroll, Earl	4	Carvalho, Solomon Solis	3
Carroll, Howard	II	Carver, George Washington	3
Carroll, James	II	Carver, John	II
Carroll, John	II	Carver, Jonathan	II
Carroll, John Lee	II	Cary, Alice	II
Carroll, Samuel Sprigg	II	Cary, Annie Louise	II
Carroll, William	II	Cary, Archibald	II
Carrora, Joseph		Cary, Edward	II
See Dundee, Johnny		Cary, Elisabeth Luther	2

Complete Index Guide

Name	Vol./Supp.	Name	Vol./Supp.
Cary, Lott	II	Cermak, Anton Joseph	1
Cary, Phoebe	II	Cerré, Jean Gabriel	II
Casanowicz, Immanuel Moses	II	Cesare, Oscar Edward	4
Case, Francis Higbee	7	Cesnola, Luigi Palma di	II
Case, Jerome Increase	II	Chace, Elizabeth Buffum	II
Case, Leonard (d. 1864)	II	Chadbourne, Paul Ansel	II
Case, Leonard (d. 1880)	II	Chadwick, French Ensor	II
Case, Shirley Jackson	4	Chadwick, George Whitefield	1
Case, William Scoville	II	Chadwick, Henry	II
Casey, Joseph	II	Chadwick, James Read	II
Casey, Silas	II	Chadwick, John White	II
Casey, Thomas Lincoln	1	Chafee, Zechariah, Jr.	6
Cash, Wilbur Joseph	3	Chaffee, Adna Romanza	
Casilear, John William	II	(d. 1914)	II
Cass, George Washington	II	Chaffee, Adna Romanza	
Cass, Lewis	II	(d. 1941)	3
Cassatt, Alexander Johnston	II	Chaffee, Jerome Bonaparte	II
Cassatt, Mary	II	Chafin, Eugene Wilder	II
Cassidy, William	II	Chaillé-Long, Charles	II
Cassin, John	II	Chalkley, Thomas	II
Cassoday, John Bolivar	1	Chalmers, James Ronald	II
Castle, Vernon Blythe	II	Chalmers, William James	2
Castle, William Richards, Jr.	7	Chamberlain, Alexander	
Caswell, Alexis	II	Francis	II
Caswell, Richard	II	Chamberlain, Charles Joseph	3
Cataldo, Joseph Maria	1	Chamberlain, Daniel Henry	II
Catesby, Mark	II	Chamberlain, George Earle	II
Cathcart, James Leander	II	Chamberlain, Henry	
Cathcart, William	II	Richardson	II
Cather, Willa	4	Chamberlain, Jacob	II
Catherwood, Mary Hartwell	II	Chamberlain, Joseph Perkins	5
Catlett, Sidney	5	Chamberlain, Joshua Lawrence	II
Catlin, George	II	Chamberlain, Mellen	II
Caton, John Dean	II	Chamberlain, Nathan Henry	II
Catron, John	II	Chamberlain, William Isaac	II
Catt, Carrie Chapman	4	Chamberlin, Thomas	
Cattell, Alexander Gilmore	II	Chrowder	II
Cattell, James McKeen	3	Chambers, Charles Julius	
Cattell, William Cassaday	II	See Chambers, James Julius	
Cawein, Madison Julius	II	Chambers, Ezekiel Forman	II
Cayvan, Georgia	II	Chambers, George	II
Cazenove, Théophile	II	Chambers, James Julius	II
Celestin, Oscar "Papa"	5	Chambers, John	II
Céloron de Blainville, Pierre		Chambers, Julius	
Joseph de	II	See Chambers, James Julius	

Complete Index Guide

Name	Vol./Supp.	Name	Vol./Supp.
Chambers, Robert William	1	Chapin, Henry Dwight	3
Chambers, Talbott Wilson	II	Chapin, James Paul	7
Chambers, Whittaker	7	Chapin, Roy Dikeman	2
Champlain, Samuel de	II	Chaplin, Jeremiah	II
Champlin, John Denison	II	Chaplin, Ralph Hosea	7
Champlin, John Wayne	II	Chapman, Alvan Wentworth	II
Champlin, Stephen	II	Chapman, Frank Michler	3
Champney, Benjamin	II	Chapman, Henry Cadwalader	II
Champney, James Wells	II	Chapman, John	II
Chanche, John Mary Joseph	II	Chapman, John Gadsby	II
Chandler, Charles Frederick	II	Chapman, John Jay	1
Chandler, Elizabeth Margaret	II	Chapman, John Wilbur	II
Chandler, Harry	3	Chapman, Maria Weston	II
Chandler, John	II	Chapman, Nathaniel	II
Chandler, John Scudder	1	Chapman, Reuben	II
Chandler, Joseph Ripley	II	Chapman, Victor Emmanuel	II
Chandler, Julian Alvin Carroll	1	Chappell, Absalom Harris	II
Chandler, Peleg Whitman	II	Charles, William	II
Chandler, Raymond Thornton	6	Charless, Joseph	II
Chandler, Seth Carlo	II	Charlevoix, Pierre François	
Chandler, Thomas Bradbury	II	Xavier de	II
Chandler, William Eaton	II	Charlton, Thomas Usher	
Chandler, Zachariah	II	Pulaski	II
Chaney, Lon	1	Chase, Edna Woolman	6
Chanfrau, Francis S.	II	Chase, George	II
Chanfrau, Henrietta Baker	II	Chase, Harry Woodburn	5
Chang and Eng	II	Chase, Irah	II
Channing, Edward	1	Chase, (Mary) Agnes Merrill	7
Channing, Edward Tyrrell	II	Chase, Philander	II
Channing, Walter	II	Chase, Pliny Earle	II
Channing, William Ellery		Chase, Salmon Portland	II
(d. 1842)	II	Chase, Samuel	II
Channing, William Ellery		Chase, Thomas	II
(d. 1901)	II	Chase, William Merritt	II
Channing, William Francis	II	Chatard, Francis Silas	II
Channing, William Henry	II	Chatterton, Ruth	7
Chanute, Octave	II	Chaumonot, Pierre Joseph	
Chapelle, Dickey	7	Marie	II
Chapelle, Placide Louis	II	Chauncey, Isaac	II
Chapin, Aaron Lucius	II	Chauncy, Charles (d. 1671/2)	II
Chapin, Alonzo Bowen	II	Chauncy, Charles (d. 1787)	II
Chapin, Calvin	II	Chauvenet, William	II
Chapin, Charles Value	3	Chavez, Dennis	7
Chapin, Chester William	II	Chavis, John	II
Chapin, Edwin Hubbell	II	Cheatham, Benjamin Franklin	II

Complete Index Guide

Name	Vol./Supp.	Name	Vol./Supp.
Checkley, John	II	Childs, George William	II
Cheesman, Forman	II	Childs, Thomas	II
Cheetham, James	II	Chilton, William Paris	II
Cheever, Ezekiel	II	Chini, Eusebio Francisco	
Cheever, George Barrell	II	See Kino, Eusebio	
Cheever, Henry Theodore	II	Francisco	
Cheney, Benjamin Pierce	II	Chipman, Daniel	II
Cheney, Charles Edward	II	Chipman, Nathaniel	II
Cheney, Ednah Dow Littlehale	II	Chipman, Ward	II
Cheney, John	II	Chisholm, Hugh Joseph	II
Cheney, John Vance	II	Chisolm, Alexander Robert	II
Cheney, Oren Burbank	II	Chisolm, John Julian	II
Cheney, Person Colby	II	Chisum, John Simpson	II
Cheney, Seth Wells	II	Chittenden, Hiram Martin	II
Cheney, Ward	II	Chittenden, Martin	II
Chennault, Claire Lee	6	Chittenden, Russell Henry	3
Cherrington, Ernest Hurst	4	Chittenden, Simeon Baldwin	II
Chesebrough, Caroline	II	Chittenden, Thomas	II
Cheshire, Joseph Blount	1	Chivers, Thomas Holley	II
Chesnut, James	II	Choate, Joseph Hodges	II
Chessman, Caryl Whittier	6	Choate, Rufus	II
Chester, Colby Mitchell		Chopin, Kate O'Flaherty	II
(d. 1932)	1	Chorpenning, George	II
Chester, Colby Mitchell		Chotzinoff, Samuel	7
(d. 1965)	7	Chouart, Medart	
Chester, George Randolph	II	See Groseilliers, Medart	
Chester, Joseph Lemuel	II	Chouart, Sieur de	
Chetlain, Augustus Louis	II	Chouteau, Auguste	
Chever, James W.	II	See Chouteau, René	
Cheverus, John Louis Ann		Auguste	
Magdalen Lefebre de	II	Chouteau, Auguste Pierre	II
Cheves, Langdon	II	Chouteau, Jean Pierre	II
Chew, Benjamin	II	Chouteau, Pierre (d. 1865)	II
Cheyney, Edward Potts	4	Chouteau, Pierre (d. 1849)	
Chickering, Jonas	II	See Chouteau, Jean Pierre	
Chiera, Edward	1	Chouteau, René Auguste	II
Child, Charles Manning	5	Chovet, Abraham	II
Child, David Lee	II	Christian, Henry Asbury	5
Child, Francis James	II	Christian, William	II
Child, Frank Samuel	II	Christiancy, Isaac Peckham	II
Child, Lydia Maria Francis	II	Christie, John Walter	3
Child, Richard Washburn	1	Christy, David	II
Child, Robert	1	Christy, Edwin P.	II
Childe, John	II	Christy, Howard Chandler	5
Childs, Cephas Grier	II	Chrysler, Walter Percy	2

Complete Index Guide

Name	Vol./Supp.	Name	Vol./Supp.
Church, Alonzo	II	Clark, Champ	II
Church, Benjamin (d. 1718)	II	Clark, Charles	II
Church, Benjamin (d. 1778?)	II	Clark, Charles Edgar	II
Church, Frederick Edwin	II	Clark, Charles Heber	II
Church, Frederick Stuart	II	Clark, Charles Hopkins	II
Church, George Earl	II	Clark, Daniel (d. 1813)	II
Church, Irving Porter	1	Clark, Daniel (d. 1891)	II
Church, John Adams	II	Clark, Francis Edward	II
Church, Pharcellus	II	Clark, George Rogers	II
Church, William Conant	II	Clark, George Whitefield	II
Churchill, Thomas James	II	Clark, Greenleaf	II
Churchill, William	II	Clark, Henry James	II
Churchill, Winston	4	Clark, Horace Francis	II
Churchman, William Henry	II	Clark, James	II
Cilley, Joseph	II	Clark, John	II
Cist, Charles (d. 1805)	II	Clark, John Bates	2
Cist, Charles (d. 1868)	II	Clark, John Maurice	7
Cist, Henry Martyn	II	Clark, Jonas	II
Cist, Jacob	II	Clark, Jonas Gilman	II
Claflin, Horace Brigham	II	Clark, Joseph Sylvester	II
Claflin, John	2	Clark, Joshua Reuben, Jr.	7
Claflin, Tennessee		Clark, Lewis Gaylord	II
See Woodhull, Victoria		Clark, Myron Holley	II
Claflin, William	II	Clark, Sheldon	II
Clagett, Wyseman	II	Clark, Thomas March	II
Claghorn, George	II	Clark, Walter	II
Claiborne, John Francis		Clark, Walter Leighton	1
Hamtramck	II	Clark, William	II
Claiborne, Nathaniel Herbert	II	Clark, William Andrews	II
Claiborne, William	II	Clark, William Bullock	II
Claiborne, William Charles		Clark, William Smith	II
Coles	II	Clark, William Thomas	II
Clap, Thomas	II	Clark, Willis Gaylord	II
Clapp, Asa	II	Clarke, Sir Caspar Purdon	II
Clapp, Charles Horace	1	Clarke, Elijah	II
Clapp, George Alfred		Clarke, Francis Devereux	II
See Dockstader, Lew		Clarke, Frank Wigglesworth	1
Clapp, William Warland	II	Clarke, George	II
Clapper, Raymond Lewis	3	Clarke, Helen Archibald	II
Clark, Abraham	II	Clarke, James Freeman	II
Clark, Alvan	II	Clarke, James Paul	II
Clark, Alvan Graham	II	Clarke, John	II
Clark, Arthur Hamilton	II	Clarke, John Hessin	3
Clark, Bennett Champ	5	Clarke, John Mason	II
Clark, Bobby	6	Clarke, John Sleeper	II

Complete Index Guide

Name	Vol./Supp.	Name	Vol./Supp.
Clarke, Jonas		Clements, Judson Claudius	II
See Clark, Jonas		Clements, William Lawrence	1
Clarke, Joseph Ignatius		Clemmer, Mary	II
Constantine	II	Clemson, Thomas Green	II
Clarke, McDonald	II	Clerc, Laurent	II
Clarke, Mary Bayard Devereux	II	Cleveland, Aaron	II
Clarke, Mary Francis	II	Cleveland, Benjamin	II
Clarke, Rebecca Sophia	II	Cleveland, Chauncey Fitch	II
Clarke, Richard	II	Cleveland, Grover	
Clarke, Robert	II	See Cleveland, Stephen	
Clarke, Thomas Benedict	1	Grover	
Clarke, Thomas Shields	II	Cleveland, Horace William	
Clarke, Walter	II	Shaler	II
Clarke, William Newton	II	Cleveland, Richard Jeffry	II
Clarkson, Coker Fifield	II	Cleveland, Stephen Grover	II
Clarkson, John Gibson	II	Clevenger, Shobal Vail	
Clarkson, Matthew	II	(d. 1843)	II
Clausen, Claus Lauritz	II	Clevenger, Shobal Vail	
Claxton, Kate	II	(d. 1920)	II
Clay, Albert Tobias	II	Clewell, John Henry	II
Clay, Cassius Marcellus	II	Clews, Henry	II
Clay, Clement Claiborne	II	Clifford, John Henry	II
Clay, Clement Comer	II	Clifford, Nathan	II
Clay, Edward Williams	II	Cliffton, William	II
Clay, Green	II	Clifton, Josephine	II
Clay, Henry	II	Clinch, Charles Powell	II
Clay, Joseph (d. 1804)	II	Cline, Genevieve Rose	6
Clay, Joseph (d. 1811)	II	Clingman, Thomas Lanier	II
Clay, Matthew	II	Clinton, DeWitt	II
Claypole, Edward Waller	II	Clinton, George (d. 1761)	II
Clayton, Augustin Smith	II	Clinton, George (d. 1812)	II
Clayton, Henry De Lamar	1	Clinton, George Wylie	II
Clayton, John	II	Clinton, James	II
Clayton, John Middleton	II	Clopton, David	II
Clayton, Joshua	II	Clopton, John	II
Clayton, Powell	II	Closson, William Baxter	II
Clayton, Thomas	II	Clothier, William Jackson	7
Cleaveland, Moses	II	Cloud, Henry Roe	4
Cleaveland, Parker	II	Cloud, Noah Bartlett	II
Cleburne, Patrick Ronayne	II	Clough, John Everett	II
Cleghorn, Sarah Norcliffe	6	Clough, William Pitt	II
Clemens, Jeremiah	II	Clyman, James	II
Clemens, Samuel Langhorne	II	Clymer, George	II
Clement, Edward Henry	II	Clymer, George E.	II
Clements, Frederic Edward	3	Coakley, Cornelius Godfrey	1

Complete Index Guide

Name	Vol./Supp.	Name	Vol./Supp.
Coalter, John		Coe, Israel	II
See Colter, John		Coerne, Louis Adolphe	II
Coan, Titus	II	Cofer, Martin Hardin	II
Coates, Florence Earle	II	Coffey, James Vincent	II
Coates, George Henry	II	Coffin, Charles Albert	II
Coates, Samuel	II	Coffin, Charles Carleton	II
Cobb, Andrew Jackson	II	Coffin, Charles Fisher	II
Cobb, David	II	Coffin, Henry Sloane	5
Cobb, Elijah	II	Coffin, Howard Earle	2
Cobb, Frank Irving	II	Coffin, Sir Isaac	II
Cobb, Howell	II	Coffin, James Henry	II
Cobb, Irvin Shrewsbury	3	Coffin, John	II
Cobb, Jonathan Holmes	II	Coffin, Levi	II
Cobb, Lyman	II	Coffin, Lorenzo S.	II
Cobb, Nathan Augustus	1	Coffin, Robert Peter Tristram	5
Cobb, Sylvanus (d. 1866)	II	Coffin, William Anderson	II
Cobb, Sylvanus (d. 1887)	II	Coffman, Lotus Delta	2
Cobb, Thomas Reade Rootes	II	Cogdell, John Stevens	II
Cobb, Tyrus Raymond ("Ty")	7	Coggeshall, George	II
Cobb, William Henry	II	Coggeshall, William Turner	II
Cobbett, William	II	Coghill, George Ellet	3
Cobo, Albert Eugene	6	Coghlan, Rose	1
Coburn, Abner	II	Cogswell, Joseph Green	II
Coburn, Foster Dwight	II	Cogswell, William Browne	II
Cochran, Alexander Smith	II	Cohan, George Michael	3
Cochran, John	II	Cohen, Felix Solomon	5
Cochrane, Elizabeth		Cohen, Jacob Da Silva Solis	II
See Seaman, Elizabeth		Cohen, John Sanford	1
Cochrane		Cohen, Mendes	II
Cochrane, Gordon Stanley		Cohen, Morris	4
("Mickey")	7	Cohen, Octavus Roy	6
Cochrane, Henry Clay	II	Cohn, Alfred A.	5
Cochrane, John	II	Cohn, Alfred Einstein	6
Cocke, John Hartwell	II	Cohn, Edwin Joseph	5
Cocke, Philip St. George	II	Cohn, Harry	6
Cocke, William	II	Coit, Henry Augustus	II
Cockerell, Theodore Dru Alison	4	Coit, Henry Leber	II
Cockerill, John Albert	II	Coit, Stanton	3
Cockran, William Bourke	II	Coit, Thomas Winthrop	II
Cockrell, Francis Marion	II	Coke, Richard	II
Coddington, William	II	Coke, Thomas	II
Codman, John	II	Coker, David Robert	2
Cody, William Frederick	II	Coker, James Lide	II
Coe, George Albert	5	Colburn, Dana Pond	II
Coe, George Simmons	II	Colburn, Irving Wightman	II

Complete Index Guide

Name	Vol./Supp.	Name	Vol./Supp.
Colburn, Warren	II	Colman, Benjamin	II
Colburn, Zerah	II	Colman, Henry	II
Colby, Bainbridge	4	Colman, John	II
Colby, Frank Moore	II	Colman, Lucy Newhall	II
Colby, Gardner	II	Colman, Norman Jay	II
Colby, Luther	II	Colman, Ronald Charles	6
Colcord, Lincoln	4	Colman, Samuel	II
Colden, Cadwallader	II	Colpitts, Edwin Henry	4
Colden, Cadwallader David	II	Colquitt, Alfred Holt	II
Colden, Jane	II	Colquitt, Walter Terry	II
Cole, Chester Cicero	II	Colston, Raleigh Edward	II
Cole, Frank Nelson	II	Colt, LeBaron Bradford	II
Cole, George Watson	2	Colt, Samuel	II
Cole, Joseph Foxcroft	II	Colter, John	II
Cole, Nat "King"	7	Colton, Calvin	II
Cole, Thomas	II	Colton, Elizabeth Avery	II
Cole, Timothy	1	Colton, Gardner Quincy	II
Coleman, Charles Caryl	II	Colton, George Radcliffe	II
Coleman, Leighton	II	Colton, Walter	II
Coleman, Lyman	II	Colver, Nathaniel	II
Coleman, William	II	Colver, William Byron	II
Coleman, William Tell	II	Colvin, Stephen Sheldon	II
Coles, Edward	II	Colvocoresses, George Musalas	II
Colfax, Schuyler	II	Colwell, Stephen	II
Colgate, James Boorman	II	Coman, Charlotte Buell	II
Colgate, William	II	Combs, Leslie	II
Collamer, Jacob	II	Combs, Moses Newell	II
Collens, Thomas Wharton	II	Comer, Braxton Bragg	II
Colles, Christopher	II	Comfort, Will Levington	1
Collier, Barron Gift	2	Comiskey, Grace Elizabeth	
Collier, Constance	5	Reidy	6
Collier, Henry Walkins	II	Commons, John Rogers	3
Collier, Hiram Price	II	Compton, Arthur Holly	7
Collier, Peter	II	Compton, Karl Taylor	5
Collier, Peter Fenelon	II	Comstock, Anthony	II
Collier, Price		Comstock, Elizabeth L.	II
See Collier, Hiram Price		Comstock, George Cary	1
Collins, Edward Knight	II	Comstock, George Franklin	II
Collins, Edward Trowbridge	5	Comstock, Henry Tompkins	
Collins, Frank Shipley	II	Paige	II
Collins, Guy N.	2	Comstock, John Henry	1
Collins, John	II	Conant, Alban Jasper	II
Collins, John Anderson	II	Conant, Charles Arthur	II
Collins, Napoleon	II	Conant, Hannah O'Brien	
Collins, Patrick Andrew	II	Chaplin	II
Collyer, Robert	II	Conant, Hezekiah	II

Complete Index Guide

Name	Vol./Supp.	Name	Vol./Supp.
Conant, Roger	II	Connor, Robert Digges	
Conant, Thomas Jefferson	II	Wimberly	4
Conaty, Thomas James	II	Conover, Harry Sayles	7
Conboy, Martin	3	Conover, Obadiah Milton	II
Conboy, Sara Agnes		Conrad, Charles Magill	II
McLaughlin	II	Conrad, Frank	3
Condit, John	II	Conrad, Holmes	II
Condon, Thomas	II	Conrad, Robert Taylor	II
Cone, Claribel	4	Conried, Heinrich	II
Cone, Etta	4	Considérant, Victor Prosper	II
Cone, Hutchinson Ingham	3	Converse, Charles Crozat	II
Cone, Moses Herman	II	Converse, Edmund Cogswell	II
Cone, Orello	II	Converse, Frederick Shepherd	2
Cone, Russell Glenn	7	Converse, James Booth	II
Cone, Spencer Houghton	II	Converse, John Heman	II
Coney, Jabez	II	Conway, Elias Nelson	II
Coney, John	II	Conway, Frederick Bartlett	II
Congdon, Charles Taber	II	Conway, James Sevier	II
Conger, Edwin Hurd	II	Conway, Martin Franklin	II
Conklin, Edwin Grant	5	Conway, Moncure Daniel	II
Conklin, Jennie Maria		Conway, Thomas	II
Drinkwater		Conwell, Henry	II
See Drinkwater, Jennie		Conwell, Russell Herman	II
Maria		Conyngham, Gustavus	II
Conkling, Alfred	II	Coode, John	II
Conkling, Roscoe	II	Cook, Albert Stanburrough	II
Connaly, Thomas Terry		Cook, Clarence Chatham	II
("Tom")	7	Cook, Flavius Josephus	II
Connelly, Cornelia	II	Cook, Frederick Albert	2
Connelly, Henry	II	Cook, George Cram	II
Connelly, Pierce Francis	II	Cook, George Hammell	II
Conner, Charlotte Mary		Cook, Isaac	II
Sanford Barnes		Cook, James Merrill	II
See Barnes, Charlotte		Cook, John Williston	II
Mary Sanford		Cook, Joseph	
Conner, David	II	See Cook, Flavius Josephus	
Conner, James	II	Cook, Martha Elizabeth	
Coney, John		Duncan Walker	II
See Coney, John		Cook, Philip	II
Connick, Charles Jay	3	Cook, Robert Johnson	II
Connolly, John (d. 1813)	II	Cook, Russell S.	II
Connolly, John (d. 1825)	1	Cook, Tennessee Celeste	
Connolly, Thomas Henry, Sr.	7	Claflin, Lady	
Connor, Henry Groves	II	See Woodhull, Victoria	
Connor, Patrick Edward	II	Cook, Walter	II
		Cook, Walter Wheeler	3

Complete Index Guide

Name	Vol./Supp.	Name	Vol./Supp.
Cook, Will Marion	3	Cooper, James	II
Cook, Zebedee	II	Cooper, James Fenimore	II
Cooke, Ebenezer	1	Cooper, James Graham	II
Cooke, Elisha (d. 1715)	II	Cooper, John Montgomery	4
Cooke, Elisha (d. 1737)	II	Cooper, Joseph Alexander	II
Cooke, George Willis	II	Cooper, Kent	7
Cooke, Henry David	II	Cooper, (Leon) Jere	6
Cooke, Jay	II	Cooper, Mark Anthony	II
Cooke, John Esten (d. 1853)	II	Cooper, Myles	II
Cooke, John Esten (d. 1886)	II	Cooper, Oswald Bruce	2
Cooke, John Rogers	II	Cooper, Peter	II
Cooke, Josiah Parsons	II	Cooper, Samuel (d. 1783)	II
Cooke, Morris Llewellyn	6	Cooper, Samuel (d. 1876)	II
Cooke, Philip Pendleton	II	Cooper, Sarah Brown Ingersoll	II
Cooke, Philip St. George	II	Cooper, Susan Fenimore	II
Cooke, Robert Anderson	6	Cooper, Theodore	II
Cooke, Rose Terry	II	Cooper, Thomas	II
Cooke, Samuel	7	Cooper, Thomas Abthorpe	II
Coolbrith, Ina Donna	II	Cooper, William	II
Cooley, Edwin Gilbert	1	Cooper, William John	1
Cooley, Lyman Edgar	II	Cooper-Poucher, Matilda S.	II
Cooley, Mortimer Elwyn	3	Coote, Richard	II
Cooley, Thomas Benton	3	Cope, Caleb	II
Cooley, Thomas McIntyre	II	Cope, Edward Drinker	II
Coolidge, Archibald Cary	II	Cope, Thomas Pym	II
Coolidge, Calvin	1	Cope, Walter	II
Coolidge, Charles Allerton	2	Copeland, Charles Townsend	5
Coolidge, Elizabeth Penn		Copeland, Charles W.	II
Sprague	5	Copeland, Royal Samuel	2
Coolidge, Julian Lowell	5	Copley, Ira Clifton	4
Coolidge, Thomas Jefferson		Copley, John Singleton	II
(d. 1920)	II	Copley, Lionel	II
Coolidge, Thomas Jefferson		Copley, Thomas	II
(d. 1959)	6	Coppée, Henry	II
Coomaraswamy, Ananda		Coppens, Charles	II
Kentish	4	Coppet, Edward J. de	
Coombe, Thomas	II	See De Coppet, Edward J.	
Coontz, Robert Edward	1	Copway, George	II
Cooper, Edward	II	Coquillett, Daniel William	II
Cooper, Elias Samuel	II	Coram, Thomas	II
Cooper, Ezekiel	II	Corbett, Harvey Wiley	5
Cooper, Gary	7	Corbett, Henry Winslow	II
Cooper, Henry Ernest	II	Corbett, James John	1
Cooper, Hugh Lincoln	2	Corbin, Austin	II
Cooper, Jacob	II	Corbin, Daniel Chase	II

Complete Index Guide

Name	Vol./Supp.	Name	Vol./Supp.
Corbin, Henry Clark	1	Cottrell, Calvert Byron	II
Corbin, Margaret	II	Cottrell, Frederick Gardner	4
Corby, William	II	Couch, Darius Nash	II
Corcoran, James Andrew	II	Couch, Harvey Crowley	3
Corcoran, William Wilson	II	Coudert, Frederic René	
Corey, Lewis	5	(d. 1903)	II
Corey, William Ellis	1	Coudert, Frederic René	
Cori, Gerty Theresa Radnitz	6	(d. 1955)	5
Coriat, Isador Henry	3	Coues, Elliott	II
Corliss, George Henry	II	Couldock, Charles Walter	II
Cornbury, Edward Hyde	II	Coulter, Ernest Kent	5
Cornell, Alonzo B.	II	Coulter, John Merle	II
Cornell, Ezekiel	II	Councilman, William Thomas	1
Cornell, Ezra	II	Couper, James Hamilton	II
Corning, Erastus	II	Courtney, Charles Edward	II
Cornoyer, Paul	II	Coutard, Henri	4
Cornstalk	II	Couzens, James	2
Cornwallis, Kinahan	II	Covici, Pascal ("Pat")	7
Coronado, Francisco Vázquez	II	Covode, John	II
Corrigan, Michael Augustine	II	Cowan, Edgar	II
Corrothers, James David	II	Cowell, Sidney Frances	
Corse, John Murray	II	See Bateman, Sidney	
Corson, Hiram	II	Frances Cowell	
Corson, Juliet	II	Cowen, John Kissig	II
Corson, Robert Rodgers	II	Cowen, Joshua Lionel	7
Cort, Edwin	4	Cowl, Jane	4
Cortambert, Louis Richard	II	Cowles, Edwin	II
Cortelyou, George Bruce	2	Cowles, Gardner	4
Corthell, Elmer Lawrence	II	Cowles, Henry Chandler	2
Cortissoz, Royal	4	Cowley, Charles	II
Corwin, Edward Samuel	7	Cox, Edward Eugene	5
Corwin, Edward Tanjore	II	Cox, George Barnsdale	II
Corwin, Thomas	II	Cox, Hannah Peirce	II
Cory, Charles Barney	II	Cox, Henry Hamilton	II
Cosby, William	II	Cox, Jacob Dolson	II
Costain, Thomas Bertram	7	Cox, James Middleton	6
Costansó, Miguel	II	Cox, Kenyon	II
Costello, Lou	6	Cox, Lemuel	II
Coster, F. Donald		Cox, Palmer	II
See Musica, Philip		Cox, Rowland	II
Mariano Fausto		Cox, Samuel Hanson	II
Costigan, Edward Prentiss	2	Cox, Samuel Sullivan	II
Costigan, George Purcell	1	Cox, William Ruffin	II
Cotton, John	II	Coxe, Arthur Cleveland	II
Cotton, Joseph Potter	1	Coxe, Daniel	II

Complete Index Guide

Name	Vol./Supp.	Name	Vol./Supp.
Coxe, Eckley Brinton	II	Cranston, Samuel	II
Coxe, John Redman	II	Crapsey, Adelaide	II
Coxe, Richard Smith	II	Crapsey, Algernon Sidney	II
Coxe, Tench	II	Crary, Isaac Edwin	II
Coxe, William	II	Cratty, Mabel	II
Coxetter, Louis Mitchell	II	Cravath, Erastus Milo	II
Coxey, Jacob Sechler	5	Cravath, Paul Drennan	2
Coyle, Grace Longwell	7	Craven, Braxton	II
Cozzens, Frederick Swartwout	II	Craven, Frank	3
Crabtree, Lotta	II	Craven, John Joseph	II
Craddock, Charles Egbert		Craven, Thomas Tingey	II
See Murfree, Mary		Craven, Tunis Augustus	
Noailles		MacDonough	II
Crafts, James Mason	II	Crawford, Francis Marion	II
Crafts, William	II	Crawford, George Walker	II
Craig, Austin	II	Crawford, James Pyle	
Craig, Daniel H.	II	Wickersham	2
Craig, Malin	3	Crawford, John	II
Craig, Thomas	II	Crawford, John Martin	II
Craig, Winchell McKendree	6	Crawford, John Wallace	
Craighead, Edwin Boone	II	(Captain Jack)	II
Craigie, Andrew	II	Crawford, Martin Jenkins	II
Craik, James	II	Crawford, Samuel Johnson	II
Cram, Ralph Adams	3	Crawford, Thomas	II
Cramer, Michael John	II	Crawford, William	II
Cramp, Charles Henry	II	Crawford, William Harris	II
Cramp, William	II	Crazy Horse	II
Cranch, Christopher Pearse	II	Creamer, David	II
Cranch, William	II	Creath, Jacob (d. 1854)	II
Crandall, Charles Henry	II	Creath, Jacob (d. 1886)	II
Crandall, Prudence	II	Creel, George	5
Crane, Anne Moncure	II	Creelman, James	II
Crane, Charles Richard	2	Creesy, Josiah Perkins	II
Crane, Frank	II	Creighton, Edward	II
Crane, Frederick Evan	4	Creighton, James Edwin	II
Crane, Harold Hart	1	Creighton, John Andrew	II
Crane, John	II	Creighton, William	II
Crane, Jonathan Townley	II	Crerar, John	II
Crane, Stephen	II	Cresap, Michael	II
Crane, Thomas Frederick	II	Cresap, Thomas	II
Crane, William Henry	II	Crespi, Juan	II
Crane, William Montgomery	II	Cresson, Elliott	II
Crane, Winthrop Murray	II	Cresson, Ezra Townsend	II
Cranston, Earl	1	Creswell, John Angel James	II
Cranston, John	II	Cret, Paul Philippe	3

Complete Index Guide

Name	Vol./Supp.	Name	Vol./Supp.
Crétin, Joseph	II	Crosby, William Otis	II
Crèvecoeur, J. Hector St. John		Crosley, Powell, Jr.	7
See Crèvecoeur,		Cross, Arthur Lyon	2
Michel-Guillaume Jean de		Cross, Charles Whitman	4
Crèvecoeur, Michel-Guillaume		Cross, Edward	II
Jean de	II	Cross, Samuel Hazzard	4
Crile, George Washington	3	Cross, Wilbur Lucius	4
Crimmins, John Daniel	II	Crosser, Robert	6
Crisp, Charles Frederick	II	Crosswaith, Frank Rudolph	7
Crissinger, Daniel Richard	3	Croswell, Edwin	II
Crittenden, George Bibb	II	Croswell, Harry	II
Crittenden, John Jordan	II	Crothers, Rachel	6
Crittenden, Thomas Leonidas	II	Crothers, Samuel McChord	II
Crittenden, Thomas Theodore	II	Crounse, Lorenzo	II
Crittenton, Charles Nelson	II	Crouter, Albert Louis Edgerton	II
Crocker, Alvah	II	Crowder, Enoch Herbert	1
Crocker, Charles	II	Crowe, Francis Trenholm	4
Crocker, Francis Bacon	II	Crowell, Luther Childs	II
Crocker, Hannah Mather	II	Crowne, John	II
Crocker, Uriel	II	Crowne, William	II
Crocker, William	4	Crowninshield, Benjamin	
Crockett, David	II	Williams	II
Croghan, George (d. 1782)	II	Crowninshield, Frank	4
Croghan, George (d. 1849)	II	Crowninshield, Frederic	II
Croix, Teodoro de	II	Crowninshield, George	II
Croker, Richard	II	Crowninshield, Jacob	II
Croly, David Goodman	II	Croy, Homer	7
Croly, Herbert David	1	Crozer, John Price	II
Croly, Jane Cunningham	II	Crozet, Claude	II
Crompton, George	II	Crozier, William	3
Crompton, William	II	Cruger, Henry	II
Cromwell, Dean Bartlett	7	Cruger, John	II
Cromwell, Gladys Louise		Crumbine, Samuel Jay	5
Husted	II	Crump, Edward Hull	5
Cromwell, William Nelson	4	Crump, William Wood	II
Crook, George	II	Crunden, Frederick Morgan	II
Crooks, George Richard	II	Cubberley, Ellwood Patterson	3
Crooks, Ramsay	II	Cubero, Pedro Rodríguez	II
Cropsey, Jaspar Francis	II	Cudahy, Michael	II
Crosby, Ernest Howard	II	Cuffe, Paul	II
Crosby, Fanny	II	Culberson, Charles Allen	II
Crosby, Howard	II	Culberson, David Browning	II
Crosby, John Schuyler	II	Culbertson, Ely	5
Crosby, Peirce	II	Culbertson, Josephine Murphy	6
Crosby, Percy Lee	7	Cullen, Countee	4

Complete Index Guide

Name	Vol./Supp.	Name	Vol./Supp.
Cullen, Hugh Roy	6	Curtis, Cyrus Hermann	
Cullen, Thomas Stephen	5	Kotzschmar	1
Cullinan, Joseph Stephen	2	Curtis, Edward Lewis	II
Cullis, Charles	II	Curtis, Edward Sheriff	5
Cullom, Shelby Moore	II	Curtis, Edwin Upton	II
Cullum, George Washington	II	Curtis, George	II
Culpeper, Thomas Lord	II	Curtis, George Ticknor	II
Cuming, Sir Alexander	II	Curtis, George William	II
Cuming, Fortescue	II	Curtis, Heber Doust	3
Cumming, Alfred	II	Curtis, John Green	II
Cummings, Amos Jay	II	Curtis, Moses Ashley	II
Cummings, Charles Amos	II	Curtis, Newton Martin	II
Cummings, Edward	II	Curtis, Olin Alfred	II
cummings, e e	7	Curtis, Samuel Ryan	II
Cummings, Homer Stillé	6	Curtis, William Eleroy	II
Cummings, John	II	Curtiss, Glenn Hammond	1
Cummings, Joseph	II	Curtiss, Samuel Ives	II
Cummings, Thomas Seir	II	Curtiz, Michael	7
Cummins, Albert Baird	II	Curwen, Samuel	II
Cummins, George David	II	Curwood, James Oliver	II
Cummins, Maria Susanna	II	Cushing, Caleb	II
Cunliffe-Owen, Philip Frederick	II	Cushing, Frank Hamilton	II
Cunningham, Ann Pamela	II	Cushing, Harvey Williams	2
Cunningham, Kate Richards		Cushing, John Perkins	II
O'Hare		Cushing, Josiah Nelson	II
See O'Hare, Kate Richards		Cushing, Luther Stearns	II
(Cunningham)		Cushing, Thomas	II
Cupples, Samuel	II	Cushing, William	II
Cuppy, Will	4	Cushing, William Barker	II
Curley, James Michael	6	Cushman, Charlotte Saunders	III
Curme, George Oliver	4	Cushman, George Hewitt	III
Curran, John Joseph	2	Cushman, Joseph Augustine	4
Curran, Thomas Jerome	6	Cushman, Joshua	III
Currier, Charles Warren	II	Cushman, Pauline	III
Currier, Moody	II	Cushman, Robert	III
Currier, Nathaniel	II	Cushman, Susan Webb	III
Curry, George Law	II	Cushman, Vera Charlotte Scott	4
Curry, Jabez Lamar Monroe	II	Cushny, Arthur Robertson	III
Curry, John Steuart	4	Custer, George Armstrong	III
Curtin, Andrew Gregg	II	Custis, George Washington	
Curtin, Jeremiah	II	Parke	III
Curtis, Alfred Allen	II	Cutbush, James	III
Curtis, Benjamin Robbins	II	Cutler, Carroll	III
Curtis, Charles	2	Cutler, Elliott Carr	4
Curtis, Charles Pelham	6	Cutler, James Goold	III

Complete Index Guide

Name	Vol./Supp.	Name	Vol./Supp.
Cutler, Lizzie Petit	III	Dallas, George Mifflin	III
Cutler, Manasseh	III	Dallin, Cyrus Edwin	3
Cutler, Timothy	III	D'Aloes, Claude Jean	
Cutter, Charles Ammi	III	See Allouez, Claude Jean	
Cutter, Ephraim	III	Dalton, John Call	III
Cutter, George Washington	III	Dalton, Robert	III
Cutting, Bronson Murray	1	Daly, Arnold	
Cutting, James Ambrose	III	See Daly, Peter Christopher	
Cutting, Robert Fulton	1	Arnold	
Cuyler, Theodore	III	Daly, Augustin	
Cuyler, Theodore Ledyard	III	See Daly, John Augustin	
		Daly, Charles Patrick	III
Dablon, Claude	III	Daly, John Augustin	III
Dabney, Charles William	3	Daly, Marcus	III
Dabney, Richard	III	Daly, Peter Christopher Arnold	III
Dabney, Robert Lewis	III	Daly, Reginald Aldworth	6
Dabney, Thomas Smith		Dalzell, John	III
Gregory	III	Dalzell, Robert M.	III
Dabney, Virginius	III	Damon, Ralph Shepard	6
Daboll, Nathan	III	Damrosch, Frank Heino	2
Dabrowski, Joseph	III	Damrosch, Leopold	III
Da Costa, Jacob Mendez	III	Damrosch, Walter	4
Da Costa, John Chalmers	1	Dana, Charles Anderson	III
Daeger, Albert Thomas	1	Dana, Charles Loomis	1
Daft, Leo	III	Dana, Edward Salisbury	1
Dagg, John Leadley	III	Dana, Francis	III
Daggett, David	III	Dana, James	III
Daggett, Ellsworth	III	Dana, James Dwight	III
Daggett, Naphtali	III	Dana, James Freeman	III
Dahl, Theodor Halvorson	III	Dana, John Cotton	III
Dahlgren, John Adolphus		Dana, Napoleon Jackson	
Bernard	III	Tecumseh	III
Dahlgren, Sarah Madeleine		Dana, Richard	III
Vinton	III	Dana, Richard Henry (d. 1879)	III
Dakin, Henry Drysdale	5	Dana, Richard Henry (d. 1882)	III
Dakin, James Harrison	1	Dana, Samuel Luther	III
Dalcho, Frederick	III	Dana, Samuel Whittelsey	III
Dale, Chester	7	Dancel, Christian	III
Dale, Maud Murray Thompson	5	Dandridge, Dorothy Jean	7
Dale, Richard	III	Dandy, Walter Edward	4
Dale, Samuel	III	Dane, Nathan	III
Dale, Sir Thomas	III	Danenhower, John Wilson	III
Dall, Caroline Wells Healey	III	Danforth, Charles	III
Dall, William Healey	III	Danforth, Moseley Isaac	III
Dallas, Alexander James	III	Danforth, Thomas (d. 1699)	III

Complete Index Guide

Name	Vol./Supp.
Danforth, Thomas (d. 1786)	III
Daniel, John Moncure	III
Daniel, John Warwick.	III
Daniel, Peter Vivian	III
Daniels, Frank Albert	1
Daniels, Fred Harris	III
Daniels, Josephus	4
Daniels, Winthrop More	3
Dannreuther, Gustav	III
Da Ponte, Lorenzo	III
Darby, John	III
Darby, William	III
Dare, Virginia	III
Dargan, Edmund Strother	III
Dargan, Edwin Preston	2
Darke, William	III
Darley, Felix Octavius Carr	III
Darling, Flora Adams	III
Darling, Henry	III
Darling, Jay Norwood ("Ding")	7
Darling, Samuel Taylor	III
Darlington, William	III
Darrow, Clarence Seward	2
Dart, Henry Plauché	1
Darton, Nelson Horatio	4
Daugherty, Harry Micajah	3
Daveis, Charles Stewart	III
Daveiss, Joseph Hamilton	III
Davenport, Charles Benedict	3
Davenport, Edward Loomis	III
Davenport, Eugene	3
Davenport, Fanny Lily Gypsy	III
Davenport, George	III
Davenport, Herbert Joseph	1
Davenport, Homer Calvin	III
Davenport, Ira Erastus	III
Davenport, James	III
Davenport, John	III
Davenport, Russell Wheeler	5
Davenport, Thomas	III
Davenport, William H.	
See Davenport, Ira Erastus	
Davey, John	III
D'Avezac, Auguste Geneviève	
Valentin	III
David, John Baptist Mary	III
Davidge, John Beale	III
Davidge, William Pleater	III
Davidson, George	III
Davidson, Israel	2
Davidson, James Wood	III
Davidson, Jo	5
Davidson, John Wynn	III
Davidson, Lucretia Maria	III
Davidson, Margaret Miller	III
Davidson, Robert	III
Davidson, Thomas	III
Davidson, William Lee	III
Davie, William Richardson	III
Davies, Arthur Bowen	III
Davies, Henry Eugene	III
Davies, John Vipond	2
Davies, Joseph Edward	6
Davies, Marion Cecilia	7
Davies, Samuel	III
Daviess, Joseph Hamilton	
See Daveiss, Joseph Hamilton	
Daviess, Maria Thompson	III
Davis, Alexander Jackson	III
Davis, Andrew Jackson	III
Davis, Andrew McFarland	III
Davis, Arthur Powell	1
Davis, Arthur Vining	7
Davis, Charles Harold	1
Davis, Charles Henry (d. 1877)	III
Davis, Charles Henry (d. 1921)	III
Davis, Charles Henry Stanley	III
Davis, Cushman Kellogg	III
Davis, David	III
Davis, Dwight Filley	3
Davis, Edmund Jackson	III
Davis, Edwin Hamilton	III
Davis, Elmer Holmes	6
Davis, Ernest R. ("Ernie")	7
Davis, Francis Breese, Jr.	7
Davis, Garret	III
Davis, George	III
Davis, George Breckenridge	III

Complete Index Guide

Name	Vol./Supp.	Name	Vol./Supp.
Davis, George Whitefield	III	Davis, Winnie	
Davis, Harvey Nathaniel	5	See Davis, Varina Anne	
Davis, Henry	III	Jefferson	
Davis, Henry Gassaway	III	Davison, George Willets	5
Davis, Henry Gassett	III	Davison, Gregory Caldwell	1
Davis, Henry Winter	III	Davison, Henry Pomeroy	III
Davis, Horace	III	Davisson, Clinton Joseph	6
Davis, James John	4	Dawes, Charles Gates	5
Davis, Jeff	III	Dawes, Henry Laurens	III
Davis, Jefferson	III	Dawes, Rufus Cutler	2
Davis, Jefferson Columbus	III	Dawes, William	III
Davis, Jerome Dean	III	Dawkins, Henry	III
Davis, John (d. 1847)	III	Dawley, Almena	6
Davis, John (d. 1838)	III	Dawson, Francis Warrington	III
Davis, John (d. 1854)	III	Dawson, Henry Barton	III
Davis, John Chandler Bancroft	III	Dawson, John	III
Davis, John Lee	III	Dawson, Thomas Cleland	III
Davis, John Staige	4	Dawson, William Crosby	III
Davis, John Wesley	III	Day, Arthur Louis	6
Davis, John William	5	Day, Benjamin Henry	III
Davis, Joseph Robert	III	Day, Clarence Shepard	1
Davis, Katharine Bement	1	Day, David Alexander	III
Davis, Mary Evelyn Moore	III	Day, David Talbot	III
Davis, Matthew Livingston	III	Day, Edmund Ezra	5
Davis, Nathan Smith	III	Day, Frank Miles	III
Davis, Noah	III	Day, George Parmly	6
Davis, Noah Knowles	III	Day, Henry Noble	III
Davis, Norman Hezekiah	3	Day, Holman Francis	1
Davis, Oscar King	1	Day, Horace H.	III
Davis, Owen Gould	6	Day, James Gamble	III
Davis, Paulina Kellogg Wright	III	Day, James Roscoe	III
Davis, Pauline Morton Sabin	5	Day, Jeremiah	III
Davis, Phineas	III	Day, Luther	III
Davis, Raymond Cazallis	III	Day, Stephen	III
Davis, Rebecca Blaine Harding	III	Day, William Rufus	III
Davis, Reuben	III	Dayton, Elias	III
Davis, Richard Harding	III	Dayton, Jonathan	III
Davis, Stuart	7	Dayton, William Lewis	III
Davis, Varina Anne Jefferson	III	Deady, Matthew Paul	III
Davis, Varina Howell	III	Dealey, George Bannerman	4
Davis, William Augustine	III	Dean, Amos	III
Davis, William Hammatt	7	Dean, Bashford	III
Davis, William Morris	1	Dean, Gordon Evans	6
Davis, William Thomas	III	Dean, James Byron	5
		Dean, Julia	III

Complete Index Guide

Name	Vol./Supp.
Dean, "Man Mountain" See Leavitt, Frank Simmons	
Dean, Sidney	III
Dean, William Henry, Jr.	5
Deane, Charles	III
Deane, Samuel	III
Deane, Silas	III
De Angelis, Thomas Jefferson	1
Dearborn, Henry	III
Dearborn, Henry Alexander Scammwell	III
Dearing, John Lincoln	III
Dearth, Henry Golden	III
Deas, Zachariah Cantey	III
Deaver, John Blair	1
De Bardeleben, Henry Fairchild	III
De Barenne, Joannes Gregorius See Dusser de Barenne, Joannes Gregorius	
De Berdt, Dennys	III
De Bow, James Dunwoody Brownson	III
De Brahm, William Gerard	III
Debs, Eugene Victor	III
De Camp, Joseph Rodefer	III
Decatur, Stephen (d. 1808)	III
Decatur, Stephen (d. 1820)	III
De Coppet, Edward J.	III
De Costa, Benjamin Franklin	III
De Cuevas, Marquis	7
Deemer, Horace Emerson	III
Deems, Charles Force	III
Deere, John	III
"Deerfoot"	III
Deering, Nathaniel	III
Deering, William	III
De Fontaine, Felix Gregory	III
De Forest, Alfred Victor	3
De Forest, David Curtis	III
De Forest, Erastus Lyman	III
De Forest, John Kinne Hyde	III
De Forest, John William	III
DeForest, Lee	7
De Forest, Robert Weeks	1
De Graffenried, Christopher See Graffenried, Christopher, Baron de	
De Haas, Jacob See Haas, Jacob Judah Aaron de	
De Haas, John Philip	III
De Haven, Edwin Jesse	III
Deindörfer, Johannes	III
Deitzler, George Washington	III
De Kay, George Colman	III
De Kay, James Ellsworth	III
De Koven, Henry Louis Reginald	III
De Koven, James	III
De Lacy, Walter Washington	III
Delafield, Edward	III
Delafield, Francis	III
Delafield, John (d. 1824)	III
Delafield, John (d. 1853)	III
Delafield, Richard	III
De Lamar, Joseph Raphael	III
Delamater, Cornelius Henry	III
De Lancey, James (d. 1760)	III
De Lancey, James (d. 1800)	III
De Lancey, James (d. 1804)	III
De Lancey, Oliver	III
De Lancey, William Heathcote	III
Deland, Margaret	3
De Langlade, Charles Michel	III
Delano, Amassa	III
Delano, Columbus	III
Delano, Jane Arminda	III
Delano, William Adams	6
Delany, Martin Robinson	III
Delany, Patrick Bernard	III
Delavan, Edward Cornelius	III
De La Warr, Thomas West	III
DeLee, Joseph Bolivar	3
De Leeuw, Adolph Lodewyk	3
De Leon, Daniel	III
De Leon, Thomas Cooper	III
Deléry, François Charles	III
Dellenbaugh, Frederick Samuel	1
Del Mar, Alexander	III
Delmas, Delphin Michael	III

Complete Index Guide

Name	Vol./Supp.	Name	Vol./Supp.
Delmonico, Lorenzo	III	Derby, Elias Hasket (d. 1880)	III
De Long, George Washington	III	Derby, George Horatio	III
Del Ruth, Roy	7	Derby, Richard	III
De Luca, Giuseppe	4	Dercum, Francis Xavier	1
De Mézières y Clugny,		Dern, George Henry	2
Athanase	III	De Rose, Peter	5
DeMille, Cecil Blount	6	De Rosset, Moses John	III
De Mille, Henry Churchill	III	De Saussure, Henry William	III
Deming, Henry Champion	III	De Schweinitz, Edmund	
Deming, Philander	III	Alexander	
Deming, William		See Schweinitz, Edmund	
See Denning, William		Alexander de	
Demme, Charles Rudolph	III	De Schweinitz, George	
Dempster, John	III	Edmund	
Demuth, Charles	1	See Schweinitz, George	
Denby, Charles	III	Edmund de	
Denby, Edwin	III	Desha, Joseph	III
Dennett, Tyler	4	De Smet, Pierre-Jean	III
Dennie, Joseph	III	De Soto, Hernando	III
Denning, William	III	De Sylva, George	4
Dennis, Alfred Lewis Pinneo	1	Detmold, Christian Edward	III
Dennis, Eugene	7	De Trobriand, Régis Denis de	
Dennis, Frederic Shepard	1	Keredern	III
Dennis, Graham Barclay	III	Dett, Robert Nathaniel	3
Dennis, James Shepard	III	Deutsch, Gotthard	III
Dennison, Aaron Lufkin	III	Devaney, John Patrick	3
Dennison, Henry Sturgis	5	De Vargas Zapata y Lujan	
Dennison, Walter	III	Ponce de Leon, Diego	III
Dennison, William	III	Devens, Charles	III
Denny, George Vernon, Jr.	6	De Vere, Maximilian Schele	
Densmore, Frances	6	See Schele de Vere,	
Dent, Frederick Tracy	III	Maximilian	
Denver, James William	III	Devereux, John Henry	III
De Palma, Ralph	6	Devin, Thomas Casimer	III
De Paolis, Alessio	7	Devine, Edward Thomas	4
De Pauw, Washington Charles	III	De Vinne, Theodore Low	III
Depew, Chauncey Mitchell	III	DeVoto, Bernard Augustine	5
De Peyster, Abraham	III	Devoy, John	III
De Peyster, John Watts	III	De Vries, David Pietersen	III
De Priest, Oscar Stanton	5	Dew, Thomas Roderick	III
De Quille, Dan		Dewees, William Potts	III
See Wright, William		Dewey, Chester	III
Derbigny, Pierre Auguste		Dewey, George	III
Charles Bourguignon	III	Dewey, John	5
Derby, Elias Hasket (d. 1799)	III	Dewey, Melvil	1
Derby, Elias Hasket (d. 1826)	III	Dewey, Orville	III

Complete Index Guide

Name	Vol./Supp.	Name	Vol./Supp.
Dewey, Richard Smith	1	Dickson, David	III
Dewing, Francis	III	Dickson, Earle Ensign	7
Dewing, Maria Richards Oakey	III	Dickson, Leonard Eugene	5
Dewing, Thomas Wilmer	2	Dickson, Robert	III
De Witt, Simeon	III	Dickson, Samuel Henry	III
De Wolf, James	III	Dickson, Thomas	III
De Wolfe, Elsie	4	Didier, Eugene Lemoine	III
Dexter, Franklin	III	Dielman, Frederick	1
Dexter, Franklin Bowditch	III	Dietrichson, Johannes Wilhelm	
Dexter, Henry (d. 1876)	III	Christian	III
Dexter, Henry (d. 1910)	III	Dietz, Peter Ernest	4
Dexter, Henry Martyn	III	Digges, Dudley	4
Dexter, Samuel (d. 1810)	III	Dike, Samuel Warren	III
Dexter, Samuel (d. 1816)	III	Dill, James Brooks	III
Dexter, Timothy	III	Dillard, James Hardy	2
Dexter, Wirt	III	Dille, John Flint	6
De Young, Michel Harry	III	Diller, Burgoyne	7
Diat, Louis Felix	6	Diller, Joseph Silas	1
Diaz, Abby Morton	III	Dillinger, John	1
Dibble, Roy Floyd	III	Dillingham, Charles Bancroft	1
Dibrell, George Gibbs	III	Dillingham, Walter Francis	7
Dick, Elisha Cullen	III	Dillingham, William Paul	III
Dick, Robert Paine	III	Dillon, John Forrest	III
Dickerson, Edward Nicoll	III	Dillon, Sidney	III
Dickerson, Mahlon	III	Diman, Jeremiah Lewis	III
Dickerson, Philemon	III	Dimitry, Alexander	III
Dickey, Theophilus Lyle	III	Dimitry, Charles Patton	III
Dickie, George William	III	Dingley, Nelson	III
Dickins, John	III	Dingman, Mary Agnes	7
Dickinson, Anna Elizabeth	1	Dinsmoor, Robert	III
Dickinson, Anson	III	Dinwiddie, Albert Bledsoe	1
Dickinson, Charles Monroe	III	Dinwiddie, Courtenay	3
Dickinson, Daniel Stevens	III	Dinwiddie, Edwin Courtland	1
Dickinson, Donald McDonald	III	Dinwiddie, Robert	III
Dickinson, Edwin De Witt	7	Disbrow, William Stephen	III
Dickinson, Emily Elizabeth	III	Disston, Henry	III
Dickinson, Jacob McGavock	III	Disturnell, John	III
Dickinson, John (d. 1808)	III	Ditmars, Raymond Lee	3
Dickinson, John (d. 1952)	5	Ditrichstein, Leo	III
Dickinson, John Woodbridge	III	Ditson, George Leighton	III
Dickinson, Jonathan	III	Ditson, Oliver	III
Dickinson, Philemon	III	Dittemore, John Valentine	2
Dickinson, Preston	1	Diven, Alexander Samuel	III
Dickinson, Robert Latou	4	Divine, Father	7
Dickman, Joseph Theodore	III	Dix, Dorothea Lynde	III

Complete Index Guide

Name	Vol./Supp.	Name	Vol./Supp.
Dix, Dorothy		Dodge, Mary Elizabeth Mapes	III
See Gilmer, Elizabeth		Dodge, Raymond	3
Meriwether		Dodge, Theodore Ayrault	III
Dix, John Adams	III	Dodge, William de Leftwich	1
Dix, John Homer	III	Dodge, William Earl	III
Dix, Morgan	III	Dods, John Bovee	III
Dixon, James	III	Doe, Charles	III
Dixon, Joseph	III	Doheny, Edward Laurence	1
Dixon, Luther Swift	III	Doherty, Henry Latham	2
Dixon, Roland Burrage	1	Dolan, Thomas	III
Dixon, Thomas	4	Dold, Jacob	III
Dixon, William	III	Dole, Charles Fletcher	III
Dixwell, John	III	Dole, James Drummond	6
Doak, Samuel	III	Dole, Nathan Haskell	1
Doane, George Washington	III	Dole, Sanford Ballard	III
Doane, Thomas	III	D'Olier, Franklin	5
Doane, William Croswell	III	Dollar, Robert	1
Dobbin, James Cochran	III	Dolliver, Jonathan Prentiss	III
Dobbs, Arthur	III	Dolph, Joseph Norton	III
Dobie, Gilmour	4	Dombrowski, Joseph	
Dobie, J(ames) Frank	7	See Dabrowski, Joseph	
Dock, Christopher	III	Dominguez, Francisco Atanasio	
Dock, Lavinia Lloyd	6	See Escalante, Silvestre	
Dockstader, Lew	III	Velez de	
Dod, Albert Baldwin	III	Donahoe, Patrick	III
Dod, Daniel	III	Donahue, Peter	III
Dod, Thaddeus	III	Donaldson, Henry Herbert	2
Dodd, Frank Howard	III	Donck, Adriaen Van der	
Dodd, Lee Wilson	1	See Van der Donck,	
Dodd, Monroe Elmon	5	Adriaen	
Dodd, Samuel Calvin Tate	III	Donelson, Andrew Jackson	III
Dodd, William Edward	2	Dongan, Thomas	III
Doddridge, Joseph	III	Doniphan, Alexander William	III
Doddridge, Philip	III	Donlevy, Harriet Farley	
Dodge, Augustus Cæsar	III	See Farley, Harriet	
Dodge, David Low	III	Donn-Byrne, Brian Oswald	III
Dodge, Ebenezer	III	Donnell, James C.	III
Dodge, Grace Hoadley	III	Donnell, Robert	III
Dodge, Grenville Mellen	III	Donnelly, Charles Francis	III
Dodge, Henry	III	Donnelly, Eleanor Cecilia	III
Dodge, Henry Chee	4	Donnelly, Ignatius	III
Dodge, Jacob Richards	III	Donoghue, John	III
Dodge, Joseph Morrell	7	Donovan, John Joseph	2
Dodge, Mary Abigail	III	Donovan, William Joseph	6

Complete Index Guide

Name	Vol./Supp.	Name	Vol./Supp.
D'Ooge, Martin Luther	III	Douglas, James	III
Dooley, Thomas Anthony III ("Tom")	7	Douglas, Lloyd Cassel	5
		Douglas, Stephen Arnold	III
Doolittle, Amos	III	Douglas, William	III
Doolittle, Charles Leander	III	Douglas, William Lewis	III
Doolittle, Eric	III	Douglass, Andrew Ellicott	7
Doolittle, James Rood	III	Douglass, David Bates	III
Doran, George Henry	6	Douglass, Frederick	III
Dorchester, Daniel	III	Douglass, William	III
Doremus, Robert Ogden	III	Doull, James Angus	7
Doremus, Sarah Platt Haines	III	Dove, Arthur Garfield	4
Dorgan, Thomas Aloysius	III	Dove, David James	III
Dorion, Marie	III	Dow, Alex	3
Dorn, Harold Fred	7	Dow, Henry	III
Dornin, Thomas Aloysius	III	Dow, Herbert Henry	1
Dorr, Julia Caroline Ripley	III	Dow, Lorenzo (d. 1834)	III
Dorr, Thomas Wilson	III	Dow, Lorenzo (d. 1899)	III
Dorrell, William	III	Dow, Neal	III
Dorsch, Eduard	III	Dowell, Greensville	III
Dorset, Marion	1	Dowie, John Alexander	III
Dorsey, Anna Hanson McKenney	III	Dowling, Austin	1
		Downer, Eliphalet	III
Dorsey, George Amos	1	Downer, Samuel	III
Dorsey, James Owen	III	Downes, (Edwin) Olin	5
Dorsey, John Syng	III	Downes, John	III
Dorsey, Sarah Anne Ellis	III	Downey, John	III
Dorsey, Stephen Wallace	III	Downey, June Etta	1
Dorsey, Thomas Francis ("Tommy")	6	Downey, Sheridan	7
		Downing, Andrew Jackson	III
Dorsheimer, William Edward	III	Downing, Charles	III
Dos Passos, John Randolph	III	Downing, George	III
Doty, Elihu	III	Dowse, Thomas	III
Doty, James Duane	III	Doyle, Alexander	III
Doubleday, Abner	III	Doyle, Alexander Patrick	III
Doubleday, Frank Nelson	1	Doyle, John Thomas	III
Doubleday, Nelson	4	Doyle, Sarah Elizabeth	III
Doubleday, Neltje de Graff	III	Drake, Alexander Wilson	III
Dougherty, Dennis Joseph	5	Drake, Benjamin	III
Dougherty, Raymond Philip	1	Drake, Charles Daniel	III
Doughton, Robert Lee	5	Drake, Daniel	III
Doughty, Thomas	III	Drake, Edwin Laurentine	III
Doughty, William Henry	III	Drake, Frances Ann Denny	III
Douglas, Amanda Minnie	III	Drake, Francis Marion	III
Douglas, Benjamin	III	Drake, Francis Samuel	III
Douglas, Henry Kyd	III	Drake, John Burroughs	III

Complete Index Guide

Name	Vol./Supp.
Drake, Joseph Rodman	III
Drake, Samuel	III
Drake, Samuel Adams	III
Drake, Samuel Gardner	III
Draper, Andrew Sloan	III
Draper, Eben Sumner	III
Draper, Henry	III
Draper, Ira	III
Draper, John	III
Draper, John William	III
Draper, Lyman Copeland	III
Draper, Margaret Green	III
Draper, Richard	III
Draper, Ruth	6
Draper, William Franklin	III
Drayton, John	III
Drayton, Percival	III
Drayton, Thomas Fenwick	III
Drayton, William (d. 1790)	III
Drayton, William (d. 1846)	III
Drayton, William Henry	III
Dreier, Katherine Sophie	5
Dreier, Margaret	
See Robins, Margaret	
Dreier	
Dreier, Mary Elisabeth	7
Dreiser, Theodore	3
Dresel, Otto	III
Dresser, Louise Kerlin	7
Dressler, Marie	1
Drew, Charles Richard	4
Drew, Daniel	III
Drew, Georgiana Emma	
See Barrymore, Georgiana	
Emma Drew	
Drew, John (d. 1862)	III
Drew, John (d. 1927)	III
Drew, Louisa Lane	III
Drexel, Anthony Joseph	III
Drexel, Francis Martin	III
Drexel, Joseph William	III
Drexel, Katharine Mary	5
Dreyfus, Max	7
Drinker, Catharine Ann	
See Janvier, Catharine Ann	

Name	Vol./Supp.
Drinker, Cecil Kent	6
Drinkwater, Jennie Maria	III
Dripps, Isaac L.	III
Drisler, Henry	III
Dromgoole, William Allen	1
Dropsie, Moses Aaron	III
Drown, Thomas Messinger	III
Druillettes, Gabriel	III
Drum, Hugh Aloysius	5
Drumgoole, John Christopher	III
Drury, John Benjamin	III
Dryden, John Fairfield	III
Dryfoos, Orvil E.	7
Duane, Alexander	III
Duane, James	III
Duane, James Chatham	III
Duane, William	III
Duane, William	1
Duane, William John	III
Dubbs, Joseph Henry	III
Dubois, Augustus Jay	III
Dubois, John	III
DuBois, William Edward	
Burghardt	7
Du Bois, William Ewing	III
Du Bose, William Porcher	III
Du Bourg, Louis Guillaume	
Valentin	III
Dubuque, Julien	III
Du Chaillu, Paul Belloni	III
Duché, Jacob	III
Duchesne, Rose Philippine	III
Duchinn, Edward Frank	
("Eddy")	5
Dudley, Benjamin Winslow	III
Dudley, Charles Benjamin	III
Dudley, Charles Edward	III
Dudley, Edward Bishop	III
Dudley, Joseph	III
Dudley, Paul	III
Dudley, Thomas	III
Dudley, William Russel	III
Duer, John	III
Duer, William	III
Duer, William Alexander	III

Complete Index Guide

Name	Vol./Supp.	Name	Vol./Supp.
Duff, Mary Ann Dyke	III	Dunlap, John	III
Duffield, George (d. 1790)	III	Dunlap, Robert Pinckney	III
Duffield, George (d. 1868)	III	Dunlap, William	III
Duffield, Samuel Augustus		Dunlop, James	III
Willoughby	III	Dunmore, John Murray, Earl of	III
Duffy, Edmund	7	Dunn, Charles	III
Duffy, Francis Patrick	1	Dunn, William McKee	III
Duffy, Hugh	5	Dunn, Williamson	III
Dufour, John James	III	Dunne, Finley Peter	2
Duganne, Augustine Joseph		Dunning, Albert Elijah	III
Hickey	III	Dunning, William Archibald	III
Dugdale, Richard Louis	III	Dunster, Henry	III
Duggar, Benjamin Minge	6	Dunwoody, William Hood	III
Dugué, Charles Oscar	III	Du Ponceau, Pierre Étienne	III
Duhring, Louis Adolphus	III	Du Pont, Alfred Irénée	1
Duke, Basil Wilson	III	Du Pont, Eleuthère Irénée	III
Duke, Benjamin Newton	III	Du Pont, Francis Irénée	3
Duke, James Buchanan	III	Du Pont, Henry	III
Dulany, Daniel (d. 1753)	III	Du Pont, Henry Algernon	III
Dulany, Daniel (d. 1797)	III	Du Pont, Irénée	7
Dulles, John Foster	6	Du Pont, Lammot	5
Duluth, Daniel Greysolon,		Du Pont, Pierre Samuel	5
Sieur	III	Du Pont, Samuel Francis	III
Dumaine, Frederic Christopher	5	Du Pont, Thomas Coleman	1
Dummer, Jeremiah (d. 1718)	III	Du Pont, Victor Marie	III
Dummer, Jeremiah (d. 1739)	III	Dupratz, Antoine Simon Le	
Dumont, Allen Balcom	7	Page	III
Dumont, Margaret	7	Dupuy, Eliza Ann	III
Dun, Robert Graham	III	Durand, Asher Brown	III
Dunbar, Charles Franklin	III	Durand, Cyrus	III
Dunbar, (Helen) Flanders	6	Durand, Élie Magloire	III
Dunbar, Moses	III	Durand, William Frederick	6
Dunbar, Paul Laurence	III	Durant, Charles Ferson	III
Dunbar, Robert	III	Durant, Henry	III
Dunbar, William	III	Durant, Henry Fowle	III
Duncan, Isadora	III	Durant, Thomas Clark	III
Duncan, James (d. 1928)	III	Durant, Thomas Jefferson	III
Duncan, James (d. 1928)	1	Durant, William Crapo	4
Duncan, Joseph	III	Duranty, Walter	6
Duncan, Robert Kennedy	III	Durbin, John Price	III
Dundee, Johnny (Joseph		Durell, Edward Henry	III
Carrora)	7	Durfee, Job	III
Dunglison, Robley	III	Durfee, Thomas	III
Dunham, Henry Morton	III	Durfee, William Franklin	III
Duniway, Abigail Jane Scott	III	Durfee, Zoheth Sherman	III

Complete Index Guide

Name	Vol./Supp.	Name	Vol./Supp.
Durham, Caleb Wheeler	III	Dyer, Isadore	III
Durivage, Francis Alexander	III	Dyer, Louis	III
Durkee, John	III	Dyer, Mary	III
Durkin, Martin Patrick	5	Dyer, Nehemiah Mayo	III
Durrett, Reuben Thomas	III	Dykstra, Clarence Addison	4
Durrie, Daniel Steele	III	Dylander, John	III
Durstine, Roy Sarles	7	Dymond, John	III
Duryea, Charles Edgar	2	Dyott, Thomas W.	III
Duryea, Hermanes Barkulo	III		
Duryée, Abram	III	Eads, James Buchanan	III
Du Simitière, Pierre Eugène	III	Eagels, Jeanne	III
Dusser de Barenne, Joannes		Eakins, Thomas	III
Gregorius	2	Eames, Charles	III
Dustin, Hannah	III	Eames, Wilberforce	2
Dutton, Clarence Edward	III	Earhart, Amelia Mary	2
Dutton, Henry	III	Earle, Alice Morse	III
Dutton, Samuel Train	III	Earle, Edward Mead	5
Duval, William Pope	III	Earle, James	III
Duvall, Gabriel	1	Earle, Mortimer Lamson	III
Duveneck, Frank	III	Earle, Pliny	III
Duyckinck, Evert Augustus	III	Earle, Pliny (son of Pliny)	III
Duyckinck, George Long	III	Earle, Ralph	III
Dwenger, Joseph	III	Earle, Ralph	2
Dwiggins, William Addison	6	Earle, Thomas	III
Dwight, Arthur Smith	4	Early, John	III
Dwight, Benjamin Woodbridge	III	Early, Jubal Anderson	III
Dwight, Edmund	III	Early, Peter	III
Dwight, Francis	III	Early, Stephen Tyree	5
Dwight, Harrison Gray Otis	III	Easley, Ralph Montgomery	2
Dwight, Henry Otis	III	East, Edward Murray	2
Dwight, John Sullivan	III	Eastman, Arthur MacArthur	III
Dwight, Nathaniel	III	Eastman, Charles Gamage	III
Dwight, Sereno Edwards	III	Eastman, Enoch Worthen	III
Dwight, Theodore (d. 1846)	III	Eastman, George	1
Dwight, Theodore (d. 1866)	III	Eastman, Harvey Gridley	III
Dwight, Theodore William	III	Eastman, John Robie	III
Dwight, Thomas	III	Eastman, Joseph Bartlett	3
Dwight, Timothy (d. 1817)	III	Eastman, Timothy Corser	III
Dwight, Timothy (d. 1916)	III	Eastman, William Reed	III
Dwight, William	III	Easton, John	III
Dworshak, Henry Clarence	7	Easton, Nicholas	III
Dyar, Harrison Gray	III	Eaton, Amos	III
Dye, William McEntyre	III	Eaton, Benjamin Harrison	III
Dyer, Alexander Brydie	III	Eaton, Charles Aubrey	5
Dyer, Eliphalet	III	Eaton, Daniel Cady	III

Complete Index Guide

Name	Vol./Supp.	Name	Vol./Supp.
Eaton, Dorman Bridgman	III	Edmondson, William	5
Eaton, Homer	III	Edmunds, Charles Wallis	3
Eaton, John	III	Edmunds, George Franklin	III
Eaton, John Henry	III	Edsall, David Linn	3
Eaton, Joseph Oriel	III	Edwards, Bela Bates	III
Eaton, Margaret L. O'Neill		Edwards, Charles	III
See O'Neale, Margaret		Edwards, Clarence Ransom	1
Eaton, Nathaniel	III	Edwards, Everett Eugene	5
Eaton, Samuel	III	Edwards, Henry Waggaman	III
Eaton, Theophilus	III	Edwards, John (d. 1746)	III
Eaton, William	III	Edwards, John (d. 1837)	III
Eaton, Wyatt	III	Edwards, Jonathan (d. 1758)	III
Eberle, Edward Walter	III	Edwards, Jonathan (d. 1801)	III
Eberle, John	III	Edwards, Julian	III
Echols, John	III	Edwards, Justin	III
Eckart, William Roberts	III	Edwards, Morgan	III
Eckels, James Herron	III	Edwards, Ninian	III
Eckert, Thomas Thompson	III	Edwards, Ninian Wirt	III
Eckford, Henry	III	Edwards, Oliver	III
Eckstein, John	III	Edwards, Pierpont	III
Eckstorm, Fannie Hardy	4	Edwards, Richard Stanislaus	6
Eddis, William	III	Edwards, Talmadge	III
Eddy, Clarence	2	Edwards, Weldon Nathaniel	III
Eddy, Daniel Clarke	III	Edwards, William	III
Eddy, Harrison Prescott	2	Edwards, William Henry	III
Eddy, Henry Turner	III	Edwin, David	III
Eddy, Manton Sprague	7	Eells, Dan Parmelee	III
Eddy, Mary Morse Baker	III	Egan, Maurice Francis	III
Eddy, Thomas	III	Egan, Michael	III
Edebohls, George Michael	III	Egan, Patrick	III
Eden, Charles	III	Eggleston, Edward	III
Eden, Robert	III	Eggleston, George Cary	III
Edes, Benjamin	III	Egle, William Henry	III
Edes, Robert Thaxter	III	Egleston, Thomas	III
Edeson, Robert	1	Ehninger, John Whetten	III
Edgar, Charles	III	Ehrlich, Arnold Bogumil	III
Edge, Walter Evans	6	Eichberg, Julius	III
Edgerton, Alfred Peck	III	Eichelberger, Robert Lawrence	7
Edgerton, Sidney	III	Eichholtz, Jacob	III
Edgrene, August Hjalmar	III	Eickemeyer, Rudolf	III
Edison, Thomas Alva	1	Eidlitz, Cyrus Lazelle Warner	III
Edman, Irwin	5	Eidlitz, Leopold	III
Edmands, John	III	Eielsen, Elling	III
Edmonds, Francis William	III	Eigenmann, Carl H.	III
Edmonds, John Worth	III	Eilers, Frederic Anton	III

Complete Index Guide

Name	Vol./Supp.	Name	Vol./Supp.
Eilshemius, Louis Michel	3	Elliott, William	III
Eimbeck, William	III	Ellis, Calvin	III
Einhorn, David	III	Ellis, Carleton	3
Einstein, Albert	5	Ellis, Edward Sylvester	III
Eisenhart, Luther Pfahler	7	Ellis, George Edward	III
Eklund, Carl Robert	7	Ellis, George Washington	III
Elbert, Samuel	III	Ellis, Henry	III
Elder, Samuel James	III	Ellis, Job Bicknell	III
Elder, Susan Blanchard	III	Ellis, John Washington	III
Elder, William	III	Ellis, John Willis	III
Elder, William Henry	III	Ellis, Powhatan	III
Eldridge, Shalor Winchell	III	Ellis, Seth Hockett	III
Eliot, Charles	III	Ellmaker, (Emmett) Lee	5
Eliot, Charles William	III	Ellsworth, Elmer Ephraim	III
Eliot, Jared	III	Ellsworth, Henry Leavitt	III
Eliot, John	III	Ellsworth, Henry William	III
Eliot, Samuel	III	Ellsworth, Lincoln	5
Eliot, Samuel Atkins	III	Ellsworth, Oliver	III
Eliot, Thomas Stearns	7	Ellsworth, William Wolcott	III
Eliot, William Greenleaf	III	Elman, Robert	6
Elkin, William Lewis	1	Elmer, Ebenezer	III
Elkins, Stephen Benton	III	Elmer, Jonathan	III
Elkins, William Lukens	III	Elmer, Lucius Quintius	
Ellery, Frank	III	Cincinnatus	III
Ellery, William	III	Elmore, Franklin Harper	III
Ellet, Charles	III	Elmslie, George Grant	5
Ellet, Elizabeth Fries Lummis	III	Elsberg, Charles Albert	4
Ellicott, Andrew	III	Elsberg, Louis	III
Ellicott, Joseph	III	Elson, Louis Charles	III
Elliot, Daniel Giraud	III	Elvehjem, Conrad Arnold	7
Elliot, James	III	Elwell, Frank Edwin	III
Elliot, Jonathan	III	Elwell, John Johnson	III
Elliott, Aaron Marshall	III	Elwyn, Alfred Langdon	III
Elliott, Benjamin	III	Ely, Hanson Edward	6
Elliott, Charles	III	Ely, Richard Theodore	3
Elliott, Charles Burke	1	Elzey, Arnold	III
Elliott, Charles Loring	III	Embree, Edwin Rogers	4
Elliott, Jesse Duncan	III	Embree, Elihu	III
Elliott, John	III	Embury, Emma Catherine	III
Elliott, John Lovejoy	3	Embury, Philip	III
Elliott, Maxine	2	Emerson, Benjamin Kendall	1
Elliott, Sarah Barnwell	III	Emerson, Edward Waldo	III
Elliott, Stephen	III	Emerson, Ellen Russell	III
Elliott, Walter Hackett Robert	III	Emerson, George Barrell	III
Elliott, Washington Lafayette	III	Emerson, Gouverneur	III

Complete Index Guide

Name	Vol./Supp.	Name	Vol./Supp.
Emerson, Haven	6	Englis, John	III
Emerson, James Ezekiel	III	English, Elbert Hartwell	III
Emerson, Joseph	III	English, George Bethune	III
Emerson, Mary Moody	III	English, James Edward	III
Emerson, Oliver Farrar	III	English, Thomas Dunn	III
Emerson, Ralph	III	English, William Hayden	III
Emerson, Ralph Waldo	III	Enneking, John Joseph	III
Emerson, Rollins	4	Eno, William Phelps	3
Emerson, William	III	Ensley, Enoch	III
Emerton, Ephraim	1	Entwistle, James	III
Emerton, James Henry	1	Eppes, John Wayles	III
Emery, Albert Hamilton	III	Epstein, Abraham	3
Emery, Charles Edward	III	Epstein, Jacob	6
Emery, Henry Crosby	III	Epstein, Philip G.	5
Emery, Lucilius Alonzo	III	Erdman, Charles Rosenbury	6
Emery, Stephen Albert	III	Ericsson, John	III
Emmet, Thomas Addis		Erlanger, Abraham Lincoln	III
(d. 1827)	III	Erlanger, Joseph	7
Emmet, Thomas Addis		Ernst, Harold Clarence	III
(d. 1919)	III	Ernst, Oswald Herbert	III
Emmet, William Le Roy	3	Errett, Isaac	III
Emmett, Burton	1	Errol, Leon	5
Emmett, Daniel Decatur	III	Erskine, John (d. 1895)	III
Emmons, Ebenezer	III	Erskine, John (d. 1951)	5
Emmons, George Foster	III	Erskine, Robert	III
Emmons, Nathanael	III	Erving, George William	III
Emmons, Samuel Franklin	III	Esbjörn, Lars Paul	III
Emory, John	III	Escalante, Silvestre Velez de	III
Emory, William Hemsley	III	Esch, John Jacob	3
Emott, James (d. 1850)	III	Esher, John Jacob	III
Emott, James (d. 1884)	III	Espejo, Antonio de	III
Endecott, John	III	Espy, James Pollard	III
Endicott, Charles Moses	III	Estabrook, Joseph	III
Endicott, John		Estaugh, Elizabeth Haddon	III
See Endecott, John		Esterbrook, Richard	III
Endicott, Mordecai Thomas	III	Esterly, George	III
Endicott, William		Estes, Dana	III
Crowninshield	III	Estey, Jacob	III
Enelow, Hyman Gerson	1	Ettwein, John	III
Engel, Carl	3	Eustis, Dorothy Harrison	4
Engelhardt, Zephyrin	1	Eustis, George (d. 1858)	III
Engelmann, George	III	Eustis, George (d. 1872)	III
Engelmann, George Julius	III	Eustis, Henry Lawrence	III
England, John	III	Eustis, James Biddle	III
Engle, Clair William Walter	7	Eustis, William	III

Complete Index Guide

Name	Vol./Supp.	Name	Vol./Supp.
Evans, Anthony Walton Whyte	III	Ewing, Charles	III
Evans, Augusta Jane	III	Ewing, Finis	III
Evans, Charles	1	Ewing, Hugh Boyle	III
Evans, Clement Anselm	III	Ewing, James (d. 1806)	III
Evans, Edward Payson	III	Ewing, James (d. 1943)	3
Evans, Evan	III	Ewing, James Caruthers Rhea	III
Evans, Frederick William	III	Ewing, John	III
Evans, George	III	Ewing, Thomas (d. 1871)	III
Evans, George Alfred	III	Ewing, Thomas (d. 1896)	III
Evans, George Henry	III	Eytinge, Rose	III
Evans, Henry Clay	III	Ezekiel, Moses Jacob	III
Evans, Hugh Davey	III		
Evans, John (fl. 1703–31)	III	Faber, John Eberhard	III
Evans, John (d. 1897)	III	Faccioli, Giuseppe	1
Evans, Lawrence Boyd	III	Fackler, David Parks	III
Evans, Lewis	III	Faesch, John Jacob	III
Evans, Nathan George	III	Fagan, James Fleming	III
Evans, Nathaniel	III	Fagan, Mark Matthew	5
Evans, Oliver	III	Fages, Pedro	III
Evans, Robley Dunglison	III	Faget, Jean Charles	III
Evans, Thomas	III	Fahnestock, Harris Charles	III
Evans, Thomas Wiltberger	III	Fair, James Graham	III
Evans, Walter	III	Fairbank, Calvin	III
Evans, Warren Felt	III	Fairbanks, Charles Warren	III
Evans, William Thomas	III	Fairbanks, Douglas	2
Evarts, Jeremiah	III	Fairbanks, Erastus	III
Evarts, William Maxwell	III	Fairbanks, Henry	III
Eve, Joseph	III	Fairbanks, Thaddeus	III
Eve, Paul Fitzsimons	III	Fairburn, William Armstrong	4
Everendon, Walter	III	Fairchild, Blair	1
Everett, Alexander Hill	III	Fairchild, Charles Stebbins	III
Everett, Charles Carroll	III	Fairchild, David Grandison	5
Everett, David	III	Fairchild, George Thompson	III
Everett, Edward	III	Fairchild, James Harris	III
Everett, Robert	III	Fairchild, Lucius	III
Everleigh, Ada	4	Fairchild, Mary Salome Cutler	III
Everleigh, Minna	4	Fairchild, Stephen Muir	4
Evermann, Barton Warren	1	Fairfax, Beatrice	
Evers, Medgar Wiley	7	See Manning, Marie	
Ewbank, Thomas	III	Fairfax, Donald McNeill	III
Ewell, Benjamin Stoddert	III	Fairfax, Thomas	III
Ewell, James	III	Fairfield, Edmund Burke	III
Ewell, Richard Stoddert	III	Fairfield, John	III
Ewell, Thomas	III	Fairfield, Sumner Lincoln	III
Ewer, Ferdinand Cartwright	III	Fairlamb, James Remington	III

Complete Index Guide

Name	Vol./Supp.	Name	Vol./Supp.
Fairless, Benjamin F.	7	Farquhar, Percival	5
Fairlie, John Archibald	4	Farragut, David Glasgow	III
Falckner, Daniel	III	Farragut, George	III
Falckner, Justus	III	Farrand, Beatrix Cadwalader	
Falk, Maurice	4	Jones	6
Falk, Otto Herbert	2	Farrand, Livingston	2
Falkner, Roland Post	2	Farrand, Max	3
Fall, Albert Bacon	3	Farrar, Edgar Howard	III
Fallows, Samuel	III	Farrar, John	III
Faneuil, Peter	III	Farrar, Timothy	III
Fannin, James Walker	III	Farrell, James Augustine	3
Fanning, Alexander Campbell		Farrer, Henry	III
Wilder	III	Farrington, Joseph Rider	5
Fanning, David	III	Farrington, Wallace Rider	1
Fanning, Edmund (d. 1818)	III	Farson, Negley	6
Fanning, Edmund (d. 1841)	III	Farwell, Arthur	5
Fanning, John Thomas	III	Farwell, Charles Benjamin	III
Fanning, Nathaniel	III	Farwell, John Villiers	III
Fanning, Tolbert	III	Fassett, Cornelia Adèle Strong	III
Farabee, William Curtis	III	Fassett, Jacob Sloat	III
Faran, James John	III	Father Divine	
Fargo, William George	III	See Divine, Father	
Faribault, Jean Baptiste	III	Faulk, Andrew Jackson	III
Farish, William Stamps	3	Faulkner, Charles James	
Farley, Harriet	III	(d. 1884)	III
Farley, John Murphy	III	Faulkner, Charles James	
Farlow, William Gilson	III	(d. 1929)	III
Farman, Elbert Eli	III	Faulkner (Falkner), William	7
Farmer, Fannie Merritt	III	Faunce, William Herbert Perry	III
Farmer, Ferdinand	III	Fauquier, Francis	III
Farmer, Hannah Tobey		Fauset, Jessie	7
Shapleigh	III	Faust, Frederick Shiller	3
Farmer, John (d. 1838)	III	Faversham, William Alfred	2
Farmer, John (d. 1859)	III	Favill, Henry Baird	III
Farmer, Moses Gerrish	III	Fawcett, Edgar	III
Farnam, Henry	III	Fay, Edward Allen	III
Farnam, Henry Walcott	1	Fay, Edwin Whitfield	III
Farnham, Eliza Woodson		Fay, Francis Anthony	
Burhans	III	("Frank")	7
Farnham, Russel	III	Fay, Jonas	III
Farnham, Thomas Jefferson	III	Fay, Theodore Sedgwick	III
Farnsworth, Elon John	III	Fayerweather, Daniel Burton	III
Farnsworth, John Franklin	III	Fayssoux, Peter	III
Farnum, Dustin Lancy	III	Fazenda, Louise Marie	7
Farnum, Franklyn	7	Fearing, Kenneth Flexner	7

Complete Index Guide

Name	Vol./Supp.	Name	Vol./Supp.
Fearn, John Walker	III	Ferguson, Samuel	4
Featherston, Winfield Scott	III	Ferguson, Thomas Barker	III
Febiger, Christian	III	Ferguson, William Jason	III
Fechter, Charles Albert	III	Ferguson, William Porter	
Fee, John Gregg	III	Frisbee	III
Feehan, Patrick Augustine	III	Fermi, Enrico	5
Feininger, Lyonel (Charles		Fernald, Charles Henry	III
Léonell Adrian)	6	Fernald, James Champlin	III
Fejos, Paul	7	Fernald, Merritt Lyndon	4
Feke, Robert	III	Fernow, Bernhard Eduard	III
Felch, Alpheus	III	Fernow, Berthold	III
Fell, John	III	Ferree, Clarence Errol	3
Fels, Joseph	III	Ferrel, William	III
Fels, Samuel Simeon	4	Ferrero, Edward	III
Felsenthal, Bernhard	III	Ferris, George Washington	
Felt, Joseph Barlow	III	Gale	III
Felton, Cornelius Conway	III	Ferris, Isaac	III
Felton, Rebecca Latimer	III	Ferris, Jean Léon Gérôme	III
Felton, Samuel Morse	III	Ferris, Woodbridge Nathan	III
Felton, William Harrell	III	Ferry, Elisha Peyre	III
Fendall, Josias	III	Ferry, Orris Sanford	III
Fenger, Christian	III	Ferry, Thomas White	III
Fenichel, Otto	4	Fersen, Hans Axel, Count von	III
Fenn, William Wallace	1	Fess, Simeon Davidson	2
Fennell, James	III	Fessenden, Francis	III
Fenneman, Nevin Melancthon	3	Fessenden, James Deering	III
Fenner, Arthur	III	Fessenden, Reginald Aubrey	1
Fenner, Burt Leslie	III	Fessenden, Samuel	III
Fenner, Charles Erasmus	III	Fessenden, Thomas Green	III
Fenner, James	III	Fessenden, William Pitt	III
Fenno, John	III	Fetter, Frank Albert	4
Fenollosa, Ernest Francisco	III	Fetterman, William Judd	III
Fenton, Reuben Eaton	III	Feuchtwanger, Lion	6
Fenwick, Benedict Joseph	III	Few, Ignatius Alphonso	III
Fenwick, Edward Dominic	III	Few, William	III
Fenwick, George	III	Few, William Preston	2
Fenwick, John	III	Fewkes, Jesse Walter	III
Fenwicke, John		Ffoulke, Charles Mather	III
See Fenwick, John		Ffrench, Charles Dominic	III
Ferguson, Alexander Hugh	III	Field, Benjamin Hazard	III
Ferguson, Elizabeth Graeme	III	Field, Charles William	III
Ferguson, James Edward	3	Field, Cyrus West	III
Ferguson, John Calvin	3	Field, David Dudley (d. 1867)	III
Ferguson, Miriam Amanda		Field, David Dudley (d. 1894)	III
Wallace	7	Field, Eugene	III

Complete Index Guide

Name	Vol./Supp.	Name	Vol./Supp.
Field, Fred Tarbell	4	Finn, Francis James	III
Field, Henry Martyn	III	Finn, Henry James William	III
Field, Herbert Haviland	III	Finney, Charles Grandison	III
Field, Joseph M.	III	Finney, John Miller Turpin	3
Field, Kate		Finotti, Joseph Maria	III
See Field, Mary Katherine		Firestone, Harvey Samuel	2
Keemle		Fischer, Emil Friedrich August	III
Field, Marshall	III	Fischer, Ruth	7
Field, Marshall, III	6	Fish, Carl Russell	1
Field, Marshall, IV	7	Fish, Hamilton	III
Field, Mary Katherine Keemle	III	Fish, Nicholas	III
Field, Maunsell Bradhurst	III	Fish, Preserved	III
Field, Richard Stockton	III	Fish, Stuyvesant	III
Field, Robert	III	Fishback, William Meade	III
Field, Roswell Martin	III	Fisher, Alfred J., and Charles	
Field, Stephen Dudley	III	T.	7
Field, Stephen Johnson	III	Fisher, Alvan	III
Field, Thomas Warren	III	Fisher, "Bud"	
Field, Walbridge Abner	III	See Fisher, Henry Conroy	
Fields, Annie Adams	III	Fisher, Clara	III
Fields, James Thomas	III	Fisher, Clarence Stanley	3
Fields, Lewis Maurice		Fisher, Clark	III
See under Weber, Joseph		Fisher, Daniel Webster	III
Morris		Fisher, Dorothea Frances	
Fields, William Claude	4	Canfield	6
Fifer, Joseph Wilson	2	Fisher, Ebenezer	III
Filene, Edward Albert	2	Fisher, Frederic John	3
Fillebrown, Thomas	III	Fisher, Frederick Bohn	2
Fillmore, Charles	4	Fisher, George Jackson	III
Fillmore, John Comfort	III	Fisher, George Park	III
Fillmore, Millard	III	Fisher, George Purnell	III
Filson, John	III	Fisher, Hammond Edward	5
Finch, Francis Miles	III	Fisher, Harrison	1
Finck, Henry Theophilus	III	Fisher, Henry Conroy	5
Findlay, James	III	Fisher, Irving	4
Findley, William	III	Fisher, John Dix	III
Fine, Henry Burchard	III	Fisher, Joshua Francis	III
Fink, Albert	III	Fisher, Philip	
Finlay, Carlos Juan	III	See Copley, Thomas	
Finlay, Hugh	III	Fisher, Sidney George	III
Finley, James Bradley	III	Fisher, Sydney George	III
Finley, John Huston	2	Fisher, Theodore Willis	III
Finley, Martha Farquharson	III	Fisher, Walter Lowrie	1
Finley, Robert	III	Fisher, William Arms	4
Finley, Samuel	III	Fisk, Clinton Bowen	III

Complete Index Guide

Name	Vol./Supp.	Name	Vol./Supp.
Fisk, James (d. 1844)	III	Fitzpatrick, Thomas	III
Fisk, James (d. 1872)	III	Fitzsimmons, Robert	
Fisk, Wilbur	III	Prometheus	III
Fiske, Amos Kidder	III	Fitzsimmons or Fitzsimins,	
Fiske, Bradley Allen	3	Thomas	III
Fiske, Daniel Willard	III	Flad, Henry	III
Fiske, Fidelia	III	Flaget, Benedict Joseph	III
Fiske, George Converse	III	Flagg, Azariah Cutting	III
Fiske, Haley	III	Flagg, Edmund	III
Fiske, Harrison Grey	3	Flagg, Ernest	4
Fiske, John (d. 1797)	III	Flagg, George Whiting	III
Fiske, John (d. 1901)	III	Flagg, James Montgomery	6
Fiske, Minnie Maddern	1	Flagg, Jared Bradley	III
Fiske, Stephen Ryder	III	Flagg, Josiah	III
Fitch, Asa	III	Flagg, Josiah Foster	III
Fitch, Clyde		Flagg, Thomas Wilson	III
See Fitch, William Clyde		Flagler, Henry Morrison	III
Fitch, John	III	Flagler, John Haldane	III
Fitch, Samuel	III	Flaherty, Robert Joseph	5
Fitch, Thomas	III	Flanagan, Edward Joseph	4
Fitch, William Clyde	III	Flanagan, Webster	III
Fite, Warner	5	Flanagin, Harris	III
Fitler, Edwin Henry	III	Flanders, Henry	III
Fitton, James	III	Flandrau, Charles Eugene	III
Fitz, Henry	III	Flandrau, Charles Macomb	2
Fitz, Reginald Heber	III	Flannagan, John Bernard	3
Fitzgerald, Alice Louise		Flannery, John	III
Florence	7	Flather, John Joseph	III
Fitzgerald, Desmond	III	Fleeming, John	
Fitzgerald, Edward	III	See Fleming, John	
Fitzgerald, Edwin		Fleet, Thomas	III
See Foy, Eddie		Flegenheimer, Arthur	1
Fitzgerald, Francis Scott Key	2	Fleischmann, Charles Louis	III
Fitzgerald, John Francis	4	Fleisher, Benjamin Wilfrid	4
Fitzgerald, Oscar Penn	III	Fleming, Aretas Brooks	III
Fitzgerald, Thomas	III	Fleming, Arthur Henry	2
Fitzgibbon, Catherine		Fleming, John (fl. 1764–1800)	III
See Irene, Sister		Fleming, John (d. 1894)	III
Fitzhugh, George	III	Fleming, John Adam	6
Fitzhugh, William	III	Fleming, Walter Lynwood	1
Fitzpatrick, Benjamin	III	Fleming, William	III
Fitzpatrick, John	4	Fleming, Williamina Paton	
Fitzpatrick, John Bernard	III	Stevens	III
Fitzpatrick, John Clement	2	Fleming, William Maybury	III
Fitzpatrick, Morgan Cassius	III	Fletcher, Alice Cunningham	III

Complete Index Guide

Name	Vol./Supp.	Name	Vol./Supp.
Fletcher, Benjamin	1	Fogg, George Gilman	III
Fletcher, Calvin	III	Fokine, Michel	3
Fletcher, Duncan Upshaw	2	Folger, Charles James	III
Fletcher, Henry Prather	6	Folger, Henry Clay	III
Fletcher, Horace	III	Folger, Peter	III
Fletcher, James Cooley	III	Folger, Walter	III
Fletcher, John Gould	4	Folin, Otto Knut Olof	1
Fletcher, Richard	III	Folk, Joseph Wingate	III
Fletcher, Robert (d. 1912)	III	Folks, Homer	7
Fletcher, Robert (d. 1936)	2	Follen, Charles	III
Fletcher, Thomas Clement	III	Follen, Eliza Lee Cabot	III
Fletcher, William Asa	III	Follen, Karl Theodor Christian	
Fletcher, William Baldwin	III	See Follen, Charles	
Flexner, Abraham	6	Follett, Mary Parker	1
Flexner, Bernard	3	Folsom, Charles	III
Flexner, Jennie Maas	3	Folsom, George	III
Flexner, Simon	4	Folsom, Nathaniel	III
Flick, Lawrence Francis	2	Folwell, Samuel	III
Flickinger, Daniel Kumler	III	Folwell, William Watts	III
Flint, Albert Stowell	III	Fonda, John H.	III
Flint, Austin (d. 1886)	III	Font, Pedro	III
Flint, Austin (d. 1915)	III	Foot, Samuel Augustus	III
Flint, Charles Louis	III	Foot, Solomon	III
Flint, Charles Ranlett	1	Foote, Andrew Hull	III
Flint, Timothy	III	Foote, Arthur William	2
Flint, Weston	III	Foote, Henry Stuart	III
Florence, Thomas Birch	III	Foote, John Ambrose	1
Florence, William Jermyn	III	Foote, Lucius Harwood	III
Flower, Benjamin Orange	III	Foote, Samuel Augustus	
Flower, George	III	See Foot, Samuel Augustus	
Flower, Lucy Louisa Coues	III	Foote, William Henry	1
Flower, Richard	III	Foraker, Joseph Benson	III
Flower, Roswell Pettibone	III	Forbes, Edwin	III
Floy, James	III	Forbes, John (d. 1759)	III
Floyd, John	III	Forbes, John (d. 1783)	III
Floyd, John Buchanan	III	Forbes, John (d. 1823)	III
Floyd, William	III	Forbes, John Murray (d. 1831)	III
Flügel, Ewald	III	Forbes, John Murray (d. 1898)	III
Flynn, Edward Joseph	5	Forbes, Robert Bennet	III
Flynn, Elizabeth Gurley	7	Forbes, Stephen Alfred	III
Flynn, Errol Leslie	6	Forbes, William Cameron	6
Flynn, John Thomas	7	Forbush, Edward Howe	III
Flynt, Josiah		Force, Juliana	4
See Willard, Josiah Flint		Force, Manning Ferguson	III

Complete Index Guide

Name	Vol./Supp.	Name	Vol./Supp.
Force, Peter	III	Foshag, William Frederick	6
Ford, Daniel Sharp	III	Foss, Cyrus David	III
Ford, Edsel Bryant	3	Foss, Sam Walter	III
Ford, George Burdett	1	Foster, Abiel	III
Ford, Gordon Lester	III	Foster, Abigail Kelley	III
Ford, Guy Stanton	7	Foster, Benjamin	III
Ford, Hannibal Choate	5	Foster, Charles	III
Ford, Henry	4	Foster, Charles James	III
Ford, Henry Jones	III	Foster, David Skaats	III
Ford, Jacob	III	Foster, Ephraim Hubbard	III
Ford, John Baptiste	III	Foster, Frank Hugh	1
Ford, John Thomson	III	Foster, Frank Pierce	III
Ford, Patrick	III	Foster, George Burman	III
Ford, Paul Leicester	III	Foster, Hannah Webster	III
Ford, Thomas	III	Foster, John	III
Ford, Worthington Chauncey	3	Foster, John Gray	III
Fordney, Joseph Warren	1	Foster, John Pierrepont	
Fordyce, John Addison	III	Codrington	III
Forepaugh, Adam	III	Foster, John Watson	III
Forester, Frank		Foster, Judith Ellen Horton	III
See Herbert, Henry		Foster, Lafayette Sabine	III
William		Foster, Murphy James	III
Foresti, Eleutario Felice	III	Foster, Randolph Sinks	III
Forgan, James Berwick	III	Foster, Robert Sanford	III
Forman, David	III	Foster, Roger Sherman Baldwin	III
Forman, Joshua	III	Foster, Stephen Collins	III
Forman, Justus Miles	III	Foster, Stephen Symonds	III
Forney, John Wien	III	Foster, Theodore	III
Forney, Matthias Nace	III	Foster, Thomas Jefferson	2
Forney, William Henry	III	Foster, William Trudant	4
Forrest, Edwin	III	Foster, William Z.	7
Forrest, French	III	Foulk, George Clayton	III
Forrest, Nathan Bedford	III	Foulke, William Dudley	1
Forrestal, James Vincent	4	Fowke, Gerard	1
Forsyth, John (d. 1841)	III	Fowle, Daniel	III
Forsyth, John (d. 1886)	III	Fowle, William Bentley	III
Forsyth, Thomas	III	Fowler, Charles Henry	III
Forten, James	III	Fowler, Frank	III
Fortescue, Charles LeGeyt	2	Fowler, Gene	6
Fortier, Alcée	III	Fowler, George Ryerson	III
Forward, Walter	III	Fowler, Joseph Smith	III
Forwood, William Henry	III	Fowler, Orin	III
Fosdick, Charles Austin	III	Fowler, Orson Squire	III
Fosdick, William Whiteman	III	Fowler, Russell Story	6

Complete Index Guide

Name	Vol./Supp.	Name	Vol./Supp.
Fox, Charles Kemble	III	Franklin, Jesse	III
Fox, Dixon Ryan	3	Franklin, Philip Albright Small	2
Fox, Fontaine Talbot, Jr.	7	Franklin, William	III
Fox, George Washington		Franklin, William Buel	III
Lafayette	III	Franz, Shepherd Ivory	1
Fox, Gilbert	III	Frasch, Herman	III
Fox, Gustavus Vasa	III	Fraser, Charles	III
Fox, Harry	III	Fraser, James Earle	5
Fox, John William	III	Fraser, Leon	3
Fox, Margaret	III	Fraunces, Samuel	IV
Fox, Richard Kyle	III	Frayne, Hugh	1
Fox, William	5	Frazee, John	IV
Fox, Williams Carlton	III	Frazer, John Fries	IV
Foxall, Henry	III	Frazer, Oliver	IV
Foy, Eddie	III	Frazer, Persifor (d. 1792)	IV
Fraina, Louis C.		Frazer, Persifor (d. 1909)	IV
See Corey, Lewis		Frazier, Charles Harrison	2
Fraley, Frederick	III	Frazier, Edward Franklin	7
Frame, Alice Seymour Browne	3	Frazier, Lynn Joseph	4
Franchère, Gabriel	III	Frear, William	IV
Francis, Charles Spencer	III	Freas, Thomas Bruce	IV
Francis, Charles Stephen	III	Frederic, Harold	IV
Francis, Convers	III	Freed, Alan J.	7
Francis, David Rowland	III	Freedman, Andrew	IV
Francis, James Bicheno	III	Freeman, Allen Weir	5
Francis, John Brown	III	Freeman, Bernardus	IV
Francis, John Morgan	III	Freeman, Douglas Southall	5
Francis, John Wakefield	III	Freeman, Frederick Kemper	IV
Francis, Joseph	III	Freeman, James	IV
Francis, Paul James	2	Freeman, James Edwards	IV
Francis, Samuel Ward	III	Freeman, John Ripley	1
Francis, Tench	III	Freeman, Joseph	7
Franck, James	7	Freeman, Mary Eleanor	
Francke, Kuno	III	Wilkins	IV
Frank, Glenn	2	Freeman, Nathaniel	IV
Frank, Jerome	6	Freeman, Thomas	IV
Frank, Tenney	2	Freer, Charles Lang	IV
Frankfurter, Alfred Moritz	7	Frelinghuysen, Frederick	IV
Frankfurter, Felix	7	Frelinghuysen, Frederick	
Frankland, Lady Agnes Surriage	III	Theodore	IV
Franklin, Benjamin (d. 1790)	III	Frelinghuysen, Theodore	IV
Franklin, Benjamin (d. 1878)	III	Frelinghuysen, Theodorus	
Franklin, Edward Curtis	2	Jacobus	IV
Franklin, Fabian	2	Frémont, Jessie Benton	IV
Franklin, James	III	Frémont, John Charles	IV

Complete Index Guide

Name	Vol./Supp.	Name	Vol./Supp.
French, Aaron	IV	Fry, Joshua	IV
French, Alice	1	Fry, Richard	IV
French, Daniel Chester	1	Fry, William Henry	IV
French, Edwin Davis	IV	Frye, Joseph	IV
French, Lucy Virginia Smith	IV	Frye, William John ("Jack")	6
French, Paul Comly	6	Frye, William Pierce	IV
French, William Henry	IV	Fryer, Douglas Henry	6
French, William Merchant		Fuertes, Estevan Antonio	IV
Richardson	IV	Fuertes, Louis Agassiz	IV
Freneau, Philip Morin	IV	Fullam, Frank L.	5
Freund, Ernst	1	Fuller, Andrew S.	IV
Frey, John Philip	6	Fuller, George	IV
Frey, Joseph Samuel Christian		Fuller, George Warren	1
Frederick	IV	Fuller, Henry Blake	IV
Frick, Henry Clay	IV	Fuller, Hiram	IV
Friday	IV	Fuller, John Wallace	IV
Friedenwald, Aaron	IV	Fuller, Joseph Vincent	1
Friedlaender, Israel	IV	Fuller, Levi Knight	IV
Fries, Francis	IV	Fuller, Loie	IV
Fries, John	IV	Fuller, Margaret	
Frieseke, Frederick Carl	2	See Fuller, Sarah Margaret	
Frieze, Henry Simmons	IV	Fuller, Melville Weston	IV
Frisbie, Levi	IV	Fuller, Richard	IV
Frissell, Hollis Burke	IV	Fuller, Robert Mason	IV
Fritschel, Conrad Sigmund	IV	Fuller, Sarah Margaret	IV
Fritschel, Gottfried Leonhard		Fuller, Thomas Charles	IV
Wilhelm	IV	Fullerton, George Stuart	IV
Fritz, John	IV	Fulton, John Farquhar	6
Frizell, Joseph Palmer	IV	Fulton, Justin Dewey	IV
Frohman, Charles	IV	Fulton, Robert	IV
Frohman, Daniel	2	Fulton, Robert Burwell	IV
Fromm-Reichmann, Frieda	6	Funk, Isaac Kauffman	IV
Frost, Arthur Burdett	IV	Funk, Wilfred John	7
Frost, Edwin Brant	1	Funston, Frederick	IV
Frost, Holloway Halstead	1	Furlow, Floyd Charles	IV
Frost, Robert Lee	7	Furman, James Clement	IV
Frost, Wade Hampton	2	Furman, Richard	IV
Frothingham, Arthur Lincoln	IV	Furnas, Robert Wilkinson	IV
Frothingham, Nathaniel		Furness, Horace Howard	
Langdon	IV	(d. 1912)	IV
Frothingham, Octavius Brooks	IV	Furness, Horace Howard	
Frothingham, Paul Revere	IV	(d. 1930)	IV
Frothingham, Richard	IV	Furness, William Henry	IV
Fry, Birkett Davenport	IV	Furst, Clyde Bowman	1
Fry, James Barnet	IV		

Complete Index Guide

Name	Vol./Supp.	Name	Vol./Supp.
Furuseth, Andrew	2	Gallaudet, Thomas Hopkins	IV
Fussell, Bartholomew	IV	Galli-Curci, Amelita	7
		Gallier, James	1
Gabb, William More	IV	Gallinger, Jacob Harold	IV
Gable, (William) Clark	6	Gallitzin, Demetrius Augustine	IV
Gabrilowitsch, Ossip	2	Galloway, Beverly Thomas	2
Gadsden, Christopher	IV	Galloway, Charles Betts	IV
Gadsden, James	IV	Galloway, Joseph	IV
Gaffney, Margaret		Galloway, Samuel	IV
See Haughery, Margaret		Gallup, Joseph Adams	IV
Gaffney		Gally, Merritt	IV
Gág, Wanda	4	Galpin, Charles Josiah	4
Gage, Frances Dana Barker	IV	Gálvez, Bernardo de	IV
Gage, Lyman Judson	IV	Gamble, Hamilton Rowan	IV
Gage, Matilda Joslyn	IV	Gambrell, James Bruton	IV
Gage, Thomas	IV	Gammon, Elijah Hedding	IV
Gaillard, David Du Bose	IV	Gannett, Ezra Stiles	IV
Gaillard, Edwin Samuel	IV	Gannett, Frank Ernest	6
Gaillard, John	IV	Gannett, Henry	IV
Gaillardet, Théodore Frédéric	IV	Gannett, William Channing	IV
Gailor, Thomas Frank	1	Gano, John	IV
Gaine, Hugh	IV	Gano, Stephen	IV
Gaines, Edmund Pendleton	IV	Gansevoort, Leonard	IV
Gaines, George Strother	IV	Gansevoort, Peter	IV
Gaines, John Pollard	IV	Ganso, Emil	3
Gaines, Reuben Reid	IV	Ganss, Henry George	IV
Gaines, Wesley John	IV	Gantt, Henry Laurence	IV
Gaither, Horace Rowan, Jr.	7	Garakonthie, Daniel	IV
Galberry, Thomas	IV	Garcelon, Alonzo	IV
Galbreath, Charles Burleigh	1	Garcés, Francisco Tomás	
Gale, Benjamin	IV	Hermenegildo	IV
Gale, Elbridge	IV	Garden, Alexander (d. 1791)	IV
Gale, George Washington	IV	Garden, Alexander (d. 1829)	IV
Gale, Henry Gordon	3	Gardener, Helen Hamilton	IV
Gale, Zona	2	Gardiner, Sir Christopher	IV
Gales, Joseph (d. 1841)	IV	Gardiner, Harry Norman	1
Gales, Joseph (d. 1860)	IV	Gardiner, James Terry	IV
Gall	IV	Gardiner, John	IV
Gallagher, Hugh Patrick	IV	Gardiner, John Sylvester John	IV
Gallagher, Ralph W.	5	Gardiner, Lion	IV
Gallagher, William Davis	IV	Gardiner, Robert Hallowell	IV
Gallatin, Abraham Alfonse		Gardiner, Silvester	IV
Albert	IV	Gardner, Caleb	IV
Gallaudet, Edward Miner	IV	Gardner, Charles Kitchel	IV
Gallaudet, Thomas	IV	Gardner, Gilson	1

Complete Index Guide

Name	Vol./Supp.	Name	Vol./Supp.
Gardner, Helen	4	Garrison, William Lloyd	IV
Gardner, Henry Joseph	IV	Garrison, William Re Tallack	IV
Gardner, Isabella Stewart	IV	Garry, Spokane	IV
Gardner, John Lane	IV	Gartrell, Lucius Jeremiah	IV
Gardner, Leroy Upson	4	Garvey, Marcus Moziah	2
Gardner, Oliver Maxwell	4	Garvin, Lucius Fayette Clark	IV
Garey, Thomas Andrew	IV	Gary, Elbert Henry	IV
Garfield, Harry Augustus	3	Gary, James Albert	IV
Garfield, James Abram	IV	Gary, Martin Witherspoon	IV
Garfield, James Rudolph	4	Gaskill, Harvey Freeman	IV
Garfield, John	5	Gass, Patrick	IV
Garis, Howard Roger	7	Gasser, Herbert Spencer	7
Garland, Augustus Hill	IV	Gasson, Thomas Ignatius	IV
Garland, Hamlin	2	Gaston, Herbert Earle	6
Garland, Landon Cabell	IV	Gaston, James McFadden	IV
Garlick, Theodatus	IV	Gaston, William (d. 1844)	IV
Garman, Charles Edward	IV	Gaston, William (d. 1894)	IV
Garman, Samuel	IV	Gates, Caleb Frank	4
Garner, James Wilford	2	Gates, Frederick Taylor	IV
Garnet, Henry Highland	IV	Gates, George Augustus	IV
Garnett, Alexander Yelverton Peyton	IV	Gates, Horatio	IV
		Gates, John Warne	IV
Garnett, James Mercer (d. 1843)	IV	Gates, Sir Thomas	IV
		Gates, Thomas Sovereign	4
Garnett, James Mercer (d. 1916)	IV	Gatling, Richard Jordan	IV
		Gatschet, Albert Samuel	IV
Garnett, Muscoe Russell Hunter	IV	Gatti-Casazza, Giulio	2
		Gaul, William Gilbert	IV
Garnett, Robert Selden	IV	Gauss, Christian Frederick	5
Garrard, James	IV	Gauss, Clarence Edward	6
Garrard, Kenner	IV	Gaut, John McReynolds	IV
Garreau, Armand	IV	Gauvreau, Emile Henry	6
Garret, William Robertson	IV	Gavin, Frank Stanton Burns	2
Garretson, Austin Bruce	1	Gaxton, William	7
Garretson, James Edmund	IV	Gay, Ebenezer	IV
Garrett, Edmund Henry	IV	Gay, Edwin Francis	4
Garrett, Finis James	6	Gay, Frederick Parker	2
Garrett, John Work	IV	Gay, Sydney Howard	IV
Garrett, Robert	IV	Gay, Winckworth Allan	IV
Garrett, Thomas	IV	Gayarré, Charles Étienne Arthur	IV
Garrettson, Freeborn	IV	Gayle, John	IV
Garrigan, Philip Joseph	IV	Gayler, Charles	IV
Garrison, Cornelius Kingsland	IV	Gayley, James	IV
Garrison, Fielding Hudson	1	Gaylord, Willis	IV
Garrison, Lindley Miller	1		

Complete Index Guide

Name	Vol./Supp.	Name	Vol./Supp.
Gaynor, William Jay	IV	Geyer, Henry Sheffie	IV
Gayoso de Lemos, Manuel	IV	Ghent, William James	3
Gear, John Henry	IV	Gherardi, Bancroft (d. 1903)	IV
Geary, John White	IV	Gherardi, Bancroft (d. 1941)	3
Geddes, James	IV	Gholson, Samuel Jameson	IV
Geddes, James Loraine	IV	Gholson, Thomas Saunders	IV
Geddes, Norman Bel	6	Gholson, William Yates	IV
Geers, Edward Franklin	IV	Giannini, Amadeo Peter	4
Gehrig, Henry Louis	3	Gibault, Pierre	IV
Geiger, Roy Stanley	4	Gibbes, Robert Wilson	IV
Gellatly, John	1	Gibbes, William Hasell	IV
Gemünder, August Martin		Gibbon, John	IV
Ludwig	IV	Gibbons, Abigail Hopper	IV
Gemünder, George		Gibbons, Floyd	2
See Gemünder,		Gibbons, Herbert Adams	1
August M. L.		Gibbons, James	IV
Genet, Edmond Charles	IV	Gibbons, James Sloan	IV
Genin, John Nicholas	IV	Gibbons, Thomas	IV
Genth, Frederick Augustus	IV	Gibbons, William (d. 1800)	IV
Genthe, Arnold	3	Gibbons, William (d. 1845)	IV
Genung, John Franklin	IV	Gibbs, Arthur Hamilton	7
George, Gladys	5	Gibbs, George (d. 1833)	IV
George, Grace	7	Gibbs, George (d. 1873)	IV
George, Henry (d. 1897)	IV	Gibbs, George (d. 1940)	2
George, Henry (d. 1916)	IV	Gibbs, James Ethan Allen	IV
George, James Zachariah	IV	Gibbs, Josiah Willard (d. 1861)	IV
George, Walter Franklin	6	Gibbs, Josiah Willard (d. 1903)	IV
George, William Reuben	2	Gibbs, Oliver Wolcott	
Gerard, James Watson	IV	(d. 1908)	IV
Gerard, James Watson	5	Gibbs, (Oliver) Wolcott	
Gerber, Daniel (Frank)	5	(d. 1958)	6
Gerber, (Daniel) Frank	5	Gibbs, Wolcott	
Gerhard, William Wood	IV	See Gibbs, Oliver Wolcott	
Gerhart, Emanuel Vogel	IV	Gibson, Charles Dana	3
Gericke, Wilhelm	IV	Gibson, Edmund Richard	
Geronimo	IV	("Hoot")	7
Gerrish, Frederic Henry	IV	Gibson, George	IV
Gerry, Elbridge	IV	Gibson, John	IV
Gerry, Elbridge Thomas	IV	Gibson, John Bannister	IV
Gershwin, George	2	Gibson, Josh	4
Gerster, Arpad Geyza Charles	IV	Gibson, Paris	IV
Gerstle, Lewis	IV	Gibson, Randall Lee	IV
Gesell, Arnold Lucius	7	Gibson, Walter Murray	IV
Gest, Morris	3	Gibson, William	IV
Getty, George Washington	IV	Gibson, William Hamilton	IV

70

Complete Index Guide

Name	Vol./Supp.	Name	Vol./Supp.
Giddings, Franklin Henry	1	Gillet, Ransom Hooker	IV
Giddings, Joshua Reed	IV	Gillett, Ezra Hall	IV
Gideon, Peter Miller	IV	Gillett, Frederick Huntington	1
Gidley, James Williams	1	Gillett, Horace Wadsworth	4
Giesler-Anneke, Mathilde		Gillette, Francis	IV
Franziska	IV	Gillette, King Camp	1
Gifford, Robert Swain	IV	Gillette, William Hooker	2
Gifford, Sanford Robinson		Gilliam, David Tod	IV
(d. 1880)	IV	Gillis, James Martin	6
Gifford, Sanford Robinson		Gilliss, James Melville	IV
(d. 1944)	3	Gilliss, Walter	IV
Gihon, Albert Leary	IV	Gillman, Henry	IV
Gilbert, Alfred Carlton	7	Gillmore, Quincy Adams	IV
Gilbert, Anne Hartley	IV	Gillon, Alexander	IV
Gilbert, Cass	1	Gilman, Arthur	IV
Gilbert, Charles Henry	IV	Gilman, Arthur Delevan	IV
Gilbert, Eliphalet Wheeler	IV	Gilman, Caroline Howard	IV
Gilbert, Grove Karl	IV	Gilman, Charlotte Perkins	
Gilbert, Henry Franklin		Stetson	1
Belknap	IV	Gilman, Daniel Coit	IV
Gilbert, John	2	Gilman, John Taylor	IV
Gilbert, John Gibbs	IV	Gilman, Lawrence	2
Gilbert, Linda	IV	Gilman, Nicholas	IV
Gilbert, Rufus Henry	IV	Gilman, Samuel	IV
Gilbert, Seymour Parker	2	Gilmer, Elizabeth Meriwether	5
Gilbert, William Lewis	IV	Gilmer, Francis Walker	IV
Gilchrist, Robert	IV	Gilmer, George Rockingham	IV
Gilchrist, William Wallace	IV	Gilmer, John Adams	IV
Gilder, Jeannette Leonard	IV	Gilmer, Thomas Walker	IV
Gilder, Richard Watson	IV	Gilmor, Harry	IV
Gilder, William Henry	IV	Gilmore, James Roberts	IV
Gildersleeve, Basil Lanneau	IV	Gilmore, Joseph Albree	IV
Gildersleeve, Virginia		Gilmore, Joseph Henry	IV
Crocheron	7	Gilmore, Patrick Sarsfield	IV
Giles, Chauncey	IV	Gilmour, Richard	IV
Giles, William Branch	IV	Gilpin, Charles Sidney	IV
Gill, John	IV	Gilpin, Edward Woodward	IV
Gill, Laura Drake	IV	Gilpin, Henry Dilworth	IV
Gill, Theodore Nicholas	IV	Gilpin, William	IV
Gillam, Bernhard	IV	Ginn, Edwin	IV
Gillem, Alvan Cullem	IV	Ginter, Lewis	IV
Gillespie, Eliza Maria		Giovannitti, Arturo	6
See Angela, Mother		Girard, Charles Frédéric	IV
Gillespie, Mabel	IV	Girard, Stephen	IV
Gillespie, William Mitchell	IV	Girardeau, John Lafayette	IV

Complete Index Guide

Name	Vol./Supp.	Name	Vol./Supp.
Girdler, Tom Mercer	7	Goddu, Louis	IV
Girsch, Frederick	IV	Godefroy, Maximilian	IV
Girty, Simon	IV	Godey, Louis Antoine	IV
Gist, Christopher	IV	Godfrey, Benjamin	IV
Gist, Mordecai	IV	Godfrey, Thomas (d. 1749)	IV
Gist, William Henry	IV	Godfrey, Thomas (d. 1763)	IV
Gitlow, Benjamin	7	Godkin, Edwin Lawrence	IV
Glackens, William James	2	Godman, John Davidson	IV
Gladden, Washington	IV	Godowsky, Leopold	2
Gladwin, Henry	IV	Godwin, Parke	IV
Glasgow, Ellen Anderson		Goebel, William	IV
Gholson	3	Goerz, David	IV
Glaspell, Susan	4	Goessmann, Charles Anthony	IV
Glass, Carter	4	Goethals, George Washington	IV
Glass, Franklin Potts	1	Goetschius, John Henry	IV
Glass, Hugh	IV	Goetschius, Percy	3
Glass, Montague Marsden	1	Goetz, George	
Glassford, Pelham Davis	6	See Calverton, Victor	
Gleason, Frederic Grant	IV	Francis	
Gleason, Kate	1	Goetz, George Washington	IV
Gleaves, Albert	2	Goff, Emmet Stull	IV
Glenn, Hugh	IV	Goff, John William	IV
Glenn, John Mark	4	Goffe, William	IV
Glennon, John Joseph	4	Goforth, William	IV
Glidden, Charles Jasper	IV	Going, Jonathan	IV
Glidden, Joseph Farwell	IV	Goldbeck, Robert	IV
Glover, John	IV	Goldberger, Joseph	IV
Glover, Samuel Taylor	IV	Golden, John	5
Glover, Townend	IV	Goldenweiser, Alexander	
Gluck, Alma	2	Alexandrovich	2
Glynn, James	IV	Goldenweiser, Emanuel	
Glynn, Martin Henry	IV	Alexander	5
Gmeiner, John	IV	Golder, Frank Alfred	IV
Gobrecht, Christian	IV	Goldin, Horace	2
Godbe, William Samuel	IV	Goldman, Edwin Franko	6
Goddard, Calvin Hooker	5	Goldman, Emma	2
Goddard, Calvin Luther	IV	Goldman, Mayer C.	2
Goddard, Henry Herbert	6	Goldmark, Henry	3
Goddard, John	IV	Goldmark, Rubin	2
Goddard, Luther Marcellus	IV	Goldsborough, Charles	IV
Goddard, Morrill	2	Goldsborough, Louis	
Goddard, Paul Beck	IV	Malesherbes	IV
Goddard, Pliny Earle	IV	Goldsborough, Robert	IV
Goddard, Robert Hutchings	3	Goldsborough, Thomas Alan	5
Goddard, William	IV	Goldschmidt, Jakob	5

Complete Index Guide

Name	Vol./Supp.	Name	Vol./Supp.
Goldsmith, Middleton	IV	Goodrich, Elizur (d. 1849)	IV
Goldstein, Max Aaron	3	Goodrich, Frank Boott	IV
Goldthwaite, George	IV	Goodrich, Samuel Griswold	IV
Goldthwaite, Henry Barnes	IV	Goodrich, Sarah	
Goldwater, Sigismund Schulz	3	See Goodridge, Sarah	
Gomberg, Moses	4	Goodrich, William Marcellus	IV
Gompers, Samuel	IV	Goodridge, Sarah	IV
Gonzales, Ambrose Elliott	IV	Goodridge, William Marcellus	
Gooch, Sir William	IV	See Goodrich, William	
Good, Adolphus Clemens	IV	Marcellus	
Good, James Isaac	IV	Goodsell, Daniel Ayres	IV
Good, Jeremiah Haak	IV	Goodspeed, Thomas Wakefield	IV
Good, John	IV	Goodwin, Daniel Raynes	IV
Goodale, George Lincoln	IV	Goodwin, Elijah	IV
Goodale, Stephen Lincoln	IV	Goodwin, Hannibal Williston	IV
Goodall, Harvey L.	IV	Goodwin, Ichabod	IV
Goodall, Thomas	IV	Goodwin, John Noble	IV
Goode, George Brown	IV	Goodwin, Nathaniel Carll	IV
Goode, John	IV	Goodwin, William Watson	IV
Goode, John Paul	1	Goodyear, Anson Conger	7
Goodell, Henry Hill	IV	Goodyear, Charles (d. 1860)	IV
Goodell, William (d. 1867)	IV	Goodyear, Charles (d. 1896)	IV
Goodell, William (d. 1878)	IV	Goodyear, William Henry	IV
Goodenow, John Milton	IV	Gookin, Daniel	IV
Goodhue, Benjamin	IV	Goold, William A.	IV
Goodhue, Bertram Grosvenor	IV	Gordin, Jacob	IV
Goodhue, James Madison	IV	Gordon, Andrew	IV
Goodloe, Daniel Reaves	IV	Gordon, George Angier	IV
Goodloe, William Cassius	IV	Gordon, George Byron	IV
Goodman, Charles	IV	Gordon, George Henry	IV
Goodman, Kenneth Sawyer	IV	Gordon, George Phineas	IV
Goodman, Louis Earl	7	Gordon, George Washington	IV
Goodnight, Charles	IV	Gordon, James	IV
Goodnough, Xanthus Henry	1	Gordon, John Brown	IV
Goodnow, Frank Johnson	2	Gordon, Laura De Force	IV
Goodnow, Isaac Tichenor	IV	Gordon, William	IV
Goodrich, Alfred John	IV	Gordon, William Fitzhugh	IV
Goodrich, Annie Warburton	5	Gordon, William Washington	IV
Goodrich, Benjamin Franklin	IV	Gordy, John Pancoast	IV
Goodrich, Charles Augustus	IV	Gore, Thomas Pryor	4
Goodrich, Chauncey (d. 1815)	IV	Gorgas, Josiah	IV
Goodrich, Chauncey (d. 1858)	IV	Gorgas, William Crawford	IV
Goodrich, Chauncey (d. 1925)	IV	Gorham, Jabez	IV
Goodrich, Chauncey Allen	IV	Gorham, John	IV
Goodrich, Elizur (d. 1797)	IV	Gorham, Nathaniel	IV

Complete Index Guide

Name	Vol./Supp.	Name	Vol./Supp.
Gorky, Arshile	4	Gräbner, August Lawrence	IV
Gorman, Arthur Pue	IV	Grace, Eugene Gifford	6
Gorman, Willis Arnold	IV	Grace, William Russell	IV
Gorrell, Edgar Staley	3	Gracie, Archibald	IV
Gorrie, John	IV	Gradle, Henry	IV
Gorringe, Henry Honeychurch	IV	Grady, Henry Francis	6
Gortner, Ross Aiken	3	Grady, Henry Woodfin	IV
Gorton, Samuel	IV	Graebner, August Lawrence	
Gosnold, Bartholomew	IV	See Gräbner, August	
Goss, Albert Simon	4	Lawrence	
Goss, James Walker	IV	Graessl, Lawrence	IV
Gossett, Benjamin Brown	5	Graff, Everett Dwight	7
Gostelowe, Jonathan	IV	Graff, Frederic	IV
Gotshall, William Charles	1	Graff, Frederick	IV
Gottheil, Gustav	IV	Graffenried, Christopher, Baron	
Gottheil, Richard James		de	IV
Horatio	2	Grafly, Charles	IV
Gottschalk, Louis Moreau	IV	Grafton, Charles Chapman	IV
Goucher, John Franklin	IV	Graham, Charles Kinnaird	IV
Goudy, Frederick William	4	Graham, David	IV
Goudy, William Charles	IV	Graham, Edward Kidder	IV
Gouge, William M.	IV	Graham, Ernest Robert	2
Gough, John Bartholomew	IV	Graham, Evarts Ambrose	6
Gould, Augustus Addison	IV	Graham, George Rex	IV
Gould, Benjamin Apthorp		Graham, Isabella Marshall	IV
(d. 1859)	IV	Graham, James	IV
Gould, Benjamin Apthorp		Graham, James Duncan	IV
(d. 1896)	IV	Graham, John (d. 1795)	IV
Gould, Edward Sherman	IV	Graham, John (d. 1820)	IV
Gould, Elgin Ralston Lovell	IV	Graham, John Andrew	IV
Gould, George Jay	IV	Graham, Joseph	IV
Gould, George Milbry	IV	Graham, Philip Leslie	7
Gould, Hannah Flagg	IV	Graham, Sylvester	IV
Gould, James	IV	Graham, William Alexander	IV
Gould, Jay	IV	Graham, William Montrose	IV
Gould, Nathaniel Duren	IV	Grainger, George Percy	7
Gould, Robert Simonton	IV	Grandgent, Charles Hall	2
Gould, Thomas Ridgeway	IV	Granger, Alfred Hoyt	2
Goulding, Francis Robert	IV	Granger, Francis	IV
Goupil, René	IV	Granger, Gideon	IV
Govan, Daniel Chevilette	IV	Granger, Gordon	IV
Gove, Aaron Estellus	IV	Granger, Walter	3
Gowans, William	IV	Grant, Albert Weston	IV
Gowen, Franklin Benjamin	IV	Grant, Asahel	IV
Grabau, Johannes Andreas		Grant, Claudius Buchanan	IV
August	IV	Grant, Frederick Dent	IV

Complete Index Guide

Name	Vol./Supp.	Name	Vol./Supp.
Grant, George Barnard	IV	Gray, John Chipman	IV
Grant, Harry Johnston	7	Gray, John Purdue	IV
Grant, James Benton	IV	Gray, Joseph W.	IV
Grant, John Thomas	IV	Gray, Robert	IV
Grant, Lewis Addison	IV	Gray, William	IV
Grant, Madison	2	Gray, William Scott, Jr.	6
Grant, Percy Stickney	IV	Graydon, Alexander	IV
Grant, Robert	2	Grayson, William	IV
Grant, Ulysses Simpson	IV	Greathouse, Clarence Ridgeby	IV
Grant, Zilpah Polly		Greaton, John	IV
See Banister, Zilpah Polly		Greaton, Joseph	IV
Grant		Greeley, Horace	IV
Grass, John	IV	Greely, Adolphus Washington	1
Grasselli, Caesar Augustin	IV	Green, Alexander Little Page	IV
Grasty, Charles Henry	IV	Green, Andrew Haswell	IV
Gratiot, Charles	IV	Green, Anna Katharine	
Gratz, Barnard	IV	See Rohlfs, Anna	
Gratz, Michael	IV	Katharine Green	
Gratz, Rebecca	IV	Green, Asa	IV
Grau, Maurice	IV	Green, Ashbel	IV
Graubau, Amadeus W.	4	Green, Bartholomew	IV
Graupner, Johann Christian		Green, Benjamin Edwards	IV
Gottlieb	IV	Green, Beriah	IV
Gravenor, John		Green, Duff	IV
See Altham, John		Green, Frances Harriet	
Graves, Alvin Cushman	7	Whipple	IV
Graves, David Bibb	3	Green, Francis	IV
Graves, Frederick Rogers	2	Green, Francis Mathews	IV
Graves, James Robinson	IV	Green, Gabriel Marcus	IV
Graves, John Temple	IV	Green, Henrietta Howland	
Graves, Rosewell Hobart	IV	Robinson	IV
Graves, William Phillips	1	Green, Henry Woodhull	IV
Graves, William Sidney	2	Green, Horace	IV
Graves, Zuinglius Calvin	IV	Green, Jacob (d. 1790)	IV
Gravier, Jacques	IV	Green, Jacob (d. 1841)	IV
Gray, Asa	IV	Green, James Stephens	IV
Gray, Carl Raymond	2	Green, John	IV
Gray, Elisha	IV	Green, John Cleve	IV
Gray, Francis Calley	IV	Green, Jonas	IV
Gray, George	IV	Green, Joseph	IV
Gray, George Alexander	IV	Green, Lewis Warner	IV
Gray, Gilda	6	Green, Nathan	IV
Gray, Glen ("Spike")	7	Green, Norvin	IV
Gray, Henry Peters	IV	Green, Samuel	IV
Gray, Horace	IV	Green, Samuel Abbott	IV
Gray, Isaac Pusey	IV	Green, Samuel Bowdlear	IV

Complete Index Guide

Name	Vol./Supp.	Name	Vol./Supp.
Green, Samuel Swett	IV	Greenslet, Ferris	6
Green, Seth	IV	Greenstreet, Sydney	5
Green, Thomas	IV	Greenup, Christopher	IV
Green, William (d. 1880)	IV	Greenwald, Emanuel	IV
Green, William (d. 1952)	5	Greenway, John Campbell	1
Green, William Henry	IV	Greenwood, Grace	
Green, William Joseph, Jr.	7	See Lippincott, Sara Jane	
Greene, Albert Gorton	IV	Clarke	
Greene, Belle da Costa	4	Greenwood, Isaac	IV
Greene, Charles Ezra	IV	Greenwood, John	IV
Greene, Charles Sumner	5	Greenwood, Miles	IV
Greene, Christopher	IV	Greer, David Hummell	IV
Greene, Daniel Crosby	IV	Greer, James Augustin	IV
Greene, Edward Lee	IV	Gregg, Alan	6
Greene, Frances Harriet		Gregg, Andrew	IV
Whipple		Gregg, David McMurtrie	IV
See Green, Frances		Gregg, John	IV
Harriet Whipple		Gregg, John Andrew	5
Greene, Francis Vinton	IV	Gregg, John Robert	4
Greene, George Sears (d. 1899)	IV	Gregg, Josiah	IV
Greene, George Sears (d. 1922)	IV	Gregg, Maxcy	IV
Greene, George Washington	IV	Gregg, William	IV
Greene, Henry Mather	5	Gregg, Willis Ray	2
Greene, Jerome Davis	6	Gregory, Caspar René	IV
Greene, Nathanael	IV	Gregory, Charles Noble	1
Greene, Nathaniel	IV	Gregory, Clifford Verne	3
Greene, Roger Sherman	4	Gregory, Daniel Seelye	IV
Greene, Samuel Dana	IV	Gregory, Eliot	IV
Greene, Samuel Stillman	IV	Gregory, John Milton	IV
Greene, William (d. 1758)	IV	Gregory, Menas Sarkas	
Greene, William (d. 1809)	IV	Boulgourjian	3
Greene, William Cornell	IV	Gregory, Samuel	IV
Greener, Richard Theodore	IV	Gregory, Stephen Strong	IV
Greenhalge, Frederic Thomas	IV	Gregory, Thomas Barger	5
Greenhow, Robert	IV	Gregory, Thomas Watt	1
Greenlaw, Edwin Almiron	1	Greist, John Milton	IV
Greenleaf, Benjamin	IV	Grellet, Stephen	IV
Greenleaf, Halbert Stevens	IV	Gresham, Walter Quintin	IV
Greenleaf, Moses	IV	Grew, Joseph Clark	7
Greenleaf, Simon	IV	Grew, Theophilus	IV
Greenleaf, Thomas	IV	Grey, Zane	2
Greenough, Henry	IV	Gridley, Charles Vernon	IV
Greenough, Horatio	IV	Gridley, Jeremiah	IV
Greenough, James Bradstreet	IV	Gridley, Richard	IV
Greenough, Richard Saltonstall	IV	Grier, Robert Cooper	IV

Complete Index Guide

Name	Vol./Supp.	Name	Vol./Supp.
Grierson, Benjamin Henry	IV	Griscom, Ludlow	6
Grierson, Francis	IV	Griswold, Alexander Viets	IV
Grieve, Miller	IV	Griswold, Alfred Whitney	7
Griffes, Charles Tomlinson	IV	Griswold, John Augustus	IV
Griffin, Appleton Prentiss Clark	IV	Griswold, Matthew	IV
Griffin, Charles	IV	Griswold, Roger	IV
Griffin, Cyrus	IV	Griswold, Rufus Wilmot	IV
Griffin, Edward Dorr	IV	Griswold, Stanley	IV
Griffin, Eugene	IV	Griswold, William McCrillis	IV
Griffin, Martin Ignatius Joseph	1	Groesbeck, William Slocum	IV
Griffin, Simon Goodell	IV	Gronlund, Laurence	IV
Griffin, Solomon Bulkley	IV	Gros, John Daniel	IV
Griffing, Josephine Sophie		Grose, William	IV
White	IV	Groseilliers, Medart Chouart,	
Griffis, William Elliot	IV	Sieur de	IV
Griffith, Benjamin	IV	Gross, Charles	IV
Griffith, Clark Calvin	5	Gross, Milt	5
Griffith, David Wark	4	Gross, Samuel David	IV
Griffith, Goldsborough		Gross, Samuel Weissell	IV
Sappington	IV	Grosscup, Peter Stenger	IV
Griffith, William	IV	Grosset, Alexander	1
Griffiths, John Willis	IV	Grossmann, Georg Martin	IV
Griggs, Everett Gallup	2	Grossmann, Louis	IV
Griggs, John William	IV	Grosvenor, Charles Henry	IV
Grigsby, Hugh Blair	IV	Grosvenor, Edwin Prescott	IV
Grim, David	IV	Grosvenor, John	
Grimes, Absalom Carlisle	IV	See Altham, John	
Grimes, James Stanley	IV	Grosvenor, William Mason	IV
Grimes, James Wilson	IV	Grosz, George	6
Grimké, Angelina Emily		Grote, Augustus Radcliffe	IV
See Grimké, Sarah Moore		Grouard, Frank	IV
Grimké, Archibald Henry	IV	Grover, Cuvier	IV
Grimké, John Faucheraud	IV	Grover, La Fayette	IV
Grimké, Sarah Moore	IV	Grow, Galusha Aaron	IV
Grimké, Thomas Smith	IV	Grube, Bernhard Adam	IV
Grinnell, Frederick	IV	Gruening, Emil	IV
Grinnell, George Bird	2	Grund, Francis Joseph	1
Grinnell, Henry	IV	Grundy, Felix	IV
Grinnell, Henry Walton	IV	Grundy, Joseph Ridgway	7
Grinnell, Joseph	IV	Gue, Benjamin T.	IV
Grinnell, Josiah Bushnell	IV	Guérin, Anne-Thérèse	IV
Grinnell, Moses Hicks	IV	Guernsey, Egbert	IV
Griscom, Clement Acton	IV	Guess, George	
Griscom, John	IV	See Sequoyah	
Griscom, Lloyd Carpenter	6	Guest, Edgar Albert	6

Complete Index Guide

Name	Vol./Supp.	Name	Vol./Supp.
Guffey, James McClurg	IV	Guthrie, George Wilkins	IV
Guffey, Joseph F.	6	Guthrie, James	IV
Guggenheim, Daniel	IV	Guthrie, Samuel	IV
Guggenheim, Meyer	IV	Guthrie, William Dameron	1
Guggenheim, Simon	3	Guy, Seymour Joseph	IV
Guggenheim, Solomon	4	Guyot, Arnold Henry	IV
Guignas, Louis Ignace		Guzik, Jack	6
See Guignas, Michel		Gwin, William McKendree	IV
Guignas, Michel	IV	Gwinnett, Button	IV
Guild, Curtis (*b. 1827*)	IV		
Guild, Curtis (*b. 1860*)	IV	Haan, William George	IV
Guild, La Fayette	1	Haarstick, Henry Christian	IV
Guild, Reuben Aldridge	IV	Haas, Francis Joseph	5
Guilday, Peter	4	Haas, Jacob Judah Aaron de	2
Guilford, Nathan	IV	Habberton, John	IV
Guiney, Louise Imogen	IV	Habersham, Alexander Wylly	IV
Guinzburg, Harold Kleinert	7	Habersham, James	IV
Guiteras, Juan	IV	Habersham, Joseph	IV
Gulick, John Thomas	IV	Hack, George	IV
Gulick, Luther Halsey		Hackett, Francis	7
(*d. 1891*)	IV	Hackett, Frank Warren	IV
Gulick, Luther Halsey		Hackett, Horatio Balch	IV
(*d. 1918*)	IV	Hackett, James Henry	IV
Gulick, Sidney Lewis	3	Hackett, James Keteltas	IV
Gummere, Francis Barton	IV	Hackley, Charles Henry	IV
Gummere, John	IV	Haddock, Charles Brickett	IV
Gummere, Samuel James	IV	Haddon, Elizabeth	
Gummere, Samuel René	IV	See Estaugh, Elizabeth	
Gummere, William Stryker	1	Haddon	
Gunn, Frederick William	IV	Hadfield, George	IV
Gunn, James Newton	IV	Hadley, Arthur Twining	IV
Gunn, Selskar Michael	3	Hadley, Henry Kimball	2
Gunnison, Foster	7	Hadley, Herbert Spencer	IV
Gunnison, John Williams	IV	Hadley, James	IV
Gunsaulus, Frank Wakeley	IV	Ha-Ga-Sa-Do-Ni	
Gunter, Archibald Clavering	IV	See Deerfoot	
Gunther, Charles Frederick	IV	Hagedorn, Hermann Ludwig	
Gunton, George	IV	Gebhard	7
Gurley, Ralph Randolph	IV	Hagen, Hermann August	IV
Gurney, Ephraim Whitman	IV	Hager, John Sharpenstein	IV
Gurowski, Adam	1	Haggerty, Melvin Everett	2
Guthe, Karl Eugen	IV	Haggin, James Ben Ali	IV
Gutherz, Carl	IV	Hagner, Peter	IV
Guthrie, Alfred	IV	Hagood, Johnson	IV
Guthrie, Edwin Ray, Jr.	6	Hague, Arnold	IV

Complete Index Guide

Name	Vol./Supp.	Name	Vol./Supp.
Hague, Frank	6	Hall, Charles Francis	IV
Hague, James Duncan	IV	Hall, Charles Henry	IV
Hague, Robert Lincoln	2	Hall, Charles Martin	IV
Hahn, Georg Michael Decker	IV	Hall, David	IV
Haid, Leo	IV	Hall, Dominick Augustin	IV
Haight, Charles Coolidge	IV	Hall, Edwin Herbert	2
Haight, Henry Huntly	IV	Hall, Fitzedward	IV
Hailmann, William Nicholas	IV	Hall, Florence Marion Howe	IV
Haines, Charles Glidden	IV	Hall, George Henry	IV
Haines, Daniel	IV	Hall, Granville Stanley	IV
Haines, Lynn	IV	Hall, Hazel	IV
Haish, Jacob	IV	Hall, Henry Bryan	IV
Haldeman, Samuel Steman	IV	Hall, Hiland	IV
Haldeman-Julius, Emanuel	5	Hall, Isaac Hollister	IV
Halderman, John A.	IV	Hall, James (d. 1826)	IV
Hale, Benjamin	IV	Hall, James (d. 1868)	IV
Hale, Charles	IV	Hall, James (d. 1898)	IV
Hale, Charles Reuben	IV	Hall, James Norman, and	
Hale, David	IV	Nordhoff, Charles Bernard	5
Hale, Edward Everett	IV	Hall, John	IV
Hale, Edward Joseph	IV	Hall, John Elihu	IV
Hale, Edwin Moses	IV	Hall, Luther Egbert	IV
Hale, Enoch	IV	Hall, Lyman	IV
Hale, Eugene	IV	Hall, Nathan Kelsey	IV
Hale, Frederick	7	Hall, Samuel (d. 1807)	IV
Hale, George Ellery	2	Hall, Samuel (d. 1870)	IV
Hale, Horatio Emmons	IV	Hall, Samuel Read	IV
Hale, John Parker	IV	Hall, Sarah Ewing	IV
Hale, Louise Closser	1	Hall, Sherman	IV
Hale, Lucretia Peabody	IV	Hall, Thomas	IV
Hale, Nathan (d. 1776)	IV	Hall, Thomas Seavey	IV
Hale, Nathan (d. 1863)	IV	Hall, Willard	IV
Hale, Philip	1	Hall, Willard Preble	IV
Hale, Philip Leslie	IV	Hall, William Whitty	IV
Hale, Robert Safford	IV	Hallam, Lewis	IV
Hale, Sarah Josepha Buell	IV	Halleck, Fitz-Greene	IV
Hale, William Bayard	IV	Halleck, Henry Wager	IV
Hale, William Gardner	IV	Hallet, Étienne Sulpice	IV
Hall, Abraham Oakey	IV	Hallet, Stephen	
Hall, Arethusa	IV	See Hallet, Étienne	
Hall, Arthur Crawshay Alliston	IV	Sulpice	
Hall, Asaph	IV	Hallett, Benjamin	IV
Hall, Baynard Rush	IV	Hallett, Benjamin Franklin	IV
Hall, Bolton	2	Hallett, Moses	IV
Hall, Charles Cuthbert	IV	Hallidie, Andrew Smith	IV

Complete Index Guide

Name	Vol./Supp.	Name	Vol./Supp.
Hallock, Charles	IV	Hamlin, Alfred Dwight Foster	IV
Hallock, Gerard	IV	Hamlin, Charles	IV
Hallock, William Allen	IV	Hamlin, Charles Sumner	2
Hallowell, Benjamin	IV	Hamlin, Cyrus	IV
Hallowell, Richard Price	IV	Hamlin, Emmons	IV
Halpine, Charles Graham	IV	Hamlin, Hannibal	IV
Halsey, Frederick Arthur	1	Hamlin, Talbot Faulkner	6
Halsey, John	IV	Hamlin, William	IV
Halsey, Thomas Lloyd	IV	Hamline, Leonidas Lent	IV
Halsey, William Frederick, Jr.	6	Hammer, William Joseph	1
Halstead, Murat	IV	Hammerstein, Oscar	IV
Halsted, George Bruce	IV	Hammerstein, Oscar, II	6
Halsted, William Stewart	IV	Hammett, Henry Pinckney	IV
Hambidge, Jay	IV	Hammett, Samuel Adams	IV
Hambleton, Thomas Edward	IV	Hammett, Samuel Dashiell	7
Hamblin, Joseph Eldridge	IV	Hammon, Jupiter	IV
Hamblin, Thomas Sowerby	IV	Hammond, Charles	IV
Hamer, Thomas Lyon	IV	Hammond, Edward Payson	IV
Hamilton, Alexander (d. 1756)	IV	Hammond, Edwin	IV
Hamilton, Alexander (d. 1804)	IV	Hammond, George Henry	IV
Hamilton, Allan McLane	IV	Hammond, Jabez Delano	IV
Hamilton, Andrew (d. 1703)	IV	Hammond, James Bartlett	IV
Hamilton, Andrew (d. 1741)	IV	Hammond, James Henry	IV
Hamilton, Andrew Jackson	IV	Hammond, John Hays	2
Hamilton, Charles Smith	IV	Hammond, Nathaniel Job	IV
Hamilton, Clayton	4	Hammond, Percy Hunter	2
Hamilton, Edith	7	Hammond, Samuel	IV
Hamilton, Edward John	IV	Hammond, William Alexander	IV
Hamilton, Frank Hastings	IV	Hammond, William Gardiner	IV
Hamilton, Gail		Hampden, Walter	5
See Dodge, Mary Abigail		Hampton, Wade (d. 1835)	IV
Hamilton, James (d. 1783)	IV	Hampton, Wade (d. 1902)	IV
Hamilton, James (d. 1857)	IV	Hamtramck, John Francis	IV
Hamilton, James Alexander	IV	Hanaford, Phoebe Ann Coffin	IV
Hamilton, John William	1	Hanby, Benjamin Russel	IV
Hamilton, Maxwell		Hanchett, Henry Granger	IV
McGaughey	6	Hancock, John (d. 1793)	IV
Hamilton, Paul	IV	Hancock, John (d. 1893)	IV
Hamilton, Peter	IV	Hancock, Thomas	IV
Hamilton, Schuyler	IV	Hancock, Winfield Scott	IV
Hamilton, Walton Hale	6	Hand, Augustus Noble	5
Hamilton, William Thomas		Hand, Daniel	IV
(d. 1888)	IV	Hand, Edward	IV
Hamilton, William Thomas		Hand, Learned	7
(d. 1908)	IV	Handerson, Henry Ebenezer	IV

Complete Index Guide

Name	Vol./Supp.	Name	Vol./Supp.
Handy, Alexander Hamilton	IV	Hardin, Martin D.	IV
Handy, William Christopher	6	Harding, Abner Clark	IV
Hanna, Edward Joseph	3	Harding, Chester	IV
Hanna, Marcus Alonzo	IV	Harding, George	IV
Hannagan, Stephen Jerome	5	Harding, Jesper	IV
Hannegan, Edward Allen	IV	Harding, Robert	IV
Hannegan, Robert Emmet	4	Harding, Seth	IV
Hansberry, Lorraine Vivian	7	Harding, Warren Gamaliel	IV
Hansen, George	IV	Harding, William Procter	
Hansen, Marcus Lee	2	Gould	IV
Hansen, Neils Ebbesen	4	Harding, William White	IV
Hansen, William Webster	4	Hardwick, Thomas William	3
Hanson, Alexander Contee		Hardwicke, Cedric Webster	7
(d. 1806)	IV	Hardy, Arthur Sherburne	IV
Hanson, Alexander Contee		Hardy, Oliver Norvell	6
(d. 1819)	IV	Hardy, Samuel	IV
Hanson, James Christian		Hardy, William Harris	IV
Meinich	3	Hare, George Emlen	IV
Hanson, John	IV	Hare, James Henry	4
Hanson, Ole	2	Hare, John Innes Clark	IV
Hanson, Roger Weightman	IV	Hare, Robert	IV
Hanus, Paul Henry	3	Hare, William Hobart	IV
Hapgood, Hutchins	3	Hargrove, Robert Kennon	IV
Hapgood, Isabel Florence	IV	Haring, Clarence	6
Hapgood, Norman	2	Harkins, William Draper	5
Happer, Andrew Patton	IV	Harkness, Albert	IV
Haraden, Jonathan	IV	Harkness, Edward Stephen	2
Harahan, James Theodore	IV	Harkness, William	IV
Harahan, William Johnson	2	Harlan, James (d. 1863)	IV
Haraszthy de Mokcsa, Agoston	IV	Harlan, James (d. 1899)	IV
Harbaugh, Henry	IV	Harlan, John Marshall	IV
Harben, William Nathaniel	IV	Harlan, Josiah	IV
Harbord, James Guthrie	4	Harlan, Richard	IV
Harby, Isaac	IV	Harland, Henry	IV
Harcourt, Alfred	5	Harland, Marion	
Hard, William	7	See Terhune, Mary	
Hardee, William Joseph	IV	Virginia	
Hardenbergh, Henry Janeway	IV	Harland, Thomas	IV
Hardenbergh, Jacob Rutsen	IV	Harlow, Jean	2
Hardey, Mother Mary Aloysia	IV	Harlow, Ralph Volney	6
Hardie, James Allen	IV	Harmar, Josiah	IV
Hardin, Ben	IV	Harmon, Daniel Williams	IV
Hardin, Charles Henry	IV	Harmon, Judson	IV
Hardin, John	IV	Harnden, William Frederick	IV
Hardin, John J.	IV	Harnett, Cornelius	IV

Complete Index Guide

Name	Vol./Supp.	Name	Vol./Supp.
Harney, Benjamin Robertson	2	Harris, Nathaniel Harrison	IV
Harney, William Selby	IV	Harris, Paul Percy	4
Harper, Fletcher	IV	Harris, Rollin Arthur	IV
Harper, Ida Husted	IV	Harris, Sam Henry	3
Harper, James	IV	Harris, Samuel	IV
Harper, John		Harris, Thaddeus Mason	IV
See Harper, James		Harris, Thaddeus William	IV
Harper, John Lyell	IV	Harris, Thomas Lake	IV
Harper, Joseph Wesley		Harris, Townsend	IV
See Harper, James		Harris, Wiley Pope	IV
Harper, Robert Francis	IV	Harris, William	IV
Harper, Robert Goodloe	IV	Harris, William Alexander	IV
Harper, William	IV	Harris, William Littleton	IV
Harper, William Rainey	IV	Harris, William Logan	IV
Harpster, John Henry	IV	Harris, William Torrey	IV
Harpur, Robert	IV	Harrison, Alexander	
Harrah, Charles Jefferson	IV	See Harrison, Thomas	
Harrell, John	IV	Alexander	
Harrigan, Edward	IV	Harrison, Benjamin (d. 1791)	IV
Harriman, Edward Henry	IV	Harrison, Benjamin (d. 1901)	IV
Harriman, Walter	IV	Harrison, Birge	
Harrington, Charles	IV	See Harrison, Lovell Birge	
Harrington, John Lyle	3	Harrison, Byron Patton	3
Harrington, Mark Walrod	IV	Harrison, Carter Henry	IV
Harrington, Samuel Maxwell	IV	Harrison, Carter Henry, Jr.	5
Harrington, Thomas Francis	IV	Harrison, Charles Custis	IV
Harris, Benjamin	IV	Harrison, Constance Cary	IV
Harris, Caleb Fiske	IV	Harrison, Elizabeth	IV
Harris, Chapin Aaron	IV	Harrison, Fairfax	2
Harris, Charles Kassell	IV	Harrison, Francis Burton	6
Harris, Daniel Lester	IV	Harrison, Gabriel	IV
Harris, Elisha	IV	Harrison, George Paul	IV
Harris, George	IV	Harrison, Gessner	IV
Harris, George Washington	IV	Harrison, Henry Baldwin	IV
Harris, Ira	IV	Harrison, Henry Sydnor	IV
Harris, Isham Green	IV	Harrison, James	IV
Harris, James Arthur	IV	Harrison, James Albert	IV
Harris, Joel Chandler	IV	Harrison, John	IV
Harris, John	IV	Harrison, Joseph	IV
Harris, John Woods	IV	Harrison, Lovell Birge	IV
Harris, Joseph	IV	Harrison, Pat	
Harris, Julian LaRose	7	See Harrison, Byron	
Harris, Maurice Henry	IV	Patton	
Harris, Merriman Colbert	IV	Harrison, Peter	IV
Harris, Miriam Coles	IV	Harrison, Richard Berry	1

Complete Index Guide

Name	Vol./Supp.	Name	Vol./Supp.
Harrison, Ross Granville	6	Harvey, Coin	
Harrison, Thomas Alexander	IV	See Harvey, William Hope	
Harrison, William Henry	IV	Harvey, George Brinton	
Harrison, William Pope	IV	McClellan	IV
Harrisse, Henry	1	Harvey, Hayward Augustus	IV
Harrod, Benjamin Morgan	IV	Harvey, Sir John	1
Harrod, James	IV	Harvey, Louis Powell	IV
Harshberger, John William	IV	Harvey, William Hope	2
Harshe, Robert Bartholow	2	Harvie, John	IV
Hart, Abraham	IV	Hasbrouck, Abraham Bruyn	IV
Hart, Albert Bushnell	3	Hasbrouck, Lydia Sayer	IV
Hart, Charles Henry	IV	Hascall, Milo Smith	IV
Hart, Edmund Hall	IV	Haseltine, James Henry	IV
Hart, Edward	1	Haselton, Seneca	IV
Hart, Edwin Bret	5	Hasenclever, Peter	IV
Hart, George Overbury	1	Haskell, Charles Nathaniel	1
Hart, Hastings Hornell	1	Haskell, Dudley Chase	IV
Hart, James MacDougal	IV	Haskell, Ella Louise Knowles	IV
Hart, James Morgan	IV	Haskell, Ernest	IV
Hart, Joel Tanner	IV	Haskell, Henry Joseph	5
Hart, John	IV	Hasket, Elias	IV
Hart, John Seely	IV	Haskins, Charles Homer	2
Hart, Lorenz Milton	3	Hassam, Frederick Childe	1
Hart, Moss	7	Hassard, John Rose Greene	IV
Hart, Samuel	IV	Hassaurek, Friedrich	IV
Hart, Virgil Chittenden	IV	Hasselquist, Tuve Nilsson	IV
Hart, William	IV	Hassler, Ferdinand Rudolph	IV
Hart, William Surrey	4	Hastings, Charles Sheldon	1
Harte, Francis Brett	IV	Hastings, Samuel Dexter	IV
Hartford, George Huntington	5	Hastings, Serranus Clinton	IV
Hartford, George Ludlum	5	Hastings, Thomas (d. 1872)	IV
Hartford, John Augustine	5	Hastings, Thomas (d. 1929)	IV
Hartley, Frank	IV	Hastings, William Wirt	2
Hartley, Jonathan Scott	IV	Haswell, Anthony	IV
Hartley, Marsden	3	Haswell, Charles Haynes	IV
Hartley, Thomas	IV	Hatch, Carl A.	7
Hartmann, Carl Sadakichi	3	Hatch, Edward	IV
Hartness, James	1	Hatch, John Porter	IV
Hartranft, Chester David	IV	Hatch, Rufus	IV
Hartranft, John Frederick	IV	Hatch, William Henry	IV
Hartshorne, Henry	IV	Hatcher, Orie Latham	4
Hartsuff, George Lucas	IV	Hatcher, Robert Anthony	3
Hartwig, Johann Christoph	IV	Hatcher, William Eldridge	IV
Hartzell, Joseph Crane	IV	Hatfield, Edwin Francis	IV
Harvard, John	IV	Hathorne, William	IV

Complete Index Guide

Name	Vol./Supp.	Name	Vol./Supp.
Hatlo, James C. ("Jimmy")	7	Hawthorne, Nathaniel	IV
Hatton, Frank	IV	Hawthorne, Rose	
Haugen, Gilbert Nelson	1	See Alphonsa, Mother	
Haugen, Nils Pederson	1	Hay, Charles Augustus	IV
Haughery, Margaret Gaffney	IV	Hay, George	IV
Haughton, Percy Duncan	IV	Hay, John Milton	IV
Hauk, Minnie	IV	Hay, Mary Garrett	IV
Haupt, Alma Cecelia	6	Hay, Oliver Perry	IV
Haupt, Herman	IV	Hayden, Amos Sutton	IV
Haupt, Paul	IV	Hayden, Charles	2
Hauser, Samuel Thomas	IV	Hayden, Charles Henry	IV
Havell, Robert	IV	Hayden, Edward Everett	1
Havemeyer, Henry Osborne	IV	Hayden, Ferdinand Vandiveer	IV
Havemeyer, William Frederick	IV	Hayden, Hiram Washington	IV
Haven, Alice B.		Hayden, Horace H.	IV
See Haven, Emily Bradley		Hayden, Joseph Shepard	IV
Neal		Hayden, William	IV
Haven, Emily Bradley Neal	IV	Hayes, Augustus Allen	IV
Haven, Erastus Otis	IV	Hayes, Carlton Joseph Huntley	7
Haven, Gilbert	IV	Hayes, Charles Willard	IV
Haven, Henry Philemon	IV	Hayes, Edward Cary	1
Haven, Joseph	IV	Hayes, Isaac Israel	IV
Havens, James Smith	IV	Hayes, John Lord	IV
Haverly, Christopher	IV	Hayes, John William	3
Haverly, Jack H.		Hayes, Max Sebastian	3
See Haverly, Christopher		Hayes, Patrick Joseph	2
Haviland, Clarence Floyd	IV	Hayes, Rutherford Birchard	IV
Haviland, John	IV	Hayes, William Henry	IV
Hawes, Charles Boardman	IV	Hayford, John Fillmore	IV
Hawes, Harriet Ann Boyd	3	Haygood, Atticus Green	IV
Hawkins, Benjamin	IV	Haygood, Laura Askew	IV
Hawkins, Dexter Arnold	IV	Hayne, Isaac	IV
Hawkins, Rush Christopher	IV	Hayne, Paul Hamilton	IV
Hawks, Francis Lister	IV	Hayne, Robert Young	IV
Hawks, John	IV	Haynes, George Edmund	6
Hawley, Gideon (d. 1807)	IV	Haynes, John	IV
Hawley, Gideon (d. 1870)	IV	Haynes, John Henry	IV
Hawley, James Henry	IV	Hays, Alexander	IV
Hawley, Joseph	IV	Hays, Arthur Garfield	5
Hawley, Joseph Roswell	IV	Hays, Harry Thompson	IV
Hawley, Paul Ramsey	7	Hays, Isaac	IV
Hawley, Willis Chatman	3	Hays, John Coffee	IV
Haworth, Joseph	IV	Hays, Will H.	5
Hawthorne, Charles Webster	IV	Hays, William Jacob	IV
Hawthorne, Julian	1	Hays, William Shakespeare	IV

Complete Index Guide

Name	Vol./Supp.	Name	Vol./Supp.
Hayward, George	IV	Hecker, Isaac Thomas	IV
Hayward, Nathaniel Manley	IV	Heckewelder, John Gottlieb	
Haywood, Allan Shaw	5	Ernestus	IV
Haywood, John	IV	Heckscher, August	3
Haywood, William Dudley	IV	Hector, Francisco Luis	
Hazard, Augustus George	IV	See Carondelet, Francisco	
Hazard, Ebenezer	IV	Luis Hector, Baron de	
Hazard, Jonathan J.	IV	Hedding, Elijah	IV
Hazard, Rowland Gibson	IV	Hedge, Frederic Henry	IV
Hazard, Samuel	IV	Hedge, Levi	IV
Hazard, Thomas	IV	Heenan, John Carmel	IV
Hazard, Thomas Robinson	IV	Heffelfinger, William Walter	
Hazelius, Ernest Lewis	IV	("Pudge")	5
Hazeltine, Mayo Williamson	IV	Heflin, James Thomas	5
Hazelton, George Cochrane	IV	Hegeman, John Rogers	IV
Hazelwood, John	IV	Heilmann, Harry	5
Hazen, Allen	1	Heilprin, Angelo	IV
Hazen, Henry Allen	IV	Heilprin, Michael	IV
Hazen, Moses	IV	Heineman, Daniel Webster	
Hazen, William Babcock	IV	("Dannie")	7
Headley, Joel Tyler	IV	Heinemann, Ernst	IV
Headley, Phineas Camp	IV	Heinrich, Antony Philip	IV
Healy, George Peter Alexander	IV	Heinrich, Max	IV
Heap, Samuel Davies	IV	Heintzelman, Samuel Peter	IV
Heard, Augustine	IV	Heintzelman, Stuart	1
Heard, Dwight Bancroft	IV	Heinz, Henry John	IV
Heard, Franklin Fiske	IV	Heinze, Frederick Augustus	IV
Hearn, Lafcadio	IV	Heinzen, Karl Peter	IV
Hearst, George	IV	Heiss, Michael	IV
Hearst, Phoebe Apperson	IV	Helbron, Peter	IV
Hearst, William Randolph	5	Helburn, Theresa	6
Heath, James Ewell	IV	Held, John, Jr.	6
Heath, Perry Sanford	IV	Helffenstein, John Albert	
Heath, Thomas Kurton		Conrad	IV
See under McIntyre,		Heller, Maximilian	IV
James		Heller, Robert	
Heath, William	IV	See Palmer, William	
Heathcote, Caleb	IV	Henry	
Heaton, John Langdon	1	Helm, Charles John	IV
Hébert, Louis	IV	Helm, John Larue	IV
Hébert, Paul Octave	IV	Helmer, Bessie Bradwell	IV
Hecht, Ben	7	Helmpraecht, Joseph	IV
Hecht, Selig	4	Helmuth, Justus Henry	
Heck, Barbara	IV	Christian	IV
Hecker, Friedrich Karl Franz	IV	Helmuth, William Tod	IV

85

Complete Index Guide

Name	Vol./Supp.	Name	Vol./Supp.
Helper, Hinton Rowan	IV	Henny, David Christiaan	1
Hemenway, Mary Porter Tileston	IV	Henri, Robert	IV
		Henrici, Arthur Trautwein	3
Hemingway, Ernest Miller	7	Henrotin, Charles	IV
Hemmeter, John Conrad	IV	Henrotin, Fernand	IV
Hempel, Charles Julius	IV	Henry, Alexander	1
Hemphill, John	IV	Henry, Alice	3
Hemphill, Joseph	IV	Henry, Andrew	IV
Hempl, George	IV	Henry, Caleb Sprague	IV
Hench, Philip Showalter	7	Henry, Edward Lamson	IV
Henchman, Daniel	1	Henry, John (d. 1794)	IV
Henck, John Benjamin	IV	Henry, John (d. 1798)	IV
Hendel, John William	IV	Henry, John (fl. 1807–20)	IV
Henderson, Archibald	IV	Henry, Joseph	IV
Henderson, Charles Richmond	IV	Henry, Morris Henry	IV
Henderson, Daniel McIntyre	IV	Henry, O.	
Henderson, David Bremner	IV	See Porter, William Sydney	
Henderson, Fletcher Hamilton	5		
Henderson, James Pinckney	IV	Henry, Patrick	IV
Henderson, John	IV	Henry, Robert	IV
Henderson, John Brooks	IV	Henry, William	IV
Henderson, Lawrence Joseph	3	Henry, William Arnon	1
Henderson, Leonard	IV	Henry, William Wirt	IV
Henderson, Paul	5	Henshall, James Alexander	IV
Henderson, Peter	IV	Henshaw, David	IV
Henderson, Richard	IV	Henshaw, Henry Wetherbee	IV
Henderson, Thomas	IV	Henson, Josiah	IV
Henderson, William James	2	Henson, Matthew Alexander	5
Henderson, Yandell	3	Hentz, Caroline Lee Whiting	IV
Hendrick	IV	Hepburn, Alonzo Barton	IV
Hendrick, Burton Jesse	4	Hepburn, James Curtis	IV
Hendrick, Ellwood	IV	Hepburn, Katharine Houghton	5
Hendricks, Thomas Andrews	IV	Hepburn, William Peters	IV
Hendricks, William	IV	Hepworth, George Hughes	IV
Hendrix, Eugene Russell	IV	Herbermann, Charles George	IV
Hendrix, Joseph Clifford	IV	Herbert, Frederick Hugh	6
Heney, Francis Joseph	2	Herbert, Henry William	IV
Hening, William Waller	IV	Herbert, Hilary Abner	IV
Henkel, Paul	IV	Herbert, Victor	IV
Henley, Robert	IV	Herdic, Peter	IV
Hennepin, Louis	IV	Herford, Oliver Brooke	1
Hennessy, John	IV	Hergesheimer, Joseph	5
Hennessy, William John	IV	Hering, Carl	IV
Henni, John Martin	IV	Hering, Constantine	IV
Henningsen, Charles Frederick	IV	Hering, Rudolph	IV

Complete Index Guide

Name	Vol./Supp.	Name	Vol./Supp.
Herkimer, Nicholas	IV	Hewett, Waterman Thomas	IV
Herman, Lebrecht Frederick	IV	Hewit, Augustine Francis	IV
Herndon, William Henry	IV	Hewit, Nathaniel Augustus	
Herndon, William Lewis	IV	See Hewit, Augustine	
Herne, Chrystal	4	Francis	
Herne, James A.	IV	Hewitt, Abram Stevens	IV
Herold, David E.		Hewitt, James	IV
See Booth, John Wilkes		Hewitt, John Hill	IV
Heron, Matilda Agnes	IV	Hewitt, Peter Cooper	IV
Heron, William	IV	Heydt, Hans Jöst	
Herr, Herbert Thacker	1	See Hite, Jost	
Herr, John	IV	Heye, George Gustav	6
Herreshoff, James Brown	IV	Heyer, John Christian	
Herreshoff, John Brown	IV	Frederick	IV
Herreshoff, Nathaniel Greene	2	Heyward, DuBose	2
Herrick, Edward Claudius	IV	Heyward, Thomas	IV
Herrick, Myron Timothy	IV	Heywood, Ezra Hervey	IV
Herrick, Robert Welch	2	Heywood, Levi	IV
Herrick, Sophia McIlvaine		Hiacoomes	IV
Bledsoe	IV	Hibbard, Freeborn Garrettson	IV
Herriman, George Joseph	3	Hibben, John Grier	1
Herring, Augustus Moore	IV	Hibben, Paxton Pattison	V
Herring, James	IV	Hibbins, Ann	V
Herring, Silas Clark	IV	Hichborn, Philip	V
Herrman, Augustine	IV	Hickenlooper, Andrew	V
Herrmann, Alexander	IV	Hickok, James Butler	V
Herron, Francis Jay	IV	Hickok, Laurens Perseus	V
Herron, George Davis	IV	Hickok, Wild Bill	
Herschel, Clemens	IV	See Hickok, James Butler	
Hersey, Evelyn Weeks	7	Hicks, Elias	V
Hershey, Milton Snavely	3	Hicks, John (d. 1890)	V
Herter, Christian	IV	Hicks, John (d. 1917)	V
Herter, Christian Archibald	IV	Hicks, Thomas Holliday	V
Herty, Charles Holmes	2	Hiester, Daniel	V
Hertz, Alfred	3	Hiester, Joseph	V
Hertz, John Daniel	7	Higgins, Andrew Jackson	5
Hess, Alfred Fabian	1	Higgins, Daniel Paul	5
Hess, Victor Franz	7	Higgins, Frank Wayland	V
Hesselius, Gustavus	IV	Higginson, Francis	V
Hesselius, John	IV	Higginson, Henry Lee	V
Hessoun, Joseph	IV	Higginson, John	V
Heth, Henry	IV	Higginson, Nathaniel	V
Hewat, Alexander	IV	Higginson, Stephen	V
Hewes, Joseph	IV	Higginson, Thomas Wentworth	V
Hewes, Robert	IV	High, Stanley Hoflund	7

Complete Index Guide

Name	Vol./Supp.	Name	Vol./Supp.
Higinbotham, Harlow Niles	V	Hilliard, Henry Washington	V
Hildreth, Richard	V	Hillis, David	V
Hildreth, Samuel Clay	V	Hillis, Newell Dwight	V
Hildreth, Samuel Prescott	V	Hillman, Sidney	4
Hilgard, Eugene Woldemar	V	Hillman, Thomas Tennessee	V
Hilgard, Julius Erasmus	V	Hillquit, Morris	1
Hilgard, Theodor Erasmus	V	Hills, Elijah Clarence	1
Hill, Ambrose Powell	V	Hillyer, Junius	V
Hill, Benjamin Harvey	V	Hillyer, Robert Silliman	7
Hill, Daniel Harvey	V	Hilprecht, Herman Volrath	V
Hill, David Bennett	V	Himes, Charles Francis	V
Hill, David Jayne	1	Himes, Joshua Vaughan	V
Hill, Edwin Conger	6	Hindman, Thomas Carmichael	V
Hill, Ernest Rowland	4	Hindman, William	V
Hill, Frank Alpine	V	Hinds, Asher Crosby	V
Hill, Frederick Trevor	V	Hine, Charles De Lano	V
Hill, Frederic Stanhope	V	Hine, Lewis Wickes	2
Hill, George Handel	V	Hines, Duncan	6
Hill, George Washington	4	Hines, Frank Thomas	6
Hill, George William	V	Hines, James J.	6
Hill, Grace Livingston	4	Hines, Walker Downer	1
Hill, Henry Barker	V	Hinkle, Beatrice Moses	5
Hill, Isaac	V	Hinman, Elisha	V
Hill, James	V	Hinman, George Wheeler	V
Hill, James Jerome	V	Hinman, Joel	V
Hill, John	V	Hinsdale, Burke Aaron	V
Hill, John Henry	V	Hinshaw, David Schull	5
Hill, Joseph Adna	2	Hires, Charles Elmer	2
Hill, Joshua	V	Hirsch, Emil Gustav	V
Hill, Louis Clarence	2	Hirsch, Isaac Seth	3
Hill, Nathaniel Peter	V	Hirschbein, Peretz	4
Hill, Patty Smith	4	Hirschensohn, Chaim	1
Hill, Richard	V	Hirst, Barton Cooke	1
Hill, Robert Andrews	V	Hirst, Henry Beck	V
Hill, Thomas (d. 1891)	V	Hirth, William Andrew	2
Hill, Thomas (d. 1908)	V	Hiscock, Frank Harris	4
Hill, Ureli Corelli	V	Hise, Elijah	V
Hill, Walter Barnard	V	Hitchcock, Charles Henry	V
Hill, William	V	Hitchcock, Edward (d. 1864)	V
Hillard, George Stillman	V	Hitchcock, Edward (d. 1911)	V
Hillebrand, William Francis	V	Hitchcock, Enos	V
Hillegas, Michael	V	Hitchcock, Ethan Allen	
Hillhouse, James	V	(d. 1870)	V
Hillhouse, James Abraham	V	Hitchcock, Ethan Allen	
Hilliard, Francis	V	(d. 1909)	V

Complete Index Guide

Name	Vol./Supp.
Hitchcock, Frank	
See Murdoch, Frank	
Hitchcock	
Hitchcock, Frank Harris	1
Hitchcock, Gilbert Monell	1
Hitchcock, Henry	V
Hitchcock, James Ripley	
Wellman	V
Hitchcock, Peter	V
Hitchcock, Phineas Warrener	V
Hitchcock, Raymond	V
Hitchcock, Ripley	
See Hitchcock, James	
Ripley Wellman	
Hitchcock, Roswell Dwight	V
Hitchcock, Thomas	3
Hite, Jost	V
Hitt, Robert Roberts	V
Hittell, John Shertzer	V
Hittell, Theodore Henry	V
Hoadley, David	V
Hoadley, John Chipman	V
Hoadly, George	V
Hoag, Joseph	V
Hoagland, Charles Lee	4
Hoagland, Dennis Robert	4
Hoan, Daniel Webster	7
Hoar, Ebenezer Rockwood	V
Hoar, George Frisbie	V
Hoar, Leonard	V
Hoar, Samuel	V
Hoard, William Dempster	V
Hoban, James	V
Hobart, Garret Augustus	V
Hobart, John Henry	V
Hobart, John Sloss	V
Hobbs, Alfred Charles	V
Hobby, William Pettus	7
Hobson, Edward Henry	V
Hobson, Richmond Pearson	2
Hoch, August	V
Hodes, Henry Irving	7
Hodge, Archibald Alexander	V
Hodge, Charles	V
Hodge, Hugh Lenox	V
Hodge, John Reed	7
Hodge, William Thomas	1
Hodgen, John Thompson	V
Hodges, George	V
Hodges, Harry Foote	V
Hodgkinson, Francis	4
Hodgkinson, John	V
Hodgson, William Brown	1
Hodson, William	3
Hodur, Francis	5
Hoe, Richard March	V
Hoe, Robert (d. 1833)	V
Hoe, Robert (d. 1909)	V
Hoecken, Christian	V
Hoen, August	V
Hoenecke, Gustav Adolf Felix Theodor	V
Hoerr, Normand Louis	6
Hoey, Clyde Roark	5
Hoff, John Van Rensselaer	V
Hoffman, Charles Fenno	V
Hoffman, David	V
Hoffman, David Murray	V
Hoffman, Eugene Augustus	V
Hoffman, Frederick Ludwig	4
Hoffman, John Thompson	V
Hoffman, Josiah Ogden	V
Hoffman, Ogden	V
Hoffman, Richard	V
Hoffman, Wickham	V
Hoffmann, Francis Arnold	V
Hofman, Heinrich Oscar	V
Hofmann, Josef Casimir	6
Hogan, John	V
Hogan, John Vincent Lawless	6
Hoge, Moses	V
Hoge, Moses Drury	V
Hogg, George	V
Hogg, James Stephen	V
Hogue, Wilson Thomas	V
Hogun, James	V
Hohfeld, Wesley Newcomb	V
Hoisington, Henry Richard	V
Hoke, Robert Frederick	V
Hokinson, Helen Elna	4

Complete Index Guide

Name	Vol./Supp.	Name	Vol./Supp.
Holabird, William	V	Holls, Frederick William	
Holbrook, Alfred	V	See Holls, George	
Holbrook, Frederick	V	Frederick William	
Holbrook, John Edwards	V	Holls, George Frederick	
Holbrook, Josiah	V	William	V
Holbrook, Stewart Hall	7	Holly, Charles Hardin	
Holcomb, Amasa	V	("Buddy")	6
Holcomb, Silas Alexander	V	Holly, James Theodore	V
Holcombe, Chester	V	Hollyer, Samuel	V
Holcombe, Henry	V	Holman, Jesse Lynch	V
Holcombe, James Philemon	V	Holman, William Steele	V
Holcombe, William Henry	V	Holme, Thomas	V
Holden, Edward Singleton	V	Holmes, Abiel	V
Holden, Hale	2	Holmes, Bayard Taylor	V
Holden, Liberty Emery	V	Holmes, Daniel Henry	V
Holden, Oliver	V	Holmes, David	V
Holden, William Woods	V	Holmes, Elias Burton	6
Holder, Charles Frederick	V	Holmes, Ezekiel	V
Holder, Joseph Bassett	V	Holmes, George Frederick	V
Holdrege, George Ward	1	Holmes, Isaac Edward	V
Holiday, Billie	6	Holmes, Israel	V
Holladay, Ben	V	Holmes, John	V
Holland, Clifford Milburn	V	Holmes, John Haynes	7
Holland, Edmund Milton	V	Holmes, Joseph Austin	V
Holland, Edwin Clifford	V	Holmes, Mary Jane Hawes	V
Holland, George	V	Holmes, Nathaniel	V
Holland, John Philip	V	Holmes, Oliver Wendell	
Holland, Joseph Jefferson	V	(d. 1894)	V
Holland, Josiah Gilbert	V	Holmes, Oliver Wendell	
Holland, William Jacob	1	(d. 1935)	1
Hollander, Jacob Harry	2	Holmes, Theophilus Hunter	V
Hollerith, Herman	1	Holmes, William Henry	1
Holley, Alexander Lyman	V	Holsey, Lucius Henry	V
Holley, Horace	V	Holst, Hermann Eduard von	V
Holley, Marietta	V	Holt, Arthur Erastus	3
Holley, Myron	V	Holt, Edwin Bissell	4
Hollick, Charles Arthur	1	Holt, Edwin Michael	V
Holliday, Cyrus Kurtz	V	Holt, Hamilton Bowen	5
Holliday, Judy	7	Holt, Henry	V
Hollingworth, Leta Stetter	2	Holt, John	V
Hollins, George Nichols	V	Holt, Joseph	V
Hollis, Ira Nelson	V	Holt, Luther Emmett	V
Hollister, Gideon Hiram	V	Holt, William Franklin	5
Holloway, John	V	Holt, Winifred	3
Holloway, Joseph Flavius	V	Holten, Samuel	V

Complete Index Guide

Name	Vol./Supp.	Name	Vol./Supp.
Holyoke, Edward Augustus	V	Hopkins, James Campbell	V
Holyoke, Samuel	V	Hopkins, John Burroughs	V
Homer, Louise Dilworth Beatty	4	Hopkins, John Henry	V
Homer, Winslow	V	Hopkins, Johns	V
Homes, Henry Augustus	V	Hopkins, Juliet Ann Opie	V
Hone, Philip	V	Hopkins, Lemuel	V
Hontan, Louis-Armand de Lom		Hopkins, Mark	V
d'Arce, Baron de la		Hopkins, Samuel (d. 1803)	V
See Lahontan,		Hopkins, Samuel (d. 1819)	V
Louis-Armand de Lom		Hopkins, Stephen	V
d'Arce		Hopkinson, Francis	V
Hood, James Walker	V	Hopkinson, Joseph	V
Hood, John Bell	V	Hoppe, William Frederick	
Hood, Raymond Mathewson	1	("Willie")	6
Hood, Washington	V	Hopper, DeWolf	1
Hooker, Donald Russell	4	Hopper, Edna Wallace	6
Hooker, Elon Huntington	2	Hopper, Isaac Tatem	V
Hooker, Isabella Beecher	V	Hoppin, Augustus	V
Hooker, Joseph	V	Hoppin, James Mason	V
Hooker, Philip	V	Hoppin, Joseph Clark	V
Hooker, Samuel Cox	1	Hoppin, William Warner	V
Hooker, Thomas	V	Hopson, Howard Colwell	4
Hooker, William	V	Hopwood, Avery	V
Hooker, Worthington	V	Horlick, William	2
Hooper, Claude Ernest	5	Hormel, George Albert	4
Hooper, Jessie Annette Jack	1	Hormel, Jay Catherwood	5
Hooper, Johnson Jones	V	Horn, Edward Traill	V
Hooper, Lucy Hamilton	V	Horn, George Henry	V
Hooper, Samuel	V	Horn, Tom	V
Hooper, William	V	Hornaday, William Temple	2
Hooton, Earnest Albert	5	Hornblower, Joseph Coerten	V
Hoover, Charles Franklin	V	Hornblower, Josiah	V
Hoover, Herbert Clark	7	Hornblower, William Butler	V
Hoover, Herbert William	5	Horner, Henry	2
Hoover, James Matthews	1	Horner, William Edmonds	V
Hope, James Barron	V	Horney, Karen Danielssen	5
Hope, John	2	Hornsby, Rogers	7
Hopkins, Arthur Francis	V	Horr, George Edwin	V
Hopkins, Cyril George	V	Horrocks, James	V
Hopkins, Edward	V	Horsfield, Thomas	V
Hopkins, Edward Augustus	V	Horsford, Eben Norton	V
Hopkins, Edward Washburn	1	Horsmanden, Daniel	V
Hopkins, Esek	V	Horst, Louis	7
Hopkins, Harry Lloyd	4	Horton, Samuel Dana	V
Hopkins, Isaac Stiles	V	Horton, Valentine Baxter	V

Complete Index Guide

Name	Vol./Supp.	Name	Vol./Supp.
Hosack, Alexander Eddy	V	Hovey, Charles Mason	V
Hosack, David	V	Hovey, Otis Ellis	3
Hoshour, Samuel Klinefelter	V	Hovey, Richard	V
Hosmer, Frederick Lucian	V	Hovgaard, William	4
Hosmer, Harriet Goodhue	V	Howard, Ada Lydia	V
Hosmer, Hezekiah Lord	V	Howard, Benjamin	V
Hosmer, James Kendall	V	Howard, Benjamin Chew	V
Hosmer, Titus	V	Howard, Blanche Willis	V
Hosmer, William Howe Cuyler	V	Howard, Bronson Crocker	V
Hotchkiss, Benjamin Berkeley	V	Howard, Charles Perry	2
Hotchkiss, Horace Leslie	V	Howard, Edgar	5
Hotz, Ferdinand Carl	V	Howard, George Elliott	V
Houdini, Harry	V	Howard, Henry	5
Houdry, Eugene Jules	7	Howard, Jacob Merritt	V
Hough, Charles Merrill	V	Howard, John Eager	V
Hough, Emerson	V	Howard, Joseph Kinsey	5
Hough, Franklin Benjamin	V	Howard, Leland Ossian	4
Hough, George Washington	V	Howard, Leslie	3
Hough, Theodore	V	Howard, Oliver Otis	V
Hough, Walter	1	Howard, Roy Wilson	7
Hough, Warwick	V	Howard, Sidney Coe	2
Houghton, Alanson Bigelow	3	Howard, Timothy Edward	V
Houghton, Douglass	V	Howard, Volney Erskine	V
Houghton, George Hendric	V	Howard, William Alanson	V
Houghton, Henry Oscar	V	Howard, William Travis	1
Houk, Leonidas Campbell	V	Howard, Willie	4
Hourwich, Isaac Aaronovich	V	Howe, Albion Parris	V
House, Edward Howard	V	Howe, Andrew Jackson	V
House, Edward Mandell	2	Howe, Edgar Watson	2
House, Henry Alonzo	V	Howe, Elias	V
House, Royal Earl	V	Howe, Frederic Clemson	2
House, Samuel Reynolds	V	Howe, Frederick Webster	V
Houston, Charles Hamilton	4	Howe, George	V
Houston, David Franklin	2	Howe, George Augustus	V
Houston, Edwin James	V	Howe, Henry	V
Houston, George Smith	V	Howe, Henry Marion	V
Houston, Henry Howard	V	Howe, Herbert Alonzo	V
Houston, Samuel	V	Howe, John Ireland	V
Houston, William Churchill	V	Howe, Julia Ward	V
Houstoun, John	V	Howe, Louis McHenry	2
Hove, Elling	V	Howe, Lucien	V
Hovenden, Thomas	V	Howe, Mark Anthony	
Hovey, Alvah	V	DeWolfe	V
Hovey, Alvin Peterson	V	Howe, Mark Antony De Wolfe	6
Hovey, Charles Edward	V	Howe, Percy Rogers	4

Complete Index Guide

Name	Vol./Supp.	Name	Vol./Supp.
Howe, Robert	V	Hubbard, Henry Guernsey	V
Howe, Samuel	V	Hubbard, John	V
Howe, Samuel Gridley	V	Hubbard, Joseph Stillman	V
Howe, Timothy Otis	V	Hubbard, Kin	
Howe, William	V	See Hubbard, Frank	
Howe, William F.	V	McKinney	
Howe, William Henry	V	Hubbard, Lucius Frederick	V
Howe, William Wirt	V	Hubbard, Richard Bennett	V
Howell, Albert Summers	5	Hubbard, Richard William	V
Howell, Clark	2	Hubbard, Thomas Hamlin	V
Howell, David	V	Hubbard, William	V
Howell, Evan Park	V	Hubbard, Wynant Davis	7
Howell, James Bruen	V	Hubbell, John Lorenzo	1
Howell, John Adams	V	Hubble, Edwin	5
Howell, Richard	V	Hubbs, Rebecca	V
Howell, Robert Boyté Crawford	V	Huber, Gotthelf Carl	1
Howell, Thomas Jefferson	V	Hubert, Conrad	V
Howell, William Henry	3	Hubner, Charles William	V
Howells, William Dean	V	Hudde, Andries	V
Howey, Walter Crawford	5	Hudson, Charles	V
Howison, George Holmes	V	Hudson, Claude Silbert	5
Howland, Alfred Cornelius	V	Hudson, Daniel Eldred	1
Howland, Emily	V	Hudson, Edward	V
Howland, Gardiner Greene	V	Hudson, Frederic	1
Howland, John	V	Hudson, Henry	V
Howley, Richard	V	Hudson, Henry Norman	V
Howry, Charles Bowen	V	Hudson, Manley Ottmer	6
Howze, Robert Lee	V	Hudson, Mary Clemmer Ames	
Hoxie, Robert Franklin	V	See Clemmer, Mary	
Hoxie, Vinnie Ream	V	Hudson, Thomson Jay	V
Hoxie, William Dixie	V	Hudson, William Smith	V
Hoyme, Gjermund	V	Huebner, Solomon Stephen	7
Hoyt, Albert Harrison	V	Huebsch, Ben W.	7
Hoyt, Charles Hale	V	Huger, Benjamin	V
Hoyt, Henry Martyn	V	Huger, Daniel Elliott	V
Hoyt, John Sherman	5	Huger, Francis Kinloch	V
Hoyt, John Wesley	V	Huger, Isaac	V
Hrdlička, Aleš	3	Huger, John	V
Hubbard, Bernard Rosecrans	7	Huggins, Miller James	V
Hubbard, David	V	Hughes, Charles Evans	4
Hubbard, Elbert	V	Hughes, Charles Frederick	1
Hubbard, Frank McKinney	V	Hughes, Christopher	V
Hubbard, Gardiner Greene	V	Hughes, David Edward	V
Hubbard, Gurdon Saltonstall	V	Hughes, Dudley Mays	V
Hubbard, Henry Griswold	V	Hughes, Edwin Holt	4

Complete Index Guide

Name	Vol./Supp.	Name	Vol./Supp.
Hughes, George Wurtz	V	Hunt, Benjamin Weeks	1
Hughes, Hector James	V	Hunt, Carleton	V
Hughes, Henry	V	Hunt, Charles Wallace	V
Hughes, Howard Robard	V	Hunt, Freeman	V
Hughes, James	V	Hunt, Gaillard	V
Hughes, John Joseph	V	Hunt, George Wylie Paul	1
Hughes, Price	V	Hunt, Harriot Kezia	V
Hughes, Robert Ball	V	Hunt, Henry Jackson	V
Hughes, Robert William	V	Hunt, Isaac	V
Hughes, Rupert	6	Hunt, Lester Callaway	5
Huidekoper, Frederic	V	Hunt, Mary Hannah Hanchett	V
Huidekoper, Harm Jan	V	Hunt, Nathan	V
Hulbert, Archer Butler	1	Hunt, Reid	4
Hulbert, Edwin James	V	Hunt, Richard Morris	V
Hull, Clark Leonard	5	Hunt, Robert	V
Hull, Cordell	5	Hunt, Robert Woolston	V
Hull, Isaac	V	Hunt, Theodore Whitefield	V
Hull, John	V	Hunt, Thomas Sterry	V
Hull, Josephine	6	Hunt, Ward	V
Hull, William	V	Hunt, Washington	V
Hullihen, Simon P.	V	Hunt, William Gibbes	V
Humbert, Jean Joseph Amable	V	Hunt, William Henry	V
Hume, Edgar Erskine	5	Hunt, William Morris	V
Hume, Robert Allen	V	Hunt, Wilson Price	V
Hume, William	V	Hunter, Andrew	V
Humes, Thomas William	V	Hunter, David	V
Humiston, William Henry	V	Hunter, Robert (d. 1734)	V
Hummel, Abraham Henry	V	Hunter, Robert (d. 1942)	3
Humphrey, Doris	6	Hunter, Robert Mercer	
Humphrey, Heman	V	Taliaferro	V
Humphreys, Alexander		Hunter, Thomas	V
Crombie	V	Hunter, Walter David	V
Humphreys, Andrew Atkinson	V	Hunter, Whiteside Godfrey	V
Humphreys, Benjamin Grubb	V	Hunter, William	V
Humphreys, David	V	Hunter, William C.	V
Humphreys, James	V	Huntington, Collis Potter	V
Humphreys, Joshua	V	Huntington, Daniel	V
Humphreys, Milton Wylie	V	Huntington, Edward Vermilye	5
Humphreys, West Hughes	V	Huntington, Elisha	V
Humphreys, William Jackson	4	Huntington, Ellsworth	4
Huneker, James Gibbons	V	Huntington, Frederic Dan	V
Hunnewell, Horatio Hollis	V	Huntington, Henry Edwards	V
Hunnewell, James	V	Huntington, Jabez	V
Hunt, Alfred Ephraim	V	Huntington, Jedediah	V

Complete Index Guide

Name	Vol./Supp.	Name	Vol./Supp.
Huntington, Jedediah Vincent	V	Hutton, Laurence	V
Huntington, Margaret Jane Evans	V	Hutton, Levi William	V
		Huxley, Aldous Leonard	7
Huntington, Samuel (*d. 1796*)	V	Hyatt, Alpheus	V
Huntington, Samuel (*d. 1817*)	V	Hyatt, John Wesley	V
Huntington, William Edwards	V	Hyde, Arthur Mastick	4
Huntington, William Reed	V	Hyde, Charles Cheney	5
Hunton, Eppa	V	Hyde, Edward (*d. 1712*)	V
Hunton, William Lee	V	Hyde, Edward (*d. 1723*)	
Hupp, Louis Gorham	7	See Cornbury, Edward	
Hurd, John Codman	V	Hyde, Viscount	
Hurd, Nathaniel	V	Hyde, Helen	V
Hurlbert, William Henry	V	Hyde, Henry Baldwin	V
Hurlbut, Jesse Lyman	V	Hyde, James Nevins	V
Hurlbut, Stephen Augustus	V	Hyde, William DeWitt	V
Hurley, Edward Nash	1	Hyer, Robert Stewart	V
Hurley, Patrick Jay	7	Hylan, John Francis	2
Hurst, John Fletcher	V	Hyrne, Edmund Massingberd	V
Hurston, Zora Neale	6	Hyslop, James Hervey	V
Husbands, Hermon	V	Hyvernat, Henri	3
Huse, Caleb	V		
Husing, Edward Britt ("Ted")	7	Iberville, Pierre Le Moyne, Sieur d'	V
Husk, Charles Ellsworth	V	Ickes, Harold Le Clair	5
Husmann, George	V	Iddings, Joseph Paxon	V
Hussey, Curtis Grubb	V	Ide, Henry Clay	V
Hussey, Obed	V	Ide, John Jay	7
Hussey, William Joseph	V	Iglesias, Santiago	2
Husting, Paul Oscar	V	Ik Marvel	
Huston, Charles	V	See Mitchell, Donald Grant	
Huston, Walter	4		
Hutcheson, Paul	6	Illington, Margaret	1
Hutcheson, William Levi	5	Ilpendam, Jan Jansen Van	
Hutchins, Harry Burns	V	See Van Ilpendam, Jan Jansen	
Hutchins, Thomas	V		
Hutchinson, Anne	V	Imber, Naphtali Herz	V
Hutchinson, Benjamin Peters	V	Imbert, Antoine	V
Hutchinson, Charles Lawrence	V	Imboden, John Daniel	V
Hutchinson, James	V	Imlay, Gilbert	V
Hutchinson, Paul	6	Ingalls, John James	V
Hutchinson, Thomas	V	Ingalls, Marilla Baker	V
Hutchinson, Woods	V	Ingalls, Melville Ezra	V
Hutson, Richard	V	Ingals, Ephraim Fletcher	V
Hutton, Edward Francis	7	Ingersoll, Charles Jared	V
Hutton, Frederick Remsen	V		

Complete Index Guide

Name	Vol./Supp.	Name	Vol./Supp.
Ingersoll, Edward	V	Irving, John Treat	V
Ingersoll, Jared (d. 1781)	V	Irving, Peter	V
Ingersoll, Jared (d. 1822)	V	Irving, Pierre Munro	V
Ingersoll, Robert Green	V	Irving, Roland Duer	V
Ingersoll, Robert Hawley	V	Irving, Washington	V
Ingersoll, Royal Rodney	V	Irving, William	V
Ingersoll, Simon	V	Irwin, Elisabeth Antoinette	3
Ingham, Charles Cromwell	V	Irwin, George Le Roy	V
Ingham, Samuel Delucenna	V	Irwin, May	2
Ingle, Richard	V	Irwin, Robert Benjamin	5
Inglis, Alexander James	V	Irwin, Will	4
Inglis, Charles	V	Isaacs, Abram Samuel	V
Ingraham, Duncan Nathaniel	V	Isaacs, Samuel Myer	V
Ingraham, Edward Duffield	V	Isbrandtsen, Hans Jeppesen	5
Ingraham, Joseph	V	Isham, Ralph Heyward	5
Ingraham, Joseph Holt	V	Isham, Samuel	V
Ingraham, Prentiss	V	Isherwood, Benjamin Franklin	V
Ingram, Jonas Howard	5	Isom, Mary Frances	V
Inman, George	V	Iverson, Alfred	V
Inman, Henry (d. 1846)	V	Ives, Charles Edward	5
Inman, Henry (d. 1899)	V	Ives, Chauncey Bradley	V
Inman, John	V	Ives, Eli	V
Inman, John Hamilton	V	Ives, Frederic Eugene	2
Inman, Samuel Martin	V	Ives, Halsey Cooley	V
Innes, Harry	V	Ives, Irving McNeil	7
Innes, James	V	Ives, James Merritt	V
Inness, George	V	Ives, Joseph Christmas	V
Innokentiï	V	Ives, Levi Silliman	V
Inshtatheamba		Ivins, Anthony Woodward	1
See Bright Eyes		Ivins, William Mills	V
Inskip, John Swanel	V	Izard, George	V
Insull, Samuel	2	Izard, Ralph	V
Ïoasaf	V		
Ioor, William	V	Jack, Captain	
Iredell, James	V	See Captain Jack	
Ireland, John (d. 1896)	V	Jackling, Daniel Cowan	6
Ireland, John (d. 1918)	V	Jackman, Wilbur Samuel	V
Ireland, Joseph Norton	V	Jackson, Abraham Reeves	V
Irene, Sister	V	Jackson, Abraham Valentine	
Ironside, Henry Allan	5	Williams	2
Irvine, James	V	Jackson, Andrew	V
Irvine, William	V	Jackson, Charles	V
Irvine, William Mann	V	Jackson, Charles Douglas	7
Irving, John Beaufain	V	Jackson, Charles Samuel	V
Irving, John Duer	V	Jackson, Charles Thomas	V

Complete Index Guide

Name	Vol./Supp.	Name	Vol./Supp.
Jackson, Chevalier	6	Jacobs, Joseph (d. 1929)	V
Jackson, Claiborne Fox	V	Jacobs, Michael	V
Jackson, Clarence Martin	4	Jacobs, Michael Strauss	5
Jackson, David	V	Jacobson, John Christian	V
Jackson, Dugald Caleb	5	Jacoby, Ludwig Sigmund	V
Jackson, Dunham	4	Jadwin, Edgar	V
Jackson, Edward	3	Jaeger, Werner Wilhelm	7
Jackson, Edward Payson	V	Jaggar, Thomas Augustus, Jr.	5
Jackson, George K.	V	James, Arthur Curtiss	3
Jackson, George Thomas	V	James, Charles	V
Jackson, Hall	V	James, Charles Tillinghast	V
Jackson, Helen Maria Fiske		James, Daniel Willis	V
Hunt	V	James, Edmund Janes	V
Jackson, Henry Rootes	V	James, Edward Christopher	V
Jackson, Howell Edmunds	V	James, Edwin	V
Jackson, James (d. 1806)	V	James, Edwin Leland	5
Jackson, James (d. 1867)	V	James, George Wharton	V
Jackson, James (d. 1887)	V	James, Henry (d. 1882)	V
Jackson, James Caleb	V	James, Henry (d. 1916)	V
Jackson, John Adams	V	James, Jesse Woodson	V
Jackson, John Brinckerhoff	V	James, Louis	V
Jackson, John Davies	V	James, Marquis	5
Jackson, John George	V	James, Ollie Murray	V
Jackson, Joseph Henry	5	James, Thomas	V
Jackson, Mercy Ruggles Bisbe	V	James, Thomas Chalkley	V
Jackson, Mortimer Melville	V	James, Thomas Lemuel	V
Jackson, Patrick Tracy	V	James, Thomas Potts	V
Jackson, Robert Houghwout	5	James, William	V
Jackson, Robert R.	3	James, Will Roderick	3
Jackson, Samuel	V	Jameson, Horatio Gates	V
Jackson, Samuel Macauley	V	Jameson, John Alexander	V
Jackson, Sheldon	V	Jameson, John Franklin	2
Jackson, Shirley Hardie	7	Jamison, Cecilia Viets Dakin	
Jackson, Thomas Jonathan	V	Hamilton	V
Jackson, William (d. 1828)	V	Jamison, David	V
Jackson, William (d. 1855)	V	Jamison, David Flavel	V
Jackson, William Alexander	7	Janauschek, Franziska	
Jackson, William Henry	3	Magdalena Romance	V
Jackson, William Hicks	V	Janes, Lewis George	V
Jacob, Richard Taylor	V	Janeway, Edward Gamaliel	V
Jacob, William Plumer	V	Janeway, Theodore Caldwell	V
Jacobi, Abraham	V	Janin, Louis	V
Jacobi, Mary Corinna Putnam	V	Janis, Elsie	6
Jacobs, Henry Eyster	1	Janney, Eli Hamilton	V
Jacobs, Joseph (d. 1916)	V	Janney, Oliver Edward	V

Complete Index Guide

Name	Vol./Supp.	Name	Vol./Supp.
Janney, Russell Dixon	7	Jeffrey, Joseph Andrew	V
Janney, Samuel McPherson	V	Jeffrey, Rosa Griffith Vertner	
Jansen, Reinier	V	Johnson	V
Jansky, Karl Guthe	4	Jeffries, Benjamin Joy	V
Janson, Kristofer Nagel	V	Jeffries, James Jackson	5
Janssens, Francis	V	Jeffries, John	V
Janvier, Catharine Ann	V	Jelliffe, Smith Ely	3
Janvier, Margaret Thomson	V	Jemison, Alice Mae Lee	7
Janvier, Thomas Allibone	V	Jemison, Mary	V
Jaquess, James Frazier	V	Jenckes, Joseph	
Jardine, William Marion	5	See Jenks, Joseph	
Jarratt, Devereux	V	Jenckes, Joseph (d. 1717)	V
Jarrell, Randall	7	Jenckes, Joseph (d. 1740)	V
Jarves, Deming	V	Jenckes, Thomas Allen	V
Jarves, James Jackson	V	Jenifer, Daniel of St. Thomas	V
Jarvis, Abraham	V	Jenkins, Albert Gallatin	V
Jarvis, Charles H.	V	Jenkins, Charles Jones	V
Jarvis, Edward	V	Jenkins, Edward Hopkins	V
Jarvis, John Wesley	V	Jenkins, Howard Malcolm	V
Jarvis, Thomas Jordan	V	Jenkins, James Graham	V
Jarvis, William	V	Jenkins, John (d. 1785)	V
Jarvis, William Chapman	V	Jenkins, John (d. 1827)	V
Jasper, William	V	Jenkins, John Stilwell	V
Jastrow, Joseph	3	Jenkins, Micah	V
Jastrow, Marcus	V	Jenkins, Nathaniel	V
Jastrow, Morris	V	Jenkins, Thornton Alexander	V
Jay, Allen	V	Jenks, George Charles	V
Jay, Sir James	V	Jenks, Jeremiah Whipple	V
Jay, John (d. 1829)	V	Jenks, Joseph	V
Jay, John (d. 1894)	V	Jenks, Tudor Storrs	V
Jay, Peter Augustus	V	Jenks, William	V
Jay, William	V	Jenney, William Le Baron	V
Jayne, Horace Fort	V	Jennings, Hennen	
Jeanes, Anna T.	V	See Jennings, James	
Jeffers, John Robinson	7	Hennen	
Jeffers, William Martin	5	Jennings, Herbert Spencer	4
Jeffers, William Nicholson	V	Jennings, James Hennen	V
Jefferson, Charles Edward	2	Jennings, John	V
Jefferson, Joseph (d. 1832)	V	Jennings, Jonathan	V
Jefferson, Joseph (d. 1905)	V	Jensen, Jens	5
Jefferson, Mark Sylvester		Jensen, Peter Laurits	7
William	4	Jepson, Willis Linn	4
Jefferson, Thomas	V	Jerome, Chauncey	V
Jeffery, Edward Turner	V	Jerome, William Travers	1
Jeffrey, Edward Charles	5	Jervis, John Bloomfield	V

Complete Index Guide

Name	Vol./Supp.	Name	Vol./Supp.
Jesse, Richard Henry	V	Johnson, Edward (d. 1672)	V
Jessup, Henry Harris	V	Johnson, Edward (d. 1873)	V
Jessup, Walter Albert	3	Johnson, Edward	6
Jesup, Morris Ketchum	V	Johnson, Edward Austin	3
Jesup, Thomas Sidney	V	Johnson, Edwin Ferry	V
Jeter, Jeremiah Bell	V	Johnson, Eldridge Reeves	3
Jewell, Harvey	V	Johnson, Elias Henry	V
Jewell, Marshall	V	Johnson, Elijah	V
Jewett, Charles Coffin	V	Johnson, Ellen Cheney	V
Jewett, Clarence Frederick	V	Johnson, Franklin	V
Jewett, David	V	Johnson, George	3
Jewett, Frank Baldwin	4	Johnson, George Francis	4
Jewett, Hugh Judge	V	Johnson, Guy	V
Jewett, John Punchard	V	Johnson, Harold Ogden	
Jewett, Milo Parker	V	("Chic")	
Jewett, Sarah Orne	V	See Olsen, John Sigvard	
Jewett, William	V	("Ole") and Johnson,	
Jewett, William Cornell	V	Harold	
Jocelyn, Nathaniel	V	Johnson, Helen Louise	
Jogues, Isaac	V	Kendrick	V
Johns, Clayton	1	Johnson, Henry	V
Johns, John	V	Johnson, Herschel Vespasian	V
Johns, Kensey (d. 1848)	V	Johnson, Hiram Warren	3
Johns, Kensey (d. 1857)	V	Johnson, Hugh Samuel	3
Johnsen, Erik Kristian	V	Johnson, Jack	4
Johnson		Johnson, James	V
See also Johnston		Johnson, James Weldon	2
Johnson, Albert	6	Johnson, Sir John	V
Johnson, Alexander	3	Johnson, John Albert	V
Johnson, Alexander Bryan	V	Johnson, John Butler	V
Johnson, Alexander Smith	V	Johnson, John Graver	V
Johnson, Allen	V	Johnson, Jonathan Eastman	V
Johnson, Andrew	V	Johnson, Joseph	V
Johnson, Benjamin Pierce	V	Johnson, Joseph French	V
Johnson, Bradley Tyler	V	Johnson, Levi	V
Johnson, Bushrod Rust	V	Johnson, Magnus	2
Johnson, Byron Bancroft	V	Johnson, Marmaduke	V
Johnson, Cave	V	Johnson, Sir Nathaniel	V
Johnson, Chapman	V	Johnson, Oliver	V
Johnson, Charles Spurgeon	6	Johnson, Osa	5
Johnson, David Bancroft	V	Johnson, Owen McMahon	5
Johnson, Douglas Wilson	3	Johnson, Reverdy	V
Johnson, Eastman		Johnson, Richard Mentor	V
See Johnson, Jonathan		Johnson, Richard W.	V
Eastman		Johnson, Robert	V

Complete Index Guide

Name	Vol./Supp.	Name	Vol./Supp.
Johnson, Robert Underwood	2	Johnston, Samuel (d. 1911)	V
Johnson, Robert Ward	V	Johnston, Thomas	V
Johnson, Samuel	V	Johnston, William Andrew	V
Johnson, Samuel	V	Johnston, William Hartshorne	1
Johnson, Samuel William	V	Johnston, William Hugh	2
Johnson, Seth Whitmore	V	Johnston, William Preston	V
Johnson, Thomas	V	Johnston, Zachariah	V
Johnson, Tom Loftin	V	Johnstone, Edward Ransom	4
Johnson, Treat Baldwin	4	Johnstone, Job	V
Johnson, Virginia Wales	V	Joline, Adrian Hoffman	V
Johnson, Walter	4	Jolliet, Louis	V
Johnson, Wendell Andrew		Jolson, Al	4
Leroy	7	Jones, Abner	V
Johnson, Sir William (b. 1715)	V	Jones, Alexander	V
Johnson, William (b. 1769)	V	Jones, Alfred	V
Johnson, William (b. 1771)	V	Jones, Allen	V
Johnson, William Bullein	V	Jones, Amanda Theodosia	V
Johnson, William Ransom	V	Jones, Anson	V
Johnson, William Samuel	V	Jones, Benjamin Allyn	7
Johnson, William Woolsey	V	Jones, Benjamin Franklin	V
Johnson, Willis Fletcher	V	Jones, Calvin	V
Johnston, Albert Sidney	V	Jones, Catesby A. P. Roger	V
Johnston, Alexander	V	Jones, Charles Colcock	V
Johnston, Annie Fellows	V	Jones, David	V
Johnston, Augustus	V	Jones, David Rumph	V
Johnston, David Claypoole	V	Jones, Ernest Lester	V
Johnston, Eric Allen	7	Jones, Evan William	V
Johnston, Frances Benjamin	5	Jones, Frank	V
Johnston, Gabriel	V	Jones, Gabriel	V
Johnston, George Ben	V	Jones, George (d. 1870)	V
Johnston, Henrietta	V	Jones, George (d. 1891)	V
Johnston, Henry Phelps	V	Jones, George Heber	V
Johnston, John (d. 1880)	V	Jones, George Wallace	V
Johnston, John (d. 1950)	4	Jones, Harry Clary	V
Johnston, John Taylor	V	Jones, Herschel Vespasian	V
Johnston, Joseph Eggleston	V	Jones, Hilary Pollard	2
Johnston, Joseph Forney	V	Jones, Hugh	V
Johnston, Josiah Stoddard	V	Jones, Hugh Bolton	V
Johnston, Mary	2	Jones, Jacob	V
Johnston, Olin DeWitt		Jones, James Chamberlayne	V
Talmadge	7	Jones, James Kimbrough	V
Johnston, Peter	V	Jones, Jehu Glancy	V
Johnston, Richard Malcolm	V	Jones, Jenkin Lloyd	V
Johnston, Robert Matteson	V	Jones, Jesse Holman	6
Johnston, Samuel (d. 1816)	V	Jones, Joel	V

Complete Index Guide

Name	Vol./Supp.	Name	Vol./Supp.
Jones, John	V	Jordan, John Woolf	V
Jones, John B.	V	Jordan, Kate	V
Jones, John Beauchamp	V	Jordan, Thomas	V
Jones, John Paul	V	Jordan, Virgil Justin	7
Jones, John Percival	V	Jordan, William George	V
Jones, John Peter	V	Joseffy, Rafael	V
Jones, John Price	7	Joseph	V
Jones, John Taylor	V	Josselyn, John	V
Jones, John William	V	Joubert de la Muraille, James	
Jones, John Winston	V	Hector Marie Nicholas	V
Jones, Joseph (d. 1805)	V	Jouett, James Edward	V
Jones, Joseph (d. 1896)	V	Jouett, John	V
Jones, Joseph Stevens	V	Jouett, Matthew Harris	V
Jones, Leonard Augustus	V	Joutel, Henri	V
Jones, Lewis Ralph	3	Joy, Agnes Eliza	
Jones, Lindley Armstrong		See Salm-Salm, Agnes	
("Spike")	7	Elisabeth Joy, Princess	
Jones, Lynds	5	Joy, Charles Turner	6
Jones, Mary Harris	V	Joy, Henry Bourne	2
Jones, Noble Wymberley	V	Joy, James Frederick	V
Jones, Richard Foster	7	Joy, Thomas	V
Jones, Robert Edmond	5	Joyce, Isaac Wilson	V
Jones, Rufus Matthew	4	Joynes, Edward Southey	V
Jones, Samuel (d. 1819)	V	Judah, Samuel	V
Jones, Samuel (d. 1853)	V	Judah, Samuel Benjamin	
Jones, Samuel Milton	1	Helbert	V
Jones, Samuel Porter	V	Judah, Theodore Dehone	V
Jones, Sybil	V	Juday, Chancey	3
Jones, Thomas	V	Judd, Charles Hubbard	4
Jones, Thomas Ap Catesby	V	Judd, Edward Starr	1
Jones, Thomas Goode	V	Judd, Gerrit Parmele	V
Jones, Thomas P.	V	Judd, Norman Buel	V
Jones, Walter	V	Judd, Orange	V
Jones, Wesley Livsey	1	Judd, Sylvester	V
Jones, William (d. 1822)	V	Judge, Thomas Augustine	1
Jones, William (d. 1831)	V	Judge, William Quan	V
Jones, William (d. 1909)	V	Judson, Adoniram	V
Jones, William Alfred	V	Judson, Adoniram Brown	V
Jones, William Palmer	V	Judson, Ann Hasseltine	V
Jones, William Patterson	V	Judson, Edward	V
Jones, William Richard	V	Judson, Edward Zane Carroll	V
Jones, Willie	V	Judson, Egbert Putnam	V
Jordan, David Starr	V	Judson, Emily Chubbuck	V
Jordan, Eben Dyer	V	Judson, Frederick Newton	V
Jordan, Edwin Oakes	2	Judson, Harry Pratt	V

Complete Index Guide

Name	Vol./Supp.	Name	Vol./Supp.
Judson, Sarah Hall Boardman	V	Katzer, Frederic Xavier	V
Juengling, Frederick	V	Kauffman, Calvin Henry	V
Juillard, Augustus D.	V	Kaufman, George S.	7
Julia, Sister	V	Kautz, August Valentine	V
Julian, George Washington	V	Kavanagh, Edward	V
Julius, Emanuel		Kay, Edgar Boyd	V
See Haldeman-Julius,		Kaye, Frederick Benjamin	V
Emanuel		Keagy, John Miller	V
Jumel, Stephen	V	Kean, Jefferson Randolph	4
June, Jennie		Keane, James John	V
See Croly, Jane		Keane, John Joseph	V
Cunningham		Kearney, Denis	V
Juneau, Solomon Laurent	V	Kearns, Jack	7
Jungman, John George	V	Kearny, Francis	V
Junkin, George	V	Kearny, Lawrence	V
Just, Ernest Everett	3	Kearny, Philip	V
		Kearny, Stephen Watts	V
Kaempffert, Waldemar		Kearsley, John	V
Bernhard	6	Keating, John McLeod	V
Kafer, John Christian	V	Keating, John Marie	V
Kah-Ge-Ga-Gah-Bowh		Keating, William Hypolitus	V
See Copway, George		Kedzie, Robert Clark	V
Kahn, Albert	3	Keefe, Daniel Joseph	V
Kahn, Florence Prag	4	Keeler, James Edward	V
Kahn, Gustav Gerson	3	Keeler, Ralph Olmstead	V
Kahn, Julius	V	Keeley, Leslie E.	V
Kahn, Otto Herman	1	Keely, John Ernst Worrell	V
Kaiser, Alois	V	Keen, Morris Longstreth	V
Kalanianaole, Jonah Kuhio	V	Keen, William Williams	1
Kalb, Johann	V	Keenan, James Francis	V
Kalisch, Isidor	V	Keene, James Robert	V
Kalisch, Samuel	V	Keene, Laura	V
Kalmus, Herbert Thomas, and		Keene, Thomas Wallace	V
Natalie Mabelle Dunfee	7	Keener, William Albert	V
Kaltenborn, Hans von	7	Keep, Henry	V
Kamaikan	V	Keep, Robert Porter	V
Kane, Elisha Kent	V	Kefauver, (Carey) Estes	7
Kane, John	1	Kefauver, Grayson Neikirk	4
Kane, John Kintzing	V	Kehew, Mary Morton Kimball	V
Kane, Thomas Leiper	V	Keifer, Joseph Warren	1
Kapp, Friedrich	V	Keimer, Samuel	V
Karfiol, Bernard	5	Keith, Arthur	3
Kármán, Theodore (Todor) von	7	Keith, Benjamin Franklin	V
Kasson, John Adam	V	Keith, George	V
Katte, Walter	V	Keith, James	V

Complete Index Guide

Name	Vol./Supp.	Name	Vol./Supp.
Keith, Minor Cooper	V	Kelton, John Cunningham	V
Keith, Sir William (d. 1749)	V	Kemble, Frances Anne	V
Keith, William (d. 1911)	V	Kemble, Gouverneur	V
Keitt, Lawrence Massillon	V	Kemeys, Edward	V
Kelland, Clarence Budington	7	Kemmerer, Edwin Walter	3
Keller, Arthur Ignatius	V	Kemp, James	V
Keller, Mathias	V	Kemp, James Furman	V
Kellerman, Karl Frederic	1	Kemp, John	V
Kellett, William Wallace	5	Kemp, Robert H.	V
Kelley, Alfred	V	Kemper, Jackson	V
Kelley, Edgar Stillman	3	Kemper, James Lawson	V
Kelley, Edith Summers	6	Kemper, Reuben	V
Kelley, Florence	1	Kempff, Louis	V
Kelley, Hall Jackson	V	Kempster, Walter	V
Kelley, James Douglas Jerrold	V	Kendall, Amos	V
Kelley, Oliver Hudson	V	Kendall, George Wilkins	V
Kelley, William Darrah	V	Kendrick, Asahel Clark	V
Kellogg, Albert	V	Kendrick, John	V
Kellogg, Clara Louise	V	Kendrick, John Benjamin	1
Kellogg, Edward	V	Kenedy, Patrick John	V
Kellogg, Elijah	V	Kenna, John Edward	V
Kellogg, Frank Billings	2	Kennan, George	V
Kellogg, John Harvey	3	Kennedy, Archibald	V
Kellogg, Martin	V	Kennedy, John Doby	V
Kellogg, Paul Underwood	6	Kennedy, John Fitzgerald	7
Kellogg, Samuel Henry	V	Kennedy, John Pendleton	V
Kellogg, William Pitt	V	Kennedy, John Stewart	V
Kellogg, Will Keith	5	Kennedy, Joseph Camp Griffith	V
Kellor, Frances (Alice)	5	Kennedy, Robert Foster	5
Kelly, Aloysius Oliver Joseph	V	Kennedy, Robert Patterson	V
Kelly, Edmond	V	Kennedy, William Sloane	V
Kelly, Edward Joseph	4	Kennelly, Arthur Edwin	2
Kelly, Eugene	V	Kenner, Duncan Farrar	V
Kelly, Howard Atwood	3	Kenney, Mary	
Kelly, John	V	See O'Sullivan, Mary	
Kelly, John Brendan	6	Kenney	
Kelly, Luther Sage	V	Kennicott, Robert	V
Kelly, Machine Gun	5	Kenrick, Francis Patrick	V
Kelly, Michael J.	V	Kenrick, Peter Richard	V
Kelly, Myra	V	Kenrick, William	V
Kelly, William	V	Kensett, John Frederick	V
Kelpius, Johann	V	Kent, Arthur Atwater	4
Kelser, Raymond Alexander	5	Kent, Charles Foster	V
Kelsey, Francis Willey	V	Kent, Edward	V
Kelsey, Rayner Wickersham	1	Kent, James	V

Complete Index Guide

Name	Vol./Supp.	Name	Vol./Supp.
Kent, Joseph	V	Kidder, Frederic	V
Kent, William	V	Kieft, Willem	V
Kenton, Simon	V	Kientpoos	
Kenyon, Josephine Hemenway	7	See Captain Jack	
Kenyon, William Squire	1	Kier, Samuel M.	V
Keokuk	V	Kilbourne, James	V
Kephart, Ezekiel Boring	V	Kilby, Christopher	1
Kephart, Isaiah Lafayette	V	Kildahl, Johan Nathan	V
Kephart, John William	3	Kilgallen, Dorothy Mae	7
Keppel, Frederick	V	Kilgore, Harley Martin	6
Keppel, Frederick Paul	3	Kilmer, Alfred Joyce	V
Keppler, Joseph	V	Kilpatrick, Hugh Judson	V
Kerby, William Joseph	2	Kilpatrick, John Reed	6
Kerens, Richard C.	V	Kilpatrick, William Heard	7
Kerfoot, John Barrett	V	Kilty, William	V
Kerlin, Isaac Newton	V	Kimball, Dexter Simpson	5
Kern, Jerome David	3	Kimball, Gilman	V
Kern, John Worth	V	Kimball, Heber Chase	V
Kernan, Francis	V	Kimball, Nathan	V
Kerney, James	1	Kimball, Richard Burleigh	V
Kerr, John Glasgow	V	Kimball, (Sidney) Fiske	5
Kerr, Robert Samuel	7	Kimball, Sumner Increase	V
Kerr, Sophie	7	Kimball, William Wirt	V
Kerr, Walter Craig	V	King, Albert Freeman	
Kerr, Washington Caruthers	V	Africanus	V
Kershaw, Joseph Brevard	V	King, Alexander	7
Kester, Paul	1	King, Austin Augustus	V
Kester, Vaughan	V	King, Basil	
Kettell, Samuel	V	See King, William	
Kettering, Charles Franklin	6	Benjamin Basil	
Key, David McKendree	V	King, Carol Weiss	5
Key, Francis Scott	V	King, Charles	V
Key, Philip Barton	V	King, Charles William	V
Key, Valdimer Orlando, Jr.	7	King, Clarence	V
Keyes, Edward Lawrence	V	King, Dan	V
Keyes, Elisha Williams	V	King, Edward Leonard	1
Keyes, Erasmus Darwin	V	King, Edward Skinner	V
Keys, Clement Melville	5	King, Edward Smith	V
Keyt, Alonzo Thrasher	V	King, Ernest Joseph	6
Kharasch, Morris Selig	6	King, Franklin Hiram	V
Kiam, Omar	5	King, Grace Elizabeth	V
Kicking Bird	V	King, Henry	V
Kidd, William	V	King, Henry Churchill	1
Kidder, Alfred Vincent	7	King, Henry Melville	V
Kidder, Daniel Parish	V	King, Horatio	V

Complete Index Guide

Name	Vol./Supp.	Name	Vol./Supp.
King, James Gore	V	Kirby, Ephraim	V
King, John	V	Kirby, George Hughes	1
King, John Alsop	V	Kirby, J. Hudson	V
King, John Pendleton	V	Kirby, Rollin	5
King, Jonas	V	Kirby-Smith, Edmund	V
King, Preston	V	Kirchhoff, Charles William	
King, Richard	V	Henry	V
King, Rufus (d. 1827)	V	Kirchmayer, John	V
King, Rufus (d. 1876)	V	Kirchwey, George Washington	3
King, Samuel	V	Kirk, Alan Goodrich	7
King, Samuel Archer	V	Kirk, Edward Norris	V
King, Samuel Ward	V	Kirk, John Foster	V
King, Stanley	5	Kirk, Norman Thomas	6
King, Thomas Butler	V	Kirkbride, Thomas Story	V
King, Thomas Starr	V	Kirkland, Caroline Matilda	
King, William	V	Stansbury	V
King, William Benjamin Basil	V	Kirkland, James Hampton	2
King, William Rufus Devane	V	Kirkland, John Thornton	V
King of William, James	V	Kirkland, Joseph	V
Kingsbury, Albert	3	Kirkland, Samuel	V
Kingsbury, John	V	Kirkman, Marshall Monroe	V
Kingsford, Thomas	V	Kirkpatrick, Andrew	V
Kingsley, Calvin	V	Kirkwood, Daniel	V
Kingsley, Darwin Pearl	1	Kirkwood, John Gamble	6
Kingsley, Elbridge	V	Kirkwood, Samuel Jordan	V
Kingsley, Elizabeth Seelman	6	Kirlin, Joseph Louis Jerome	V
Kingsley, James Luce	V	Kirstein, Louis Edward	3
Kingsley, Norman William	V	Kirtland, Jared Potter	V
Kinkead, Edgar Benton	V	Kitchin, Claude	V
Kinloch, Cleland	V	Kitchin, William Walton	V
Kinloch, Robert Alexander	V	Kittredge, George Lyman	3
Kinne, La Vega George	V	Kittson, Norman Wolfred	V
Kinnersley, Ebenezer	V	Klauder, Charles Zeller	2
Kinney, Elizabeth Clementine		Klaw, Marc	2
Dodge Stedman	V	Klein, August Clarence	4
Kinney, William Burnet	V	Klein, Bruno Oscar	V
Kinnicutt, Leonard Parker	V	Klein, Charles	V
Kino, Eusebio Francisco	V	Klein, Charles Herbert	
Kinsella, Thomas	V	("Chuck")	6
Kinsey, Alfred Charles	6	Klein, Joseph Frederic	V
Kinsey, John	V	Klem, William J. (Bill)	5
Kintpuash		Kline, Franz Josef	7
See Captain Jack		Kline, George	V
Kinzie, John	V	Klingelsmith, Margaret Center	V
Kip, William Ingraham	V	Klippart, John Hancock	V

Complete Index Guide

Name	Vol./Supp.	Name	Vol./Supp.
Klipstein, Louis Frederick	V	Knox, Frank	3
Klopsch, Louis	V	Knox, George William	V
Knab, Frederick	V	Knox, Henry	V
Knabe, Valentine Wilhelm		Knox, John Jay	V
Ludwig	V	Knox, Philander Chase	V
Knapp, Bradford	2	Knox, Rose Markward	4
Knapp, George	V	Knox, Samuel	V
Knapp, Herman	V	Knox, Thomas Wallace	V
Knapp, Joseph Palmer	5	Knudsen, William S.	4
Knapp, Martin Augustine	V	Knutson, Harold	5
Knapp, Philip Coombs	V	Kobbé, Gustav	V
Knapp, Samuel Lorenzo	V	Kober, George Martin	V
Knapp, Seaman Asahel	V	Koch, Fred Conrad	4
Knapp, William Ireland	V	Koch, Frederick Henry	3
Knappen, Theodore Temple	5	Koch, Vivienne	7
Knauth, Oswald Whitman	7	Kocherthal, Josua von	V
Kneass, Samuel Honeyman	V	Koehler, Robert	V
Kneass, Strickland	V	Koehler, Sylvester Rosa	V
Kneass, William	V	Koemmenich, Louis	V
Kneeland, Abner	V	Koenig, George Augustus	V
Kneeland, Samuel (d. 1769)	V	Koenigsberg, Moses	3
Kneeland, Samuel (d. 1888)	V	Koerner, Gustave Philip	
Kneeland, Stillman Foster	V	See Körner, Gustav	
Kneisel, Franz	V	Philipp	
Knickerbocker, Herman	V	Koffka, Kurt	3
Knight, Austin Melvin	V	Kofoid, Charles Atwood	4
Knight, Daniel Ridgway	V	Kohlberg, Alfred	6
Knight, Edward Collings	V	Kohler, Elmer Peter	2
Knight, Edward Henry	V	Kohler, Kaufmann	V
Knight, Frederick Irving	V	Kohler, Max James	1
Knight, Henry Cogswell	V	Kohler, Walter Jodok	2
Knight, Jonathan (d. 1858)	V	Kohlmann, Anthony	V
Knight, Jonathan (d. 1864)	V	Kohlsaat, Herman Henry	V
Knight, Lucian Lamar	1	Kohut, Alexander	V
Knight, Ridgway		Kohut, George Alexander	1
See Knight, Daniel		Kolb, Dielman	V
Ridgway		Kolb, Reuben Francis	V
Knight, Sarah Kemble	V	Kolle, Frederick Strange	V
Knott, Aloysius Leo	V	Koller, Carl	3
Knott, James Proctor	V	Kollock, Shepard	V
Knowles, Lucius James	V	Koopman, Augustus	V
Knowlton, Charles	V	Kooweskowe	
Knowlton, Frank Hall	V	See Ross, John	
Knowlton, Marcus Perrin	V	Koren, John	V
Knowlton, Thomas	V	Koren, Ulrik Vilhelm	V
Knox, Dudley Wright	6	Körner, Gustav Philipp	V

Complete Index Guide

Name	Vol./Supp.	Name	Vol./Supp.
Korngold, Erich Wolfgang	6	Kunze, John Christopher	V
Kościuszko, Tadeusz Andrzej		Kunze, Richard Ernest	V
Bonawentura	V	Kurtz, Benjamin	V
Koussevitzky, Serge		Kuskov, Ivan Aleksandrovich	V
Alexandrovich	5	Kuykendall, Ralph Simpson	7
Kovacs, Ernie	7	Kyle, David Braden	V
Koyl, Charles Herschel	V	Kyle, James Henderson	V
Kraemer, Henry	V	Kyne, Peter Bernard	6
Kraft, James Lewis	5	Kynett, Alpha Jefferson	V
Krantz, Philip			
See Rombro, Jacob		La Barge, Joseph	V
Krapp, George Philip	1	La Borde, Maximilian	V
Kraus, John	V	Lacey, John	V
Kraus-Boelté, Maria	V	Lacey, John Fletcher	V
Krause, Allen Kramer	3	Lachaise, Gaston	1
Krauskopf, Joseph	V	Lackaye, Wilton	1
Krauth, Charles Philip	V	Laclede, Pierre	V
Krauth, Charles Porterfield	V	Lacock, Abner	V
Krehbiel, Christian	V	Lacy, Drury	V
Krehbiel, Henry Edward	V	Lacy, Ernest	V
Kreisler, Fritz	7	Ladd, Alan Walbridge	7
Kremers, Edward	3	Ladd, Carl Edwin	3
Kress, Samuel Henry	5	Ladd, Catherine	V
Krez, Konrad	V	Ladd, Edwin Fremont	V
Krimmel, John Lewis	V	Ladd, George Trumbull	V
Kroeber, Alfred Louis	6	Ladd, Joseph Brown	V
Kroeger, Adolph Ernst	V	Ladd, Kate Macy	3
Kroeger, Ernest Richard	1	Ladd, William	V
Kroger, Bernard Henry	2	Ladd, William Sargent	V
Krol, Bastiaen Jansen	V	Ladd-Franklin, Christine	V
Kruell, Gustav	V	Laemmle, Carl	2
Kruesi, John	V	La Farge, Christopher Grant	
Krüsi, Hermann		(d. 1938)	2
See Krüsi, Johann		La Farge, Christopher Grant	
Heinrich Hermann		(d. 1956)	6
Krüsi, Johann Heinrich		La Farge, Grant	
Hermann	V	See La Farge, Christopher	
Kugelman, Frederick Benjamin		Grant	
See Kaye, Frederick		La Farge, John (d. 1910)	V
Benjamin		LaFarge, John (d. 1963)	7
Kuhn, Adam	V	La Farge, Oliver Hazard Perry	7
Kuhn, Joseph Ernst	1	Lafayette, Marie Joseph Paul	
Kuhn, Walt	4	Yves Roch Gilbert du	
Kumler, Henry	V	Motier, Marquis de	V
Kuniyoshi, Yasuo	5	Lafever, Minard	1
Kunz, George Frederick	1	Laffan, William Mackay	V

Complete Index Guide

Name	Vol./Supp.	Name	Vol./Supp.
Laffite, Jean	V	Lamoureux, Andrew Jackson	V
Lafitte, Jean		Lampson, Sir Curtis Miranda	V
See Laffite, Jean		Lamy, John Baptist	V
La Flesche, Susette		Lancaster, Henry Carrington	5
See Bright Eyes		Landais, Pierre	V
La Follette, Philip Fox	7	Lander, Edward	V
La Follette, Robert Marion	V	Lander, Frederick West	V
La Follette, Robert Marion, Jr.	5	Lander, Jean Margaret	
Lafon, Thomy	V	Davenport	V
La Guardia, Fiorello Henry	4	Landis, Henry Robert Murray	2
Laguna, Theodore de Leo de	V	Landis, James McCauley	7
Lahey, Frank Howard	5	Landis, Kenesaw Mountain	3
Lahontan, Louis-Armand de		Landis, Walter Savage	3
Lom d'Arce, Baron de		Landon, Melville de Lancy	V
Laimbeer, Nathalie Schenck	V	Landowska, Wanda Aleksandra	6
Lait, Jacquin Leonard (Jack)	5	Landreth, David	V
Lajoie, Napoleon ("Larry")	6	Landsteiner, Karl	3
Lake, Kirsopp	4	Lane, Arthur Bliss	6
Lake, Simon	3	Lane, Franklin Knight	V
Lalor, Alice		Lane, George Martin	V
See Teresa, Mother		Lane, Gertrude Battles	3
Lamar, Gazaway Bugg	V	Lane, Henry Smith	V
Lamar, Joseph Rucker	V	Lane, Horace M.	V
Lamar, Lucius Quintus		Lane, James Henry (d. 1866)	V
Cincinnatus	V	Lane, James Henry (d. 1907)	V
Lamar, Mirabeau Buonaparte	V	Lane, John	V
Lamb, Arthur Becket	5	Lane, Joseph	V
Lamb, Isaac Wixom	V	Lane, Levi Cooper	V
Lamb, John	V	Lane, Sir Ralph	V
Lamb, Martha Joanna Reade		Lane, Tidence	V
Nash	V	Lane, Walter Paye	V
Lamb, William Frederick	5	Lane, William Carr	V
Lambdin, James Reid	V	Lang, Benjamin Johnson	V
Lambeau, Earl Louis ("Curly")	7	Lang, Henry Roseman	1
Lambert, Louis Aloisius	V	Lang, Lucy Fox Robins	7
Lamberton, Benjamin Peffer	V	Langdeel, Christopher	
Lambing, Andrew Arnold	V	Columbus	V
Lambuth, James William	V	Langdon, Courtney	V
Lambuth, Walter Russell	V	Langdon, Harry Philmore	3
Lamme, Benjamin Garver	V	Langdon, John	V
Lamon, Ward Hill	V	Langdon, Samuel	V
Lamont, Daniel Scott	V	Langdon, William Chauncy	V
Lamont, Hammond	V	Langdon, Woodbury	V
Lamont, Thomas William	4	Lange, Alexis Frederick	V
La Mountain, John	V	Lange, Dorothea	7

Complete Index Guide

Name	Vol./Supp.	Name	Vol./Supp.
Lange, Louis	V	Larrabee, Charles Hathaway	VI
Langer, William	6	Larrabee, William	VI
Langford, Nathaniel Pitt	V	Larrabee, William Clark	VI
Langford, Samuel	6	Larrazolo, Octaviano Ambrosio	VI
Langlade, Charles Michel de		Larrínaga, Tulio	VI
See De Langlade, Charles		Larsen, Peter Laurentius	VI
Michel		Larson, Laurence Marcellus	2
Langley, John Williams	V	La Salle, Robert Cavelier, Sieur	
Langley, Samuel Pierpont	V	de	VI
Langmuir, Irving	6	Lasater, Edward Cunningham	VI
Langner, Lawrence	7	Lashley, Karl Spencer	6
Langston, John Mercer	V	Lasker, Albert Davis	5
Langstroth, Lorenzo Lorraine	V	Lasky, Jesse Louis	6
Langworthy, Edward	V	Lasser, Jacob Kay	5
Langworthy, James Lyon	V	Latané, John Holladay	1
Lanham, Frederick Garland		Latham, Milton Slocum	VI
("Fritz")	7	Lathbury, Mary Artemisia	VI
Lanier, James Franklin		Lathrop, Francis Augustus	VI
Doughty	V	Lathrop, George Parsons	VI
Lanier, Sidney	V	Lathrop, John	VI
Lanigan, George Thomas	V	Lathrop, John Hiram	VI
Lanman, Charles	V	Lathrop, Julia Clifford	1
Lanman, Charles Rockwell	3	Lathrop, Rose Hawthorne	
Lanman, Joseph	V	See Alphonsa, Mother	
Lansing, Gulian	V	Latil, Alexandre	VI
Lansing, John	V	Latimer, Mary Elizabeth	
Lansing, Robert	V	Wormeley	VI
Lanston, Tolbert	V	Latimer, Wendell Mitchell	5
Lapham, Increase Allen	V	La Tour, Le Blond de	VI
Lapham, William Berry	V	Latrobe, Benjamin Henry	
Laramie, Jacques	V	(d. 1820)	VI
Larcom, Lucy	V	Latrobe, Benjamin Henry	
Lard, Moses E.	V	(d. 1878)	VI
Lardner, James Lawrence	V	Latrobe, Charles Hazlehurst	VI
Lardner, John Abbott	6	Latrobe, John Hazlehurst	
Lardner, Ringgold Wilmer	1	Boneval	VI
Larkin, John	V	Latta, Alexander Bonner	VI
Larkin, Thomas Oliver	V	Lattimore, William	VI
Larned, Joseph Gay Eaton	VI	Laudonnière, René Goulaine de	VI
Larned, Josephus Nelson	VI	Laufer, Berthold	1
Larned, William Augustus	VI	Laughlin, Harry Hamilton	3
LaRoche, René	VI	Laughlin, James Laurence	1
La Ronde, Louis Denis, Sieur		Laughton, Charles	7
de	VI	Launitz, Robert Eberhard	
Larpenteur, Charles	VI	Schmidt von der	VI

109

Complete Index Guide

Name	Vol./Supp.	Name	Vol./Supp.
Laurance, John	VI	Lawson, Thomas William	VI
Laurel, Stan	7	Lawson, Victor Freemont	VI
Laurens, Henry	VI	Lawton, Alexander Robert	VI
Laurens, John	VI	Lawton, Henry Ware	VI
Laurie, James	VI	Lay, Benjamin	VI
La Vérendrye, Pierre Gaultier		Lay, Henry Champlin	VI
de Varennes, Sieur de	VI	Lay, John Louis	VI
Law, Andrew	VI	Lazarus, Emma	VI
Law, Evander McIvor	VI	Lazear, Jesse William	VI
Law, George	VI	Lea, Henry Charles	VI
Law, John	VI	Lea, Homer	VI
Law, Jonathan	VI	Lea, Isaac	VI
Law, Richard	VI	Lea, Luke	3
Law, Sallie Chapman Gordon	VI	Lea, Mathew Carey	VI
Lawes, Lewis Edward	4	Leach, Abby	VI
Lawley, George Frederick	VI	Leach, Daniel Dyer	VI
Lawrance, Charles Lanier	4	Leach, Shepherd	VI
Lawrance, John		Leahy, William Daniel	6
See Laurance, John		Leaming, Jacob Spicer	VI
Lawrance, Marion		Leaming, Jeremiah	VI
See Lawrance, Uriah		Leaming, Thomas	VI
Marion		Lear, Tobias	VI
Lawrance, Uriah Marion	VI	Learned, Ebenezer	VI
Lawrence, Abbott	VI	Learned, Marion Dexter	VI
Lawrence, Amos	VI	Leary, John	VI
Lawrence, Amos Adams	VI	Lease, Mary Elizabeth Clyens	1
Lawrence, Ernest Orlando	6	Leathers, Walter Smith	4
Lawrence, George Newbold	VI	Leavenworth, Francis Preserved	VI
Lawrence, Gertrude	5	Leavenworth, Henry	VI
Lawrence, James	VI	Leavitt, Dudley	VI
Lawrence, Richard Smith	VI	Leavitt, Erasmus Darwin	VI
Lawrence, William (d. 1848)	VI	Leavitt, Frank McDowell	VI
Lawrence, William (d. 1899)	VI	Leavitt, Frank Simmons	5
Lawrence, William (d. 1941)	3	Leavitt, Henrietta Swan	VI
Lawrence, William Beach	VI	Leavitt, Humphrey Howe	VI
Lawrie, Alexander	VI	Leavitt, Joshua	VI
Laws, Samuel Spahr	VI	Leavitt, Mary Greenleaf	
Lawson, Alexander	VI	Clement	VI
Lawson, Andrew Cowper	5	Lebrun, Federico ("Rico")	7
Lawson, Ernest	2	Le Brun, Napoléon Eugène	
Lawson, James	VI	Henry Charles	VI
Lawson, John	VI	Lechford, Thomas	VI
Lawson, Leonidas Merion	VI	Le Clear, Thomas	VI
Lawson, Robert Ripley	6	Le Conte, John	VI
Lawson, Thomas	VI	Le Conte, John Lawrence	VI

Complete Index Guide

Name	Vol./Supp.	Name	Vol./Supp.
Le Conte, Joseph	VI	Lee, William Little	VI
Ledbetter, Huddie		Lee, Willis Augustus	3
("Leadbelly")	4	Leeds, Daniel	VI
Lederer, John	VI	Leeds, John	VI
Le Duc, William Gates	VI	Lees, Ann	
Ledyard, John	VI	See Lee, Ann	
Ledyard, William	VI	Leeser, Isaac	VI
Lee, Alfred	VI	Leete, William	VI
Lee, Ann	VI	Lefevere, Peter Paul	VI
Lee, Arthur	VI	Leffel, James	VI
Lee, Canada	5	Lefferts, George Morewood	VI
Lee, Charles (d. 1782)	VI	Lefferts, Marshall	VI
Lee, Charles (d. 1815)	VI	Leffingwell, Russell Cornell	6
Lee, Charles Alfred	VI	Leffler, Isaac	VI
Lee, Eliza Buckminister	VI	Leffler, Shepherd	VI
Lee, Fitzhugh	VI	Leffmann, Henry	VI
Lee, Francis Lightfoot	VI	Leflore, Greenwood	VI
Lee, Frederic Schiller	2	Legaré, Hugh Swinton	VI
Lee, George Washington		LeGendre, Charles William	VI
Custis	VI	Legge, Alexander	1
Lee, Hannah Farnham Sawyer	VI	Leggett, Mortimer Dormer	VI
Lee, Henry (b. 1756)	VI	Leggett, William	VI
Lee, Henry (b. 1782)	VI	Legler, Henry Eduard	VI
Lee, Henry (b. 1787)	VI	Lehman, Adele Lewisohn	7
Lee, Ivy Ledbetter	1	Lehman, Arthur	2
Lee, James Melvin	VI	Lehman, Herbert Henry	7
Lee, James Wideman	VI	Lehman, Irving	3
Lee, Jason	VI	Lehmann, Frederick William	VI
Lee, Jesse	VI	Leib, Michael	VI
Lee, John Clifford Hodges	6	Leiber, Fritz	4
Lee, John Doyle	VI	Leidy, Joseph	VI
Lee, Joseph	2	Leigh, Benjamin Watkins	VI
Lee, Luther	VI	Leigh, William Robinson	5
Lee, Porter Raymond	2	Leighton, William	VI
Lee, Richard	VI	Leiper, Thomas	VI
Lee, Richard Bland	VI	Leipzig, Nate	2
Lee, Richard Henry	VI	Leipziger, Henry Marcus	VI
Lee, Robert Edward	VI	Leiserson, William Morris	6
Lee, Samuel Phillips	VI	Leishman, John G. A.	VI
Lee, Stephen Dill	VI	Leisler, Jacob	VI
Lee, Thomas	VI	Leiter, Joseph	1
Lee, Thomas Sim	VI	Leiter, Levi Zeigler	VI
Lee, William	VI	Le Jau, Francis	VI
Lee, William Granville	VI	Lejeune, John Archer	3
Lee, William Henry Fitzhugh	VI	Leland, Charles Godfrey	VI

Complete Index Guide

Name	Vol./Supp.	Name	Vol./Supp.
Leland, George Adams	VI	Leschi	VI
Leland, John	VI	Lesley, J. Peter	
Lemke, Peter Henry	VI	See Lesley, Peter	
Lemke, William Frederick	4	Lesley, Peter	VI
Lemmon, John Gill	VI	Leslie, Charles Robert	VI
LeMoyne, Francis Julius	VI	Leslie, Eliza	VI
Le Moyne, Jean Baptiste		Leslie, Frank	VI
See Bienville, Jean		Leslie, Miriam Florence Folline	VI
Baptiste Le Moyne, Sieur		Lesquereux, Leo	VI
de		Lester, Charles Edwards	VI
Le Moyne, Pierre		Lesueur, Charles Alexandre	VI
See Iberville, Pierre Le		Le Sueur, Pierre	VI
Moyne, Sieur d'		Letcher, John	VI
Le Moyne, William J.	VI	Letcher, Robert Perkins	VI
Leney, William Satchwell	VI	Letchworth, William Pryor	VI
L'Enfant, Pierre Charles	VI	Letterman, Jonathan	VI
Lenker, John Nicholas	VI	Leupp, Francis Ellington	VI
Lennon, John Brown	VI	Leutze, Emanuel	VI
Lennox, Charlotte Ramsay	VI	Levene, Phoebus Aaron	
Lenox, James	VI	Theodore	2
Lenroot, Irvine Luther	4	Lever, Asbury Francis	2
Lenthall, John	VI	Leverett, Frank	3
Lenz, Sidney Samuel	6	Leverett, John (d. 1679)	VI
Leonard, Charles Lester	VI	Leverett, John (d. 1724)	VI
Leonard, Daniel	VI	Levering, Joseph Mortimer	VI
Leonard, George	VI	Levermore, Charles Herbert	VI
Leonard, Harry Ward	VI	Levin, Lewis Charles	VI
Leonard, Helen Louise		Levins, Thomas C.	VI
See Russell, Lillian		Levinson, Salmon Oliver	3
Leonard, Levi Washburn	VI	Levitt, Abraham	7
Leonard, Robert Josselyn	VI	Levy, Joseph Leonard	VI
Leonard, Sterling Andrus	VI	Levy, Louis Edward	VI
Leonard, William Andrew	VI	Levy, Max	VI
Leonard, William Ellery	3	Levy, Uriah Phillips	VI
Leonard, Zenas	VI	Lewelling, Henderson	
Leonty, Metropolitan	7	See Luelling, Henderson	
Leopold, Aldo	4	Lewelling, Lorenzo Dow	VI
Le Page Du Pratz, Antoine		Lewin, Kurt	4
Simon		Lewis, Alfred Henry	VI
See Dupratz, Antoine		Lewis, Andrew	VI
Simon Le Page		Lewis, Arthur	VI
Le Roux, Bartholomew	VI	Lewis, Charles Bertrand	VI
Le Roux, Charles	VI	Lewis, Charlton Thomas	VI
Léry, Joseph Gaspard		Lewis, Clarence Irving	7
Chaussegros de	VI	Lewis, Dean De Witt	3

Complete Index Guide

Name	Vol./Supp.	Name	Vol./Supp.
Lewis, Dioclesian	VI	L'Halle, Nicolas Bénoit	
Lewis, Dixon Hall	VI	Constantin de	
Lewis, Edmund Darch	VI	See L'Halle, Constantin de	
Lewis, Ellis	VI	Lhévinne, Josef	3
Lewis, Enoch	VI	L'Hommedieu, Ezra	VI
Lewis, Estelle Anna Blanche		Libbey, Edward Drummond	VI
Robinson	VI	Libby, Orin Grant	5
Lewis, Exum Percival	VI	Libman, Emmanuel	4
Lewis, Fielding	VI	Lick, James	VI
Lewis, Francis	VI	Lie, Jonas	2
Lewis, Francis Park	2	Lieb, John William	VI
Lewis, George William	4	Lieber, Francis	VI
Lewis, Gilbert Newton	4	Liebling, Abbott Joseph	7
Lewis, Harry Sinclair	5	Liebling, Emil	VI
Lewis, Isaac Newton	VI	Liebman, Joshua Loth	4
Lewis, James	VI	Lienau, Detlef	1
Lewis, James Hamilton	2	Liggett, Hunter	1
Lewis, John Francis	VI	Liggett, Louis Kroh	4
Lewis, Joseph Horace	VI	Liggett, Walter William	1
Lewis, Lawrence	VI	Lightburn, Joseph Andrew	
Lewis, Lloyd Downs	4	Jackson	VI
Lewis, Meriwether	VI	Ligon, Thomas Watkins	VI
Lewis, Morgan	VI	Lile, William Minor	1
Lewis, Orlando Faulkland	VI	Lilienthal, Max	VI
Lewis, Samuel	VI	Lillie, Frank Rattray	4
Lewis, Sinclair		Lillie, Gordon William	3
See Lewis, Harry Sinclair		Lilly, Josiah Kirby	4
Lewis, Tayler	VI	Lincecum, Gideon	VI
Lewis, Wilfred	1	Lincoln, Abraham	VI
Lewis, William	VI	Lincoln, Benjamin	VI
Lewis, William Berkeley	VI	Lincoln, Enoch	VI
Lewis, William David	VI	Lincoln, John Larkin	VI
Lewis, William Draper	4	Lincoln, Joseph Crosby	3
Lewis, William Gaston	VI	Lincoln, Levi (d. 1820)	VI
Lewis, William Henry	4	Lincoln, Levi (d. 1868)	VI
Lewis, Winslow	VI	Lincoln, Mary Johnson Bailey	VI
Lewisohn, Adolph	2	Lincoln, Mary Todd	VI
Lewisohn, Ludwig	5	Lincoln, Robert Todd	VI
Lewisohn, Sam Adolph	5	Lincoln, Rufus Pratt	VI
Lexow, Clarence	VI	Lind, John	VI
Leyendecker, Joseph Christian	5	Lindabury, Richard Vliet	VI
Leyner, John George	VI	Lindberg, Conrad Emil	VI
Leypoldt, Frederick	VI	Lindbergh, Charles Augustus	VI
L'Halle, Constantin de	VI	Linde, Christian	VI
		Lindeman, Eduard Christian	5

Complete Index Guide

Name	Vol./Supp.	Name	Vol./Supp.
Lindenkohl, Adolph	VI	Little, Charles Joseph	VI
Lindenthal, Gustav	1	Little, Charles Sherman	2
Linderman, Henry Richard	VI	Little, George	VI
Lindgren, Waldemar	2	Little Crow V	VI
Lindheimer, Ferdinand Jacob	VI	Littledale, Clara Savage	6
Lindley, Curtis Holbrook	VI	Littlefield, George Washington	VI
Lindley, Daniel	1	Littlejohn, Abram Newkirk	VI
Lindley, Jacob	VI	Littlepage, Lewis	VI
Lindsay, Nicholas Vachel	VI	Littleton, Martin Wiley	1
Lindsay, Vachel		Little Turtle	VI
See Lindsay, Nicholas		Liveright, Horace Brisbin	1
Vachel		Livermore, Abiel Abbot	VI
Lindsay, William	VI	Livermore, Arthur	VI
Lindsey, Benjamin Barr	3	Livermore, Edward St. Loe	VI
Lindsey, William	VI	Livermore, George	VI
Lindsley, John Berrien	VI	Livermore, Mary Ashton Rice	VI
Lindsley, Philip	VI	Livermore, Samuel (d. 1803)	VI
Lingelbach, Anna Lane	5	Livermore, Samuel (d. 1833)	VI
Lining, John	VI	Livingston, Burton Edward	4
Link, Henry Charles	5	Livingston, Edward	VI
Linn, John Blair	VI	Livingston, Henry Brockholst	VI
Linn, Lewis Fields	VI	Livingston, James	VI
Linn, William Alexander	VI	Livingston, John Henry	VI
Lintner, Joseph Albert	VI	Livingston, John William	VI
Linton, Ralph	5	Livingston, Peter Van Brugh	VI
Linton, William James	VI	Livingston, Philip	VI
Lipman, Jacob Goodale	2	Livingston, Robert	VI
Lippard, George	VI	Livingston, Robert R. (d. 1775)	VI
Lippincott, James Starr	VI	Livingston, Robert R. (d. 1813)	VI
Lippincott, Joshua Ballinger	VI	Livingston, William	VI
Lippincott, Sara Jane Clarke	VI	Livingstone, Belle	6
Lippitt, Henry	VI	Livingstone, William	VI
Lipscomb, Abner Smith	VI	Llewellyn, Karl Nickerson	7
Lipscomb, Andrew Adgate	VI	Lloyd, Alfred Henry	VI
Lisa, Manuel	VI	Lloyd, David	VI
List, Georg Friedrich	VI	Lloyd, Edward (d. 1796)	VI
Listemann, Bernhard	VI	Lloyd, Edward (d. 1834)	VI
Litchfield, Electus Backus	VI	Lloyd, Henry Demarest	VI
Litchfield, Paul Weeks	6	Lloyd, James	VI
Littauer, Lucius Nathan	3	Lloyd, John Uri	2
Littell, Eliakim	VI	Lloyd, Marshall Burns	VI
Littell, Squier	VI	Lloyd, Thomas	VI
Littell, William	VI	Lochman, John George	VI
Little, Arthur Dehon	1	Locke, Alain Leroy	5
Little, Charles Coffin	VI	Locke, Bessie	5

114

Complete Index Guide

Name	Vol./Supp.
Locke, David Ross	VI
Locke, John	VI
Locke, Matthew	VI
Locke, Richard Adams	VI
Lockhart, Charles	VI
Lockheed, Malcolm	6
Lockrey, Sarah Hunt	VI
Lockwood, Belva Ann Bennett	VI
Lockwood, James Booth	VI
Lockwood, Ralph Ingersoll	VI
Lockwood, Robert Wilton	VI
Lockwood, Samuel Drake	VI
Lockwood, Wilton	
See Lockwood, Robert	
Wilton	
Locy, William Albert	VI
Lodge, George Cabot	VI
Lodge, Henry Cabot	VI
Lodge, John Ellerton	3
Loeb, Jacques	VI
Loeb, James	1
Loeb, Leo	6
Loeb, Louis	VI
Loeb, Morris	VI
Loeb, Sophie Irene Simon	VI
Loeffler, Charles Martin	1
Loew, Marcus	VI
Loewenthal, Isidor	VI
Loewi, Otto	7
Logan, Benjamin	VI
Logan, Cornelius Ambrose	VI
Logan, Cornelius Ambrosius	VI
Logan, Deborah Norris	VI
Logan, George	VI
Logan, James (d. 1751)	VI
Logan, James (d. 1780)	VI
Logan, James Harvey	VI
Logan, John Alexander	VI
Logan, Olive	VI
Logan, Stephen Trigg	VI
Logan, Thomas Muldrup	
(d. 1876)	VI
Logan, Thomas Muldrup	
(d. 1914)	VI
Loguen, Jermain Wesley	VI
Lomax, John Avery	4
Lomax, John Tayloe	VI
Lomax, Lunsford Lindsay	VI
Lombard, Carole	3
Lombard, Warren Plimpton	2
London, Jack	VI
London, Meyer	VI
Lonesome Charley	
See Reynolds, Charles	
Alexander	
Long, Armistead Lindsay	VI
Long, Breckinridge	6
Long, Charles Chaillé	
See Chaillé-Long, Charles	
Long, Crawford Williamson	VI
Long, Earl Kemp	6
Long, Huey Pierce	1
Long, James	VI
Long, John Davis	VI
Long, John Harper	VI
Long, John Luther	VI
Long, Joseph Ragland	1
Long, Perrin Hamilton	7
Long, Stephen Harriman	VI
Longacre, James Barton	VI
Longcope, Warfield Theobald	5
Longfellow, Ernest Wadsworth	VI
Longfellow, Henry Wadsworth	VI
Longfellow, Samuel	VI
Longfellow, Stephen	VI
Longfellow, William Pitt Preble	VI
Longley, Alcander	VI
Longstreet, Augustus Baldwin	VI
Longstreet, James	VI
Longstreet, William	VI
Longworth, Nicholas (d. 1863)	VI
Longworth, Nicholas (d. 1931)	VI
Longyear, John Munroe	VI
Loomis, Arphaxed	VI
Loomis, Charles Battell	VI
Loomis, Dwight	VI
Loomis, Elias	VI
Loomis, Elmer Howard	VI
Loomis, Mahlon	VI
Loop, Henry Augustus	VI

Complete Index Guide

Name	Vol./Supp.	Name	Vol./Supp.
Loos, Charles Louis	VI	Lotka, Alfred James	4
Lopez, Aaron	VI	Lotta	
Loras, Jean Mathias Pierre	VI	See Crabtree, Lotta	
Lord, Asa Dearborn	VI	Loucks, Henry Langford	VI
Lord, Chester Sanders	1	Loudon, Samuel	VI
Lord, Daniel	VI	Loudoun, John Campbell,	
Lord, David Nevins	VI	Fourth Earl of	VI
Lord, Eleazar	VI	Loughridge, Robert McGill	VI
Lord, Henry Curwen	VI	Louis, Morris	7
Lord, Herbert Mayhew	VI	Lounsbury, Thomas Raynesford	VI
Lord, Jeremy		Love, Alfred Henry	VI
See Redman, Benjamin		Love, Emanuel King	VI
Ray		Love, Robertus Donnell	VI
Lord, John	VI	Lovejoy, Arthur Oncken	7
Lord, Nathan	VI	Lovejoy, Asa Lawrence	VI
Lord, Otis Phillips	VI	Lovejoy, Elijah Parish	VI
Lord, Pauline	4	Lovejoy, Owen	VI
Lord, William Paine	VI	Lovejoy, Owen Reed	7
Lord, William Wilberforce	VI	Lovelace, Francis	VI
Loree, Leonor Fresnel	2	Loveland, William Austin	
Lorillard, Pierre	VI	Hamilton	VI
Lorimer, George Claude	VI	Lovell, James	VI
Lorimer, George Horace	2	Lovell, John	VI
Lorimer, William	1	Lovell, John Epy	VI
Lorimier, Pierre Louis	VI	Lovell, Joseph	VI
Loring, Charles Harding	VI	Lovell, Mansfield	VI
Loring, Charles Morgridge	VI	Loveman, Amy	5
Loring, Edward Greely	VI	Lovering, Joseph	VI
Loring, Ellis Gray	VI	Lovett, Robert Morss	6
Loring, Frederick Wadsworth	VI	Lovett, Robert Scott	1
Loring, George Bailey	VI	Lovett, Robert Williamson	VI
Loring, Joshua (d. 1781)	VI	Lovewell, John	VI
Loring, Joshua (d. 1789)	VI	Low, Abiel Abbot	VI
Loring, William Wing	VI	Low, Frederick Ferdinand	VI
Lorre, Peter	7	Low, Isaac	VI
Loskiel, George Henry	VI	Low, John Gardner	VI
Lossing, Benson John	VI	Low, Juliette Gordon	VI
Lothrop, Alice Louise Higgins	VI	Low, Nicholas	VI
Lothrop, Amy		Low, Seth	VI
See Warner, Anna Bartlett		Low, Will Hicok	1
Lothrop, Daniel	VI	Lowden, Frank Orren	3
Lothrop, George Van Ness	VI	Lowe, Charles	VI
Lothrop, Harriett Mulford		Lowe, Ralph Phillips	VI
Stone	VI	Lowe, Thaddeus Sobieski	
Lothropp, John	VI	Coulincourt	VI

Complete Index Guide

Name	Vol./Supp.	Name	Vol./Supp.
Lowell, Abbott Lawrence	3	Luce, Stephen Bleecker	VI
Lowell, Amy	VI	Luciano, Charles ("Lucky")	7
Lowell, Edward Jackson	VI	Luckenbach, J(ohn) Lewis	5
Lowell, Francis Cabot	VI	Ludeling, John Theodore	VI
Lowell, Guy	VI	Ludlow, Daniel	VI
Lowell, James Russell	VI	Ludlow, Fitz Hugh	VI
Lowell, John (b. 1743)	VI	Ludlow, Gabriel George	VI
Lowell, John (b. 1769)	VI	Ludlow, George Duncan	VI
Lowell, John (b. 1799)	VI	Ludlow, Noah Miller	VI
Lowell, John (b. 1824)	VI	Ludlow, Roger	VI
Lowell, Josephine Shaw	VI	Ludlow, Thomas William	VI
Lowell, Percival	VI	Ludlow, William	VI
Lowell, Robert Traill Spence	VI	Ludlowe, Roger	
Lower, William Edgar	4	See Ludlow, Roger	
Lowery, Woodbury	VI	Ludwell, Philip	VI
Lowes, John Livingston	3	Ludwick, Christopher	VI
Lowie, Robert Harry	6	Luelling, Henderson	VI
Lowndes, Lloyd	VI	Lufbery, Raoul Gervais Victor	VI
Lowndes, Rawlins	VI	Lugosi, Bela	6
Lowndes, William	VI	Luhan, Mabel Dodge	7
Lowrey, Mark Perrin	VI	Lukeman, Henry Augustus	1
Lowrie, James Walter	VI	Lukens, Rebecca Webb	
Lowrie, Walter	VI	Pennock	VI
Lowry, Hiram Harrison	VI	Luks, George Benjamin	1
Lowry, Robert	VI	Lull, Edward Phelps	VI
Lowry, Thomas	VI	Lumbrozo, Jacob	VI
Loy, Matthias	VI	Lummis, Charles Fletcher	VI
Loyd, Samuel	VI	Lumpkin, Joseph Henry	VI
Lozier, Clemence Sophia		Lumpkin, Wilson	VI
Harned	VI	Luna y Arellano, Tristan de	VI
Lubbock, Francis Richard	VI	Lunceford, James	4
Lubin, David	VI	Lundeberg, Harry	6
Lubitsch, Ernst	4	Lundeen, Ernest	2
Lucas, Anthony Francis	VI	Lundie, John	VI
Lucas, Daniel Bedinger	VI	Lundin, Carl Axel Robert	VI
Lucas, Eliza		Lundy, Benjamin	VI
See Pinckney, Elizabeth		Lunn, George Richard	4
Lucas		Lunt, George	VI
Lucas, Frederic Augustus	VI	Lunt, Orrington	VI
Lucas, James H.	VI	Lurton, Horace Harmon	VI
Lucas, John Baptiste Charles	VI	Lusk, Graham	1
Lucas, Jonathan (d. 1821)	VI	Lusk, William Thompson	VI
Lucas, Jonathan (d. 1832)	VI	Luther, Seth	VI
Lucas, Robert	VI	Lutkin, Peter Christian	VI
Luce, Henry Winters	3	Lutz, Frank Eugene	3

Complete Index Guide

Name	Vol./Supp.	Name	Vol./Supp.
Lyall, James	VI	Maas, Anthony J.	VI
Lybrand, William Mitchell	6	Mabery, Charles Frederic	VI
Lydenberg, Harry Miller	6	Mabie, Hamilton Wright	VI
Lydston, George Frank	VI	McAdams, Clark	1
Lyman, Albert Josiah	VI	McAdie, Alexander George	3
Lyman, Benjamin Smith	VI	McAdoo, William Gibbs	3
Lyman, Chester Smith	VI	McAfee, John Armstrong	VI
Lyman, Eugene William	4	McAfee, Robert Breckinridge	VI
Lyman, Joseph Bardwell	VI	Macalester, Charles (d. 1832)	VI
Lyman, Phineas	VI	Macalester, Charles (d. 1873)	VI
Lyman, Theodore (d. 1849)	VI	McAlexander, Ulysses Grant	2
Lyman, Theodore (d. 1897)	VI	MacAlister, James	VI
Lyman, Theodore (d. 1954)	5	McAllister, Charles Albert	VI
Lynch, Anne Charlotte		McAllister, Hall	VI
See Botta, Anne Charlotte		McAllister, Matthew Hall	VI
Lynch		McAllister, Samuel Ward	VI
Lynch, Charles	VI	McAlpine, William Jarvis	VI
Lynch, James Daniel	VI	McAnally, David Rice	VI
Lynch, James Mathew	VI	McAndrew, William	2
Lynch, John Roy	2	MacArthur, Arthur	1
Lynch, Patrick Neeson	VI	MacArthur, Charles Gordon	6
Lynch, Robert Clyde	VI	MacArthur, Douglas	7
Lynch, Thomas (b. 1727)	VI	McArthur, Duncan	VI
Lynch, Thomas (b. 1749)	VI	McArthur, John (d. 1890)	VI
Lynch, William Francis	VI	McArthur, John (d. 1906)	VI
Lynde, Benjamin	VI	MacArthur, Robert Stuart	VI
Lynde, Francis	VI	McArthur, William Pope	VI
Lynds, Elam	VI	Macauley, Edward Yorke	
Lyon, Caleb	VI	See McCauley, Edward	
Lyon, David Gordon	1	Yorke	
Lyon, David Willard	4	McAuley, Jeremiah	VI
Lyon, Francis Strother	VI	McAuley, Thomas	VI
Lyon, Harris Merton	VI	McBain, Howard Lee	2
Lyon, James	VI	McBride, F(rancis) Scott	5
Lyon, James Benjamin	VI	McBride, Henry	7
Lyon, Mary	VI	McBryde, John McLaren	VI
Lyon, Matthew	VI	McBurney, Charles	VI
Lyon, Nathaniel	VI	McBurney, Robert Ross	VI
Lyon, Theodatus Timothy	VI	McCabe, Charles Cardwell	VI
Lyon, William Penn	VI	McCabe, John Collins	VI
Lyons, Peter	VI	McCabe, William Gordon	VI
Lyster, Henry Francis Le		McCaffrey, John	VI
Hunte	VI	McCaine, Alexander	VI
Lytle, William Haines	VI	McCaleb, Theodore Howard	VI
Lyttelton, William Henry	VI	McCall, Edward Rutledge	VI
		McCall, John Augustine	VI

Complete Index Guide

Name	Vol./Supp.	Name	Vol./Supp.
McCall, Samuel Walker	VI	McClintock, Oliver	VI
McCalla, Bowman Hendry	VI	McCloskey, John	VI
McCalla, William Latta	VI	McCloskey, William George	VI
McCallum, Daniel Craig	VI	McClung, Clarence Erwin	4
MacCallum, William George	3	McClure, Alexander Kelly	VI
MacCameron, Robert	VI	McClure, Alexander Wilson	VI
McCann, Alfred Watterson	VI	McClure, George	VI
McCann, William Penn	VI	McClure, Robert Alexis	6
McCardell, Claire	6	McClure, Samuel Sidney	4
McCarran, Patrick Anthony	5	McClurg, Alexander Caldwell	VI
McCarren, Patrick Henry	VI	McClurg, James	VI
McCarroll, James	VI	McClurg, Joseph Washington	VI
McCartee, Divie Bethune	VI	McComas, Louis Emory	VI
McCarthy, Charles	VI	McComb, John	VI
McCarthy, Charles Louis		McConnel, John Ludlum	VI
("Clem")	7	McConnell, Francis John	5
McCarthy, Daniel Joseph	6	McConnell, Ira Welch	1
McCarthy, Joseph Raymond	6	McCook, Alexander McDowell	VI
McCartney, Washington	VI	McCook, Anson George	VI
McCauley, Charles Stewart	VI	McCook, Edward Moody	VI
MacCauley, Clay	VI	McCook, Henry Christopher	VI
McCauley, Edward Yorke	VI	McCook, John James	VI
McCauley, Mary Ludwig Hays	VI	McCord, David James	VI
McCausland, John	VI	McCord, James Bennett	4
McCaw, James Brown	VI	McCord, Louisa Susanna	
McCawley, Charles Grymes	VI	Cheves	VI
McCawley, Charles Laurie	1	McCormack, John Francis	3
McCay, Charles Francis	VI	McCormack, Joseph Nathaniel	VI
McCay, Henry Kent	VI	McCormick, Anne Elizabeth	
McClain, Emlin	VI	O'Hare	5
McClatchy, Charles Kenny	2	McCormick, Cyrus Hall	
McClellan, George (d. 1847)	VI	(d. 1884)	VI
McClellan, George (d. 1913)	VI	McCormick, Cyrus Hall	
McClellan, George Brinton		(d. 1936)	2
(d. 1885)	VI	McCormick, Joseph Medill	VI
McClellan, George Brinton		McCormick, Leander James	VI
(d. 1940)	2	McCormick, Lynde Dupuy	6
McClellan, Henry Brainerd	VI	McCormick, Medill	
McClellan, Robert	VI	See McCormick, Joseph	
McClelland, Robert	VI	Medill	
McClenahan, Howard	1	McCormick, Richard	
McClernand, John Alexander	VI	Cunningham	VI
McClintic, Guthrie	7	McCormick, Robert	VI
McClintock, Emory	VI	McCormick, Robert Rutherford	5
McClintock, James Harvey	1	McCormick, Robert Sanderson	VI
M'Clintock, John	VI		

Complete Index Guide

Name	Vol./Supp.	Name	Vol./Supp.
McCormick, Ruth Hanna		McDougall, Alexander	
See Simms, Ruth Hanna		(d. 1786)	VI
McCormick		McDougall, Alexander	
McCormick, Samuel Black	VI	(d. 1923)	VI
McCormick, Stephen	VI	McDougall, Frances Harriet	
McCosh, Andrew James	VI	See Green, Frances	
McCosh, James	VI	Harriet Whipple	
McCoy, Elijah	VI	McDougall, William	2
McCoy, Isaac	VI	McDowell, Charles	VI
McCoy, Joseph Geating	VI	MacDowell, Edward Alexander	VI
MacCracken, Henry Mitchell	VI	McDowell, Ephraim	VI
McCracken, Joan	7	McDowell, Irvin	VI
McCrady, Edward	VI	McDowell, James	VI
McCrae, Thomas	1	McDowell, John (d. 1820)	VI
McCrary, George Washington	VI	McDowell, John (d. 1863)	VI
McCreary, James Bennett	VI	McDowell, Joseph	VI
McCreery, Charles	VI	MacDowell, Katherine	
McCreery, James Work	VI	Sherwood Bonner	VI
McCullagh, Joseph Burbridge	VI	McDowell, Mary Eliza	2
McCulloch, Ben	VI	McDowell, William Fraser	2
McCulloch, Hugh	VI	McDuffie, George	VI
McCulloch, Oscar Carleton	VI	McElrath, Thomas	VI
McCullough, Ernest	VI	McElroy, John (d. 1877)	VI
McCullough, John	VI	McElroy, John (d. 1929)	VI
McCullough, John Griffith	VI	McElroy, Robert McNutt	6
McCumber, Porter James	1	McElwaine, William Howe	VI
MacCurdy, George Grant	4	McEnery, Samuel Douglas	VI
McCurdy, Richard Aldrich	VI	McEntee, James Joseph	6
McCutcheon, George Barr	VI	McEntee, Jervis	VI
McDaniel, Hattie	5	Macfadden, Bernarr	5
McDaniel, Henry Dickerson	VI	McFadden, Louis Thomas	2
McDill, James Wilson	VI	McFarland, George Bradley	3
MacDonald, Betty	6	McFarland, John Horace	4
Macdonald, Charles Blair	2	McFarland, John Thomas	VI
McDonald, Charles James	VI	McFarland, Samuel Gamble	VI
McDonald, James Grover	7	McFarland, Thomas Bard	VI
MacDonald, James Wilson		Macfarlane, Charles William	VI
Alexander	VI	Macfarlane, Robert	VI
MacDonald, Jeanette Anna	7	McFaul, James Augustine	VI
McDonald, John Bartholomew	VI	McFerrin, John Berry	VI
McDonald, Joseph Ewing	VI	MacGahan, Januarius Aloysius	VI
MacDonald, Ranald	VI	McGarrah, Gates White	2
McDonogh, John	VI	McGarvey, John William	VI
MacDonough, Thomas	VI	McGee, William John	VI
McDougal, David Stockton	VI	McGeehan, William O'Connell	1

Complete Index Guide

Name	Vol./Supp.	Name	Vol./Supp.
McGhee, Charles McClung	VI	McKay, Claude	4
McGiffert, Arthur Cushman	1	McKay, Donald	VI
McGiffin, Philo Norton	VI	McKay, Gordon	VI
McGill, John	VI	Mackay, James	VI
McGillivray, Alexander	VI	McKay, (James) Douglas	6
McGilvary, Daniel	VI	McKay, James Iver	VI
McGivney, Michael Joseph	VI	Mackay, John William	VI
McGlothlin, William Joseph	1	MacKaye, James Morrison	
McGlynn, Edward	VI	Steele	VI
McGovern, John	VI	MacKaye, Percy Wallace	6
McGowan, Samuel	VI	MacKaye, Steele	
McGranery, James Patrick	7	See MacKaye, James	
McGrath, James	VI	Morrison Steele	
McGrath, Matthew J.	3	McKean, James W.	4
McGraw, James Herbert	4	McKean, Joseph Borden	VI
McGraw, John Harte	VI	McKean, Samuel	VI
McGraw, John Joseph	1	McKean, Thomas	VI
McGready, James	VI	McKean, William Wister	VI
McGroarty, Susan		McKechnie, William Boyd	7
See Julia, Sister		McKee, John	VI
McGuffey, William Holmes	VI	McKeen, Joseph	VI
McGuire, Charles Bonaventure	VI	McKellar, Kenneth Douglas	6
McGuire, Hunter Holmes	VI	Mackellar, Patrick	VI
McGuire, Joseph Deakins	VI	MacKellar, Thomas	VI
McHale, Kathryn	6	McKelway, St. Clair	VI
Machebeuf, Joseph Projectus	VI	McKendree, William	VI
Machen, John Gresham	2	McKenna, Charles Hyacinth	VI
McHenry, James (d. 1816)	VI	McKenna, Joseph	VI
McHenry, James (d. 1845)	VI	McKennan, Thomas McKean	
McHugh, Rose John	5	Thompson	VI
McIlvaine, Charles Pettit	VI	McKenney, Thomas Loraine	VI
McIlwaine, Richard	VI	McKenzie, Alexander	VI
McIntire, Ross	6	Mackenzie, Alexander Slidell	VI
McIntire, Samuel	VI	Mackenzie, Donald	VI
Macintosh, Douglas Clyde	4	Mackenzie, George Henry	VI
McIntosh, John Baillie	VI	Mackenzie, James Cameron	VI
McIntosh, Lachlan	VI	Mackenzie, John Noland	VI
McIntosh, William	VI	Mackenzie, Kenneth	VI
McIntyre, Alfred Robert	4	Mackenzie, Murdo	2
McIntyre, James	2	Mackenzie, Ranald Slidell	VI
McIntyre, Oscar Odd	2	Mackenzie, Robert Shelton	VI
McIver, Charles Duncan	VI	McKenzie, Robert Tait	2
Mack, Connie	6	Mackenzie, William	VI
Mack, Julian William	3	Mackey, Albert Gallatin	VI
Mackay, Clarence Hungerford	2	McKim, Charles Follen	VI

Complete Index Guide

Name	Vol./Supp.	Name	Vol./Supp.
McKim, Isaac	VI	McLoughlin, Maurice Evans	6
McKim, James Miller	VI	Maclure, William	VI
McKinley, Albert Edward	2	McMahon, Bernard	VI
McKinley, Carlyle	VI	McMahon, Brien	5
McKinley, John	VI	McMahon, John Van Lear	VI
McKinley, William	VI	McManes, James	VI
McKinley, William Brown	1	McManus, George	5
McKinly, John	VI	McMaster, Guy Humphreys	VI
McKinstry, Alexander	VI	McMaster, James Alphonsus	VI
McKinstry, Elisha Williams	VI	McMaster, John Bach	VI
McKnight, Robert	VI	McMath, Robert Emmet	VI
Mackubin, Florence	VI	McMichael, Morton	VI
McLaglen, Victor	6	McMillan, James	VI
McLane, Allan	VI	McMillan, James Winning	VI
McLane, Louis	VI	McMillin, Alvin Nugent	5
McLane, Robert Milligan	VI	McMillin, Benton	1
McLaren, John	3	McMinn, Joseph	VI
McLaren, William Edward	VI	MacMonnies, Frederick	
McLaughlin, Andrew		William	2
Cunningham	4	McMurrich, James Playfair	2
McLaughlin, Hugh	VI	McMurry, Frank Morton	2
McLaughlin, James	VI	McMurtrie, Douglas Crawford	3
McLaurin, Anselm Joseph	VI	McMurtrie, William	VI
Maclaurin, Richard Cockburn	VI	McNair, Alexander	VI
McLaws, Lafayette	VI	McNair, Frederick Vallette	VI
Maclay, Edgar Stanton	VI	McNair, Fred Walter	VI
Maclay, Robert Samuel	VI	MacNair, Harley Farnsworth	4
Maclay, Samuel	VI	McNair, Lesley James	3
Maclay, William	VI	McNamee, Graham	3
Maclay, William Brown	VI	McNary, Charles Linza	3
McLean, Angus Wilton	1	Macnaughtan, Myra Kelly	
McLean, Archibald	VI	See Kelly, Myra	
McLean, Edward Beale	3	MacNeil, Hermon Atkins	4
MacLean, George Edwin	2	McNeill, Daniel	VI
Maclean, John (d. 1814)	VI	McNeill, George Edwin	VI
McLean, John (d. 1861)	VI	McNeill, Hector	VI
Maclean, John (d. 1886)	VI	McNeill, John Hanson	VI
McLean, Walter	VI	McNeill, William Gibbs	VI
McLean, William Lippard	VI	MacNeven, William James	VI
McLellan, Isaac	VI	MacNicholas, John Timothy	4
McLeod, Alexander	VI	McNulty, Frank Joseph	VI
McLeod, Hugh	VI	McNulty, John Augustine	6
McLeod, Martin	VI	McNutt, Alexander	VI
McLevy, Jasper	7	McNutt, Paul Vories	5
McLoughlin, John	VI	Macomb, Alexander	VI

Complete Index Guide

Name	Vol./Supp.	Name	Vol./Supp.
Macomber, Mary Lizzie	VI	Magee, Christopher Lyman	VI
Macon, Nathaniel	VI	Magie, William Jay	VI
McPherson, Aimee Semple	3	Magill, Edward Hicks	VI
McPherson, Edward	VI	Maginnis, Charles Donagh	5
McPherson, James Birdseye	VI	Maginnis, Martin	VI
McPherson, Logan Grant	VI	Magnes, Judah Leon	4
McPherson, Smith	VI	Magoffin, Beriah	VI
McQuaid, Bernard John	VI	Magoffin, James Wiley	VI
McQuillen, John Hugh	VI	Magonigle, Harold Van Buren	1
McRae, Duncan Kirkland	VI	Magoon, Charles Edward	VI
Macrae, John	3	Magoun, George Frederic	VI
McRae, Milton Alexander	VI	Magrath, Andrew Gordon	VI
McRae, Thomas Chipman	VI	Magruder, George Lloyd	VI
McReynolds, James Clark	4	Magruder, John Bankhead	VI
McReynolds, Samuel Davis	2	Magruder, Julia	VI
MacSparran, James	VI	Maguire, Charles Bonaventure	
McTammany, John	VI	See McGuire, Charles	
McTyeire, Holland Nimmons	VI	Bonaventure	
Macune, Charles William	2	Mahan, Alfred Thayer	VI
MacVeagh, Charles	1	Mahan, Asa	VI
MacVeagh, Franklin	1	Mahan, Dennis Hart	VI
MacVeagh, Isaac Wayne	VI	Mahan, Milo	VI
McVey, Frank LeRond	5	Mahler, Herbert	7
MacVicar, Malcolm	VI	Mahone, William	VI
McVickar, John	VI	Mahoney, John Friend	6
McVickar, William Neilson	VI	Maier, Walter Arthur	4
McVicker, James Hubert	VI	Mailly, William	VI
MacWhorter, Alexander	VI	Main, Charles Thomas	3
Macy, Jesse	VI	Main, John Hanson Thomas	1
Macy, John Albert	VI	Maisch, John Michael	VI
Macy, Josiah	VI	Major, Charles	VI
Macy, Valentine Everit	VI	Majors, Alexander	VI
Madden, John Edward	VI	Ma-Ka-Tai-Me-She-Kia-Kiak	
Madden, Martin Barnaby	VI	See Black Hawk	
Madden, Owen Victor		Makemie, Francis	VI
("Owney")	7	Malbone, Edward Greene	VI
Madigan, LaVerne	7	Malcolm, Daniel	VI
Madison, Dolly Payne	VI	Malcolm, James Peller	VI
Madison, James (d. 1812)	VI	Malcolm X	7
Madison, James (d. 1836)	VI	Malcom, Daniel	
Maeder, Clara Fisher		See Malcolm, Daniel	
See Fisher, Clara		Malcom, Howard	VI
Maes, Camillus Paul	VI	Malcom, James Peller	
Maffitt, David	VI	See Malcolm, James Peller	
Maffitt, John Newland	VI	Malin, Patrick Murphy	7

Complete Index Guide

Name	Vol./Supp.	Name	Vol./Supp.
Mall, Franklin Paine	VI	Manning, James	VI
Mallary, Rollin Carolas	VI	Manning, Marie	3
Mallery, Garrick	VI	Manning, Richard Irvine	
Mallet, John William	VI	(d. 1836)	VI
Mallinckrodt, Edward	VI	Manning, Richard Irvine	
Mallory, Anna Margrethe		(d. 1931)	VI
("Molla") Bjurstedt	6	Manning, Robert	VI
Mallory, Clifford Day	3	Manning, Thomas Courtland	VI
Mallory, Frank Burr	3	Manning, Vannoy Hartrog	VI
Mallory, Stephen Russell	VI	Manning, William Thomas	4
Malone, Dudley Field	4	Mansell, William Albert	VI
Malone, Sylvester	VI	Mansfield, Edward Deering	VI
Malone, Walter	VI	Mansfield, Jared	VI
Maloney, Martin	VI	Mansfield, Joseph King Fenno	VI
Malter, Henry	VI	Mansfield, Richard (d. 1820)	VI
Manatt, James Irving	VI	Mansfield, Richard (d. 1907)	VI
Manderson, Charles Frederick	VI	Manson, Otis Frederick	VI
Maney, George Earl	VI	Mantell, Robert Bruce	VI
Mangin, Joseph François	VI	Mantle, Robert Burns	4
Mangum, Willie Person	VI	Mapes, Charles Victor	VI
Manigault, Arthur Middleton	VI	Mapes, James Jay	VI
Manigault, Gabriel	VI	Mappa, Adam Gerard	VI
Manigault, Peter	VI	Maranville, Walter James	
Manigault, Pierre	VI	Vincent	5
Mankiewicz, Herman Jacob	5	Marble, Albert Prescott	VI
Manley, John	VI	Marble, Danforth	VI
Manley, Joseph Homan	VI	Marble, Manton Malone	VI
Manly, Basil (d. 1868)	VI	Marburg, Theodore	4
Manly, Basil (d. 1892)	VI	Marbury, Elisabeth	1
Manly, Basil Maxwell	4	Marbut, Curtis Fletcher	1
Manly, Charles Matthews	VI	Marcantonio, Vito Anthony	5
Manly, John Matthews	2	March, Alden	VI
Mann, Ambrose Dudley	VI	March, Francis Andrew	
Mann, Horace	VI	(d. 1911)	VI
Mann, James	VI	March, Francis Andrew	
Mann, James Robert	VI	(d. 1928)	VI
Mann, Louis	VI	March, Peyton Conway	5
Mann, Mary Tyler Peabody	VI	March, William Edward	
Mann, Newton	VI	See Campbell, William	
Mann, William Julius	VI	Edward March	
Manners, John Hartley	VI	Marchand, John Bonnett	VI
Mannes, Clara Damrosch	4	Marchant, Henry	VI
Mannes, David	6	Marcosson, Isaac Frederick	7
Mannes, Leopold Damrosch	7	Marcou, Jules	VI
Manning, Daniel	VI	Marcus, Bernard Kent	5

Complete Index Guide

Name	Vol./Supp.	Name	Vol./Supp.
Marcy, Henry Orlando	VI	Marsh, Sylvester	VI
Marcy, Randolph Barnes	VI	Marsh, William Wallace	VI
Marcy, William Learned	VI	Marshall, Benjamin	VI
Marden, Charles Carroll	VI	Marshall, Charles Henry	VI
Marden, Orison Swett	VI	Marshall, Christopher	VI
Maréchal, Ambrose	VI	Marshall, Clara	VI
Marest, Piérre Gabriel	VI	Marshall, Daniel	VI
Maretzek, Max	VI	Marshall, Frank James	3
Margolis, Max Leopold	VI	Marshall, George Catlett, Jr.	6
Marigny, Bernard	VI	Marshall, Henry Rutgers	VI
Marin, John (Cheri)	5	Marshall, Humphrey (d. 1841)	VI
Marion, Francis	VI	Marshall, Humphrey (d. 1872)	VI
Markham, Charles Henry	VI	Marshall, Humphry (d. 1801)	VI
Markham, Edwin	2	Marshall, James Fowle Baldwin	VI
Markham, William	VI	Marshall, James Markham	VI
Markoe, Abraham	VI	Marshall, James Wilson	VI
Markoe, Peter	VI	Marshall, John	VI
Marks, Amasa Abraham	VI	Marshall, Louis (d. 1866)	VI
Marks, Elias	VI	Marshall, Louis (d. 1929)	VI
Marland, Ernest Whitworth	3	Marshall, Thomas	VI
Marlatt, Abby Lillian	3	Marshall, Thomas Alexander	VI
Marling, Alfred Erskine	1	Marshall, Thomas Riley	VI
Marling, John Leake	VI	Marshall, William Edgar	VI
Marlowe, Julia (Sothern)	4	Marshall, William Louis	VI
Marmaduke, John Sappington	VI	Marshall, William Rainey	VI
Marquand, Allan	VI	Martel, Charles	3
Marquand, Henry Gurdon	VI	Martin, Alexander	VI
Marquand, John Phillips	6	Martin, Anne Henrietta	5
Marquett, Turner Mastin	VI	Martin, Artemas	VI
Marquette, Jacques	VI	Martin, Edward Sandford	2
Marquis, Albert Nelson	3	Martin, Elizabeth Price	1
Marquis, Donald Robert Perry	2	Martin, Everett Dean	3
Marquis, John Abner	VI	Martin, François-Xavier	VI
Marquis de Cuevas		Martin, Franklin Henry	1
See De Cuevas, Marquis		Martin, Frederick Townsend	VI
Marriott, Williams McKim	2	Martin, Glenn Luther ("Cy")	5
Marsh, Charles Wesley	VI	Martin, Henry Austin	VI
Marsh, Frank Burr	2	Martin, Henry Newell	VI
Marsh, George Perkins	VI	Martin, Homer Dodge	VI
Marsh, Grant Prince	VI	Martin, James Green	VI
Marsh, James	VI	Martin, John Alexander	VI
Marsh, John (b. 1788)	VI	Martin, John Hill	VI
Marsh, John (b. 1799)	VI	Martin, John Leonard	
Marsh, Othniel Charles	VI	Roosevelt ("Pepper")	7
Marsh, Reginald	5	Martin, Josiah	VI

Complete Index Guide

Name	Vol./Supp.	Name	Vol./Supp.
Martin, Luther	VI	Mason, Luther Whiting	VI
Martin, Thomas Commerford	VI	Mason, Max	7
Martin, Thomas Staples	VI	Mason, Otis Tufton	VI
Martin, Victoria Claflin		Mason, Richard Barnes	VI
Woodhull		Mason, Samuel	VI
See Woodhull, Victoria		Mason, Stevens Thomson	
Claflin		(d. 1803)	VI
Martin, William Alexander		Mason, Stevens Thomson	
Parsons	VI	(d. 1843)	VI
Martin, William Thompson	VI	Mason, Thomson	VI
Martindale, John Henry	VI	Mason, Walt	2
Martiny, Philip	VI	Mason, William (d. 1883)	VI
Marty, Martin	VI	Mason, William (d. 1908)	VI
Martyn, Sarah Towne Smith	VI	Mason, William Ernest	VI
Marvel, Ik		Masquerier, Lewis	VI
See Mitchell, Donald		Massassoit	VI
Grant		Massey, George Betton	VI
Marvin, Charles Frederick	3	Massey, John Edward	VI
Marvin, Dudley	VI	Masson, Thomas Lansing	1
Marvin, Enoch Mather	VI	Mast, Phineas Price	VI
Marwedel, Emma Jacobina		Masters, Edgar Lee	4
Christiana	VI	Masterson, William Barclay	VI
Marx, Adolf Arthur ("Harpo")	7	Mastin, Claudius Henry	VI
Marx, Leonard ("Chico")	7	Masury, John Wesley	VI
Marzo, Eduardo	VI	Matas, Rudolph	6
Maschke, Heinrich	VI	Mateer, Calvin Wilson	VI
Masliansky, Zvi Hirsch	3	Mather, Cotton	VI
Mason, Arthur John	1	Mather, Frank Jewett, Jr.	5
Mason, Charles	VI	Mather, Fred	VI
Mason, Claibourne Rice	VI	Mather, Increase	VI
Mason, Daniel Gregory	5	Mather, Richard	VI
Mason, Francis	VI	Mather, Samuel (d. 1785)	VI
Mason, Frank Stuart	VI	Mather, Samuel (d. 1931)	VI
Mason, George (d. c. 1686)	VI	Mather, Samuel Holmes	VI
Mason, George (d. 1792)	VI	Mather, Samuel Livingston	VI
Mason, Henry	VI	Mather, Stephen Tyng	VI
Mason, James Murray	VI	Mather, William Williams	VI
Mason, Jeremiah	VI	Mather, Winifred Holt	
Mason, John (d. 1672)	VI	See Holt, Winifred	
Mason, John (d. 1919)	VI	Matheson, William John	VI
Mason, John Mitchell	VI	Mathews, Albert	VI
Mason, John Young	VI	Mathews, Cornelius	VI
Mason, Jonathan	VI	Mathews, George	VI
Mason, Lowell	VI	Mathews, Henry Mason	VI
Mason, Lucy Randolph	6	Mathews, John	VI

Complete Index Guide

Name	Vol./Supp.	Name	Vol./Supp.
Mathews, John Alexander	1	Maverick, Peter	VI
Mathews, Samuel	VI	Maverick, Samuel	VI
Mathews, Shailer	3	Maxcy, Jonathan	VI
Mathews, William	VI	Maxcy, Virgil	VI
Mathews, William Smythe		Maxey, Samuel Bell	VI
Babcock	VI	Maxim, Hiram Percy	2
Mathewson, Christopher	VI	Maxim, Hiram Stevens	VI
Mathewson, Edward Payson	4	Maxim, Hudson	VI
Matignon, Francis Anthony	VI	Maxwell, Augustus Emmett	VI
Matlack, Timothy	VI	Maxwell, David Hervey	VI
Matteson, Joel Aldrich	VI	Maxwell, Elsa	7
Matteson, Tompkins Harrison	VI	Maxwell, George Hebard	4
Matthes, François Emile	4	Maxwell, George Troup	VI
Matthes, Gerard Hendrik	6	Maxwell, Hugh	VI
Matthew, William Diller	VI	Maxwell, Lucien Bonaparte	VI
Matthews, Brander		Maxwell, Samuel	VI
See Matthews, James		Maxwell, William (d. 1796)	VI
Brander		Maxwell, William (d. 1809)	VI
Matthews, Claude	VI	Maxwell, William (d. 1857)	VI
Matthews, Francis Patrick	5	Maxwell, William Henry	VI
Matthews, Franklin	VI	May, Andrew Jackson	6
Matthews, James Brander	VI	May, Edward Harrison	VI
Matthews, John	VI	May, Samuel Joseph	VI
Matthews, Joseph Merritt	VI	May, Sophie	
Matthews, Nathan	VI	See Clarke, Rebecca	
Matthews, Stanley	VI	Sophia	
Matthews, Washington	VI	Maybank, Burnet Rhett	5
Matthews, William	VI	Maybeck, Bernard Ralph	6
Matthiessen, Francis Otto	4	Mayer, Alfred Goldsborough	
Matthiessen, Frederick William	VI	See Mayor, Alfred	
Mattice, Asa Martines	VI	Goldsborough	
Mattingly, Garrett	7	Mayer, Alfred Marshall	VI
Mattison, Hiram	VI	Mayer, Brantz	VI
Mattocks, John	VI	Mayer, Constant	VI
Mattoon, Stephen	VI	Mayer, Emil	VI
Mattson, Hans	VI	Mayer, Lewis	VI
Matzeliger, Jan Ernst	VI	Mayer, Louis Burt	6
Mauran, John Lawrence	1	Mayer, Oscar Gottfried	7
Maurer, James Hudson	3	Mayer, Philip Frederick	VI
Maurin, Peter	4	Mayes, Edward	VI
Maury, Dabney Herndon	VI	Mayes, Joel Bryan	VI
Maury, Francis Fontaine	VI	Mayhew, Experience	VI
Maury, Matthew Fontaine	VI	Mayhew, Jonathan	VI
Maus, Marion Perry	VI	Mayhew, Thomas (b. 1593)	VI
Maverick, (Fontaine) Maury	5	Mayhew, Thomas (b. c. 1621)	VI

Complete Index Guide

Name	Vol./Supp.	Name	Vol./Supp.
Maynard, Charles Johnson	VI	Mears, Helen Farnsworth	VI
Maynard, Edward	VI	Mears, John William	VI
Maynard, George William	VI	Mears, Otto	VI
Maynard, George Willoughby	VI	Mease, James	VI
Maynard, Horace	VI	Meason, Isaac	VI
Mayo, Amory Dwight	VI	Mechem, Floyd Russell	VI
Mayo, Frank	VI	Mecom, Benjamin	VI
Mayo, George Elton	4	Medary, Milton Bennett	VI
Mayo, Henry Thomas	2	Medary, Samuel	VI
Mayo, Mary Anne Bryant	VI	Medill, Joseph	VI
Mayo, Sarah Carter Edgarton	VI	Meehan, Thomas	VI
Mayo, William	VI	Meek, Alexander Beaufort	VI
Mayo, William James	2	Meek, Fielding Bradford	VI
Mayo, William Kennon	VI	Meek, Joseph L.	VI
Mayo, William Starbuck	VI	Meeker, Ezra	VI
Mayo, William Worrell	VI	Meeker, Jotham	VI
Mayor, Alfred Goldsborough	VI	Meeker, Moses	VI
Mayo-Smith, Richmond	VI	Meeker, Nathan Cook	VI
Maytag, Frederick Louis	2	Meerschaert, Théophile	VI
Mazureau, Étienne	VI	Mees, Arthur	VI
Mazzei, Philip	VI	Mees, Charles Edward Kenneth	6
Mazzuchelli, Samuel Charles	VI	Megapolensis, Johannes	VI
Mead, Charles Marsh	VI	Megrue, Roi Cooper	VI
Mead, Edwin Doak	2	Meière, Marie Hildreth	7
Mead, Elwood	2	Meiggs, Henry	VI
Mead, George Herbert	1	Meigs, Arthur Vincent	VI
Mead, James Michael	7	Meigs, Charles Delucena	VI
Mead, Larkin Goldsmith	VI	Meigs, James Aitken	VI
Mead, William Rutherford	VI	Meigs, John	VI
Meade, George	VI	Meigs, John Forsyth	VI
Meade, George Gordon	VI	Meigs, Josiah	VI
Meade, Richard Kidder	VI	Meigs, Montgomery	
Meade, Richard Worsam		Cunningham	VI
(d. 1828)	VI	Meigs, Return Jonathan	
Meade, Richard Worsam		(b. 1740)	VI
(d. 1870)	VI	Meigs, Return Jonathan	
Meade, Richard Worsam		(b. 1764)	VI
(d. 1897)	VI	Meigs, Return Jonathan	
Meade, Robert Leamy	VI	(b. 1801)	VI
Meade, William	VI	Meigs, William Montgomery	VI
Meagher, Thomas Francis	VI	Meiklejohn, Alexander	7
Means, Gaston Bullock	2	Meinzer, Oscar Edward	4
Meany, Edmond Stephen	1	Melcher, Frederic Gershom	7
Mearns, Edgar Alexander	VI	Melchers, Gari	VI
Mears, David Otis	VI	Melish, John	VI

Complete Index Guide

Name	Vol./Supp.	Name	Vol./Supp.
Mell, Patrick Hues (d. 1888)	VI	Mercier, Charles Alfred	VI
Mell, Patrick Hues (d. 1918)	VI	Merck, George Wilhelm	6
Mellen, Charles Sanger	VI	Mercur, Ulysses	VI
Mellen, Grenville	VI	Meredith, Edna C. Elliott	7
Mellen, Prentiss	VI	Meredith, Edwin Thomas	VI
Mellette, Arthur Calvin	VI	Meredith, Samuel	VI
Mellon, Andrew William	2	Meredith, William Morris	VI
Mellon, William Larimer	4	Mergenthaler, Ottmar	VI
Melsheimer, Friedrich Valentin	VI	Mergler, Marie Josepha	VI
Melton, James	7	Merriam, Augustus Chapman	VI
Meltzer, Samuel James	VI	Merriam, Charles	VI
Melville, David	VI	Merriam, Charles Edward, Jr.	5
Melville, George Wallace	VI	Merriam, Clinton Hart	3
Melville, Herman	VI	Merriam, Henry Clay	VI
Membré, Zenobius	VI	Merriam, John Campbell	3
Memminger, Christopher		Merriam, William Rush	VI
Gustavus	VI	Merrick, Edwin Thomas	VI
Menard, Michel Branamour	VI	Merrick, Frederick	VI
Menard, Pierre	VI	Merrick, Pliny	VI
Ménard, René	VI	Merrick, Samuel Vaughan	VI
Mencken, Henry Louis	6	Merrill, Charles Edward	6
Mendel, Lafayette Benedict	1	Merrill, Daniel	VI
Mendelsohn, Erich (or Eric)	5	Merrill, Elmer Drew	6
Mendenhall, Charles Elwood	1	Merrill, Elmer Truesdell	2
Mendenhall, Thomas Corwin	VI	Merrill, Frank Dow	5
Mendes, Frederic de Sola	VI	Merrill, George Edmands	VI
Mendes, Henry Pereira	2	Merrill, George Perkins	VI
Meneely, Andrew	VI	Merrill, Gretchen Van Zandt	7
Menéndez de Avilés, Pedro	VI	Merrill, James Cushing	VI
Menetrey, Joseph	VI	Merrill, James Griswold	VI
Menewa	VI	Merrill, Joshua	VI
Mengarini, Gregory	VI	Merrill, Samuel	VI
Menjou, Adolphe Jean	7	Merrill, Selah	VI
Menken, Adah Isaacs	VI	Merrill, Stephen Mason	VI
Menninger, Charles Frederick	5	Merrill, Stuart Fitzrandolph	VI
Menocal, Aniceto Garcia	VI	Merrill, William Bradford	VI
Menoher, Charles Thomas	VI	Merrill, William Emery	VI
Mercer, Charles Fenton	VI	Merrimon, Augustus	
Mercer, Henry Chapman	VI	Summerfield	VI
Mercer, Hugh	VI	Merritt, Anna Lea	VI
Mercer, James	VI	Merritt, Israel John	VI
Mercer, Jesse	VI	Merritt, Leonidas	VI
Mercer, John Francis	VI	Merritt, Wesley	VI
Mercer, Lewis Pyle	VI	Merry, Ann Brunton	VI
Mercer, Margaret	VI	Merry, William Lawrence	VI

Complete Index Guide

Name	Vol./Supp.	Name	Vol./Supp.
Mervine, William	VI	Middleton, Arthur (d. 1737)	VI
Merz, Karl	VI	Middleton, Arthur (d. 1787)	VI
Meserve, Frederick Hill	7	Middleton, Henry (d. 1784)	VI
Meserve, Nathaniel	VI	Middleton, Henry (d. 1846)	VI
Messer, Asa	VI	Middleton, John Izard	VI
Messersmith, George Strausser	6	Middleton, Nathaniel Russell	VI
Messler, Thomas Doremus	VI	Middleton, Peter	VI
Messmer, Sebastian Gebhard	VI	Middleton, Thomas Cooke	VI
Meštrović, Ivan	7	Midgley, Thomas	3
Metalious, Grace	7	Mielatz, Charles Frederick	
Metcalf, Henry Harrison	VI	William	VI
Metcalf, Joel Hastings	VI	Mielziner, Moses	VI
Metcalf, Theron	VI	Mifflin, Lloyd	VI
Metcalf, Willard Leroy	VI	Mifflin, Thomas	VI
Metcalf, William	VI	Mifflin, Warner	VI
Metcalfe, Samuel Lytler	VI	Mignot, Louis Remy	VI
Metcalfe, Thomas	VI	Milburn, William Henry	VI
Mettauer, John Peter	VI	Miles, Edward	VI
Metz, Christian	VI	Miles, George Henry	VI
Meyer, Adolph	4	Miles, Henry Adolphus	VI
Meyer, Albert Gregory	7	Miles, Manly	VI
Meyer, Annie Nathan	5	Miles, Nelson Appleton	VI
Meyer, Eugene Isaac	6	Miles, Richard Pius	VI
Meyer, George von Lengerke	VI	Miles, William Porcher	VI
Meyer, Henry Coddington	1	Milholland, Inez	
Meyer, Martin Abraham	VI	See Boissevain, Inez	
Meyerhof, Otto	5	Milholland	
Mezes, Sidney Edward	VI	Millay, Edna St. Vincent	4
Miantonomo	VI	Milledge, John	VI
Mich, Daniel Danforth	7	Milledoler, Philip	VI
Michael, Arthur	3	Miller, Charles Henry	VI
Michaelis, Leonor	4	Miller, Charles Ransom	VI
Michaëlius, Jonas	VI	Miller, Cincinnatus Hiner	VI
Michaux, André	VI	Miller, David Hunter	7
Michaux, François André	VI	Miller, Dayton Clarence	3
Micheaux, Oscar	5	Miller, Edward	VI
Michel, Virgil George	2	Miller, Emily Clark Huntington	VI
Michel, William Middleton	VI	Miller, Ezra	VI
Michelson, Albert Abraham	VI	Miller, George	VI
Michelson, Charles	4	Miller, George Abram	5
Michener, Ezra	VI	Miller, Gerrit Smith, Jr.	6
Michie, Peter Smith	VI	Miller, Glenn	3
Michikinikwa		Miller, Harriet Mann	VI
See Little Turtle		Miller, Heinrich	
Michler, Nathaniel	1	See Miller, John Henry	

Complete Index Guide

Name	Vol./Supp.	Name	Vol./Supp.
Miller, Henry (d. 1874)	VI	Mills, Benjamin Fay	VII
Miller, Henry (d. 1926)	VI	Mills, Charles Karsner	VII
Miller, James Alexander	4	Mills, Charles Wright	7
Miller, James Russell	VI	Mills, Clark	VII
Miller, Joaquin		Mills, Cyrus Taggart	VII
See Miller, Cincinnatus		Mills, Darius Ogden	VII
Hiner		Mills, Elijah Hunt	VII
Miller, John (d. 1846)	VI	Mills, Enos Abijah	1
Miller, John (d. 1895)	VI	Mills, Hiram Francis	VII
Miller, John Franklin	VI	Mills, Lawrence Heyworth	VII
Miller, John Henry	VI	Mills, Ogden Livingston	2
Miller, John Peter	VI	Mills, Robert (d. 1855)	VII
Miller, Jonathan Peckham	VI	Mills, Robert (d. 1888)	VII
Miller, Kelly	2	Mills, Roger Quarles	VII
Miller, Kempster Blanchard	1	Mills, Samuel John	VII
Miller, Kenneth Hayes	5	Mills, Susan Lincoln Tolman	VII
Miller, Leslie William	VI	Millspaugh, Charles Frederick	VII
Miller, Lewis	VI	Milner, John Turner	VII
Miller, Nathan Lewis	5	Milner, Moses Embree	
Miller, Oliver	VI	See California Joe	
Miller, Olive Thorne		Milner, Thomas Picton	
See Miller, Harriet Mann		See Picton, Thomas	
Miller, Perry Gilbert Eddy	7	Milroy, Robert Huston	VII
Miller, Peter		Milton, George Fort	5
See Miller, John Peter		Milton, John	VII
Miller, Samuel (d. 1850)	VI	Miner, Alonzo Ames	VII
Miller, Samuel (d. 1901)	VI	Miner, Charles	VII
Miller, Samuel Freeman	VI	Miner, Myrtilla	VII
Miller, Stephen Decatur	VI	Ming, John Joseph	VII
Miller, Warner	VI	Minnigerode, Lucy	1
Miller, Webb	2	Minor, Benjamin Blake	VII
Miller, William	VI	Minor, John Barbee	VII
Miller, William Henry Harrison	VI	Minor, Lucian	VII
Miller, William Snow	2	Minor, Raleigh Colston	VII
Miller, Willoughby Dayton	VI	Minor, Robert	5
Millet, Francis Davis	VI	Minor, Robert Crannell	VII
Milligan, Robert	VI	Minor, Virginia Louisa	VII
Milligan, Robert Wiley	VI	Minot, Charles Sedgwick	VII
Millikan, Robert Andrews	5	Minot, George Richards	
Millikin, Eugene Donald	6	(d. 1802)	VII
Millington, John	VI	Minot, George Richards	
Millis, Harry Alvin	4	(d. 1950)	4
Millmore, Martin	VII	Minto, Walter	VII
Mills, Anson	VII	Minton, Sherman	7
Mills, Benjamin	VII	Minturn, Robert Bowne	VII

131

Complete Index Guide

Name	Vol./Supp.	Name	Vol./Supp.
Minty, Robert Horatio George	VII	Mitchell, William (b. 1798)	VII
Minuit, Peter	VII	Mitchell, William (b. 1801)	VII
Miranda, Carmen	5	Mitchell, William (b. 1832)	VII
Miró, Esteban Rodríguez	VII	Mitchell, William (b. 1879)	2
Mitchel, John	VII	Mitchell, William DeWitt	5
Mitchel, John Purroy	VII	Mitchill, Samuel Latham	VII
Mitchel, Ormsby MacKnight	VII	Mitropoulos, Dimitri	6
Mitchell, Albert Graeme	3	Mitscher, Marc Andrew	4
Mitchell, Alexander	VII	Mitten, Thomas Eugene	VII
Mitchell, David Brydie	VII	Mix, Tom	2
Mitchell, David Dawson	VII	Mixter, Samuel Jason	VII
Mitchell, Donald Grant	VII	Mizner, Addison	1
Mitchell, Edward Cushing	VII	Modjeska, Helena	VII
Mitchell, Edward Page	VII	Modjeski, Ralph	2
Mitchell, Edwin Knox	1	Moeller, Henry	VII
Mitchell, Elisha	VII	Moffat, David Halliday	VII
Mitchell, George Edward	VII	Moffat, James Clement	VII
Mitchell, Henry	VII	Moffat, Jay Pierrepont	3
Mitchell, Hinckley Gilbert		Moffatt, James	3
Thomas	VII	Moffett, Cleveland Langston	VII
Mitchell, Isaac	VII	Moffett, William Adger	1
Mitchell, James Paul	7	Moholy-Nagy, László	4
Mitchell, James Tyndale	VII	Mohr, Charles Theodore	VII
Mitchell, John, d. 1768	VII	Moïse, Penina	VII
Mitchell, John, 1870–1919	VII	Moisseiff, Leon Solomon	3
Mitchell, John Ames	VII	Moldehnke, Edward Frederick	VII
Mitchell, John Hipple	VII	Moldenke, Richard George	
Mitchell, John Kearsley	VII	Gottlob	VII
Mitchell, Jonathan	VII	Mollenhauer, Emil	VII
Mitchell, Langdon Elwyn	1	Möllhausen, Heinrich Baldwin	VII
Mitchell, Lucy Myers Wright	VII	Molyneux, Robert	VII
Mitchell, Margaret Julia	VII	Mombert, Jacob Isidor	VII
Mitchell, Margaret Munnelyn	4	Monckton, Robert	VII
Mitchell, Maria	VII	Moncure, Richard Cassius Lee	VII
Mitchell, Nahum	VII	Mondell, Frank Wheeler	2
Mitchell, Nathaniel	VII	Monette, John Wesley	VII
Mitchell, Robert Byington	VII	Money, Hernando De Soto	VII
Mitchell, Samuel Augustus	VII	Monis, Judah	VII
Mitchell, Sidney Zollicoffer	3	Monroe, Harriet	2
Mitchell, Silas Weir	VII	Monroe, James	VII
Mitchell, Stephen Mix	VII	Monroe, Marilyn	7
Mitchell, Thomas Duché	VII	Monroe, Paul	4
Mitchell, Thomas Gregory	7	Monsky, Henry	4
Mitchell, Wesley Clair	4	Montague, Andrew Jackson	2
Mitchell, William (b. 1791)	VII	Montague, Gilbert Holland	7

Complete Index Guide

Name	Vol./Supp.	Name	Vol./Supp.
Montague, Henry James	VII	Moore, Ely	VII
Montague, William Pepperell	5	Moore, Frank	VII
Montefiore, Joshua	VII	Moore, Frederick Randolph	3
Monteux, Pierre Benjamin	7	Moore, Gabriel	VII
Montgomery, David Henry	VII	Moore, George Fleming	VII
Montgomery, Edmund Duncan	VII	Moore, George Foot	VII
Montgomery, George		Moore, George Henry	VII
Washington	VII	Moore, Grace	4
Montgomery, James	VII	Moore, Sir Henry	VII
Montgomery, James Alan	4	Moore, Henry Ludwell	6
Montgomery, John Berrien	VII	Moore, Jacob Bailey	VII
Montgomery, Richard	VII	Moore, James (d. 1706)	VII
Montgomery, Thomas Harrison	VII	Moore, James (d. 1777)	VII
Montgomery, William Bell	VII	Moore, James (d. 1814)	VII
Montrésor, James Gabriel	VII	Moore, James Edward	VII
Montrésor, John	VII	Moore, John (d. 1732)	VII
Mood, Francis Asbury	VII	Moore, John (d. 1901)	VII
Moody, (Arthur Edson) Blair	5	Moore, John Bassett	4
Moody, Dwight Lyman	VII	Moore, John Trotwood	VII
Moody, James	VII	Moore, John Weeks	VII
Moody, John	6	Moore, Joseph Earle	6
Moody, Paul	VII	Moore, Joseph Haines	4
Moody, William Henry	VII	Moore, Maurice	VII
Moody, William Vaughan	VII	Moore, Nathaniel Fish	VII
Moon, Parker Thomas	2	Moore, Nicholas	
Mooney, James	VII	See More, Nicholas	
Mooney, Thomas Joseph	3	Moore, Philip North	VII
Mooney, William	VII	Moore, Richard Bishop	VII
Moore, Addison Webster	VII	Moore, Richard Channing	VII
Moore, Alfred	VII	Moore, Samuel Preston	VII
Moore, Andrew	VII	Moore, Thomas Overton	VII
Moore, Anne Carroll	7	Moore, Thomas Patrick	VII
Moore, Annie Aubertine		Moore, Veranus Alva	VII
Woodward	VII	Moore, Victor Frederick	7
Moore, (Austin) Merrill	6	Moore, William (d. 1783)	VII
Moore, Bartholomew Figures	VII	Moore, William (d. 1793)	VII
Moore, Benjamin	VII	Moore, William Henry	VII
Moore, Charles	3	Moore, William Thomas	VII
Moore, Charles Herbert	VII	Moore, Zephaniah Swift	VII
Moore, Clarence Lemuel Elisha	VII	Moorehead, William Gallogly	VII
Moore, Clement Clarke	VII	Moorhead, James Kennedy	VII
Moore, Clifford Herschel	VII	Moosmüller, Oswald William	VII
Moore, Edward Mott	VII	Morais, Sabato	VII
Moore, Edwin Ward	VII	Moran, Benjamin	VII
Moore, Eliakim Hastings	1	Moran, Daniel Edward	2

Complete Index Guide

Name	Vol./Supp.	Name	Vol./Supp.
Moran, Edward	VII	Morgan, John Tyler	VII
Moran, Eugene Francis	7	Morgan, Julia	6
Moran, Peter	VII	Morgan, Junius Spencer	VII
Moran, Thomas	VII	Morgan, Justin	VII
Morawetz, Victor	2	Morgan, Lewis Henry	VII
Mordecai, Alfred	VII	Morgan, Matthew Somerville	VII
Mordecai, Moses Cohen	VII	Morgan, Morris Hicky	VII
More, Nicholas	VII	Morgan, Philip Hicky	VII
More, Paul Elmer	2	Morgan, Thomas Hunt	3
Moreau de Saint-Méry,		Morgan, Thomas Jefferson	VII
Médéric-Louis-Élie	VII	Morgan, William	VII
Moreau-Lislet, Louis Casimir		Morgenthau, Henry	4
Elisabeth	VII	Moriarity, Patrick Eugene	VII
Morehead, Charles Slaughter	VII	Morini, Austin John	VII
Morehead, James Turner	VII	Morison, George Shattuck	VII
Morehead, John Motley		Morley, Christopher Darlington	6
(d. 1866)	VII	Morley, Edward Williams	VII
Morehead, John Motley		Morley, Frank	2
(d. 1965)	7	Morley, Margaret Warner	VII
Morehouse, Henry Lyman	VII	Morley, Sylvanus Griswold	4
Morell, George Webb	VII	Morphy, Paul Charles	VII
Morey, Samuel	VII	Morrell, Benjamin	VII
Morfit, Campbell	VII	Morril, David Lawrence	VII
Morford, Henry	VII	Morrill, Anson Peaslee	VII
Morgan, Abel	VII	Morrill, Edmund Needham	VII
Morgan, Anne	5	Morrill, Justin Smith	VII
Morgan, Charles	VII	Morrill, Lot Myrick	VII
Morgan, Charles Hill	VII	Morris, Anthony (d. 1721)	VII
Morgan, Daniel	VII	Morris, Anthony (d. 1860)	VII
Morgan, Edwin Barber	VII	Morris, Cadwalader	VII
Morgan, Edwin Denison	VII	Morris, Caspar	VII
Morgan, Edwin Vernon	1	Morris, Charles	VII
Morgan, George	VII	Morris, Clara	VII
Morgan, George Washington	VII	Morris, Edmund	VII
Morgan, Helen	3	Morris, Edward Dafydd	VII
Morgan, James Dada	VII	Morris, Edward Joy	VII
Morgan, James Morris	VII	Morris, Elizabeth	VII
Morgan, John	VII	Morris, George Pope	VII
Morgan, John Harcourt		Morris, George Sylvester	VII
Alexander	4	Morris, Gouverneur	VII
Morgan, John Hunt	VII	Morris, John Gottlieb	VII
Morgan, John Pierpont		Morris, Lewis (d. 1746)	VII
(d. 1913)	VII	Morris, Lewis (d. 1798)	VII
Morgan, John Pierpont		Morris, Lewis Richard	VII
(d. 1943)	3	Morris, Luzon Burritt	VII

Complete Index Guide

Name	Vol./Supp.	Name	Vol./Supp.
Morris, Mary Philipse	VII	Morton, Henry	VII
Morris, Nelson	VII	Morton, James St. Clair	VII
Morris, Mrs. Owen		Morton, Jelly Roll	
See Morris, Elizabeth		See Morton, Ferdinand	
Morris, Richard	VII	Joseph	
Morris, Richard Valentine	VII	Morton, John	VII
Morris, Robert (d. 1806)	VII	Morton, Julius Sterling	VII
Morris, Robert (d. 1815)	VII	Morton, Levi Parsons	VII
Morris, Robert (d. 1888)	VII	Morton, Marcus (d. 1864)	VII
Morris, Robert Hunter	VII	Morton, Marcus (d. 1891)	VII
Morris, Roger	VII	Morton, Nathaniel	VII
Morris, Thomas	VII	Morton, Oliver Perry	VII
Morris, Thomas Armstrong	VII	Morton, Paul	VII
Morris, William Hopkins	VII	Morton, Samuel George	VII
Morrison, DeLesseps Story	7	Morton, Sarah Wentworth	
Morrison, Frank	4	Apthorp	VII
Morrison, John Irwin	VII	Morton, Thomas	VII
Morrison, Nathan Jackson	VII	Morton, William James	VII
Morrison, William	VII	Morton, William Thomas	
Morrison, William McCutchan	VII	Green	VII
Morrison, William Ralls	VII	Morwitz, Edward	VII
Morrissey, John	VII	Mosby, John Singleton	VII
Morrow, Dwight Whitney	VII	Moscoso De Alvarado, Luis de	VII
Morrow, Edwin Porch	1	Moseley, Edward Augustus	VII
Morrow, Jeremiah	VII	Moser, Christopher Otto	1
Morrow, Prince Albert	VII	Moses, Anna Mary Robertson	
Morrow, Thomas Vaughan	VII	("Grandma")	7
Morrow, William W.	VII	Moses, Bernard	VII
Morse, Anson Daniel	VII	Moses, Franklin J.	VII
Morse, Charles Wyman	VII	Moses, George Higgins	3
Morse, Edward Sylvester	VII	Moses, Montrose Jonas	1
Morse, Freeman Harlow	VII	Mosessohn, David Nehemiah	VII
Morse, Harmon Northrop	VII	Mosher, Eliza Maria	VII
Morse, Henry Dutton	VII	Mosher, Thomas Bird	VII
Morse, Jedidiah	VII	Moskowitz, Belle Lindner	
Morse, John Lovett	2	Israels	1
Morse, John Torrey	2	Mosler, Henry	VII
Morse, Samuel Finley Breese	VII	Moss, Frank	VII
Morse, Sidney Edwards	VII	Moss, John Calvin	VII
Mortimer, Mary	VII	Moss, Lemuel	VII
Morton, Charles	VII	Moss, Sanford Alexander	4
Morton, Charles Gould	1	Most, Johann Joseph	VII
Morton, Ferdinand Joseph	3	Motley, John Lothrop	VII
Morton, Ferdinand Quintin	4	Motley, Willard Francis	7
Morton, George	VII	Moton, Robert Russa	2

Complete Index Guide

Name	Vol./Supp.	Name	Vol./Supp.
Mott, Frank Luther	7	Muldoon, William	1
Mott, Gershom	VII	Mulford, Clarence Edward	6
Mott, James	VII	Mulford, Elisha	VII
Mott, John R.	5	Mulford, Prentice	VII
Mott, Lucretia Coffin	VII	Mulholland, St. Clair Augustin	VII
Mott, Valentine	VII	Mulholland, William	1
Moulton, Ellen Louise		Mullan, John	VII
Chandler	VII	Mullany, James Robert	
Moulton, Forest Ray	5	Madison	VII
Moulton, Richard Green	VII	Mullany, Patrick Francis	
Moultrie, John	VII	See Azarias, Brother	
Moultrie, William	VII	Müller, Wilhelm Max	VII
Mount, William Sidney	VII	Mulligan, Charles J.	VII
Mourt, George		Mulliken, Samuel Parsons	1
See Morton, George		Mullins, Edgar Young	VII
Mouton, Alexander	VII	Mulry, Thomas Maurice	VII
Mowatt, Anna Cora Ogden	VII	Mumford, James Gregory	VII
Mowbray, George Mordey	VII	Mundé, Paul Fortunatus	VII
Mowbray, Henry Siddons	VII	Mundelein, George William	2
Mower, Joseph Anthony	VII	Munford, Robert	VII
Mowry, William Augustus	VII	Munford, William	VII
Moxham, Arthur James	VII	Munger, Robert Sylvester	VII
Moxom, Philip Stafford	VII	Munger, Theodore Thornton	VII
Moylan, Stephen	VII	Munn, Orson Desaix	VII
Mozier, Joseph	VII	Muñoz-Rivera, Luis	VII
Mudd, Samuel A.		Munro, Dana Carleton	VII
See Booth, John Wilkes		Munro, George	VII
Mudge, Enoch	VII	Munro, Henry	VII
Mudge, James	VII	Munro, William Bennett	6
Muhlenberg, Frederick		Munroe, Charles Edward	2
Augustus	VII	Munsell, Joel	VII
Muhlenberg, Frederick		Munsey, Frank Andrew	VII
Augustus Conrad	VII	Munson, Thomas Volney	VII
Mühlenberg, Gotthilf Henry		Munson, Walter David	VII
Ernest	VII	Münsterberg, Hugo	VII
Muhlenberg, Henry Augustus		Murat, Achille	VII
Philip	VII	Murdoch, Frank Hitchcock	VII
Mühlenberg, Henry Melchior	VII	Murdock, James	VII
Muhlenberg, John Peter		Murdock, James Edward	VII
Gabriel	VII	Murdock, Joseph Ballard	VII
Muhlenberg, William		Murdock, Victor	3
Augustus	VII	Murel, John A.	
Muir, Charles Henry	1	See Murrell, John A.	
Muir, John	VII	Murfee, James Thomas	VII

Complete Index Guide

Name	Vol./Supp.	Name	Vol./Supp.
Murfree, Mary Noailles	VII	Murrieta, Joaquin	VII
Murietta (Murieta), Joaquin		Murrow, Edward (Egbert)	
See Murrieta, Joaquin		Roscoe	7
Murphey, Archibald De Bow	VII	Murrow, Joseph Samuel	VII
Murphy, Charles Francis	VII	Musica, Philip Mariano Fausto	2
Murphy, Dominic Ignatius	VII	Musin, Ovide	VII
Murphy, Edgar Gardner	VII	Mussey, Ellen Spencer	2
Murphy, Francis	VII	Mussey, Reuben Dimond	VII
Murphy, Frank	4	Muybridge, Eadweard	VII
Murphy, Franklin	VII	Muzzey, David Saville	7
Murphy, Frederick E.	2	Myer, Albert James	VII
Murphy, Gerald Clery	7	Myers, Abraham Charles	VII
Murphy, Henry Cruse	VII	Myers, Gustavus	3
Murphy, Isaac	VII	Myers, Jerome	2
Murphy, James Bumgardner	4	Myerson, Abraham	4
Murphy, John	VII	Myles, John	VII
Murphy, John Benjamin	VII	Myrick, Herbert	VII
Murphy, John Francis	VII		
Murphy, John W.	VII	Nack, James M.	VII
Murphy, Michael Charles	VII	Nadal, Ehrman Syme	VII
Murphy, William Sumter	VII	Nadelman, Elie	4
Murphy, William Walton	VII	Nairne, Thomas	VII
Murray, Alexander	VII	Naismith, James	2
Murray, David	VII	Nancrède, Charles Beylard	
Murray, James Edward	7	Guérard de	VII
Murray, James Ormsbee	VII	Nancrède, Paul Joseph Guérard	
Murray, John (d. 1808)	VII	de	VII
Murray, John (d. 1815)	VII	Nanuntenoo	
Murray, John Gardner	VII	See Canonchet	
Murray, Joseph	VII	Napton, William Barclay	VII
Murray, Judith Sargent Stevens	VII	Narváez, Pánfilo de	VII
Murray, Lindley	VII	Nasby, Petroleum V.	
Murray, Louise Shipman		See Locke, David Ross	
Welles	VII	Nash, Abner	VII
Murray, Mae	7	Nash, Arthur	VII
Murray, Philip	5	Nash, Charles Sumner	VII
Murray, Robert	VII	Nash, Charles Williams	4
Murray, Thomas Edward		Nash, Daniel	VII
(d. 1929)	VII	Nash, Francis	VII
Murray, Thomas Edward		Nash, Frederick	VII
(d. 1961)	7	Nash, Henry Sylvester	VII
Murray, William Henry David	6	Nash, John Henry	4
Murray, William Vans	VII	Nash, Simeon	VII
Murrell, John A.	VII	Nason, Elias	VII

Complete Index Guide

Name	Vol./Supp.	Name	Vol./Supp.
Nason, Henry Bradford	VII	Nelson, Marjorie Maxine	7
Nassau, Robert Hamill	VII	Nelson, Nels Christian	7
Nast, Condé Montrose	3	Nelson, Nelson Olsen	VII
Nast, Thomas	VII	Nelson, Rensselaer Russell	VII
Nast, William	VII	Nelson, Reuben	VII
Nathan, George Jean	6	Nelson, Roger	VII
Nathan, Maud	4	Nelson, Samuel	VII
Nation, Carry Amelia Moore	VII	Nelson, Thomas	VII
Navarre, Pierre	VII	Nelson, Thomas Henry	VII
Nazimova, Alla	3	Nelson, William (d. 1772)	VII
Neagle, John	VII	Nelson, William (d. 1862)	VII
Neal, Alice Bradley		Nelson, William (d. 1914)	VII
See Haven, Emily Bradley		Nelson, William Rockhill	VII
Neal		Nerinckx, Charles	VII
Neal, David Dalhoff	VII	Nesbitt, John Maxwell	VII
Neal, John	VII	Nesmith, James Willis	VII
Neal, Joseph Clay	VII	Nesmith, John	VII
Neal, Josephine Bicknell	5	Nessler, Karl Ludwig	5
Neale, Leonard	VII	Nestle, Charles	
Needham, James	VII	See Nessler, Karl Ludwig	
Neef, Francis Joseph Nicholas	VII	Nestor, Agnes	4
Neely, Matthew Mansfield	6	Nettleton, Alvred Bayard	VII
Neely, Thomas Benjamin	VII	Nettleton, Asahel	VII
Nef, John Ulric	VII	Nettleton, Edwin S.	VII
Negley, James Scott	VII	Neuberger, Richard Lewis	6
Nehrling, Henry	VII	Neuendorff, Adolph Heinrich	
Neidhard, Charles	VII	Anton Magnus	VII
Neighbors, Robert Simpson	VII	Neumann, Franz Leopold	5
Neill, Edward Duffield	VII	Neumann, John Nepomucene	VII
Neill, John	VII	Neumann, John von	
Neill, Thomas Hewson	VII	See Von Neumann, John	
Neill, William	VII	Neumark, David	VII
Neilson, John	VII	Nevada, Emma	2
Neilson, William Allan	4	Neville, John	VII
Neilson, William George	VII	Neville, Wendell Cushing	VII
Nell, William Cooper	VII	Nevin, Alfred	VII
Nelson, Charles Alexander	VII	Nevin, Edwin Henry	VII
Nelson, David	VII	Nevin, Ethelbert Woodbridge	VII
Nelson, Donald Marr	6	Nevin, George Balch	VII
Nelson, Edward William	1	Nevin, John Williamson	VII
Nelson, Henry Loomis	VII	Nevin, Robert Peebles	VII
Nelson, Hugh	VII	Nevius, John Livingston	VII
Nelson, John	VII	New, Harry Stewart	2
Nelson, Julius	VII	Newberry, John Stoughton	VII
Nelson, Knute	VII	Newberry, John Strong	VII

Complete Index Guide

Name	Vol./Supp.	Name	Vol./Supp.
Newberry, Oliver	VII	Neyland, Robert Reese, Jr.	7
Newberry, Truman Handy	3	Ng Poon Chew	VII
Newberry, Walter Loomis	VII	Niblack, Albert Parker	VII
Newbold, William Romaine	VII	Niblack, William Ellis	VII
Newbrough, John Ballou	VII	Niblo, William	VII
Newcomb, Charles Leonard	VII	Nicholas, George	VII
Newcomb, Harvey	VII	Nicholas, John	VII
Newcomb, Josephine Louise		Nicholas, Philip Norborne	VII
LeMonnier	VII	Nicholas, Robert Carter	VII
Newcomb, Simon	VII	Nicholas, Wilson Cary	VII
Newcomer, Christian	VII	Nicholls, Francis Redding	
Newel, Stanford	VII	Tillou	VII
Newell, Edward Theodore	3	Nicholls, Rhoda Holmes	VII
Newell, Frederick Haynes	VII	Nichols, Charles Henry	VII
Newell, Peter Sheaf Hersey	VII	Nichols, Charles Lemuel	VII
Newell, Robert	VII	Nichols, Clarina Irene Howard	VII
Newell, Robert Henry	VII	Nichols, Dudley	6
Newell, William Augustus	VII	Nichols, Edward Leamington	2
Newell, William Wells	VII	Nichols, Ernest Fox	VII
Newhouse, Samuel	VII	Nichols, George Ward	VII
Newlands, Francis Griffith	VII	Nichols, James Robinson	VII
Newlon, Jesse Homer	3	Nichols, Mary Sargeant Neal	
Newman, Albert Henry	1	Gove	VII
Newman, Henry	VII	Nichols, Ruth Rowland	6
Newman, Henry Roderick	VII	Nichols, Thomas Low	VII
Newman, John Philip	VII	Nichols, William Ford	VII
Newman, Robert Loftin	VII	Nicholson, Alfred Osborne	
Newman, Samuel Phillips	VII	Pope	VII
Newman, William H.	1	Nicholson, Eliza Jane Poitevent	
Newman, William Truslow	VII	Holbrook	VII
Newport, Christopher	VII	Nicholson, Francis	VII
Newsam, Albert	VII	Nicholson, James	VII
Newton, Henry Jotham	VII	Nicholson, James Bartram	VII
Newton, Hubert Anson	VII	Nicholson, James William	
Newton, Isaac (d. 1858)	VII	Augustus	VII
Newton, Isaac (d. 1867)	VII	Nicholson, John	VII
Newton, John	VII	Nicholson, Joseph Hopper	VII
Newton, Joseph Fort	4	Nicholson, Meredith	4
Newton, Richard	VII	Nicholson, Samuel	VII
Newton, Richard Heber	VII	Nicholson, Samuel Danford	VII
Newton, Robert Safford	VII	Nicholson, Seth Barnes	7
Newton, Thomas (d. 1721)	VII	Nicholson, Timothy	VII
Newton, Thomas (d. 1847)	VII	Nicholson, William Jones	VII
Newton, William Wilberforce	VII	Nicholson, William Thomas	VII
Ney, Elisabet	VII	Nicola, Lewis	VII

Complete Index Guide

Name	Vol./Supp.	Name	Vol./Supp.
Nicolay, John George	VII	Noble, James	VII
Nicolet, Jean	VII	Noble, John Willock	VII
Nicoll		Noble, Samuel	VII
See also Nicolls		Nock, Albert Jay	3
Nicoll, De Lancey	VII	Noeggerath, Emil Oscar Jacob	
Nicoll, James Craig	VII	Bruno	VII
Nicollet, Joseph Nicolas	VII	Noguchi, Hideyo	VII
Nicolls, Matthias	VII	Nolan, Philip	VII
Nicolls, Richard	VII	Nolen, John	2
Nicolls, William	VII	Noll, John Francis	6
Niebuhr, Helmut Richard	7	Noonan, James Patrick	VII
Niedringhaus, Frederick		Norbeck, Peter	2
Gottlieb	VII	Norcross, Orlando Whitney	VII
Niehaus, Charles Henry	1	Nordberg, Bruno Victor	VII
Nielsen, Alice	3	Norden, Carl Lukas	7
Nieman, Lucius William	1	Nordheimer, Isaac	VII
Niemeyer, John Henry	VII	Nordhoff, Charles	VII
Nies, James Buchanan	VII	Nordhoff, Charles B.	
Nies, Konrad	VII	See under Hall, James	
Nieuwland, Julius Arthur	2	Norman	
Niles, David K.	5	Nordica, Lillian	VII
Niles, Hezekiah	VII	Norelius, Eric	VII
Niles, John Milton	VII	Norman, John	VII
Niles, Nathaniel (d. 1828)	VII	Norris, Benjamin Franklin	VII
Niles, Nathaniel (d. 1869)	VII	Norris, Charles Gilman Smith	3
Niles, Samuel	VII	Norris, Edward	VII
Nipher, Francis Eugene	VII	Norris, Frank	
Nisbet, Charles	VII	See Norris, Benjamin	
Nisbet, Eugenius Aristides	VII	Franklin	
Nitchie, Edward Bartlett	VII	Norris, George Washington	VII
Nitschmann, David	VII	Norris, George William	3
Nixon, John (b. 1727)	VII	Norris, Isaac (d. 1735)	VII
Nixon, John (b. 1733)	VII	Norris, Isaac (d. 1766)	VII
Nixon, John Thompson	VII	Norris, James Flack	2
Nixon, William Penn	VII	Norris, John Franklin	5
Niza, Marcos de	VII	Norris, Mary Harriott	VII
Nizza, Marcos de		Norris, William	VII
See Niza, Marcos de		Norris, William Fisher	VII
Noah, Mordecai Manuel	VII	Norsworthy, Naomi	VII
Noailles, Louis Marie, Vicomte		North, Edward	VII
de	VII	North, Elisha	VII
Nobili, John	VII	North, Frank Joshua	VII
Noble, Alfred	VII	North, Frank Mason	1
Noble, Frederick Alphonso	VII	North, Simeon (d. 1852)	VII
Noble, Gladwyn Kingsley	2	North, Simeon (d. 1884)	VII

Complete Index Guide

Name	Vol./Supp.	Name	Vol./Supp.
North, Simon Newton Dexter	VII	Noyes, La Verne	VII
North, William	VII	Noyes, Walter Chadwick	VII
Northen, William Jonathan	VII	Noyes, William Albert	3
Northend, Charles	VII	Noyes, William Curtis	VII
Northrop, Birdsey Grant	VII	Nugent, John Frost	VII
Northrop, Cyrus	VII	Núñez, Cabeza de Vaca, Alvar	VII
Northrop, Lucius Bellinger	VII	Nunó, Jaime	VII
Norton, Alice Peloubet		Nurse, Rebecca	VII
See Norton, Mary Alice		Nuthead, William	VII
Peloubet		Nuttall, Thomas	VII
Norton, Andrews	VII	Nutting, Charles Cleveland	VII
Norton, Charles Eliot	VII	Nutting, Mary Adelaide	4
Norton, Charles Hotchkiss	3	Nutting, Wallace	3
Norton, Elijah Hise	VII	Nye, Edgar Wilson	VII
Norton, John	VII	Nye, James Warren	VII
Norton, John Nicholas	VII		
Norton, John Pitkin	VII	Oakes, George Washington	
Norton, Mary Alice Peloubet	VII	Ochs	VII
Norton, Mary Teresa Hopkins	6	Oakes, Thomas Fletcher	VII
Norton, William Edward	VII	Oakes, Urian	VII
Norton, William Warder	3	Oakley, Annie	VII
Norwood, Robert Winkworth	VII	Oakley, Thomas Jackson	VII
Noss, Theodore Bland	VII	Oates, William Calvin	VII
Nott, Abraham	VII	Oatman, Johnson	VII
Nott, Charles Cooper	VII	Ober, Frederick Albion	VII
Nott, Eliphalet	VII	Oberhoffer, Emil Johann	1
Nott, Henry Junius	VII	Oberholser, Harry Church	7
Nott, Josiah Clark	VII	Oberholtzer, Ellis Paxson	2
Nott, Samuel	VII	Oberholtzer, Sara Louisa	
Notz, Frederick William		Vickers	VII
Augustus	VII	Oberndorf, Clarence Paul	5
Novy, Frederick George	6	O'Brien, Edward Charles	VII
Noyan, Gilles-Augustin Payen		O'Brien, Fitz-James	VII
de	VII	O'Brien, Frederick	VII
Noyan, Pierre-Jacques Payen de	VII	O'Brien, Jeremiah	VII
Noyes, Alexander Dana	3	O'Brien, Matthew Anthony	VII
Noyes, Arthur Amos	2	O'Brien, Morgan Joseph	2
Noyes, Clara Dutton	2	O'Brien, Richard	VII
Noyes, Crosby Stuart	VII	O'Brien, Robert Lincoln	5
Noyes, Edward Follansbee	VII	O'Brien, Thomas James	1
Noyes, Frank Brett	4	O'Brien, William Shoney	VII
Noyes, George Rapall	VII	O'Brien, Willis Harold	7
Noyes, Henry Drury	VII	O'Callaghan, Edmund Bailey	VII
Noyes, John Humphrey	VII	O'Callaghan, Jeremiah	VII

Complete Index Guide

Name	Vol./Supp.	Name	Vol./Supp.
O'Callahan, Joseph Timothy	7	Ogden, Peter Skene	VII
Occidente, Maria del		Ogden, Robert Curtis	VII
See Brooks, Maria Gowen		Ogden, Rollo	2
Occom, Samson	VII	Ogden, Samuel	VII
Occonostota		Ogden, Thomas Ludlow	VII
See Oconostota		Ogden, Uzal	VII
Ochs, Adolph Simon	1	Ogden, William Butler	VII
Ochs, Julius	VII	Ogg, Frederick Austin	5
Ochsner, Albert John	VII	Ogilvie, James	VII
Ockerson, John Augustus	VII	Ogilvie, John	VII
O'Connell, William Henry	3	Ogle, Samuel	VII
O'Connor, James	VII	Oglesby, Richard James	VII
O'Connor, Mary Flannery	7	Oglethorpe, James Edward	VII
O'Connor, Michael	VII	O'Gorman, Thomas	VII
O'Connor, William Douglas	VII	O'Hara, James	VII
O'Conor, Charles	VII	O'Hara, Theodore	VII
Oconostota	VII	O'Hare, Kate Richards	
Odell, Benjamin Barker	VII	(Cunningham)	4
Odell, George Clinton		O'Higgins, Harvey Jerrold	VII
Densmore	4	Ohlmacher, Albert Philip	VII
Odell, Jonathan	VII	O'Kelly, James	VII
Odenbach, Frederick Louis	1	Okey, John Waterman	VII
Odenheimer, William Henry	VII	O'Laughlin, Michael	
Odets, Clifford	7	See Booth, John Wilkes	
Odin, John Mary	VII	Olcott, Chancellor John	
O'Donnell, Thomas Jefferson	VII	See Olcott, Chauncey	
O'Donovan, William Rudolf	VII	Olcott, Chauncey	VII
Odum, Howard Washington	5	Olcott, Eben Erskine	VII
O'Dwyer, Joseph	VII	Olcott, Henry Steel	VII
O'Dwyer, William	7	Olden, Charles Smith	VII
Oehmler, Leo Carl Martin	VII	Older, Fremont	1
Oemler, Arminius	VII	Oldfather, William Abbott	3
Oertel, Johannes Adam Simon	VII	Oldfield, Barney	4
O'Fallon, Benjamin	VII	Oldham, John	VII
O'Fallon, James	VII	Oldham, William Fitzjames	2
O'Fallon, John	VII	Oldham, Williamson Simpson	VII
O'Ferrall, Charles Triplett	VII	Olds, Irving S.	7
Offley, David	VII	Olds, Leland	6
Oftedal, Sven	VII	Olds, Ransom	4
Ogburn, William Fielding	6	Olds, Robert Edwin	1
Ogden, Aaron	VII	Oldschool, Oliver	
Ogden, David	VII	See Sargent, Nathan	
Ogden, David Bayard	VII	O'Leary, Daniel	1
Ogden, Francis Barber	VII	Olin, Stephen	VII
Ogden, Herbert Gouverneur	VII	Oliphant, Herman	2

Complete Index Guide

Name	Vol./Supp.	Name	Vol./Supp.
Oliver, Andrew (d. 1774)	VII	O'Neill, Eugene	5
Oliver, Andrew (d. 1799)	VII	O'Neill, James	VII
Oliver, Charles Augustus	VII	O'Neill, John	VII
Oliver, Fitch Edward	VII	O'Neill, Margaret L.	
Oliver, George Tener	VII	See O'Neale, Margaret L.	
Oliver, Henry Kemble	VII	O'Neill, Rose Cecil	3
Oliver, Henry William	VII	Opdyke, George	VII
Oliver, James	VII	Oppenheim, James	VII
Oliver, Joseph	2	Opper, Frederick Burr	2
Oliver, King		Optic, Oliver	
See Oliver, Joseph		See Adams, William	
Oliver, Paul Ambrose	VII	Taylor	
Oliver, Peter	VII	Orcutt, Hiram	VII
Olmstead, Albert Ten Eyck	3	Ord, Edward Otho Cresap	VII
Olmstead, Gideon		Ord, George	VII
See Olmsted, Gideon		Ordronaux, John	VII
Olmsted, Denison	VII	Ordway, John	VII
Olmsted, Frederick Law		O'Reilly, Alexander	VII
(d. 1903)	VII	O'Reilly, Henry	VII
Olmsted, Frederick Law		O'Reilly, John Boyle	VII
(d. 1957)	6	O'Reilly, Robert Maitland	VII
Olmsted, Gideon	VII	O'Rielly, Henry	
Olmsted, John Charles	VII	See O'Reilly, Henry	
Olmsted, Marlin Edgar	VII	Ormsby, Waterman Lilly	VII
Olney, Jesse	VII	Orne, John	VII
Olney, Richard	VII	Orr, Alexander Ector	VII
Olsen, John Sigvard ("Ole"),		Orr, Gustavus John	VII
and Johnson, Harold		Orr, Hugh	VII
Ogden ("Chic")	7	Orr, James Lawrence	VII
Olson, Floyd Bjerstjerne	2	Orr, Jehu Amaziah	VII
Olyphant, David Washington		Orry-Kelly	7
Cincinnatus	VII	Orth, Godlove Stein	VII
Olyphant, Robert Morrison	VII	Orthwein, Charles F.	VII
O'Mahoney, Joseph		Orton, Edward Francis Baxter	VII
Christopher	7	Orton, Harlow South	VII
O'Mahony, John	VII	Orton, Helen Fuller	5
O'Malley, Frank Ward	VII	Orton, James	VII
Oñate, Juan de	VII	Orton, William	VII
Onderdonk, Benjamin Tredwell	VII	Ortynsky, Stephen Soter	VII
Onderdonk, Henry	VII	Osborn, Charles	VII
Onderdonk, Henry Ustick	VII	Osborn, Chase Salmon	4
O'Neal, Edward Asbury	VII	Osborn, Henry Fairfield	1
O'Neal, Edward Asbury, III	6	Osborn, Henry Stafford	VII
O'Neale, Margaret L.	VII	Osborn, Laughton	VII
O'Neall, John Belton	VII	Osborn, Norris Galpin	VII

Complete Index Guide

Name	Vol./Supp.	Name	Vol./Supp.
Osborn, Selleck	VII	Otis, Fessenden Nott	VII
Osborn, Thomas Andrew	VII	Otis, George Alexander	VII
Osborn, Thomas Ogden	VII	Otis, Harrison Gray (d. 1848)	VII
Osborn, William Henry	VII	Otis, Harrison Gray (d. 1917)	VII
Osborne, James Walker	VII	Otis, James	VII
Osborne, Thomas Burr	VII	Ott, Isaac	VII
Osborne, Thomas Mott	VII	Ott, Melvin Thomas ("Mel")	6
Osceola	VII	Ottassite	
Osgood, Frances Sargent Locke	VII	See Outacity	
Osgood, George Laurie	VII	Ottendorfer, Anna Behr Uhl	VII
Osgood, Herbert Levi	VII	Ottendorfer, Oswald	VII
Osgood, Howard	VII	Otterbein, Philip William	VII
Osgood, Jacob	VII	Ottley, Roi	6
Osgood, Samuel	VII	Otto, Bodo	VII
Osgood, William Fogg	3	Otto, John Conrad	VII
O'Shaughnessy, Michael		Otto, William Tod	VII
Maurice	1	Ouconnastote	
O'Shaughnessy, Nelson Jarvis		See Oconostota	
Waterbury	1	Ouray	VII
O'Shea, Michael Vincent	VII	Oursler, (Charles) Fulton	5
Osler, William	VII	Outacity	VII
Ossoli, Margaret Fuller		Outcault, Richard Felton	VII
See Fuller, Sarah Margaret		Outerbridge, Alexander Ewing	VII
Ostenaco		Outerbridge, Eugenius Harvey	1
See Outacity		Overman, Frederick	VII
Osten Sacken, Carl Robert		Overman, Lee Slater	VII
Romanovich von der	VII	Overton, John	VII
Osterhaus, Peter Joseph	VII	Owen, David Dale	VII
Osterhout, Winthrop John		Owen, Edward Thomas	VII
Vanleuven	7	Owen, Griffith	VII
Ostromislensky, Iwan		Owen, Robert Dale	VII
Iwanowich	2	Owen, Robert L.	4
O'Sullivan, John Louis	VII	Owen, Stephen Joseph	7
O'Sullivan, Mary Kenney	3	Owen, Thomas McAdory	1
Oswald, Lee Harvey	7	Owen, William Florence	VII
Otacite		Owens, John Edmond	VII
See Outacity		Owens, Michael Joseph	VII
Otermín, Antonio de	VII	Owre, Alfred	1
Otey, James Hervey	VII	Owsley, Frank Lawrence	6
Otis, Arthur Sinton	7	Owsley, William	VII
Otis, Bass	VII	Oxnam, Garfield Bromley	7
Otis, Charles Eugene	VII		
Otis, Charles Rollin	VII	Paca, William	VII
Otis, Elisha Graves	VII	Pace, Edward Aloysius	2
Otis, Elwell Stephen	VII	Pacheco, Romualdo	VII

Complete Index Guide

Name	Vol./Supp.	Name	Vol./Supp.
Pack, Charles Lathrop	2	Painter, William	VII
Packard, Alpheus Spring		Paley, John	VII
(d. 1884)	VII	Palfrey, John Carver	VII
Packard, Alpheus Spring		Palfrey, John Gorham	VII
(d. 1905)	VII	Palladino, Lawrence Benedict	VII
Packard, Frederick Adolphus	VII	Pallen, Condé Benoist	VII
Packard, James Ward	VII	Palmer, Albert Marshman	VII
Packard, John Hooker	VII	Palmer, Alexander Mitchell	2
Packard, Joseph	VII	Palmer, Alice Elvira Freeman	VII
Packard, Silas Sadler	VII	Palmer, Alonzo Benjamin	VII
Packer, Asa	VII	Palmer, Benjamin Morgan	VII
Packer, William Fisher	VII	Palmer, Bertha Honoré	VII
Paddock, Algernon Sidney	VII	Palmer, Daniel David	VII
Paddock, Benjamin Henry	VII	Palmer, Elihu	VII
Paddock, John Adams	VII	Palmer, Erastus Dow	VII
Padilla, Juan de	VII	Palmer, George Herbert	VII
Page, Charles Grafton	VII	Palmer, Henry Wilbur	VII
Page, David Perkins	VII	Palmer, Horatio Richmond	VII
Page, John	VII	Palmer, Innis Newton	VII
Page, Leigh	5	Palmer, James Croxall	VII
Page, Mann	VII	Palmer, James Shedden	VII
Page, Oran Thaddeus	5	Palmer, Joel	VII
Page, Richard Lucian	VII	Palmer, John McAuley	
Page, Thomas Jefferson	VII	(d. 1900)	VII
Page, Thomas Nelson	VII	Palmer, John McAuley	
Page, Thomas Walker	2	(d. 1955)	5
Page, Walter Hines	VII	Palmer, John Williamson	VII
Page, William	VII	Palmer, Joseph	VII
Paine, Albert Bigelow	2	Palmer, Nathaniel Brown	VII
Paine, Byron	VII	Palmer, Potter	VII
Paine, Charles	VII	Palmer, Mrs. Potter	
Paine, Charles Jackson	VII	See Palmer, Bertha	
Paine, Elijah	VII	Honoré	
Paine, Halbert Eleazer	VII	Palmer, Ray	VII
Paine, Henry Warren	VII	Palmer, Thomas Witherell	VII
Paine, John Alsop	VII	Palmer, Walter Launt	VII
Paine, John Knowles	VII	Palmer, Walter Walker	4
Paine, Martyn	VII	Palmer, William Adams	VII
Paine, Ralph Delahaye	VII	Palmer, William Henry	VII
Paine, Robert	VII	Palmer, William Jackson	VII
Paine, Robert Treat (b. 1731)	VII	Palmore, William Beverly	VII
Paine, Robert Treat (b. 1773)	VII	Palóu, Francisco	VII
Paine, Robert Treat (b. 1835)	VII	Pammel, Louis Hermann	VII
Paine, Thomas	VII	Pancoast, Henry Khunrath	2
Painter, Gamaliel	VII	Pancoast, Joseph	VII

Complete Index Guide

Name	Vol./Supp.	Name	Vol./Supp.
Pancoast, Seth	VII	Parker, Jane Marsh	VII
Pangborn, Clyde Edward	6	Parker, Joel (*b. 1795*)	VII
Pansy		Parker, Joel (*b. 1799*)	VII
See Alden, Isabella		Parker, Joel (*b. 1816*)	VII
Macdonald		Parker, John	VII
Panton, William	VII	Parker, John Cortlandt	VII
Papanicolaou, George Nicholas	7	Parker, John Johnston	6
Pardee, Ario	VII	Parker, John Milliken	2
Pardee, Don Albert	VII	Parker, Josiah	VII
Pardow, William O'Brien	VII	Parker, Peter	VII
Paris, Walter	VII	Parker, Quanah	
Parish, Elijah	VII	See Quanah	
Park, Edwards Amasa	VII	Parker, Richard Elliot	VII
Park, James	VII	Parker, Richard Green	VII
Park, Maud Wood	5	Parker, Samuel	VII
Park, Robert Ezra	3	Parker, Samuel Chester	VII
Park, Roswell (*d. 1869*)	VII	Parker, Theodore	VII
Park, Roswell (*d. 1914*)	VII	Parker, Theodore Bissell	3
Park, Trenor William	VII	Parker, Thomas	VII
Park, William Hallock	2	Parker, Willard	VII
Parke, Benjamin	VII	Parker, William Harwar	VII
Parke, John	VII	Parkhurst, Charles	VII
Parke, John Grubb	VII	Parkhurst, Charles Henry	VII
Parker, Alton Brooks	VII	Parkhurst, John Adelbert	VII
Parker, Alvin Pierson	VII	Parkinson, Thomas Ignatius	6
Parker, Amasa Junius	VII	Parkman, Francis	VII
Parker, Arthur Caswell	5	Parks, William	VII
Parker, Carleton Hubbell	VII	Parley, Peter	
Parker, Charlie ("Bird")	5	See Goodrich, Samuel	
Parker, Cortlandt		Griswold	
See Parker, John Cortlandt		Parmentier, Andrew	1
Parker, Edwin Brewington	VII	Parmly, Eleazar	VII
Parker, Edwin Pond	VII	Parr, Samuel Wilson	VII
Parker, Edwin Wallace	VII	Parrington, Vernon Louis	VII
Parker, Ely Samuel	VII	Parris, Albion Keith	VII
Parker, Foxhall Alexander	VII	Parris, Alexander	VII
Parker, Francis Wayland	VII	Parris, Samuel	VII
Parker, George Howard	5	Parrish, Anne	VII
Parker, Henry Taylor	1	Parrish, Celestia Susannah	VII
Parker, Horatio William	VII	Parrish, Charles	VII
Parker, Isaac	VII	Parrish, Edward	VII
Parker, Isaac Charles	VII	Parrish, Joseph	VII
Parker, James (*d. 1770*)	VII	Parrott, Enoch Greenleafe	VII
Parker, James (*d. 1868*)	VII	Parrott, Robert Parker	VII
Parker, James Cutler Dunn	VII	Parry, Charles Christopher	VII

Complete Index Guide

Name	Vol./Supp.	Name	Vol./Supp.
Parry, Charles Thomas	VII	Paton, Lewis Bayles	VII
Parry, John Stubbs	VII	Patri, Angelo	7
Parsons, Albert Richard	VII	Patrick, Edwin Hill ("Ted")	7
Parsons, Albert Ross	VII	Patrick, Hugh Talbot	2
Parsons, Elsie Worthington		Patrick, Marsena Rudolph	VII
Clews	3	Patrick, Mary Mills	2
Parsons, Frank	VII	Patrick, Mason Mathews	3
Parsons, John Edward	VII	Patten, Gilbert	3
Parsons, Lewis Baldwin	VII	Patten, James A.	VII
Parsons, Lewis Eliphalet	VII	Patten, Simon Nelson	VII
Parsons, Samuel Bowne	VII	Patten, William	VII
Parsons, Samuel Holden	VII	Patterson, Alicia	7
Parsons, Theophilus (d. 1813)	VII	Patterson, Daniel Todd	VII
Parsons, Theophilus (d. 1882)	VII	Patterson, Eleanor Medill	4
Parsons, Thomas William	VII	Patterson, James Kennedy	VII
Parsons, Usher	VII	Patterson, James Willis	VII
Parsons, William Barclay	VII	Patterson, John Henry	VII
Partington, Mrs.		Patterson, Joseph Medill	4
See Shillaber, Benjamin		Patterson, Morris	VII
Penhallow		Patterson, Robert (d. 1824)	VII
Parton, Arthur	VII	Patterson, Robert (d. 1881)	VII
Parton, James	VII	Patterson, Robert Mayne	VII
Parton, Sara Payson Willis	VII	Patterson, Robert Porter	5
Partridge, Alden	VII	Patterson, Rufus Lenoir	3
Partridge, James Rudolph	VII	Patterson, Thomas Harman	VII
Partridge, Richard	VII	Patterson, Thomas MacDonald	VII
Partridge, William Ordway	VII	Patterson, William	VII
Parvin, Theodore Sutton	VII	Pattie, James Ohio	VII
Parvin, Theophilus	VII	Pattison, Granville Sharp	VII
Pascalis-Ouvrière, Felix	VII	Pattison, James William	VII
Paschal, George Washington	VII	Pattison, John M.	VII
Pasco, Samuel	VII	Pattison, Robert Emory	VII
Pasquin, Anthony		Pattison, Thomas	VII
See Williams, John		Patton, Francis Landey	VII
(d. 1818)		Patton, George Smith	3
Passavant, William Alfred	VII	Patton, John Mercer	VII
Pastor, Antonio	VII	Patton, William	VII
Pastorius, Francis Daniel	VII	Pauger, Adrien de	VII
Pasvolsky, Leo	5	Paul, Elliot Harold	6
Patch, Alexander McCarrell	3	Paul, Father	
Patch, Sam	VII	See Francis, Paul James	
Pate, Maurice	7	Paul, Henry Martyn	VII
Paterson, John	VII	Paul, John	
Paterson, William	VII	See Webb, Charles Henry	
Patillo, Henry	VII	Paul, Josephine Bay	7

Complete Index Guide

Name	Vol./Supp.	Name	Vol./Supp.
Paulding, Hiram	VII	Pearce, Stephen Austen	VII
Paulding, James Kirke	VII	Pearl, Raymond	2
Pavy, Octave	VII	Pearse, John Barnard Sweet	VII
Pawnee Bill		Pearson, Edmund Lester	2
See Lillie, Gordon William		Pearson, Edward Jones	VII
Payne, Bruce Ryburn	2	Pearson, Eliphalet	VII
Payne, Christopher Harrison	VII	Pearson, Fred Stark	VII
Payne, Daniel Alexander	VII	Pearson, Leonard	VII
Payne, Henry B.	VII	Pearson, Raymond Allen	2
Payne, Henry Clay	VII	Pearson, Richmond Mumford	VII
Payne, John Barton	1	Pearson, Thomas Gilbert	3
Payne, John Howard	VII	Pearsons, Daniel Kimball	VII
Payne, Lewis Thornton Powell		Peary, Josephine Diebitsch	5
See Booth, John Wilkes		Peary, Robert Edwin	VII
Payne, Oliver Hazard	VII	Pease, Alfred Humphreys	VII
Payne, Sereno Elisha	VII	Pease, Calvin	VII
Payne, William Harold	VII	Pease, Elisha Marshall	VII
Payne, William Morton	VII	Pease, Joseph Ives	VII
Payson, Edward	VII	Peaslee, Edmund Randolph	VII
Payson, Seth	VII	Peattie, Donald Culross	7
Peabody, Andrew Preston	VII	Peavey, Frank Hutchinson	VII
Peabody, Cecil Hobart	1	Peay, Austin	VII
Peabody, Elizabeth Palmer	VII	Peck, Charles Horton	VII
Peabody, Endicott	3	Peck, Charles Howard	VII
Peabody, Francis Greenwood	2	Peck, George	VII
Peabody, George	VII	Peck, George Record	VII
Peabody, George Foster	2	Peck, George Washington	VII
Peabody, Joseph	VII	Peck, George Wilbur	VII
Peabody, Josephine Preston	VII	Peck, Harry Thurston	VII
Peabody, Lucy Whitehead	4	Peck, James Hawkins	VII
Peabody, Nathaniel	VII	Peck, Jesse Truesdell	VII
Peabody, Oliver William Bourn	VII	Peck, John James	VII
Peabody, Robert Swain	VII	Peck, John Mason	VII
Peabody, Selim Hobart	VII	Peck, Lillie	6
Peabody, William Bourn Oliver	VII	Peck, Thomas Ephraim	VII
Peale, Anna Claypoole	VII	Peck, Tracy	VII
Peale, Charles Willson	VII	Peck, William Dandridge	VII
Peale, James	VII	Peckham, George Williams	VII
Peale, Raphael	VII	Peckham, Rufus Wheeler	VII
Peale, Rembrandt	VII	Peckham, Stephen Farnum	VII
Peale, Sarah Miriam	VII	Peckham, Wheeler Hazard	VII
Peale, Titian Ramsay	VII	Pedder, James	VII
Pearce, Charles Sprague	VII	Peek, Frank William	VII
Pearce, James Alfred	VII	Peek, George Nelson	3
Pearce, Richard	VII	Peers, Benjamin Orrs	VII
Pearce, Richard Mills	VII	Peerson, Cleng	VII

Complete Index Guide

Name	Vol./Supp.	Name	Vol./Supp.
Peet, Harvey Prindle	VII	Penn, John (b. 1729)	VII
Peet, Isaac Lewis	VII	Penn, John (b. 1740)	VII
Peet, Stephen Denison	VII	Penn, Richard	VII
Peffer, William Alfred	VII	Penn, Thomas	VII
Pegram, George Braxton	6	Penn, William	VII
Peirce, Benjamin	VII	Pennell, Joseph	VII
Peirce, Benjamin Osgood	VII	Penniman, James Hosmer	VII
Peirce, Bradford Kinney	VII	Pennington, James W. C.	VII
Peirce, Charles Sanders	VII	Pennington, William	VII
Peirce, Cyrus	VII	Pennington, William Sandford	VII
Peirce, Henry Augustus	VII	Pennock, Alexander Mosely	VII
Peirce, James Mills	VII	Pennoyer, Sylvester	VII
Peirce, William	VII	Pennypacker, Elijah Funk	VII
Peixotto, Benjamin Franklin	VII	Pennypacker, Galusha	VII
Pelham, Henry	VII	Pennypacker, Samuel Whitaker	VII
Pelham, John	VII	Penrose, Boies	VII
Pelham, Peter	VII	Penrose, Charles Bingham	VII
Pelham, Robert A.	3	Penrose, Richard Alexander	
Pellew, Henry Edward	VII	Fullerton	VII
Peloubet, Francis Nathan	VII	Penrose, Spencer	2
Pelz, Paul Johannes	VII	Pentecost, George Frederick	VII
Pemberton, Brock	4	Pepper, George Seckel	VII
Pemberton, Israel	VII	Pepper, George Wharton	7
Pemberton, James	VII	Pepper, William (d. 1864)	VII
Pemberton, John	VII	Pepper, William (d. 1898)	VII
Pemberton, John Clifford	VII	Pepper, William (d. 1947)	4
Peñalosa Briceño, Diego		Pepperrell, Sir William	VII
Dioniso de	VII	Perabo, Johann Ernst	VII
Pender, William Dorsey	VII	Peralta, Pedro de	VII
Pendergast, Thomas Joseph	3	Perché, Napoleon Joseph	VII
Pendleton, Edmund	VII	Percival, James Gates	VII
Pendleton, Edmund Monroe	VII	Percival, John	VII
Pendleton, Ellen Fitz	2	Percy, George	VII
Pendleton, George Hunt	VII	Percy, William Alexander	3
Pendleton, James Madison	VII	Perham, Josiah	VII
Pendleton, John B.	VII	Periam, Jonathan	VII
Pendleton, John Strother	VII	Perin, Charles Page	2
Pendleton, William Kimbrough	VII	Perkins, Charles Callahan	VII
Pendleton, William Nelson	VII	Perkins, Charles Elliott	VII
Penfield, Edward	VII	Perkins, Dwight Heald	3
Penfield, Frederic Courtland	VII	Perkins, Eli	
Penfield, William Lawrence	VII	See Landon, Melville De	
Penhallow, Samuel	VII	Lancey	
Penick, Charles Clifton	VII	Perkins, Elisha	VII
Penington, Edward (d. 1701)	VII	Perkins, Frances	7
Penington, Edward (d. 1796)	VII		

Complete Index Guide

Name	Vol./Supp.	Name	Vol./Supp.
Perkins, Frederic Beecher	VII	Perry, William Flake	VII
Perkins, George Clement	VII	Perry, William Stevens	VII
Perkins, George Douglas	VII	Pershing, John Joseph	4
Perkins, George Hamilton	VII	Person, Thomas	VII
Perkins, George Henry	VII	Persons, Warren Milton	2
Perkins, George Walbridge	VII	Peter, Hugh	VII
Perkins, Jacob	VII	Peter, John Frederick	VII
Perkins, James Breck	VII	Peter, Robert	VII
Perkins, James Handasyd		Peter, Sarah Worthington King	VII
(d. 1849)	VII	Peterkin, George William	VII
Perkins, James Handasyd		Peterkin, Julia Mood	7
(d. 1940)	2	Peters, Absalom	VII
Perkins, Justin	VII	Peters, Christian Henry	
Perkins, Marion	7	Frederick	VII
Perkins, Maxwell	4	Peters, Edward Dyer	VII
Perkins, Samuel Elliott	VII	Peters, John Andrew	VII
Perkins, Thomas Handasyd	VII	Peters, John Charles	VII
Perkins, Thomas Nelson	2	Peters, John Punnett	VII
Perley, Ira	VII	Peters, Madison Clinton	VII
Perlman, Philip Benjamin	6	Peters, Phillis Wheatley	
Perlman, Selig	6	See Wheatley, Phillis	
Perrin, Bernadotte	VII	Peters, Richard (d. 1776)	VII
Perrine, Charles Dillon	5	Peters, Richard (d. 1828)	VII
Perrine, Frederic Auten Combs	VII	Peters, Richard (d. 1889)	VII
Perrine, Henry	VII	Peters, Samuel Andrew	VII
Perrot, Nicolas	VII	Peters, William Cumming	VII
Perry, Antoinette	4	Peterson, Charles Jacobs	VII
Perry, Arthur Latham	VII	Peterson, Henry	VII
Perry, Benjamin Franklin	VII	Petigru, James Louis	VII
Perry, Bliss	5	Petri, Angelo	7
Perry, Christopher Raymond	VII	Pettigrew, Charles	VII
Perry, Clarence Arthur	3	Pettigrew, James Johnston	VII
Perry, Edward Aylesworth	VII	Pettigrew, Richard Franklin	VII
Perry, Edward Baxter	VII	Pettit, Charles	VII
Perry, Enoch Wood	VII	Pettit, Thomas McKean	VII
Perry, Matthew Calbraith	VII	Pettus, Edmund Winston	VII
Perry, Nora	VII	Pew, Joseph Newton, Jr.	7
Perry, Oliver Hazard	VII	Peyton, John Lewis	VII
Perry, Pettis	7	Pfahler, George Edward	6
Perry, Ralph Barton	6	Pfister, Alfred	7
Perry, Rufus Lewis	VII	Pfund, August Herman	4
Perry, Stuart	VII	Phelan, David Samuel	VII
Perry, Thomas Sergeant	VII	Phelan, James (b. 1824)	VII
Perry, Walter Scott	1	Phelan, James (b. 1856)	VII
Perry, William	VII	Phelan, James Duval	VII

Complete Index Guide

Name	Vol./Supp.	Name	Vol./Supp.
Phelps, Almira Hart Lincoln	VII	Phips, Sir William	VII
Phelps, Anson Greene	VII	Phisterer, Frederick	VII
Phelps, Austin	VII	Phoenix, John	
Phelps, Charles Edward	VII	See Derby, George	
Phelps, Edward John	VII	Horatio	
Phelps, Elizabeth Stuart		Phyfe, Duncan	VII
(d. 1852), and Phelps,		Physick, Philip Syng	VII
Elizabeth Stuart (d. 1911)		Piatt, Donn	VII
See Ward, Elizabeth		Piatt, John James	VII
Stuart Phelps		Piatt, Sarah Morgan Bryan	VII
Phelps, Guy Rowland	VII	Piccard, Jean Felix	7
Phelps, John Smith	VII	Pick, Lewis Andrew	6
Phelps, Oliver	VII	Pickard, Samuel Thomas	VII
Phelps, Thomas Stowell	VII	Pickens, Andrew	VII
Phelps, William Franklin	VII	Pickens, Francis Wilkinson	VII
Phelps, William Lyon	3	Pickens, Israel	VII
Phelps, William Walter	VII	Pickens, William	5
Philip (d. 1676)	VII	Pickering, Charles	VII
Philip, John Woodward	VII	Pickering, Edward Charles	VII
Philipp, Emanuel Lorenz	VII	Pickering, John (d. 1805)	VII
Philips, John Finis	VII	Pickering, John (d. 1846)	VII
Philips, Martin Wilson	VII	Pickering, Timothy	VII
Philipse, Frederick	VII	Picket, Albert	VII
Philipson, David	4	Pickett, Albert James	VII
Phillips, David Graham	VII	Pickett, George Edward	VII
Phillips, Francis Clifford	VII	Pickett, James Chamberlayne	VII
Phillips, Frank	4	Picknell, William Lamb	VII
Phillips, George	VII	Picton, Thomas	VII
Phillips, Harry Irving	7	Pidgin, Charles Felton	VII
Phillips, Henry	VII	Pieper, Franz August Otto	VII
Phillips, John	VII	Pierce, Benjamin	VII
Phillips, John Sanburn	4	Pierce, Edward Lillie	VII
Phillips, Lena Madesin	5	Pierce, Franklin	VII
Phillips, Philip	VII	Pierce, George Foster	VII
Phillips, Samuel	VII	Pierce, Gilbert Ashville	VII
Phillips, Thomas Wharton	VII	Pierce, Henry Lillie	VII
Phillips, Ulrich Bonnell	1	Pierce, John Davis	VII
Phillips, Walter Polk	VII	Pierce, William Leigh	VII
Phillips, Wendell	VII	Pierpont, Francis Harrison	VII
Phillips, Willard	VII	Pierpont, James	VII
Phillips, William	VII	Pierpont, John	VII
Phillips, William Addison	VII	Pierrepont, Edwards	VII
Phinizy, Ferdinand	VII	Pierson, Abraham (d. 1678)	VII
Phipps, Henry	VII	Pierson, Abraham (d. 1707)	VII
Phipps, Lawrence Cowle	6	Pierson, Arthur Tappan	VII

Complete Index Guide

Name	Vol./Supp.	Name	Vol./Supp.
Pierson, Hamilton Wilcox	VII	Pinney, Norman	VII
Pierz, Franz	VII	Pino, José	
Piez, Charles	1	See Son of Many Beads	
Piggot, Robert	VII	Pintard, John	VII
Piggott, James	VII	Pintard, Lewis	VII
Pike, Albert	VII	Pinto, Isaac	VII
Pike, James Shepherd	VII	Pinza, Ezio	6
Pike, Mary Hayden Green	VII	Piper, Charles Vancouver	VII
Pike, Nicolas	VII	Pippin, Horace	4
Pike, Robert	VII	Pirsson, Louis Valentine	VII
Pike, Zebulon Montgomery	VII	Pise, Charles Constantine	VII
Pilat, Ignaz Anton	VII	Pitcairn, John (d. 1775)	VII
Pilcher, Joshua	VII	Pitcairn, John (d. 1916)	VII
Pilcher, Lewis Stephen	1	Pitcher, Molly	
Pilcher, Paul Monroe	VII	See McCauley, Mary	
Pilkington, James	VII	Ludwig Hays	
Pilling, James Constantine	VII	Pitcher, Zina	VII
Pillow, Gideon Johnson	VII	Pitchlynn, Peter Perkins	VII
Pillsbury, Charles Alfred	VII	Pitkin, Frederick Walker	VII
Pillsbury, Harry Nelson	VII	Pitkin, Timothy	VII
Pillsbury, John Elliott	VII	Pitkin, Walter Boughton	5
Pillsbury, John Sargent	VII	Pitkin, William (d. 1694)	VII
Pillsbury, Parker	VII	Pitkin, William (d. 1769)	VII
Pilmore, Joseph	VII	Pitkin, William (d. 1789)	VII
Pilsbury, Amos	VII	Pitman, Benn	VII
Pinchback, Pinckney Benton		Pitney, Mahlon	VII
Stewart	VII	Pittman, Key	2
Pinchot, Amos Richards Eno	3	Pittock, Henry Lewis	VII
Pinchot, Cornelia Elizabeth		Pitts, Hiram Avery	VII
Bryce	6	Pitts, ZaSu	7
Pinchot, Gifford	4	Placide, Henry	VII
Pinckney, Charles	VII	Plaisted, Harris Merrill	VII
Pinckney, Charles Cotesworth	VII	Plant, Henry Bradley	VII
Pinckney, Elizabeth Lucas	VII	Plater, George	VII
Pinckney, Henry Laurens	VII	Plath, Sylvia	7
Pinckney, Thomas	VII	Platner, Samuel Ball	VII
Pine, Robert Edge	VII	Platt, Charles Adams	VIII
Piñero Jiménez, Jesús Toribio	5	Platt, Orville Hitchcock	VIII
Pingree, Hazen Stuart	VII	Platt, Thomas Collier	VIII
Pinkerton, Allan	VII	Pleasants, James	VIII
Pinkerton, Lewis Letig	VII	Pleasants, John Hampden	VIII
Pinkham, Lydia Estes	VII	Pleasonton, Alfred	VIII
Pinkney, Edward Coote	VII	Plimpton, George Arthur	2
Pinkney, Ninian	VII	Plotz, Harry	4
Pinkney, William	VII	Plowman, George Taylor	VIII

Complete Index Guide

Name	Vol./Supp.	Name	Vol./Supp.
Plumb, Glenn Edward	VIII	Pond, Enoch	VIII
Plumb, Preston B.	VIII	Pond, Frederick Eugene	VIII
Plumbe, John	VIII	Pond, George Edward	VIII
Plumer, William	VIII	Pond, Irving Kane	2
Plumer, William Swan	VIII	Pond, James Burton	VIII
Plumley, Frank	VIII	Pond, Peter	VIII
Plummer, Henry	VIII	Pond, Samuel William	VIII
Plummer, Henry Stanley	2	Pontiac	VIII
Plummer, Jonathan	VIII	Pool, John	VIII
Plummer, Mary Wright	VIII	Pool, Maria Louise	VIII
Plunkett, Charles Peshall	VIII	Poole, Ernest	4
Pocahontas	VIII	Poole, Fitch	VIII
Poe, Edgar Allan	VIII	Poole, William Frederick	VIII
Poe, Orlando Metcalfe	VIII	Poor, Charles Henry	VIII
Poindexter, George	VIII	Poor, Daniel	VIII
Poindexter, Miles	4	Poor, Enoch	VIII
Poinsett, Joel Roberts	VIII	Poor, Henry Varnum	VIII
Polak, John Osborn	VIII	Poor, John	VIII
Poland, Luke Potter	VIII	Poor, John Alfred	VIII
Polk, Frank Lyon	3	Poore, Benjamin Perley	VIII
Polk, James Knox	VIII	Pope, Albert Augustus	VIII
Polk, Leonidas	VIII	Pope, Franklin Leonard	VIII
Polk, Leonidas Lafayette	VIII	Pope, John	VIII
Polk, Lucius Eugene	VIII	Pope, John Russell	2
Polk, Thomas	VIII	Pope, Nathaniel	VIII
Polk, Trusten	VIII	Popham, George	VIII
Polk, William	VIII	Porcher, Francis Peyre	VIII
Polk, William Mecklenburg	VIII	Pormort, Philemon	VIII
Polk, Willis Jefferson	VIII	Porter, Albert Gallatin	VIII
Pollak, Gustav	VIII	Porter, Alexander	VIII
Pollak, Walter Heilprin	2	Porter, Andrew	VIII
Pollard, Edward Alfred	VIII	Porter, Arthur Kingsley	1
Pollard, Joseph Percival	VIII	Porter, Benjamin Curtis	VIII
Pollock, Channing	4	Porter, Cole	7
Pollock, James	VIII	Porter, David	VIII
Pollock, Oliver	VIII	Porter, David Dixon	VIII
Pollock, (Paul) Jackson	6	Porter, David Rittenhouse	VIII
Polock, Moses	VIII	Porter, Ebenezer	VIII
Pomerene, Atlee	2	Porter, Edwin Stanton	3
Pomeroy, John Norton	VIII	Porter, Fitz-John	VIII
Pomeroy, Marcus Mills	VIII	Porter, Gene Stratton	1
Pomeroy, Samuel Clarke	VIII	Porter, Holbrook Fitz-John	VIII
Pomeroy, Seth	VIII	Porter, Horace	VIII
Ponce de León, Juan	VIII	Porter, James Davis	VIII
Pond, Allen Bartlit	VIII	Porter, James Madison	VIII

Complete Index Guide

Name	Vol./Supp.	Name	Vol./Supp.
Porter, Jermain Gildersleeve	VIII	Potter, Henry Codman	VIII
Porter, John Addison	VIII	Potter, Horatio	VIII
Porter, John Luke	VIII	Potter, James	VIII
Porter, Noah	VIII	Potter, Louis McClellan	VIII
Porter, Peter Buell	VIII	Potter, Nathaniel	VIII
Porter, Robert Percival	VIII	Potter, Paul Meredith	VIII
Porter, Rufus	VIII	Potter, Platt	VIII
Porter, Russell Williams	4	Potter, Robert	VIII
Porter, Samuel	VIII	Potter, Robert Brown	VIII
Porter, Sarah	VIII	Potter, William Bancroft	1
Porter, Stephen Geyer	VIII	Potter, William James	VIII
Porter, Thomas Conrad	VIII	Potts, Benjamin Franklin	VIII
Porter, William Sydney	VIII	Potts, Charles Sower	VIII
Porter, William Townsend	4	Potts, Jonathan	VIII
Porter, William Trotter	VIII	Potts, Richard	VIII
Portier, Michael	VIII	Pou, Edward William	1
Portolá, Gaspar de	VIII	Poulson, Niels	VIII
Pory, John	VIII	Poulson, Zachariah	VIII
Posey, Alexander Lawrence	VIII	Pound, Cuthbert Winfred	1
Posey, Thomas	VIII	Pound, Roscoe	7
Post, Augustus	5	Pound, Thomas	VIII
Post, Charles William	VIII	Pourtalès, Louis François de	VIII
Post, Christian Frederick	VIII	Powderly, Terence Vincent	VIII
Post, Emily Price	6	Powel, John Hare	VIII
Post, George Adams	VIII	Powell	
Post, George Browne	VIII	See Osceola	
Post, George Edward	VIII	Powell, Adam Clayton, Sr.	5
Post, Isaac	VIII	Powell, Alma Webster	VIII
Post, Louis Freeland	VIII	Powell, Edward Payson	VIII
Post, Melville Davisson	VIII	Powell, George Harold	VIII
Post, Truman Marcellus	VIII	Powell, John Benjamin	4
Post, Wiley	1	Powell, John Wesley	VIII
Post, Wright	VIII	Powell, Lazarus Whitehead	VIII
Postl, Carl		Powell, Lucien Whiting	VIII
See Sealsfield, Charles		Powell, Maud	VIII
Poston, Charles Debrill	VIII	Powell, Richard Ewing	
Potamian, Brother	VIII	("Dick")	7
Pott, Francis Lister Hawks	4	Powell, Snelling	VIII
Pott, John	VIII	Powell, Thomas	VIII
Potter, Alonzo	VIII	Powell, Thomas Reed	5
Potter, Charles Francis	7	Powell, William Bramwell	VIII
Potter, Edward Clark	VIII	Powell, William Byrd	VIII
Potter, Eliphalet Nott	VIII	Powell, William Henry	VIII
Potter, Elisha Reynolds	VIII	Power, Frederick Belding	VIII
Potter, Ellen Culver	6	Power, Frederick Dunglison	VIII

Complete Index Guide

Name	Vol./Supp.	Name	Vol./Supp.
Power, Frederick Tyrone	VIII	Prentice, George Dennison	VIII
Power, John	VIII	Prentice, Samuel Oscar	VIII
Power, Tyrone (d. 1931)		Prentis, Henning Webb, Jr.	6
See Power, Frederick		Prentiss, Benjamin Mayberry	VIII
Tyrone		Prentiss, Elizabeth Payson	VIII
Power, Tyrone (d. 1958)	6	Prentiss, George Lewis	VIII
Powers, Daniel William	VIII	Prentiss, Samuel	VIII
Powers, Hiram	VIII	Prentiss, Seargent Smith	VIII
Powhatan	VIII	Presbrey, Eugene Wiley	VIII
Pownall, Thomas	VIII	Prescott, Albert Benjamin	VIII
Poydras, Julien de Lalande	VIII	Prescott, George Bartlett	VIII
Poznanski, Gustavus	VIII	Prescott, Oliver	VIII
Prall, David Wight	2	Prescott, Samuel	VIII
Prang, Louis	VIII	Prescott, Samuel Cate	7
Prang, Mary Amelia Dana		Prescott, William	VIII
Hicks	VIII	Prescott, William Hickling	VIII
Pratt, Bela Lyon	VIII	Presser, Theodore	VIII
Pratt, Charles	VIII	Preston, Ann	VIII
Pratt, Daniel (d. 1873)	VIII	Preston, Harriet Waters	VIII
Pratt, Daniel (d. 1887)	VIII	Preston, John Smith	VIII
Pratt, Eliza Anna Farman	VIII	Preston, Jonas	VIII
Pratt, Enoch	VIII	Preston, Margaret Junkin	VIII
Pratt, Francis Ashbury	VIII	Preston, Thomas Scott	VIII
Pratt, James Bissett	3	Preston, William	VIII
Pratt, John	VIII	Preston, William Ballard	VIII
Pratt, Matthew	VIII	Preston, William Campbell	VIII
Pratt, Orson	1	Preus, Christian Keyser	VIII
Pratt, Parley Parker	VIII	Prevost, François Marie	VIII
Pratt, Richard Henry	VIII	Priber, Christian	VIII
Pratt, Sereno Stansbury	VIII	Price, Bruce	VIII
Pratt, Silas Gamaliel	VIII	Price, Eli Kirk (d. 1884)	VIII
Pratt, Thomas George	VIII	Price, Eli Kirk (d. 1933)	1
Pratt, Thomas Willis	VIII	Price, George Edward	
Pratt, Waldo Selden	2	McCready	7
Pratt, William Veazie	6	Price, George Moses	3
Pratt, Zadock	VIII	Price, Hiram	VIII
Pratte, Bernard	VIII	Price, Joseph	VIII
Pray, Isaac Clark	VIII	Price, Rodman McCamley	VIII
Preber, Christian		Price, Stephen	VIII
See Priber, Christian		Price, Sterling	VIII
Preble, Edward	VIII	Price, Theodore Hazeltine	1
Preble, George Henry	VIII	Price, Thomas Frederick	VIII
Preble, William Pitt	VIII	Price, Thomas Lawson	VIII
Preetorius, Emil	VIII	Price, Thomas Randolph	VIII
Prendergast, Maurice Brazil	VIII	Price, William Cecil	VIII

Complete Index Guide

Name	Vol./Supp.	Name	Vol./Supp.
Price, William Thompson	VIII	Pruyn, John Van Shaick	
Priest, Edward Dwight	VIII	Lansing	VIII
Priestley, James	VIII	Pruyn, Robert Hewson	VIII
Priestley, Joseph	VIII	Pryber, Christian	
Prime, Benjamin Youngs	VIII	See Priber, Christian	
Prime, Edward Dorr Griffin	VIII	Pryor, Arthur W.	3
Prime, Samuel Irenaeus	VIII	Pryor, Nathaniel	VIII
Prime, William Cowper	VIII	Pryor, Roger Atkinson	VIII
Prince, Frederick Henry	5	Puget, Peter Richings	
Prince, Le Baron Bradford	VIII	See Richings, Peter	
Prince, Morton	VIII	Pugh, Ellis	VIII
Prince, Thomas	VIII	Pugh, Evan	VIII
Prince, William (d. 1802)	VIII	Pugh, George Ellis	VIII
Prince, William (d. 1842)	VIII	Pujo, Arsène Paulin	2
Prince, William Robert	VIII	Pulaski, Casimir	VIII
Pring, Martin	VIII	Pulitzer, Joseph	VIII
Pringle, Cyrus Guernsey	VIII	Pulitzer, Joseph, Jr.	5
Pringle, Henry Fowles	6	Pulitzer, Ralph	2
Pringle, Joel Roberts Poinsett	VIII	Pullman, George Mortimer	VIII
Pringle, John Julius	VIII	Pulte, Joseph Hippolyt	VIII
Printz, Johan Björnsson	VIII	Pumpelly, Raphael	VIII
Pritchard, Frederick John	VIII	Pupin, Michael Idvorsky	1
Pritchard, Jeter Connelly	VIII	Purcell, John Baptist	VIII
Pritchett, Henry Smith	2	Purdue, John	VIII
Procter, John Robert	VIII	Purdy, Corydon Tyler	3
Procter, William	VIII	Purdy, Lawson	6
Procter, William Cooper	1	Purnell, Benjamin	1
Proctor, Frederick Francis	VIII	Purnell, William Henry	VIII
Proctor, Henry Hugh	VIII	Purple, Samuel Smith	VIII
Proctor, Joseph	VIII	Purry, Jean Pierre	VIII
Proctor, Lucien Brock	VIII	Pursh, Frederick	VIII
Proctor, Redfield	VIII	Purviance, David	VIII
Profaci, Joseph	7	Puryear, Bennet	VIII
Prokosch, Eduard	2	Pusey, Caleb	VIII
Prophet		Pusey, William Allen	2
See Tenskwatawa		Pushmataha	VIII
Prosser, Charles Smith	VIII	Putnam, Arthur	VIII
Proud, Robert	VIII	Putnam, Charles Pickering	VIII
Prouty, Charles Azro	VIII	Putnam, Eben	VIII
Provoost, Samuel	VIII	Putnam, Frederic Ward	VIII
Provost, Etienne	VIII	Putnam, George Haven	VIII
Provosty, Olivier Otis	VIII	Putnam, (George) Herbert	5
Prudden, Theophil Mitchell	VIII	Putnam, George Palmer	VIII
Prud'homme, John Francis		Putnam, Gideon	VIII
Eugene	VIII	Putnam, Helen Cordelia	5

Complete Index Guide

Name	Vol./Supp.
Putnam, Israel	VIII
Putnam, James Jackson	VIII
Putnam, James Osborne	VIII
Putnam, Nina Wilcox	7
Putnam, Rufus	VIII
Putnam, Ruth	VIII
Putnam, William Le Baron	VIII
Pye, Watts Orson	VIII
Pyle, Ernest Taylor	3
Pyle, Howard	VIII
Pyle, Robert	5
Pyle, Walter Lytle	VIII
Pynchon, John	VIII
Pynchon, Thomas Ruggles	VIII
Pynchon, William	VIII
Quackenbush, Stephen Platt	VIII
Quanah	VIII
Quantrill, William Clarke	VIII
Quarter, William	VIII
Quartley, Arthur	VIII
Quay, Matthew Stanley	VIII
Quayle, William Alfred	VIII
Queen, Walter W.	VIII
Quelch, John	VIII
Quesnay, Alexandre-Marie	VIII
Quezon, Manuel Luis	3
Quick, John Herbert	VIII
Quidor, John	VIII
Quigg, Lemuel Ely	VIII
Quigley, James Edward	VIII
Quimby, Phineas Parkhurst	VIII
Quinan, John Russell	VIII
Quinby, Isaac Ferdinand	VIII
Quincy, Edmund	VIII
Quincy, Josiah (d. 1775)	VIII
Quincy, Josiah (d. 1864)	VIII
Quincy, Josiah Phillips	VIII
Quine, William Edward	1
Quinn, Arthur Hobson	6
Quinn, Edmond Thomas	VIII
Quintard, Charles Todd	VIII
Quintard, George William	VIII
Quitman, John Anthony	VIII

Name	Vol./Supp.
Raby, James Joseph	VIII
Rachford, Benjamin Knox	VIII
Rachmaninoff, Sergei Vasilyevich	3
Radcliff, Jacob	VIII
Radford, William	VIII
Radin, Max	4
Radin, Paul	6
Radisson, Pierre Esprit	VIII
Rae, John	VIII
Raffeiner, John Stephen	VIII
Rafinesque, Constantine Samuel	VIII
Rafter, George W.	VIII
Raguet, Condy	VIII
Raht, August Wilhelm	VIII
Raines, John	VIII
Rainey, Gertrude Malissa Nix Pridgett	2
Rainey, Henry Thomas	1
Rainey, Joseph Hayne	VIII
Rainey, Ma See Rainey, Gertrude Malissa Nix Pridgett	
Rains, Gabriel James	VIII
Rains, George Washington	VIII
Rainsford, William Stephen	1
Râle, Sébastien	VIII
Ralph, James	VIII
Ralph, Julian	VIII
Ralston, Samuel Moffett	VIII
Ralston, William Chapman	VIII
Ramage, John	VIII
Rambaut, Mary Lucinda Bonney	VIII
Ramée, Joseph Jacques	VIII
Ramsay, Alexander	VIII
Ramsay, David	VIII
Ramsay, Erskine	5
Ramsay, Francis Munroe	VIII
Ramsay, George Douglas	VIII
Ramsay, Nathaniel	VIII
Ramseur, Stephen Dodson	VIII
Ramsey, Alexander	VIII

Complete Index Guide

Name	Vol./Supp.	Name	Vol./Supp.
Ramsey, James Gettys McGready	VIII	Ransohoff, Joseph	VIII
Rand, Addison Crittenden	VIII	Ransom, Matt Whitaker	VIII
Rand, Benjamin	1	Ransom, Thomas Edward Greenfield	VIII
Rand, Edward Kennard	3	Ransome, Frederick Leslie	1
Rand, Edward Sprague	VIII	Ranson, Stephen Walter	3
Rand, James Henry	3	Rantoul, Robert (b. 1778)	VIII
Randall, Alexander Williams	VIII	Rantoul, Robert (b. 1805)	VIII
Randall, Benjamin	VIII	Rapaport, David	6
Randall, Burton Alexander	VIII	Raphall, Morris Jacob	VIII
Randall, Henry Stephens	VIII	Rapp, George	VIII
Randall, James Garfield	5	Rapp, Wilhelm	VIII
Randall, James Ryder	VIII	Rarey, John Solomon	VIII
Randall, Robert Richard	VIII	Raskob, John Jakob	4
Randall, Samuel	VIII	Rasle, Sébastien	
Randall, Samuel Jackson	VIII	See Râle, Sébastien	
Randall, Samuel Sidwell	VIII	Rathbone, Justus Henry	VIII
Randall, Wyatt William	VIII	Rathbun, Richard	VIII
Randolph, Alfred Magill	VIII	Rattermann, Heinrich Armin	VIII
Randolph, Edmund (d. 1813)	VIII	Rau, Charles	VIII
Randolph, Edmund (d. 1861)	VIII	Rauch, Frederick Augustus	VIII
Randolph, Edward	VIII	Rauch, John Henry	VIII
Randolph, Epes	VIII	Raue, Charles Gottlieb	VIII
Randolph, George Wythe	VIII	Raulston, John Tate	6
Randolph, Isham	VIII	Raum, Green Berry	VIII
Randolph, Jacob	VIII	Rauschenbusch, Walter	VIII
Randolph, Sir John (d. 1736/37)	VIII	Rautenstrauch, Walter	5
Randolph, John (d. 1784)	VIII	Ravalli, Antonio	VIII
Randolph, John (d. 1833)	VIII	Ravenel, Edmund	VIII
Randolph, Peyton	VIII	Ravenel, Harriott Horry Rutledge	VIII
Randolph, Sarah Nicholas	VIII	Ravenel, Henry William	VIII
Randolph, Theodore Fitz	VIII	Ravenel, Mazÿck Porcher	4
Randolph, Thomas Jefferson	VIII	Ravenel, St. Julien	VIII
Randolph, Thomas Mann	VIII	Ravenscroft, John Stark	VIII
Randolph, William	VIII	Ravoux, Augustin	VIII
Raney, George Pettus	VIII	Rawle, Francis (d. 1726/27)	VIII
Ranger, Henry Ward	VIII	Rawle, Francis (d. 1930)	VIII
Rankin, Jeremiah Eames	VIII	Rawle, William	VIII
Rankin, John Elliott	6	Rawle, William Henry	VIII
Rankin, McKee	VIII	Rawlings, Marjorie Kinnan	5
Rankine, William Birch	VIII	Rawlins, John Aaron	VIII
Ranney, Ambrose Loomis	VIII	Rawlinson, Frank Joseph	2
Ranney, Rufus Percival	VIII	Ray, Charles Bennett	VIII
Ranney, William Tylee	VIII	Ray, Isaac	VIII

Complete Index Guide

Name	Vol./Supp.	Name	Vol./Supp.
Rayburn, Samuel Taliaferro ("Sam")	7	Redfield, Isaac Fletcher	VIII
		Redfield, Justus Starr	VIII
Raymond, Alexander Gillespie	6	Redfield, Robert	6
Raymond, Benjamin Wright	VIII	Redfield, William C.	VIII
Raymond, Charles Walker	VIII	Redfield, William Cox	VIII
Raymond, Daniel	VIII	Red Jacket	VIII
Raymond, George Lansing	VIII	Redman, Benjamin Ray	7
Raymond, Harry Howard	1	Redman, John	VIII
Raymond, Henry Jarvis	VIII	Redpath, James	VIII
Raymond, John Howard	VIII	Red Wing	VIII
Raymond, John T.	VIII	Redwood, Abraham	VIII
Raymond, Miner	VIII	Reece, B(razilla) Carroll	7
Raymond, Rossiter Worthington	VIII	Reed, Daniel Alden	6
		Reed, David	VIII
Rayner, Isidor	VIII	Reed, David Aiken	5
Rayner, Kenneth	VIII	Reed, Earl Howell	VIII
Rea, Samuel	VIII	Reed, Elizabeth Armstrong	VIII
Reach, Alfred James	VIII	Reed, Henry Hope	VIII
Read, Charles	VIII	Reed, James (d. 1807)	VIII
Read, Charles William	VIII	Reed, James (d. 1921)	VIII
Read, Conyers	6	Reed, James Alexander	3
Read, Daniel (d. 1836)	VIII	Reed, James Hay	VIII
Read, Daniel (d. 1878)	VIII	Reed, John (d. 1845)	VIII
Read, George	VIII	Reed, John (d. 1920)	VIII
Read, George Campbell	VIII	Reed, Joseph	VIII
Read, George Windle	1	Reed, Luman	VIII
Read, Jacob	VIII	Reed, Mary	3
Read, John (d. 1749)	VIII	Reed, Myrtle	VIII
Read, John (d. 1854)	VIII	Reed, Richard Clark	VIII
Read, John Meredith (d. 1874)	VIII	Reed, Sampson	VIII
Read, John Meredith (d. 1896)	VIII	Reed, Simeon Gannett	VIII
Read, Nathan	VIII	Reed, Thomas Brackett	VIII
Read, Opie Pope	2	Reed, Walter	VIII
Read, Thomas	VIII	Reed, William Bradford	VIII
Read, Thomas Buchanan	VIII	Reeder, Andrew Horatio	VIII
Reade, Edwin Godwin	VIII	Reedy, William Marion	VIII
Reagan, John Henninger	VIII	Rees, James	VIII
Realf, Richard	VIII	Rees, John Krom	VIII
Ream, Norman Bruce	VIII	Reese, Abram	VIII
Record, Samuel James	3	Reese, Charles Lee	2
Rector, Henry Massey	VIII	Reese, Isaac	VIII
Red Cloud	VIII	Reese, Jacob	VIII
Red Eagle		Reese, John James	VIII
See Weatherford, William		Reese, Lizette Woodworth	1
Redfield, Amasa Angell	VIII	Reeve, Tapping	VIII

Complete Index Guide

Name	Vol./Supp.	Name	Vol./Supp.
Reeves, Arthur Middleton	VIII	Remond, Charles Lenox	VIII
Reeves, Joseph Mason	4	Remsen, Ira	VIII
Regan, Agnes Gertrude	3	Rémy, Henri	VIII
Rehan, Ada	VIII	Renick, Felix	VIII
Rehn, Frank Knox Morton	VIII	Reno, Jesse Lee	VIII
Reichel, Charles Gotthold	VIII	Reno, Milo	2
Reichel, William Cornelius	VIII	Renwick, Edward Sabine	VIII
Reichenbach, Hans	5	Renwick, Henry Brevoort	VIII
Reick, William Charles	VIII	Renwick, James (d. 1863)	VIII
Reid, Christian		Renwick, James (d. 1895)	VIII
See Tiernan, Frances		Repplier, Agnes	4
Christine Fisher		Requa, Mark Lawrence	2
Reid, David Boswell	VIII	Requier, Augustus Julian	VIII
Reid, David Settle	VIII	Rese, Frederick	VIII
Reid, Gilbert	VIII	Resor, Stanley Burnet	7
Reid, James L.	VIII	Restarick, Henry Bond	1
Reid, John Morrison	VIII	Reuling, George	VIII
Reid, Mayne		Reuter, Dominic	VIII
See Reid, Thomas Mayne		Reuterdahl, Henry	VIII
Reid, Mont Rogers	3	Revel, Bernard	2
Reid, Ogden Mills	4	Revell, Fleming Hewitt	VIII
Reid, Robert	VIII	Revell, Nellie MacAleney	6
Reid, Samuel Chester	VIII	Revels, Hiram Rhoades	VIII
Reid, Thomas Mayne	VIII	Revere, Joseph Warren	VIII
Reid, Whitelaw	VIII	Revere, Paul	VIII
Reid, William Shields	VIII	Reynolds, Alexander Welch	VIII
Reid, William Wharry	VIII	Reynolds, Charles Alexander	VIII
Reiersen, Johan Reinert	VIII	Reynolds, Edwin	VIII
Reilly, Marion	VIII	Reynolds, George McClelland	2
Reinagle, Alexander	VIII	Reynolds, John (d. 1788)	VIII
Reiner, Fritz	7	Reynolds, John (d. 1865)	VIII
Reinhardt, Aurelia Isabel Henry	4	Reynolds, John Fulton	VIII
Reinhart, Benjamin Franklin	VIII	Reynolds, Joseph Jones	VIII
Reinhart, Charles Stanley	VIII	Reynolds, Quentin James	7
Reinsch, Paul Samuel	VIII	Reynolds, Richard Samuel, Sr.	5
Reisinger, Hugo	VIII	Reynolds, Robert Rice	7
Reisner, George Andrew	3	Reynolds, Samuel Godfrey	VIII
Reitzel, Robert	VIII	Reynolds, William	VIII
Rellstab, John	VIII	Reynolds, William Neal	5
Remey, George Collier	VIII	Rezanov, Nikolai Petrovich	VIII
Remington, Eliphalet	VIII	Rhea, John	VIII
Remington, Frederic	VIII	Rhees, Morgan John	1
Remington, Joseph Price	VIII	Rhees, Rush	2
Remington, Philo	VIII	Rhees, William Jones	VIII
Remington, William Walter	5	Rhett, Robert Barnwell	VIII

Complete Index Guide

Name	Vol./Supp.	Name	Vol./Supp.
Rhind, Alexander Colden	VIII	Richards, Vincent	6
Rhind, Charles	VIII	Richards, William	VIII
Rhoads, Cornelius Packard	6	Richards, William Trost	VIII
Rhoads, James E.	VIII	Richards, Zalmon	VIII
Rhodes, Eugene Manlove	1	Richardson, Albert Deane	VIII
Rhodes, James Ford	VIII	Richardson, Anna Euretta	VIII
Ribaut, Jean	VIII	Richardson, Charles Francis	VIII
Rice, Alexander Hamilton	VIII	Richardson, Charles	
Rice, Alice Caldwell Hegan	3	Williamson	VIII
Rice, Calvin Winsor	1	Richardson, Edmund	VIII
Rice, Charles	VIII	Richardson, Henry Hobson	VIII
Rice, Charles Allen Thorndike	VIII	Richardson, Israel Bush	VIII
Rice, Dan	VIII	Richardson, James Daniel	VIII
Rice, David	VIII	Richardson, Joseph	VIII
Rice, Edmund	VIII	Richardson, Maurice Howe	VIII
Rice, Edwin Wilbur (d. 1929)	VIII	Richardson, Robert	VIII
Rice, Edwin Wilbur (d. 1935)	1	Richardson, Rufus Byam	VIII
Rice, Fenelon Bird	VIII	Richardson, Sid Williams	6
Rice, George Samuel	4	Richardson, Tobias Gibson	VIII
Rice, (Henry) Grantland	5	Richardson, Wilds Preston	VIII
Rice, Henry Mower	VIII	Richardson, Willard	VIII
Rice, Isaac Leopold	VIII	Richardson, William Adams	VIII
Rice, John Holt	VIII	Richardson, William Lambert	VIII
Rice, Luther	VIII	Richardson, William Merchant	VIII
Rice, Nathan Lewis	VIII	Richberg, Donald Randall	6
Rice, Richard Henry	VIII	Richings, Peter	VIII
Rice, Thomas Dartmouth	VIII	Richmond, Charles Wallace	VIII
Rice, Victor Moreau	VIII	Richmond, Dean	VIII
Rice, William Marsh	VIII	Richmond, John Lambert	VIII
Rice, William North	VIII	Richmond, John Wilkes	VIII
Rich, Isaac	VIII	Richmond, Mary Ellen	VIII
Rich, Obadiah	VIII	Richtmyer, Floyd Karker	2
Richard, Gabriel	VIII	Rickard, George Lewis	VIII
Richard, James William	VIII	Rickert, Martha Edith	2
Richards, Charles Brinckerhoff	VIII	Ricketson, Daniel	VIII
Richards, Charles Herbert	VIII	Ricketts, Claude Vernon	7
Richards, Ellen Henrietta		Ricketts, Howard Taylor	1
Swallow	VIII	Ricketts, James Brewerton	VIII
Richards, John Kelvey	VIII	Ricketts, Palmer Chamberlaine	1
Richards, Joseph William	VIII	Rickey, Wesley Branch	7
Richards, Laura Elizabeth		Ricord, Frederick William	VIII
Howe	3	Ricord, Philippe	VIII
Richards, Robert Hallowell	3	Riddell, John Leonard	VIII
Richards, Theodore William	VIII	Ridder, Herman	VIII
Richards, Thomas Addison	VIII	Riddle, Albert Gallatin	VIII

Complete Index Guide

Name	Vol./Supp.	Name	Vol./Supp.
Riddle, George Peabody	VIII	Ripley, William Zebina	3
Riddle, Matthew Brown	VIII	Rising, Johan Classon	VIII
Riddle, Samuel Doyle	5	Rister, Carl Coke	5
Rideing, William Henry	VIII	Ritchey, George Willis	3
Rideout, Henry Milner	VIII	Ritchie, Albert Cabell	2
Ridgaway, Henry Bascom	VIII	Ritchie, Alexander Hay	VIII
Ridge, Major	VIII	Ritchie, Anna Cora	
Ridgely, Charles Goodwin	VIII	See Mowatt, Anna Cora	
Ridgely, Daniel Bowly	VIII	Ogden	
Ridgely, Nicholas	VIII	Ritchie, Thomas	VIII
Ridgway, Robert (d. 1929)	VIII	Ritner, Joseph	VIII
Ridgway, Robert (d. 1938)	2	Rittenhouse, David	VIII
Ridpath, John Clark	VIII	Rittenhouse, Jesse Belle	4
Rieger, Johann Georg Joseph		Rittenhouse, William	VIII
Anton	VIII	Ritter, Frédéric Louis	VIII
Riegger, Wallingford	7	Ritter, William Emerson	3
Rigdon, Sidney	VIII	Rivera, Luis Muñoz	
Rigge, William Francis	VIII	See Muñoz-Rivera, Luis	
Riggs, Elias	VIII	Rivers, Thomas Milton	7
Riggs, George Washington	VIII	Rivers, William James	VIII
Riggs, John Mankey	VIII	Rives, George Lockhart	VIII
Riggs, Stephen Return	VIII	Rives, Hallie Erminie	6
Riggs, William Henry	VIII	Rives, John Cook	VIII
Riis, Jacob August	VIII	Rives, William Cabell	VIII
Riley, Benjamin Franklin	VIII	Rivington, James	VIII
Riley, Bennet	VIII	Rix, Julian Walbridge	VIII
Riley, Charles Valentine	VIII	Roach, John	VIII
Riley, Isaac Woodbridge	VIII	Roane, Archibald	VIII
Riley, James Whitcomb	VIII	Roane, John Selden	VIII
Riley, William Bell	4	Roane, Spencer	VIII
Rimmer, William	VIII	Roark, Ruric Nevel	VIII
Rindge, Frederick Hastings	VIII	Robb, James	VIII
Rinehart, Mary Roberts	6	Robb, William Lispenard	1
Rinehart, William Henry	VIII	Robbins, Chandler	VIII
Ringgold, Cadwalader	VIII	Robbins, Thomas	VIII
Ringling, Charles	VIII	Roberdeau, Daniel	VIII
Riordan, Patrick William	VIII	Roberdeau, Isaac	VIII
Ripley, Edward Hastings	VIII	Robert, Christopher	
Ripley, Edward Payson	VIII	Rhinelander	VIII
Ripley, Eleazar Wheelock	VIII	Robert, Henry Martyn	1
Ripley, Ezra	VIII	Roberts, Benjamin Stone	VIII
Ripley, George	VIII	Roberts, Benjamin Titus	VIII
Ripley, James Wolfe	VIII	Roberts, Brigham Henry	VIII
Ripley, Robert LeRoy	4	Roberts, Edmund	VIII
Ripley, Roswell Sabine	VIII	Roberts, Elizabeth Madox	3

Complete Index Guide

Name	Vol./Supp.	Name	Vol./Supp.
Roberts, Elizabeth Wentworth	VIII	Robinson, Boardman	5
Roberts, Ellis Henry	VIII	Robinson, Charles	VIII
Roberts, George Brooke	VIII	Robinson, Charles Mulford	VIII
Roberts, Howard	VIII	Robinson, Charles Seymour	VIII
Roberts, Issachar Jacob	VIII	Robinson, Christopher	VIII
Roberts, Job	VIII	Robinson, Claude Everett	7
Roberts, Jonathan	VIII	Robinson, Conway	VIII
Roberts, Joseph Jenkins	VIII	Robinson, Edward (d. 1863)	VIII
Roberts, Kenneth Lewis	6	Robinson, Edward (d. 1931)	VIII
Roberts, Marshall Owen	VIII	Robinson, Edward Mott	VIII
Roberts, Nathan S.	VIII	Robinson, Edward Stevens	2
Roberts, Oran Milo	VIII	Robinson, Edward Van Dyke	VIII
Roberts, Owen Josephus	5	Robinson, Edwin Arlington	1
Roberts, Robert Richford	VIII	Robinson, Ezekiel Gilman	VIII
Roberts, Solomon White	VIII	Robinson, Frederick Byron	VIII
Roberts, Theodore	VIII	Robinson, George Canby	6
Roberts, William Charles	VIII	Robinson, Harriet Jane Hanson	VIII
Roberts, William Henry	VIII	Robinson, Henry Cornelius	VIII
Roberts, William Milnor	VIII	Robinson, Henry Morton	7
Roberts, William Randall	VIII	Robinson, James Harvey	2
Robertson, Alice Mary	VIII	Robinson, John	VIII
Robertson, Archibald	VIII	Robinson, John Cleveland	VIII
Robertson, Ashley Herman	VIII	Robinson, John Mitchell	VIII
Robertson, George	VIII	Robinson, Joseph Taylor	2
Robertson, James (b. 1740)	VIII	Robinson, Moncure	VIII
Robertson, James (b. 1742)	VIII	Robinson, Moses	VIII
Robertson, James Alexander	2	Robinson, Rowland Evans	VIII
Robertson, Jerome Bonaparte	VIII	Robinson, Solon	VIII
Robertson, John	VIII	Robinson, Stillman Williams	VIII
Robertson, Morgan Andrew	VIII	Robinson, Stuart	VIII
Robertson, Thomas Bolling	VIII	Robinson, Theodore	VIII
Robertson, William Henry	VIII	Robinson, Therese Albertine	
Robertson, William Joseph	VIII	Louise von Jakob	VIII
Robertson, William Schenck	VIII	Robinson, William	VIII
Robertson, William Spence	5	Robinson, William Callyhan	VIII
Robertson, Wyndham	VIII	Robinson, William Erigena	VIII
Robeson, George Maxwell	VIII	Robinson, William Stevens	VIII
Robidou, Antoine	VIII	Robinson-Smith, Gertrude	7
Robins, Henry Ephraim	VIII	Robot, Isidore	VIII
Robins, Margaret Dreier	3	Robson, May	3
Robins, Raymond	5	Robson, Stuart	VIII
Robinson, Albert Alonzo	VIII	Rochambeau, Jean Baptiste	
Robinson, Benjamin Lincoln	1	Donatien de Vimeur,	
Robinson, Beverley	VIII	Comte de	VIII
Robinson, Bill (Bojangles)	4	Roche, Arthur Somers	1

Complete Index Guide

Name	Vol./Supp.	Name	Vol./Supp.
Roche, James Jeffrey	VIII	Rogers, Henry Darwin	VIII
Rochester, Nathaniel	VIII	Rogers, Henry Huttleston	VIII
Rock, John	VIII	Rogers, Henry J.	VIII
Rockefeller, Abby Greene		Rogers, Henry Wade	VIII
Aldrich	4	Rogers, Isaiah	VIII
Rockefeller, John Davison	2	Rogers, James Blythe	VIII
Rockefeller, John Davison, Jr.	6	Rogers, James Gamble	4
Rockefeller, William	VIII	Rogers, James Harris	VIII
Rockhill, William Woodville	VIII	Rogers, James Harvey	2
Rockne, Knute Kenneth	VIII	Rogers, John (d. 1721)	VIII
Rockwell, Alphonso David	VIII	Rogers, John (d. 1904)	VIII
Rockwell, Kiffin Yates	VIII	Rogers, John Almanza Rowley	VIII
Roddey, Philip Dale	VIII	Rogers, John Ignatius	VIII
Rodenbough, Theophilus		Rogers, John Rankin	VIII
Francis	VIII	Rogers, John Raphael	VIII
Rodes, Robert Emmett	VIII	Rogers, Mary Josephine	5
Rodgers, Christopher Raymond		Rogers, Moses	VIII
Perry	VIII	Rogers, Randolph	VIII
Rodgers, George Washington		Rogers, Robert	VIII
(d. 1832)	VIII	Rogers, Robert Empie	VIII
Rodgers, George Washington		Rogers, Robert William	VIII
(d. 1863)	VIII	Rogers, Stephen	VIII
Rodgers, John (d. 1811)	VIII	Rogers, Thomas	VIII
Rodgers, John (d. 1838)	VIII	Rogers, Will	1
Rodgers, John (d. 1882)	VIII	Rogers, William Allen	VIII
Rodgers, John (d. 1926)	VIII	Rogers, William Augustus	VIII
Rodman, Isaac Peace	VIII	Rogers, William Barton	VIII
Rodman, Thomas Jackson	VIII	Rogers, William Crowninshield	VIII
Rodney, Cæsar	VIII	Rohde, Ruth Bryan Owen	5
Rodney, Cæsar Augustus	VIII	Rohé, George Henry	VIII
Rodney, Thomas	VIII	Roheim, Geza	5
Rodzinski, Artur	6	Rohlfs, Anna Katharine Green	1
Roe, Edward Payson	VIII	Rolette, Jean Joseph	VIII
Roe, Francis Asbury	VIII	Rolfe, John	VIII
Roe, Gilbert Ernstein	VIII	Rolfe, William James	VIII
Roebling, John Augustus	VIII	Rollins, Alice Marland	
Roebling, Washington		Wellington	VIII
Augustus	VIII	Rollins, Edward Henry	VIII
Roeding, George Christian	VIII	Rollins, Frank West	VIII
Roemer, Karl Ferdinand	VIII	Rollins, James Sidney	VIII
Roethke, Theodore Huebner	7	Rollinson, William	VIII
Rogers, Clara Kathleen Barnett	VIII	Rolph, James	1
Rogers, Edith Nourse	6	Rolshoven, Julius	VIII
Rogers, Edward Staniford	VIII	Rölvaag, Ole Edvart	VIII
Rogers, Harriet Burbank	VIII	Roman, André Bienvenu	VIII

Complete Index Guide

Name	Vol./Supp.	Name	Vol./Supp.
Romans, Bernard	VIII	Rose, Wickliffe	1
Romayne, Nicholas	VIII	Rosecrans, Sylvester Horton	VIII
Rombauer, Irma S.	7	Rosecrans, William Starke	VIII
Romberg, Sigmund	5	Roselins, Christian	VIII
Rombro, Jacob	VIII	Rosen, Joseph A.	4
Romeike, Henry	VIII	Rosenau, Milton Joseph	4
Rondthaler, Edward	VIII	Rosenbach, Abraham Simon	
Rood, Ogden Nicholas	VIII	Wolf	5
Rooney, Pat	7	Rosenbach, Philip Hyman	5
Roosa, Daniel Bennett St. John	VIII	Rosenberg, Abraham Hayyim	VIII
Roosevelt, Anna Eleanor	7	Rosenberg, Ethel	5
Roosevelt, Franklin Delano	3	Rosenberg, Henry	VIII
Roosevelt, Hilborne Lewis	VIII	Rosenberg, Julius	5
Roosevelt, Kermit	3	Rosenberg, Paul	6
Roosevelt, Nicholas J.	VIII	Rosenblatt, Joseph	VIII
Roosevelt, Robert Barnwell	VIII	Rosenfeld, Morris	VIII
Roosevelt, Theodore (d. 1919)	VIII	Rosenfeld, Paul	4
Roosevelt, Theodore (d. 1944)	3	Rosenthal, Herman	VIII
Root, Amos Ives	VIII	Rosenthal, Max	VIII
Root, Elihu	2	Rosenthal, Toby Edward	VIII
Root, Elisha King	VIII	Rosenwald, Julius	VIII
Root, Erastus	VIII	Rosewater, Edward	VIII
Root, Frank Albert	VIII	Rosewater, Victor	2
Root, Frederic Woodman	VIII	Ross, Abel Hastings	VIII
Root, George Frederick	VIII	Ross, Alexander	VIII
Root, Jesse	VIII	Ross, Alexander Coffman	VIII
Root, John Wellborn	VIII	Ross, Araminta	
Root, Joseph Pomeroy	VIII	See Tubman, Harriet	
Roper, Daniel Calhoun	3	Ross, Betsy	VIII
Ropes, James Hardy	VIII	Ross, Charles Griffith	4
Ropes, John Codman	VIII	Ross, Denman Waldo	1
Ropes, Joseph	VIII	Ross, Edmund Gibson	VIII
Rorer, David	VIII	Ross, Edward Alsworth	5
Rosa, Edward Bennett	VIII	Ross, Erskine Mayo	VIII
Rosati, Joseph	VIII	Ross, George	VIII
Rose, Aquila	VIII	Ross, Harold Wallace	5
Rose, Chauncey	VIII	Ross, James	VIII
Rose, Edward	VIII	Ross, James Delmage	
Rose, Ernestine Louise		McKenzie	2
Siismondi Potowski	VIII	Ross, John	VIII
Rose, John Carter	VIII	Ross, Lawrence Sullivan	VIII
Rose, Joseph Nelson	VIII	Ross, Martin	VIII
Rose, Mary Davies Swartz	3	Rosser, Thomas Lafayette	VIII
Rose, Uriah Milton	VIII	Rossiter, Thomas Prichard	VIII
Rose, Walter Malins	VIII	Rossiter, William Sidney	VIII

Complete Index Guide

Name	Vol./Supp.	Name	Vol./Supp.
Rostovtzeff, Michael Ivanovitch	5	Ruditsky, Barney	7
Rotch, Abbott Lawrence	VIII	Ruef, Abraham	2
Rotch, Arthur	VIII	Ruffin, Edmund	VIII
Rotch, Thomas Morgan	VIII	Ruffin, Thomas	VIII
Rotch, William	VIII	Ruffner, Henry	VIII
Rothafel, Samuel Lionel	2	Ruffner, William Henry	VIII
Rothermel, Peter Frederick	VIII	Ruger, Thomas Howard	VIII
Rothrock, Joseph Trimble	VIII	Rugg, Arthur Prentice	2
Rothwell, Richard Pennefather	VIII	Rugg, Harold Ordway	6
Roulstone, George	VIII	Ruggles, Samuel Bulkley	VIII
Round, William Marshall Fitts	VIII	Ruggles, Timothy	VIII
Rouquette, Adrien Emmanuel	VIII	Ruhl, Arthur Brown	1
Rouquette, François Dominique	VIII	Ruhräh, John	1
Rourke, Constance Mayfield	3	Rumford, Benjamin Thompson,	
Rousseau, Harry Harwood	VIII	Count	
Rousseau, Lovell Harrison	VIII	See Thompson, Benjamin	
Rovenstine, Emery Andrew	6	Ruml, Beardsley	6
Rowan, John	VIII	Rummel, Joseph Francis	7
Rowan, Stephen Clegg	VIII	Rumsey, Charles Cary	VIII
Rowe, Leo Stanton	4	Rumsey, James	VIII
Rowe, Lynwood Thomas	7	Rumsey, Mary Harriman	1
Rowell, Chester Harvey	4	Rumsey, William	VIII
Rowell, George Presbury	VIII	Runcie, Constance Faunt Le	
Rowland, Henry Augustus	VIII	Roy	VIII
Rowland, Henry Cottrell	VIII	Runkle, John Daniel	VIII
Rowland, Thomas Fitch	VIII	Runyon, Damon	4
Rowlands, William	VIII	Rupp, Israel Daniel	VIII
Rowlandson, Mary White	VIII	Rupp, William	VIII
Rowse, Samuel Worcester	VIII	Ruppert, Jacob	2
Rowson, Susanna Haswell	VIII	Rusby, Henry Hurd	2
Roxy		Rush, Benjamin	VIII
See Rothafel, Samuel		Rush, James	VIII
Lionel		Rush, Richard	VIII
Royall, Anne Newport	VIII	Rush, William	VIII
Royce, Josiah	VIII	Rusk, Jeremiah McClain	VIII
Royce, Ralph	7	Rusk, Thomas Jefferson	VIII
Roye, Edward James	VIII	Russ, John Dennison	VIII
Royster, James Finch	VIII	Russell, Annie	2
Ruark, Robert Chester	7	Russell, Benjamin	VIII
Rubin, Isidor Clinton	6	Russell, Charles Edward	3
Rubinow, Isaac Max	2	Russell, Charles Taze	VIII
Rubinstein, Helena	7	Russell, Charles Wells	VIII
Rublee, George	6	Russell, David Allen	VIII
Rublee, Horace	VIII	Russell, Henry Norris	6
Ruckstull, Frederick Wellington	3	Russell, Irwin	VIII
Rudge, William Edwin	VIII	Russell, Israel Cook	VIII

Complete Index Guide

Name	Vol./Supp.	Name	Vol./Supp.
Russell, James Earl	3	Sabin, Florence Rena	5
Russell, James Solomon	1	Sabin, Joseph	VIII
Russell, John Henry	VIII	Sabine, Lorenzo	VIII
Russell, Jonathan	VIII	Sabine, Wallace Clement Ware	VIII
Russell, Joseph	VIII	Sacagawea	VIII
Russell, Lillian	VIII	Sacco, Nicola	VIII
Russell, Mother Mary Baptist	VIII	Sachs, Bernard	3
Russell, Osborne	VIII	Sachs, Hanns	4
Russell, Sol Smith	VIII	Sachs, Julius	VIII
Russell, William	VIII	Sachs, Paul Joseph	7
Russell, William Eustis	VIII	Sachs, Theodore Bernard	VIII
Russell, William Henry	VIII	Sachse, Julius Friedrich	VIII
Russell, William Hepburn	VIII	Sack, Israel	6
Russwurm, John Brown	VIII	Sackett, Henry Woodward	VIII
Rust, John Daniel	5	Sadlier, Denis	VIII
Rust, Richard Sutton	VIII	Sadlier, Mary Anne Madden	VIII
Ruter, Martin	VIII	Sadtler, John Philip Benjamin	VIII
Rutgers, Henry	VIII	Sadtler, Samuel Philip	VIII
Ruth, George Herman		Saenderl, Simon	VIII
("Babe")	4	Safford, James Merrill	VIII
Rutherford, Joseph Franklin	3	Safford, Truman Henry	VIII
Rutherfurd, Lewis Morris	VIII	Safford, William Edwin	VIII
Rutledge, Edward	VIII	Sage, Bernard Janin	VIII
Rutledge, John	VIII	Sage, Henry Williams	VIII
Rutledge, Wiley Blount	4	Sage, Margaret Olivia Slocum	VIII
Ryan, Abram Joseph	VIII	Sage, Russell	VIII
Ryan, Arthur Clayton	VIII	St. Ange de Bellerive, Louis	VIII
Ryan, Edward George	VIII	St. Clair, Arthur	VIII
Ryan, Harris Joseph	1	St. Denis (Denys), Louis	
Ryan, John Augustine	3	Juchereau de	VIII
Ryan, John Dennis	VIII	Saint-Gaudens, Augustus	VIII
Ryan, Patrick John	VIII	St. John, Charles Edward	3
Ryan, Stephen Vincent	VIII	St. John, Isaac Munroe	VIII
Ryan, Thomas Fortune	VIII	St. John, John Pierce	VIII
Ryan, Walter D'Arcy	VIII	St. Lusson, Simon François	
Rybner, Martin Cornelius	VIII	Daumont, Sieur de	VIII
Rydberg, Per Axel	VIII	Saint-Mémin, Charles Balthazar	
Ryder, Albert Pinkham	VIII	Julien Fevret de	VIII
Ryerson, Martin Antoine	VIII	Saint-Méry, Moreau de	
Ryland, Robert	VIII	See Moreau de	
Rynning, Ole	VIII	Saint-Méry,	
		Médéric-Louis-Elie	
Saarinen, Eero	7	St. Vrain, Ceran de Hault de	
Saarinen, Eliel	4	Lassus de	VIII
Sabath, Adolph J.	5	Sajous, Charles Euchariste de	
Sabin, Charles Hamilton	VIII	Médicis	VIII

Complete Index Guide

Name	Vol./Supp.	Name	Vol./Supp.
Sakel, Manfred Joshua	6	Sands, Benjamin Franklin	VIII
Salisbury, Albert	VIII	Sands, Comfort	VIII
Salisbury, Edward Elbridge	VIII	Sands, David	VIII
Salisbury, James Henry	VIII	Sands, Joshua Ratoon	VIII
Salisbury, Rollin D.	VIII	Sands, Robert Charles	VIII
Salmon, Daniel Elmer	VIII	Sandys, George	VIII
Salmon, Lucy Maynard	VIII	Sanford, Edmund Clark	VIII
Salmon, Thomas William	VIII	Sanford, Edward Terry	VIII
Salm-Salm, Agnes Elisabeth		Sanford, Elias Benjamin	VIII
Winona Leclercq Joy,		Sanford, Henry Shelton	VIII
Princess	VIII	Sanford, Nathan	VIII
Salomon, Haym	VIII	Sanger, Charles Robert	VIII
Salter, William	VIII	Sanger, George Partridge	VIII
Salter, William Mackintire	VIII	Sangster, Margaret Elizabeth	
Saltonstall, Dudley	VIII	Munson	VIII
Saltonstall, Gurdon	VIII	Sankey, Ira David	VIII
Saltonstall, Richard	VIII	Santayana, George	5
Saltus, Edgar Evertson	VIII	Sapir, Edward	2
Samaroff, Olga	4	Sappington, John	VIII
Sampson, Martin Wright	VIII	Sarg, Tony	3
Sampson, William	VIII	Sargent, Aaron Augustus	VIII
Sampson, William Thomas	VIII	Sargent, Charles Sprague	VIII
Samuels, Edward Augustus	VIII	Sargent, Dudley Allen	VIII
Samuels, Samuel	VIII	Sargent, Epes	VIII
Sanborn, Edwin David	VIII	Sargent, Fitzwilliam	VIII
Sanborn, Franklin Benjamin	VIII	Sargent, Frank Pierce	VIII
Sanborn, Katherine Abbott	VIII	Sargent, Frederick	VIII
Sanborn, Walter Henry	VIII	Sargent, George Henry	VIII
Sandeman, Robert	VIII	Sargent, Henry	VIII
Sanders, Billington McCarter	VIII	Sargent, Henry Winthrop	VIII
Sanders, Charles Walton	VIII	Sargent, James	VIII
Sanders, Daniel Clarke	VIII	Sargent, John Osborne	VIII
Sanders, Daniel Jackson	VIII	Sargent, John Singer	VIII
Sanders, Elizabeth Elkins	VIII	Sargent, Lucius Manlius	VIII
Sanders, Frank Knight	VIII	Sargent, Nathan	VIII
Sanders, George Nicholas	VIII	Sargent, Winthrop (d. 1820)	VIII
Sanders, James Harvey	VIII	Sargent, Winthrop (d. 1870)	VIII
Sanders, Thomas	VIII	Sarpy, Peter A.	VIII
Sanders, Wilbur Fisk	VIII	Sartain, Emily	VIII
Sanderson, Ezra Dwight	3	Sartain, John	VIII
Sanderson, John	VIII	Sartain, Samuel	VIII
Sanderson, Robert	VIII	Sartain, William	VIII
Sanderson, Sibyl	VIII	Sarton, George Alfred Léon	6
Sandham, Henry	VIII	Sartwell, Henry Parker	VIII
Sandler, Jacob Koppel	VIII	Saslavsky, Alexander	VIII

Complete Index Guide

Name	Vol./Supp.	Name	Vol./Supp.
Sassacus	VIII	Say, Thomas	VIII
Satterlee, Henry Yates	VIII	Sayles, John	VIII
Satterlee, Richard Sherwood	VIII	Sayre, Lewis Albert	VIII
Sauganash	VIII	Sayre, Reginald Hall	VIII
Saugrain de Vigni, Antoine		Sayre, Robert Heysham	VIII
François	VIII	Sayre, Stephen	VIII
Saulsbury, Eli	VIII	Scammell, Alexander	VIII
Saulsbury, Gove	VIII	Scammon, Jonathan Young	VIII
Saulsbury, Willard (d. 1892)	VIII	Scanlan, Lawrence	VIII
Saulsbury, Willard (d. 1927)	VIII	Scarborough, Dorothy	1
Saunders, Alvin	VIII	Scarborough, Lee Rutland	3
Saunders, Clarence	5	Scarborough, William Saunders	VIII
Saunders, Frederick	VIII	Scarbrough, William	VIII
Saunders, Prince	VIII	Scattergood, Thomas	VIII
Saunders, Romulus Mitchell	VIII	Schadle, Jacob Evans	VIII
Saunders, William	VIII	Schaeberle, John Martin	VIII
Saunders, William Laurence		Schaeffer, Charles Frederick	VIII
(d. 1891)	VIII	Schaeffer, Charles William	VIII
Saunders, William Lawrence		Schaeffer, David Frederick	VIII
(d. 1931)	VIII	Schaeffer, Frederick Christian	VIII
Saur, Christopher		Schaeffer, Frederick David	VIII
See Sower, Christopher		Schaeffer, Nathan Christ	VIII
Sauveur, Albert	2	Schaff, Philip	VIII
Savage, Edward	VIII	Schall, Thomas David	1
Savage, Henry Wilson	VIII	Schamberg, Jay Frank	VIII
Savage, James	VIII	Scharf, John Thomas	VIII
Savage, John	VIII	Schauffler, Henry Albert	VIII
Savage, Minot Judson	VIII	Schauffler, William Gottlieb	VIII
Savage, Philip Henry	VIII	Schechter, Solomon	VIII
Savage, Thomas Staughton	VIII	Scheel, Fritz	VIII
Savery, William (d. 1787)	VIII	Schele de Vere, Maximilian	VIII
Savery, William (d. 1804)	VIII	Schell, Augustus	VIII
Saville, Marshall Howard	1	Schelling, Ernest Henry	2
Sawyer, Leicester Ambrose	VIII	Schelling, Felix Emanuel	3
Sawyer, Lemuel	VIII	Schem, Alexander Jacob	VIII
Sawyer, Lorenzo	VIII	Schenandoa	
Sawyer, Philetus	VIII	See Skenandoa	
Sawyer, Sylvanus	VIII	Schenck, Ferdinand Schureman	VIII
Sawyer, Thomas Jefferson	VIII	Schenck, James Findlay	VIII
Sawyer, Walter Howard	VIII	Schenck, Robert Cumming	VIII
Sawyer, Wilbur Augustus	5	Schereschewsky, Samuel Isaac	
Saxe, John Godfrey	VIII	Joseph	VIII
Saxton, Eugene Francis	3	Scheve, Edward Benjamin	VIII
Saxton, Joseph	VIII	Schevill, Randolph	4
Say, Benjamin	VIII		

Complete Index Guide

Name	Vol./Supp.	Name	Vol./Supp.
Schickillemy		Schomer, Nahum Meir	VIII
See Shikellamy		Schoolcraft, Henry Rowe	VIII
Schieren, Charles Adolph	VIII	Schöpf, Johann David	VIII
Schiff, Jacob Henry	VIII	Schott, Charles Anthony	VIII
Schildkraut, Joseph	7	Schouler, James	VIII
Schilling, Hugo Karl	VIII	Schouler, William	VIII
Schillinger, Joseph	3	Schradieck, Henry	VIII
Schindler, Kurt	1	Schrembs, Joseph	3
Schindler, Rudolph Michael	5	Schrieck, Sister Louise van der	VIII
Schindler, Solomon	VIII	Schriver, Edmund	VIII
Schinz, Albert	3	Schroeder, John Frederick	VIII
Schirmer, Gustav	VIII	Schroeder, Rudolph William	5
Schirmer, Rudolph Edward	VIII	Schroeder, Seaton	VIII
Schlatter, Michael	VIII	Schuchert, Charles	3
Schlesinger, Benjamin	VIII	Schuessele, Christian	
Schlesinger, Frank	3	See Schussele, Christian	
Schlessinger, Arthur Maier, Sr.	7	Schultz, Dutch	
Schley, Winfield Scott	VIII	See Flegenheimer, Arthur	
Schmauk, Theodore Emanuel	VIII	Schultz, Henry	2
Schmidt, Arthur Paul	VIII	Schultze, Augustus	VIII
Schmidt, Carl Louis August	4	Schumann-Heink, Ernestine	2
Schmidt, Friedrich August	VIII	Schumpeter, Joseph Alois	4
Schmidt, Nathaniel	2	Schurman, Jacob Gould	3
Schmucker, Beale Melanchthon	VIII	Schurz, Carl	VIII
Schmucker, John George	VIII	Schussele, Christian	VIII
Schmucker, Samuel Simon	VIII	Schuttler, Peter	VIII
Schnabel, Artur	5	Schuyler, Eugene	VIII
Schnauffer, Carl Heinrich	VIII	Schuyler, George Washington	VIII
Schneider, Albert	VIII	Schuyler, James Dix	VIII
Schneider, Benjamin	VIII	Schuyler, Louisa Lee	VIII
Schneider, George	VIII	Schuyler, Margarita	VIII
Schneider, Herman	2	Schuyler, Montgomery	VIII
Schneider, Theodore	VIII	Schuyler, Peter	VIII
Schneller, George Otto	VIII	Schuyler, Philip John	VIII
Schnerr, Leander	VIII	Schwab, Charles Michael	2
Schodde, George Henry	VIII	Schwab, John Christopher	VIII
Schoenberg, Arnold	5	Schwartz, Maurice	6
Schoenheimer, Rudolph	3	Schwarz, Eugene Amandus	VIII
Schoenhof, Jacob	VIII	Schwatka, Frederick	VIII
Schoeppel, Andrew Frank	7	Schweinitz, Edmund Alexander	
Schoff, Stephen Alonzo	VIII	de	VIII
Schofield, Henry	VIII	Schweinitz, Emil Alexander de	VIII
Schofield, John McAllister	VIII	Schweinitz, George Edmund de	2
Schofield, William Henry	VIII	Schweinitz, Lewis David von	VIII
Scholte, Hendrik Peter	VIII	Schwellenbach, Lewis Baxter	4

Complete Index Guide

Name	Vol./Supp.	Name	Vol./Supp.
Schwidetzky, Oscar Otto Rudolf	7	Screws, William Wallace	VIII
Schwimmer, Rosika	4	Scribner, Charles (d. 1871)	VIII
Scidmore, Eliza Ruhamah	VIII	Scribner, Charles (d. 1930)	VIII
Scollard, Clinton	VIII	Scribner, Charles (d. 1952)	5
Scott, Allen Cecil	7	Scripps, Edward Wyllis	VIII
Scott, Austin	VIII	Scripps, Ellen Browning	VIII
Scott, Charles	VIII	Scripps, James Edmund	VIII
Scott, Colin Alexander	VIII	Scripps, Robert Paine	2
Scott, Dred	VIII	Scripps, William Edmund	5
Scott, Emmett Jay	6	Scruggs, William Lindsay	VIII
Scott, Fred Newton	VIII	Scrymser, James Alexander	VIII
Scott, Gustavus	VIII	Scudder, Horace Elisha	VIII
Scott, Harvey Whitefield	VIII	Scudder, John	VIII
Scott, Hugh Lenox	1	Scudder, John Milton	VIII
Scott, Irving Murray	VIII	Scudder, (Julia) Vida Dutton	5
Scott, James Brown	3	Scudder, Nathaniel	VIII
Scott, James Wilmot	VIII	Scudder, Samuel Hubbard	VIII
Scott, Job	VIII	Scull, John	VIII
Scott, John	VIII	Scullin, John	VIII
Scott, John Adams	4	Seabury, George John	VIII
Scott, John Morin	VIII	Seabury, Samuel (d. 1796)	VIII
Scott, John Prindle	VIII	Seabury, Samuel (d. 1872)	VIII
Scott, Leroy	VIII	Seabury, Samuel (d. 1958)	6
Scott, Orange	VIII	Seager, Henry Rogers	VIII
Scott, Robert Kingston	VIII	Seagrave, Gordon Stifler	7
Scott, Samuel Parsons	VIII	Sealsfield, Charles	VIII
Scott, Thomas Alexander	VIII	Seaman, Elizabeth Cochrane	VIII
Scott, Thomas Fielding	VIII	Searing, Laura Catherine Redden	VIII
Scott, Walter	VIII	Searle, Arthur	VIII
Scott, Walter Dill	5	Searle, James	VIII
Scott, Walter Edward	5	Searle, John Preston	VIII
Scott, William	VIII	Sears, Barnas	VIII
Scott, William Anderson	VIII	Sears, Edmund Hamilton	VIII
Scott, William Berryman	4	Sears, Isaac	VIII
Scott, W(illiam) Kerr	6	Sears, Richard Dudley	3
Scott, William Lawrence	VIII	Sears, Richard Warren	VIII
Scott, Winfield	VIII	Sears, Robert	VIII
Scovel, Henry Sylvester	VIII	Seashore, Carl Emil	4
Scovel, Sylvester See Scovel, Henry Sylvester		Seaton, William Winston	VIII
		Seattle	VIII
		Seawell, Molly Elliot	VIII
Scovell, Melville Amasa	VIII	Sebastian, Benjamin	VIII
Scoville, Joseph Alfred	VIII	Seccomb, John	VIII
Scranton, George Whitfield	VIII	Seddon, James Alexander	VIII

Complete Index Guide

Name	Vol./Supp.	Name	Vol./Supp.
Sedella, Antoine		Selikovitsch, Goetzel	VIII
See Antoine, Père		Sellers, Coleman	VIII
Sedgwick, Anne Douglas	1	Sellers, Isaiah	VIII
Sedgwick, Arthur George	VIII	Sellers, Matthew Bacon	VIII
Sedgwick, Catharine Maria	VIII	Sellers, William	VIII
Sedgwick, Ellery	6	Sellstedt, Lars Gustaf	VIII
Sedgwick, John	VIII	Selyns, Henricus	
Sedgwick, Robert	VIII	See Selijns, Henricus	
Sedgwick, Theodore (d. 1813)	VIII	Selznick, David Oliver	7
Sedgwick, Theodore (d. 1839)	VIII	Sembrich, Marcella	1
Sedgwick, Theodore (d. 1859)	VIII	Semmes, Alexander Jenkins	VIII
Sedgwick, William Thompson	VIII	Semmes, Raphael	VIII
Sedley, William Henry		Semmes, Thomas Jenkins	VIII
See Smith, William Henry		Semple, Ellen Churchill	VIII
See, Horace	VIII	Seney, George Ingraham	VIII
Seed, Miles Ainscough	VIII	Senn, Nicholas	VIII
Seeger, Alan	VIII	Sennett, George Burritt	VIII
Seelye, Julius Hawley	VIII	Sennett, Mack	6
Seelye, Laurenus Clark	VIII	Sequoyah	VIII
Seevers, William Henry	VIII	Sergeant, Henry Clark	VIII
Seghers, Charles Jean	VIII	Sergeant, John (d. 1749)	VIII
Seguin, Edouard	VIII	Sergeant, John (d. 1852)	VIII
Seguin, Edward Constant	VIII	Sergeant, Jonathan Dickinson	VIII
Seiberling, Frank Augustus	5	Sergeant, Thomas	VIII
Seibold, Louis	3	Serra, Junípero	VIII
Seidel, Emil	4	Serrell, Edward Wellman	VIII
Seidensticker, Oswald	VIII	Service, Robert William	6
Seidl, Anton	VIII	Servoss, Thomas Lowery	VIII
Seiler, Carl	VIII	Sessions, Henry Howard	VIII
Seip, Theodore Lorenzo	VIII	Sestini, Benedict	VIII
Seiss, Joseph Augustus	VIII	Setchell, William Albert	3
Seitz, Don Carlos	1	Seth, James	VIII
Seixas, Gershom Mendes	VIII	Seton, Elizabeth Ann Bayley	VIII
Séjour, Victor	VIII	Seton, Ernest Thompson	4
Selby, William	VIII	Seton, Grace Gallatin	
Selden, George Baldwin	VIII	Thompson	6
Selfridge, Thomas Oliver	VIII	Seton, Robert	VIII
Selig, William Nicholas	4	Seton, William	VIII
Seligman, Arthur	VIII	Settle, Thomas	VIII
Seligman, Edwin Robert		Severance, Caroline Maria	
Anderson	2	Seymour	VIII
Seligman, Isaac Newton	VIII	Severance, Frank Hayward	VIII
Seligman, Jesse	VIII	Severance, Louis Henry	VIII
Seligman, Joseph	VIII	Sevier, Ambrose Hundley	VIII
Selijns, Henricus	VIII	Sevier, John	VIII

Complete Index Guide

Name	Vol./Supp.	Name	Vol./Supp.
Sewall, Arthur	VIII	Sharp, Katharine Lucinda	IX
Sewall, Frank	VIII	Sharp, William Graves	IX
Sewall, Harold Marsh	VIII	Sharpe, Horatio	IX
Sewall, Jonathan	VIII	Sharples, James	IX
Sewall, Jonathan Mitchell	VIII	Sharpless, Isaac	IX
Sewall, Joseph Addison	VIII	Sharswood, George	IX
Sewall, May Eliza Wright	VIII	Shattuck, Aaron Draper	IX
Sewall, Samuel	VIII	Shattuck, Frederick Cheever	IX
Sewall, Stephen	VIII	Shattuck, George Brune	IX
Seward, Frederick William	VIII	Shattuck, George Cheyne	
Seward, George Frederick	VIII	(d. 1854)	IX
Seward, Theodore		Shattuck, George Cheyne	
Frelinghuysen	VIII	(d. 1893)	IX
Seward, William Henry	VIII	Shattuck, Lemuel	IX
Sewell, William Joyce	IX	Shaubena	
Seybert, Adam	IX	See Shabonee	
Seybert, Henry	IX	Shauck, John Allen	IX
Seybert, John	IX	Shaw, Albert	4
Seyffarth, Gustavus	IX	Shaw, Anna Howard	IX
Seymour, Charles	7	Shaw, Edward Richard	IX
Seymour, George Franklin	IX	Shaw, Elijah	IX
Seymour, Horatio	IX	Shaw, Henry	IX
Seymour, Horatio Winslow	IX	Shaw, Henry Wheeler	IX
Seymour, Thomas Day	IX	Shaw, Howard Van Doren	IX
Seymour, Thomas Hart	IX	Shaw, John (b. 1773)	IX
Seymour, Truman	IX	Shaw, John (b. 1778)	IX
Seymour, William	IX	Shaw, Lemuel	IX
Shabonee	IX	Shaw, Leslie Mortier	IX
Shafer, Helen Almira	IX	Shaw, Mary	IX
Shafroth, John Franklin	IX	Shaw, Nathaniel	IX
Shafter, William Rufus	IX	Shaw, Oliver	IX
Shahan, Thomas Joseph	IX	Shaw, Pauline Agassiz	IX
Shaikewitz, Nahum Meir		Shaw, Samuel	IX
See Schomer, Nahum		Shaw, Thomas	IX
Meir		Shaw, (Warren) Wilbur	5
Shakallamy		Shaw, William Smith	IX
See Shikellamy		Shays, Daniel	IX
Shaler, Nathaniel Southgate	IX	Shea, John Dawson Gilmary	IX
Shaler, William	IX	Shean, Al	4
Shannon, Fred Albert	7	Shear, Theodore Leslie	3
Shannon, Wilson	IX	Shearman, Thomas Gaskell	IX
Sharkey, William Lewis	IX	Shecut, John Linnaeus Edward	
Sharp, Dallas Lore	IX	Whitridge	IX
Sharp, Daniel	IX	Shedd, Fred Fuller	2
Sharp, John	IX	Shedd, Joel Herbert	IX

Complete Index Guide

Name	Vol./Supp.	Name	Vol./Supp.
Shedd, John Graves	IX	Sherman, Henry Clapp	5
Shedd, William Ambrose	IX	Sherman, James Schoolcraft	IX
Shedd, William Greenough		Sherman, John (d. 1685)	IX
Thayer	IX	Sherman, John (d. 1900)	IX
Sheedy, Dennis	IX	Sherman, Roger	IX
Sheeler, Charles R.	7	Sherman, Stuart Pratt	IX
Sheffield, Devello Zelotes	IX	Sherman, Thomas West	IX
Sheffield, Joseph Earl	IX	Sherman, William Tecumseh	IX
Shelby, Evan	IX	Sherry, Louis	IX
Shelby, Isaac	IX	Sherwin, Thomas	IX
Shelby, Joseph Orville	IX	Sherwood, Adiel	IX
Sheldon, Charles Monroe	4	Sherwood, Isaac Ruth	IX
Sheldon, Edward Austin	IX	Sherwood, Katharine Margaret	
Sheldon, Edward Stevens	IX	Brownlee	IX
Sheldon, Henry Newton	IX	Sherwood, Mary Elizabeth	
Sheldon, Mary Downing		Wilson	IX
See Barnes, Mary		Sherwood, Robert Emmet	5
Downing Sheldon		Sherwood, Thomas Adiel	IX
Sheldon, Walter Lorenzo	IX	Sherwood, William Hall	IX
Sheldon, William Evarts	IX	Shick, Calamys	
Shelekhov, Grigoriĭ Ivanovich	IX	See Shikellamy	
Shellabarger, Samuel	5	Shields, Charles Woodruff	IX
Shelton, Albert Leroy	IX	Shields, George Howell	IX
Shelton, Edward Mason	IX	Shields, George Oliver	IX
Shelton, Frederick William	IX	Shields, James	IX
Shepard, Charles Upham	IX	Shields, John Knight	1
Shepard, Edward Morse	IX	Shields, Thomas Edward	IX
Shepard, Fred Douglas	IX	Shikellamy	IX
Shepard, James Edward	4	Shillaber, Benjamin Penhallow	IX
Shepard, James Henry	IX	Shinn, Asa	IX
Shepard, Jesse		Shinn, Everett	5
See Grierson, Francis		Shipherd, John Jay	IX
Shepard, Seth	IX	Shipman, Andrew Jackson	IX
Shepard, Thomas	IX	Shipp, Albert Micajah	IX
Shepard, William	IX	Shipp, Scott	IX
Shepherd, Alexander Robey	IX	Shippen, Edward (d. 1712)	IX
Shepherd, William Robert	1	Shippen, Edward (d. 1806)	IX
Shepley, Ether	IX	Shippen, William	IX
Shepley, George Foster	IX	Shipstead, Henrik	6
Sheppard, John Morris	3	Shiras, George	IX
Sheppard, Samuel Edward	4	Shiras, Oliver Perry	IX
Sheridan, Philip Henry	IX	Shirlaw, Walter	IX
Sherman, Forrest Percival	5	Shirley, William	IX
Sherman, Frank Dempster	IX	Shobonier	
Sherman, Frederick Carl	6	See Shabonee	

Complete Index Guide

Name	Vol./Supp.	Name	Vol./Supp.
Sholes, Christopher Latham	IX	Sicard, Montgomery	IX
Shonts, Theodore Perry	IX	Sickels, Frederick Ellsworth	IX
Shook, Alfred Montgomery	IX	Sickles, Daniel Edgar	IX
Shorey, Paul	IX	Sidell, William Henry	IX
Short, Charles	IX	Sidis, Boris	IX
Short, Charles Wilkins	IX	Sidney, Margaret	
Short, Joseph Hudson, Jr.	5	See Lothrop, Harriett	
Short, Sidney Howe	IX	Mulford Stone	
Short, Walter Campbell	4	Sieber, Al	1
Short, William	IX	Sigel, Franz	IX
Shorter, John Gill	IX	Sigerist, Henry Ernest	6
Shotwell, James Thomson	7	Sigman, Morris	IX
Shoup, Francis Asbury	IX	Sigourney, Lydia Howard	
Shoup, George Laird	IX	Huntley	IX
Showerman, Grant	1	Sigsbee, Charles Dwight	IX
Shrady, George Frederick	IX	Sikes, William Wirt	IX
Shrady, Henry Merwin	IX	Silcox, Ferdinand Augustus	2
Shreve, Henry Miller	IX	Sill, Anna Peck	IX
Shreve, Thomas Hopkins	IX	Sill, Edward Rowland	IX
Shubert, Lee	5	Silliman, Benjamin (d. 1864)	IX
Shubrick, John Templer	IX	Silliman, Benjamin (d. 1885)	IX
Shubrick, William Branford	IX	Sills, Milton	IX
Shuck, Jehu Lewis	IX	Siloti, Alexander Ilyitch	3
Shuey, Edwin Longstreet	IX	Silsbee, Nathaniel	IX
Shuey, William John	IX	Silver, Abba Hillel	7
Shufeldt, Robert Wilson	IX	Silver, Gray	1
Shull, George Harrison	5	Silver, Thomas	IX
Shull, Lee	5	Silverman, Joseph	IX
Shulze, John Andrew	IX	Silverman, Sime	IX
Shunk, Francis Rawn	IX	Silvers, Louis	5
Shurtleff, Nathaniel Bradstreet	IX	Simkhovitch, Mary Melinda	
Shurtleff, Roswell Morse	IX	Kingsbury	5
Shuster, W(illiam) Morgan	6	Simmons (Szymanski), Aloysius	
Shute, Samuel	IX	Harry	6
Siamese Twins		Simmons, Edward	IX
See Chang and Eng		Simmons, Franklin	IX
Sibert, William Luther	1	Simmons, Furnifold McLendel	2
Sibley, George Champlain	IX	Simmons, George Henry	2
Sibley, Henry Hastings	IX	Simmons, James Stevens	5
Sibley, Hiram	IX	Simmons, Roscoe Conkling	
Sibley, John	IX	Murray	5
Sibley, John Langdon	IX	Simmons, Thomas Jefferson	IX
Sibley, Joseph Crocker	IX	Simmons, William Joseph	3
Sicalamous		Simms, Ruth Hanna	
See Shikellamy		McCormick	3

Complete Index Guide

Name	Vol./Supp.	Name	Vol./Supp.
Simms, William Elliott	IX	Skinner, Otis	3
Simms, William Gilmore	IX	Skinner, Thomas Harvey	IX
Simon, Richard Leo	6	Skinner, William	IX
Simonds, Frank Herbert	2	Skouras, George Panagiotes	7
Simons, Algie Martin	4	Slade, Joseph Alfred	IX
Simons, Harry Calvert	4	Slade, William	IX
Simonton, Charles Henry	IX	Slafter, Edmund Farwell	IX
Simonton, James William	IX	Slater, John Fox	IX
Simpson, Albert Benjamin	IX	Slater, Samuel	IX
Simpson, Charles Torrey	1	Slattery, Charles Lewis	IX
Simpson, Edmund Shaw	IX	Slaughter, Philip	IX
Simpson, Edward	IX	Sleeper, Jacob	IX
Simpson, James Hervey	IX	Slemp, Campbell Bascom	3
Simpson, Jerry	IX	Slicer, Thomas Roberts	IX
Simpson, John Andrew	IX	Slichter, Sumner Huber	6
Simpson, Matthew	IX	Slidell, John	IX
Simpson, Michael Hodge	IX	Sloan, George Arthur	5
Simpson, Stephen	IX	Sloan, Harold Paul	7
Simpson, William Dunlap	IX	Sloan, James Forman	IX
Simpson, William Kelly	IX	Sloan, John French	5
Sims, Charles N.	IX	Sloan, Matthew Scott	3
Sims, James Marion	IX	Sloan, Richard Elihu	IX
Sims, William Sowden	2	Sloan, Samuel	IX
Sims, Winfield Scott	IX	Sloan, Tod	
Sinclair, Harry Ford	6	See Sloan, James Forman	
Singer, Isaac Merrit	IX	Sloane, Isabel Dodge	7
Singer, Israel Joshua	3	Sloane, William Milligan	IX
Singerly, William Miskey	IX	Sloat, John Drake	IX
Singleton, Esther	IX	Slocum, Frances	IX
Singleton, James Washington	IX	Slocum, Henry Warner	IX
Siringo, Charles A.	IX	Slocum, Joshua	IX
Sitting Bull	IX	Slocum, Samuel	IX
Sizer, Nelson	IX	Sloss, James Withers	IX
Skaniadariio	IX	Sloss, Louis	IX
Skenandoa	IX	Slosson, Edwin Emery	IX
Skene, Alexander Johnston		Small, Albion Woodbury	IX
Chalmers	IX	Small, Alvan Edmond	IX
Skidmore, Louis	7	Smalley, Eugene Virgil	IX
Skillern, Ross Hall	IX	Smalley, George Washburn	IX
Skinner, Aaron Nichols	IX	Smalls, Robert	IX
Skinner, Alanson Buck	IX	Smallwood, William	IX
Skinner, Charles Rufus	IX	Smart, David Archibald	5
Skinner, Halcyon	IX	Smart, James Henry	IX
Skinner, Harry	IX	Smedley, Agnes	4
Skinner, John Stuart	IX	Smedley, William Thomas	IX

Complete Index Guide

Name	Vol./Supp.	Name	Vol./Supp.
Smibert, John	IX	Smith, Elihu Hubbard	IX
Smiley, Albert Keith	IX	Smith, Elizabeth Oakes Prince	IX
Smillie, George Henry	IX	Smith, Eliza Roxey Snow	
Smillie, James	IX	See Snow, Eliza Roxey	
Smillie, James David	IX	Smith, Ellison DuRant	3
Smillie, Ralph	6	Smith, Erasmus Darwin	IX
Smith, Abby Hadassah	IX	Smith, Erminnie Adelle Platt	IX
Smith, Albert Holmes	IX	Smith, Erwin Frink	IX
Smith, Alexander	IX	Smith, Eugene Allen	IX
Smith, Alfred Emanuel	3	Smith, Francis Henney	IX
Smith, Alfred Holland	IX	Smith, Francis Hopkinson	IX
Smith, Andrew Jackson	IX	Smith, Francis Marion	IX
Smith, Archibald Cary	IX	Smith, Frank Leslie	4
Smith, Arthur Henderson	IX	Smith, Fred Burton	2
Smith, Asa Dodge	IX	Smith, George	IX
Smith, Ashbel	IX	Smith, George Albert	5
Smith, Azariah	IX	Smith, George Henry	IX
Smith, Benjamin Eli	IX	Smith, George Otis	3
Smith, Benjamin Mosby	IX	Smith, Gerald Birney	IX
Smith, Bessie	2	Smith, Gerrit	IX
Smith, Bruce	5	Smith, Giles Alexander	IX
Smith, Buckingham	IX	Smith, Gustavus Woodson	IX
Smith, Byron Caldwell	IX	Smith, Hamilton	IX
Smith, Caleb Blood	IX	Smith, Hannah Whitall	IX
Smith, Charles Alphonso	IX	Smith, Harold Babbitt	IX
Smith, Charles Emory	IX	Smith, Harold Dewey	4
Smith, Charles Ferguson	IX	Smith, Harry Bache	2
Smith, Charles Forster	IX	Smith, Harry James	IX
Smith, Charles Henry (b. 1826)	IX	Smith, Henry Augustus	
Smith, Charles Henry (b. 1827)	IX	Middleton	IX
Smith, Charles Perrin	IX	Smith, Henry Boynton	IX
Smith, Charles Shaler	IX	Smith, Henry Justin	2
Smith, Charles Sprague	IX	Smith, Henry Louis	5
Smith, Chauncey	IX	Smith, Henry Preserved	IX
Smith, Daniel	IX	Smith, Hezekiah	IX
Smith, Daniel B.	IX	Smith, Hiram	IX
Smith, David	7	Smith, Hoke	IX
Smith, David Eugene	3	Smith, Homer William	7
Smith, Edgar Fahs	IX	Smith, Horace	IX
Smith, Edmund Kirby		Smith, Horatio Elwin	4
See Kirby-Smith, Edmund		Smith, Horton	7
Smith, Edmund Munroe	IX	Smith, Israel	IX
Smith, Edward Hanson	7	Smith, James (d. 1806)	IX
Smith, Eli	IX	Smith, James (d. c. 1814)	IX
Smith, Elias	IX	Smith, James (d. 1927)	IX

Complete Index Guide

Name	Vol./Supp.	Name	Vol./Supp.
Smith, James Allen	IX	Smith, Meriwether	IX
Smith, James Francis	IX	Smith, Milton Hannibal	IX
Smith, James McCune	IX	Smith, Morgan Lewis	IX
Smith, James Perrin	IX	Smith, Nathan (*d. 1829*)	IX
Smith, James Youngs	IX	Smith, Nathan (*d. 1835*)	IX
Smith, Jedediah Strong	IX	Smith, Nathaniel	IX
Smith, Jeremiah	1	Smith, Nathan Ryno	IX
Smith, Jeremiah (*d. 1842*)	IX	Smith, Oliver	IX
Smith, Jeremiah (*d. 1921*)	IX	Smith, Oliver Hampton	IX
Smith, Job Lewis	IX	Smith, Ormond Gerald	1
Smith, Joel West	IX	Smith, Persifor Frazer	IX
Smith, John (*d. 1631*)	IX	Smith, Peter	IX
Smith, John (*d. c. 1824*)	IX	Smith, Preserved	3
Smith, John Augustine	IX	Smith, Richard	IX
Smith, John Bernhard	IX	Smith, Richard Penn	IX
Smith, John Blair	IX	Smith, Richard Somers	IX
Smith, John Cotton (*d. 1845*)	IX	Smith, Robert (*d. 1777*)	IX
Smith, John Cotton (*d. 1882*)	IX	Smith, Robert (*d. 1801*)	IX
Smith, John Eugene	IX	Smith, Robert (*d. 1842*)	IX
Smith, John Gregory	IX	Smith, Robert Alexander C.	IX
Smith, John Jay	IX	Smith, Robert Barnwell	
Smith, John Lawrence	IX	See Rhett, Robert	
Smith, John Merlin Powis	IX	Barnwell	
Smith, John Rowson	IX	Smith, Robert Hardy	IX
Smith, John Rubens	IX	Smith, Robert Sidney	1
Smith, Jonas Waldo	IX, 1	Smith, Roswell	IX
Smith, Jonathan Bayard	IX	Smith, Russell	IX
Smith, Joseph (*b. 1790*)	IX	Smith, Samuel	IX
Smith, Joseph (*b. 1805*)	IX	Smith, Samuel Francis	IX
Smith, Joseph (*b. 1832*)	IX	Smith, Samuel Harrison	IX
Smith, Joseph Fielding	IX	Smith, Samuel Stanhope	IX
Smith, Judson	IX	Smith, Seba	IX
Smith, Julia Evelina		Smith, Solomon Franklin	IX
See Smith,		Smith, Sophia	IX
Abby Hadassah		Smith, Stephen	IX
Smith, Junius	IX	Smith, Theobald	1
Smith, Justin Harvey	IX	Smith, Theodate Louise	IX
Smith, Lloyd Pearsall	IX	Smith, Thomas Adams	1
Smith, Logan Pearsall	4	Smith, Thomas Vernor	7
Smith, Lucy Harth	5	Smith, Truman	IX
Smith, Marcus	IX	Smith, Uriah	IX
Smith, Margaret Bayard	IX	Smith, Walter Bedell	7
Smith, Martin Luther	IX	Smith, Walter Inglewood	IX
Smith, Melancton (*d. 1798*)	IX	Smith, William (*b. 1697*)	IX
Smith, Melancton (*d. 1893*)	IX	Smith, William (*b. 1727*)	IX

Complete Index Guide

Name	Vol./Supp.	Name	Vol./Supp.
Smith, William (b. 1728)	IX	Snyder, John Francis	IX
Smith, William (b. c. 1754)	IX	Snyder, Simon	IX
Smith, William (b. c. 1762)	IX	Sobolewski, J. Friedrich Eduard	IX
Smith, William (b. 1797)	IX	Sokolsky, George Ephraim	7
Smith, William Andrew	IX	Soldan, Frank Louis	IX
Smith, William Farrar	IX	Soley, James Russell	IX
Smith, William Henry		Solger, Reinhold	IX
(d. 1872)	IX	Solis-Cohen, Jacob da Silva	
Smith, William Henry		See Cohen, Jacob da Silva	
(d. 1896)	IX	Solis	
Smith, William Loughton	IX	Solomons, Adolphus Simeon	IX
Smith, William Nathan Harrell	IX	Somers, Richard	IX
Smith, William Russell	IX	Somervell, Brehon Burke	5
Smith, William Sooy	IX	Sonneck, Oscar George	
Smith, William Stephens	IX	Theodore	IX
Smith, William Waugh	IX	Sonnichsen, Albert	IX
Smith, Winchell	IX	Son of Many Beads	5
Smith, Xanthus Russell	IX	Sooysmith, Charles	IX
Smohalla	IX	Sophocles, Evangelinus	
Smott, Reed Owen	3	Apostolides	IX
Smyth, Albert Henry	IX	Sorge, Friedrich Adolph	IX
Smyth, Alexander	IX	Sorin, Edward Frederick	IX
Smyth, Egbert Coffin	IX	Sothern, Edward Askew	IX
Smyth, Herbert Weir	2	Sothern, Edward Hugh	IX
Smyth, John Henry	IX	Sothern, Julia Marlowe	
Smyth, Julian Kennedy	IX	See Marlowe, Julia	
Smyth, Newman	IX	Soto, Hernando de	
Smyth, Thomas	IX	See De Soto, Hernando	
Smyth, William	IX	Souchon, Edmond	IX
Snead, Thomas Lowndes	IX	Soulé, George	IX
Snell, Bertrand Hollis	6	Soule, Joshua	IX
Snelling, Henry Hunt	IX	Soulé, Pierre	IX
Snelling, Josiah	IX	Sousa, John Philip	IX
Snelling, William Joseph	IX	Southack, Cyprian	IX
Snethen, Nicholas	IX	Southall, James Cocke	IX
Snider, Denton Jaques	IX	Southard, Elmer Ernest	IX
Snow, Carmel White	7	Southard, Lucien H.	IX
Snow, Eliza Roxey	IX	Southard, Samuel Lewis	IX
Snow, Francis Huntington	IX	Southgate, Horatio	1
Snow, Jesse Baker	4	Southmayd, Charles Ferdinand	IX
Snow, Lorenza	IX	Southwick, Solomon	IX
Snow, William Freeman	4	Southworth, Emma Dorothy	
Snowden, James Ross	IX	Eliza Nevitte	IX
Snowden, Thomas	IX	Sower, Christopher (d. 1758)	IX
Snyder, Edwin Reagan	IX	Sower, Christopher (d. 1784)	IX

Complete Index Guide

Name	Vol./Supp.	Name	Vol./Supp.
Sower, Christopher (*d. 1799*)	IX	Spencer, Elihu	IX
Spaeth, Adolph	IX	Spencer, Jesse Ames	IX
Spaeth, John Duncan	5	Spencer, John Canfield	IX
Spaeth, Sigmund	7	Spencer, Joseph	IX
Spahr, Charles Barzillai	IX	Spencer, Pitman Clemens	IX
Spaight, Richard Dobbs	IX	Spencer, Platt Rogers	IX
Spalding, Albert	5	Spencer, Robert	IX
Spalding, Albert Goodwill	IX	Spencer, Samuel	IX
Spalding, Catherine	IX	Sperry, Elmer Ambrose	IX
Spalding, Franklin Spencer	IX	Sperry, Nehemiah Day	IX
Spalding, John Lancaster	IX	Sperry, Willard Learoyd	5
Spalding, Lyman	IX	Speyer, James Joseph	3
Spalding, Martin John	IX	Spicker, Max	IX
Spalding, Thomas	IX	Spier, Leslie	7
Spalding, Volney Morgan	IX	Spiering, Theodore	IX
Spangenberg, Augustus Gottlieb	IX	Spillman, William Jasper	IX
Spangler, Edward		Spilsbury, Edmund Gybbon	IX
See Booth, John Wilkes		Spingarn, Joel Elias	2
Spangler, Henry Wilson	IX	Spink, (John George) Taylor	7
Sparks, Edwin Erle	IX	Spinner, Francis Elias	IX
Sparks, Jared	IX	Spitzka, Edward Anthony	IX
Sparks, William Andrew		Spitzka, Edward Charles	IX
Jackson	IX	Spivak, Charles David	IX
Sparrow, William	IX	Spofford, Ainsworth Rand	IX
Spaulding, Charles Clinton	5	Spofford, Harriet Elizabeth	
Spaulding, Edward Gleason	2	Prescott	IX
Spaulding, Elbridge Gerry	IX	Spooner, John Coit	IX
Spaulding, Levi	IX	Spooner, Lysander	IX
Spaulding, Oliver Lyman	IX	Spooner, Shearjashub	IX
Speaker, Tris E.	6	Spotswood, Alexander	IX
Speaks, Oley	4	Spotted Tail	IX
Spear, Charles	IX	Sprague, Achsa W.	IX
Spear, William Thomas	IX	Sprague, Charles	IX
Speck, Frank Gouldsmith	4	Sprague, Charles Ezra	IX
Speed, James	IX	Sprague, Frank Julian	1
Speer, Emma Bailey	7	Sprague, Homer Baxter	IX
Speer, Emory	IX	Sprague, Kate Chase	IX
Speer, Robert Elliott	4	Sprague, Oliver Mitchell	
Speer, William	IX	Wentworth	5
Speir, Samuel Fleet	IX	Sprague, Peleg	IX
Speiser, Ephraim Avigdor	7	Sprague, William (*d. 1836*)	IX
Spencer, Ambrose	IX	Sprague, William (*d. 1915*)	IX
Spencer, Anna Garlin	IX	Sprague, William Buell	IX
Spencer, Christopher Miner	IX	Sprecher, Samuel	IX
Spencer, Cornelia Phillips	IX	Spreckels, Claus	IX

Complete Index Guide

Name	Vol./Supp.	Name	Vol./Supp.
Spreckels, John Diedrich	IX	Stanley, Augustus Owsley	6
Spreckels, Rudolph	6	Stanley, David Sloane	IX
Spring, Gardiner	IX	Stanley, Francis Edgar	IX
Spring, Leverett Wilson	IX	Stanley, Harold	7
Spring, Samuel	IX	Stanley, Henry Morton	IX
Springer, Charles	1	Stanley, John Mix	IX
Springer, Frank	IX	Stanley, Robert Crooks	5
Springer, Reuben Runyan	IX	Stanley, William	IX
Springer, William McKendree	IX	Stanly, Edward	IX
Sproul, William Cameron	IX	Stansbury, Howard	IX
Sproule, William	1	Stansbury, Joseph	IX
Sproull, Thomas	IX	Stanton, Edwin McMasters	IX
Sprunt, James	IX	Stanton, Elizabeth Cady	IX
Spurr, Josiah Edward	4	Stanton, Frank Lebby	IX
Squanto	IX	Stanton, Frederick Perry	IX
Squibb, Edward Robinson	IX	Stanton, Henry Brewster	IX
Squier, Ephraim George	IX	Stanton, Richard Henry	IX
Squier, George Owen	IX	Stanwood, Edward	IX
Squiers, Herbert Goldsmith	IX	Staples, Waller Redd	IX
Squire, Watson Carvosso	IX	Staples, William Read	IX
Stacy, Walter Parker	5	Starbuck, Edwin Diller	4
Stager, Anson	IX	Starin, John Henry	IX
Stagg, Amos Alonzo	7	Stark, Edward Josef	IX
Stahel, Julius	IX	Stark, John	IX
Stahlman, Edward Bushrod	IX	Stark, Louis	5
Stahr, John Summers	IX	Starks, Edwin Chapin	1
Staley, Cady	IX	Starr, Eliza Allen	IX
Stallo, Johann Bernhard	IX	Starr, Frederick	IX
Stanard, Mary Mann Page		Starr, Louis	IX
Newton	IX	Starr, Merritt	IX
Stanard, William Glover	IX	Starr, Moses Allen	IX
Stanbery, Henry	IX	Starrett, Laroy S.	IX
Stanchfield, John Barry	IX	Starrett, Paul	6
Standerren, Ann Lee		Starrett, William Aiken	IX
See Lee, Ann		Statler, Ellsworth Milton	IX
Standish, Burt L.		Stauffer, David McNeely	IX
See Patten, Gilbert		Staughton, William	IX
Standish, Myles	IX	Stayton, John William	IX
Standley, William Harrison	7	Steagall, Henry Bascom	3
Stanford, John	IX	Stearns, Abel	IX
Stanford, Leland	IX	Stearns, Asahel	IX
Stang, William	IX	Stearns, Eben Sperry	IX
Stanley, Albert Augustus	IX	Stearns, Frank Ballou	5
Stanley, Ann Lee		Stearns, Frank Waterman	2
See Lee, Ann		Stearns, Frederic Pike	IX

Complete Index Guide

Name	Vol./Supp.	Name	Vol./Supp.
Stearns, George Luther	IX	Stelzle, Charles	3
Stearns, Harold Edmund	3	Stengel, Alfred	2
Stearns, Henry Putnam	IX	Stephens, Alexander Hamilton	IX
Stearns, Irving Ariel	IX	Stephens, Alice Barber	IX
Stearns, John Newton	IX	Stephens, Ann Sophia	IX
Stearns, Oliver	IX	Stephens, Charles Asbury	IX
Stearns, Robert Edwards Carter	IX	Stephens, Edwin William	IX
Stearns, Shubal	IX	Stephens, Henry Morse	IX
Stearns, William Augustus	IX	Stephens, John Lloyd	IX
Stebbins, Horatio	IX	Stephens, Linton	IX
Stebbins, Rufus Phineas	IX	Stephens, Uriah Smith	IX
Steck, George	IX	Stephenson, Benjamin Franklin	IX
Stedman, Edmund Clarence	IX	Stephenson, Carl	5
Steedman, Charles	IX	Stephenson, Isaac	IX
Steedman, James Blair	IX	Stephenson, John	IX
Steele, Daniel	IX	Stephenson, Nathaniel Wright	1
Steele, Frederick	IX	Sterett, Andrew	IX
Steele, Joel Dorman	IX	Sterki, Victor	IX
Steele, John	IX	Sterling, George	IX
Steendam, Jacob	IX	Sterling, James	IX
Steenwijck, Cornelis van		Sterling, John Whalen	IX
See Steenwyck, Cornelis		Sterling, John William	IX
Steenwyck, Cornelis	IX	Sterling, Ross Shaw	4
Steers, George	IX	Stern, Joseph William	IX
Steffansson, Vilhjalmur	7	Stern, Kurt Guenter	6
Steffens, Lincoln	2	Sternberg, Constantin	
Stehle, Aurelius Aloysius	IX	Ivanovich, Edler von	IX
Stein, Evaleen	IX	Sternberg, George Miller	IX
Stein, Gertrude	4	Sterne, Maurice	6
Stein, Leo	4	Sterne, Simon	IX
Steiner, Bernard Christian	IX	Sterne, Stuart	
Steiner, Lewis Henry	IX	See Bloede, Gertrude	
Steinert, Morris	IX	Sterrett, James Macbride	IX
Steinhardt, Laurence Adolph	4	Sterrett, John Robert Sitlington	IX
Steinitz, William	IX	Stetefeldt, Carl August	IX
Steinman, David Barnard	6	Stetson, Augusta Emma	
Steinmetz, Charles Proteus	IX	Simmons	IX
Steinmeyer, Ferdinand		Stetson, Charles Augustus	IX
See Farmer, Ferdinand		Stetson, Charles Walter	IX
Steinway, Christian Friedrich		Stetson, Francis Lynde	IX
Theodore	IX	Stetson, Henry Crosby	5
Steinway, Henry Engelhard	IX	Stetson, John Batterson	IX
Steinway, William	IX	Stetson, William Wallace	IX
Stejneger, Leonard Hess	3	Stettinius, Edward Reilly	4
Stella, Joseph	4	Stettinius, Edward Riley	IX

Complete Index Guide

Name	Vol./Supp.
Steuben, Friedrich Wilhelm Ludolf Gerhard Augustin, Baron von	IX
Steuben, John	6
Steuer, Max David	2
Stevens, Abel	IX
Stevens, Alexander Hodgdon	IX
Stevens, Ashton	5
Stevens, Benjamin Franklin	IX
Stevens, Clement Hoffman	IX
Stevens, Doris	7
Stevens, Edwin Augustus	IX
Stevens, Emily	IX
Stevens, Frank Mozley	7
Stevens, George Barker	IX
Stevens, George Washington	IX
Stevens, Harry Mozley	7
Stevens, Henry	IX
Stevens, Hiram Fairchild	IX
Stevens, Isaac Ingalls	IX
Stevens, John	IX
Stevens, John Austin (d. 1874)	IX
Stevens, John Austin (d. 1910)	IX
Stevens, John Frank	3
Stevens, John Harrington	IX
Stevens, John Leavitt	IX
Stevens, Robert Livingston	IX
Stevens, Thaddeus	IX
Stevens, Thomas Holdup (d. 1841)	IX
Stevens, Thomas Holdup (d. 1896)	IX
Stevens, Wallace	5
Stevens, Walter Husted	IX
Stevens, William Arnold	IX
Stevens, William Bacon	IX
Stevenson, Adlai Ewing	IX
Stevenson, Adlai Ewing, II	7
Stevenson, Andrew	IX
Stevenson, Carter Littlepage	IX
Stevenson, James	IX
Stevenson, John James	IX
Stevenson, John White	IX
Stevenson, Matilda Coxe Evans	IX
Stevenson, Sara Yorke	IX
Steward, Ira	IX
Stewardson, John	IX
Stewart, Alexander Peter	IX
Stewart, Alexander Turney	IX
Stewart, Alvan	IX
Stewart, Andrew	IX
Stewart, Charles	IX
Stewart, Edwin	IX
Stewart, Eliza Daniel	IX
Stewart, George Neil	IX
Stewart, Humphrey John	IX
Stewart, John Aikman	IX
Stewart, Philo Penfield	IX
Stewart, Robert	IX
Stewart, Robert Marcellus	IX
Stewart, Walter Winne	6
Stewart, William Morris	IX
Stewart, William Rhinelander	IX
Stickney, Alpheus Beede	IX
Stiegel, Henry William	IX
Stieglitz, Alfred	4
Stieglitz, Julius	2
Stigler, William Grady	5
Stiles, Charles Wardell	3
Stiles, Ezra	IX
Stiles, Henry Reed	IX
Still, Andrew Taylor	IX
Still, William	IX
Stillé, Alfred	IX
Stillé, Charles Janeway	IX
Stillman, James	IX
Stillman, Samuel	IX
Stillman, Thomas Bliss	IX
Stillman, Thomas Edgar	IX
Stillman, William James	IX
Stilwell, Silas Moore	IX
Stilwell, Simpson Everett	IX
Stimpson, William	IX
Stimson, Alexander Lovett	IX
Stimson, Frederic Jesup	3
Stimson, Henry Lewis	4
Stimson, Julia Catherine	4
Stimson, Lewis Atterbury	IX
Stine, Charles Milton Altland	5
Stiness, John Henry	IX

Complete Index Guide

Name	Vol./Supp.	Name	Vol./Supp.
Stirling, Lord William		Stokes, Caroline Phelps	
See Alexander, William		See Stokes, Olivia Egleston	
Stith, William	IX	Phelps	
Stitt, Edward Rhodes	4	Stokes, Frederick Abbot	2
Stobo, Robert	IX	Stokes, Isaac Newton Phelps	3
Stock, Frederick August	3	Stokes, Montfort	IX
Stockard, Charles Rupert	2	Stokes, Olivia Egleston Phelps	IX
Stockbridge, Henry	IX	Stokes, Rose Harriet Pastor	IX
Stockbridge, Henry Smith	IX	Stokes, Thomas Lunsford, Jr.	6
Stockbridge, Horace Edward	IX	Stokes, William Earl Dodge	IX
Stockbridge, Levi	IX	Stolberg, Benjamin	5
Stockdale, Thomas Ringland	IX	Stone, Abraham	6
Stöckhardt, Karl Georg	IX	Stone, Amasa	IX
Stockton, Charles G.	IX	Stone, Barton Warren	IX
Stockton, Charles Herbert	IX	Stone, Charles Augustus	3
Stockton, Frank Richard	IX	Stone, Charles Pomeroy	IX
Stockton, John Potter	IX	Stone, David	IX
Stockton, Richard (d. 1781)	IX	Stone, David Marvin	IX
Stockton, Richard (d. 1828)	IX	Stone, Ellen Maria	IX
Stockton, Robert Field	IX	Stone, George Washington	IX
Stockton, Thomas Hewlings	IX	Stone, Harlan Fiske	4
Stockwell, John Nelson	IX	Stone, Horatio	IX
Stoddard, Amos	IX	Stone, James Kent	IX
Stoddard, Charles Warren	IX	Stone, John Augustus	IX
Stoddard, David Tappan	IX	Stone, John Marshall	IX
Stoddard, Elizabeth Drew		Stone, John Seely	IX
Barstow	IX	Stone, John Stone	3
Stoddard, John Fair	IX	Stone, John Wesley	IX
Stoddard, John Lawson	IX	Stone, Lucy	IX
Stoddard, John Tappan	IX	Stone, Melville Elijah	IX
Stoddard, Joshua C.	IX	Stone, Ormond	1
Stoddard, Lothrop	4	Stone, Richard French	IX
Stoddard, Richard Henry	IX	Stone, Samuel	IX
Stoddard, Solomon	IX	Stone, Thomas	IX
Stoddard, William Osborn	IX	Stone, Warren	IX
Stoddart, James Henry	IX	Stone, Warren Sanford	IX
Stoddart, Joseph Marshall	IX	Stone, Wilbur Fisk	IX
Stoddert, Benjamin	IX	Stone, William	IX
Stoeckel, Carl	IX	Stone, William Joel	IX
Stoek, Harry Harkness	IX	Stone, William Leete (d. 1844)	IX
Stoessel, Albert Frederic	3	Stone, William Leete (d. 1908)	IX
Stoever, Martin Luther	IX	Stone, William Oliver	IX
Stokes, Anson Phelps (d. 1913)	IX	Stone, Witmer	2
Stokes, Anson Phelps (d. 1958)	6	Stoneman, George	IX

Complete Index Guide

Name	Vol./Supp.	Name	Vol./Supp.
Stong, Phil(lip Duffield)	6	Straus, Roger W(illiams)	6
Storer, Bellamy	IX	Straus, Simon William	IX
Storer, David Humphreys	IX	Strauss, Joseph Baermann	2
Storer, Francis Humphreys	IX	Strawbridge, Robert	IX
Storer, Horatio Robinson	IX	Strawn, Jacob	IX
Storey, Moorfield	IX	Strawn, Silas Hardy	4
Storey, Wilbur Fisk	IX	Street, Alfred Billings	IX
Storrow, Charles Storer	IX	Street, Augustus Russell	IX
Storrow, James Jackson	IX	Street, Joseph Montfort	IX
Storrs, Richard Salter (d. 1873)	IX	Streeter, George Linius	4
Storrs, Richard Salter (d. 1900)	IX	Stribling, Thomas Sigismund	7
Story, Isaac	IX	Strickland, William	IX
Story, Joseph	IX	Stringfellow, Franklin	IX
Story, Julian Russell	IX	Stringham, Silas Horton	IX
Story, William Edward	IX	Stringham, Washington Irving	IX
Story, William Wetmore	IX	Stritch, Samuel Alphonsus	6
Stotesbury, Edward Townsend	2	Strobel, Charles Louis	2
Stott, Henry Gordon	IX	Strobel, Edward Henry	IX
Stouffer, Samuel Andrew	6	Stroheim, Erich von	
Stoughton, Edwin Wallace	IX	See Von Stroheim, Erich	
Stoughton, William	IX	Stromme, Peer Olsen	IX
Stovall, Pleasant Alexander	1	Strong, Augustus Hopkins	IX
Stow, Baron	IX	Strong, Benjamin	IX
Stowe, Calvin Ellis	IX	Strong, Caleb	IX
Stowe, Harriet Elizabeth		Strong, Charles Augustus	2
Beecher	IX	Strong, Charles Lyman	IX
Strachey, William	IX	Strong, Harriet Williams	
Straight, Willard Dickerman	IX	Russell	IX
Strain, Isaac G.	IX	Strong, James	IX
Stranahan, James Samuel		Strong, James Hooker	IX
Thomas	IX	Strong, James Woodward	IX
Strang, James Jesse	IX	Strong, Josiah	IX
Strange, Michael	4	Strong, Moses McCure	IX
Stratemeyer, Edward	IX	Strong, Richard Pearson	4
Straton, John Roach	IX	Strong, Theodore	IX
Stratton, Charles Sherwood	IX	Strong, Walter Ansel	IX
Stratton, Samuel Wesley	IX	Strong, William	IX
Stratton-Porter, Gene		Strong, William Barstow	IX
See Porter, Gene Stratton		Strong, William Lafayette	IX
Straus, Isidor	IX	Strother, David Hunter	IX
Straus, Jesse Isidor	2	Strubberg, Friedrich Armand	IX
Straus, Nathan	IX	Strudwick, Edmund Charles	
Straus, Oscar Solomon	IX	Fox	IX
Straus, Percy Selden	3	Strunsky, Simeon	4

Complete Index Guide

Name	Vol./Supp.	Name	Vol./Supp.
Struve, Gustav	IX	Sullivan, James Edward	IX
Struve, Otto	7	Sullivan, James William	2
Stryker, Lloyd Paul	5	Sullivan, John	IX
Stryker, Melancthon Woolsey	IX	Sullivan, John Florence	
Stuart, Alexander Hugh Holmes	IX	See Allen, Fred	
Stuart, Archibald	IX	Sullivan, John Lawrence	IX
Stuart, Charles	IX	Sullivan, Louis Henri	IX
Stuart, Charles Beebe	IX	Sullivan, Louis Robert	IX
Stuart, Charles Macaulay	IX	Sullivan, Mark	5
Stuart, Elbridge Amos	3	Sullivan, Timothy Daniel	IX
Stuart, Francis Lee	1	Sullivan, William	IX
Stuart, Gilbert	IX	Sullivan, William Henry	IX
Stuart, Granville	IX	Sullivant, William Starling	IX
Stuart, Henry Robson		Sully, Daniel John	IX
See Robson, Stuart		Sully, Thomas	IX
Stuart, Isaac William	IX	Sulzberger, Cyrus Lindauer	IX
Stuart, James Ewell Brown	IX	Sulzberger, Mayer	IX
Stuart, John	IX	Sulzer, William	3
Stuart, John Leighton	7	Summerall, Charles Pelot	5
Stuart, John Todd	IX	Summers, Edith	
Stuart, Moses	IX	See Kelley, Edith Summers	
Stuart, Robert	IX	Summers, George William	IX
Stuart, Robert Leighton	IX	Summers, Thomas Osmond	IX
Stuart, Ruth McEnery	IX	Sumner, Charles	IX
Stub, Hans Gerhard	IX	Sumner, Edwin Vose	IX
Stubbs, Walter Roscoe	1	Sumner, Francis Bertody	3
Stuck, Hudson	IX	Sumner, Increase	IX
Stuckenberg, John Henry		Sumner, James Batcheller	5
Wilbrandt	IX	Sumner, Jethro	IX
Studebaker, Clement	IX	Sumner, Walter Taylor	1
Stuhldreher, Harry A.	7	Sumner, William Graham	IX
Sturges, Preston	6	Sumners, Hatton William	7
Sturgis, Russell	IX	Sumter, Thomas	IX
Sturgis, Samuel Davis	IX	Sunday, William Ashley	1
Sturgis, William	IX	Sunderland, Eliza Jane Read	IX
Sturtevant, Benjamin Franklin	IX	Sunderland, La Roy	IX
Sturtevant, Edward Lewis	IX	Surratt, John H.	
Sturtevant, Julian Monson	IX	See Booth, John Wilkes	
Stutz, Harry Clayton	IX	Surratt, Mary E.	
Stuyvesant, Petrus	IX	See Booth, John Wilkes	
Sublette, William Lewis	IX	Sutherland, Edwin Hardin	4
Sullavan, Margaret	6	Sutherland, George	3
Sullivan, George	IX	Sutherland, Joel Barlow	IX
Sullivan, Harry Stack	4	Sutro, Adolph Heinrich Joseph	IX
Sullivan, James	IX	Sutter, John Augustus	IX

Complete Index Guide

Name	Vol./Supp.	Name	Vol./Supp.
Sutton, William Seneca	IX	Sylvester, Frederick Oakes	IX
Suzzallo, Henry	IX	Sylvester, James Joseph	IX
Sverdrup, Georg	IX	Sylvis, William H.	IX
Swain, Clara A.	IX	Symmes, John Cleves	IX
Swain, David Lowry	IX	Symons, George Gardner	IX
Swain, George Fillmore	1	Symons, Thomas William	IX
Swain, James Barrett	IX	Syms, Benjamin	IX
Swallow, George Clinton	IX	Syndor, Charles Sackett	5
Swallow, Silas Comfort	IX	Syng, Philip	IX
Swan, James	IX	Syzk, Arthur	5
Swan, Joseph Rockwell	IX	Szilard, Leo	7
Swan, Timothy	IX	Szold, Benjamin	IX
Swank, James Moore	IX	Szold, Henrietta	3
Swann, Thomas	IX		
Swanson, Claude Augustus	2	Tabb, John Banister	IX
Swanton, John Reed	6	Taber, John	7
Swartwout, Samuel	IX	Tabor, Horace Austin Warner	IX
Swasey, Ambrose	2	Taft, Alphonso	IX
Swayne, Noah Haynes	IX	Taft, Charles Phelps	IX
Swayne, Wager	IX	Taft, Henry Waters	3
Sweeney, Martin Leonard	6	Taft, Lorado Zadoc	2
Sweeny, Peter Barr	IX	Taft, Robert Alphonso	5
Sweeny, Thomas William	IX	Taft, William Howard	IX
Sweet, John Edson	IX	Taggard, Genevieve	4
Swenson, David Ferdinand	2	Taggart, Thomas	IX
Swensson, Carl Aaron	IX	Tagliabue, Giuseppe	IX
Swett, John	IX	Tait, Arthur Fitzwilliam	IX
Swift, Gustavus Franklin	IX	Tait, Charles	IX
Swift, John Franklin	IX	Takamine, Jokichi	IX
Swift, Joseph Gardner	IX	Talbot, Arthur Newell	3
Swift, Lewis	IX	Talbot, Emily Fairbanks	IX
Swift, Linton Bishop	4	Talbot, Ethelbert	IX
Swift, Louis Franklin	2	Talbot, Francis Xavier	5
Swift, Lucius Burrie	IX	Talbot, Henry Paul	IX
Swift, William Henry	IX	Talbot, Israel Tisdale	IX
Swift, Zephaniah	IX	Talbot, John	IX
Swing, David	IX	Talbot, Silas	IX
Swinton, John	IX	Talbott, Harold Elstner	6
Swinton, William	IX	Talcott, Andrew	IX
Swisshelm, Jane Grey Cannon	IX	Talcott, Eliza	IX
Switzler, William Franklin	IX	Talcott, Joseph	IX
Swope, Gerard	6	Taliaferro, Lawrence	IX
Swope, Herbert Bayard	6	Taliaferro, William Booth	IX
Sydenstricker, Edgar	2	Tallmadge, Benjamin	IX
Sykes, George	IX	Tallmadge, James	IX

Complete Index Guide

Name	Vol./Supp.	Name	Vol./Supp.
Talmadge, Eugene	4	Tatlock, John Strong Perry	4
Talmadge, Norma	6	Tattnall, Josiah	IX
Talmage, James Edward	IX	Tatum, Art	6
Talmage, John Van Nest	IX	Taussig, Frank William	2
Talmage, Thomas DeWitt	IX	Taussig, Frederick Joseph	3
Talvj		Taussig, Joseph Knefler	4
See Robinson, Therese		Taussig, William	IX
Albertine Louise von Jakob		Tawney, James Albertus	IX
Tamarkin, Jacob David	3	Taylor, Alfred Alexander	IX
Tamarón, Pedro	IX	Taylor, Archibald Alexander	
Tammany	IX	Edward	IX
Tammen, Harry Heye		Taylor, Bayard	IX
See under Bonfils,		Taylor, Benjamin Franklin	IX
Frederick Gilmer		Taylor, Bert Leston	IX
Taney, Roger Brooke	IX	Taylor, Charles Alonzo	3
Tanguay, Eva	4	Taylor, Charles Fayette	IX
Tanneberger, David	IX	Taylor, Charles Henry	IX
Tanner, Benjamin	IX	Taylor, Charlotte De Bernier	IX
Tanner, Benjamin Tucker	IX	Taylor, Creed	IX
Tanner, Henry Ossawa	2	Taylor, David Watson	2
Tanner, Henry Schenck	IX	Taylor, Edward	1
Tanner, James	IX	Taylor, Edward Thompson	IX
Tansill, Charles Callan	7	Taylor, Francis Henry	6
Tappan, Arthur	IX	Taylor, Frank Bursley	2
Tappan, Benjamin	IX	Taylor, Frank Walter	IX
Tappan, Eli Todd	IX	Taylor, Frederick Winslow	IX
Tappan, Eva March	IX	Taylor, Fred Manville	IX
Tappan, Henry Philip	IX	Taylor, George	IX
Tappan, Lewis	IX	Taylor, George Boardman	IX
Tappen, Frederick Dobbs	IX	Taylor, Graham	2
Tapper, Bertha Feiring	IX	Taylor, Hannis	IX
Tarbell, Edmund Charles	2	Taylor, Harry	IX
Tarbell, Frank Bigelow	IX	Taylor, Henry Osborn	3
Tarbell, Ida Minerva	3	Taylor, James Barnett	IX
Tarbell, Joseph	IX	Taylor, James Bayard	
Tarbox, Increase Niles	IX	See Taylor, Bayard	
Tarkington, Booth	4	Taylor, James Monroe	IX
Tarr, Ralph Stockman	IX	Taylor, James Wickes	IX
Tashrak		Taylor, John (b. 1752)	IX
See Zevin, Israel Joseph		Taylor, John (b. 1753)	IX
Tashunca-Uitco		Taylor, John (b. 1808)	IX
See Crazy Horse		Taylor, John Louis	IX
Tate, George Henry Hamilton	5	Taylor, John W.	IX
Tate, John Torrence	4	Taylor, Joseph Wright	IX
Tatham, William	IX	Taylor, Laurette	4

Complete Index Guide

Name	Vol./Supp.	Name	Vol./Supp.
Taylor, Marshall William	IX	Tenney, William Jewett	IX
Taylor, Moses	IX	Tenskwatawa	IX
Taylor, Myron Charles	6	Teresa, Mother	IX
Taylor, Nathaniel William	IX	Terhune, Albert Payson	3
Taylor, Raynor	IX	Terhune, Mary Virginia Hawes	IX
Taylor, Richard	IX	Terman, Lewis Madison	6
Taylor, Richard Cowling	IX	Terrell, Edwin Holland	IX
Taylor, Robert Love	IX	Terrell, Mary Eliza Church	5
Taylor, Robert Tunstall	IX	Terry, Alfred Howe	IX
Taylor, Samuel Harvey	IX	Terry, David Smith	IX
Taylor, Stevenson	IX	Terry, Eli	IX
Taylor, William	IX	Terry, Marshall Orlando	IX
Taylor, William Chittenden	6	Terry, Milton Spenser	IX
Taylor, William Ladd	IX	Tesla, Nikola	3
Taylor, William Mackergo	IX	Testut, Charles	IX
Taylor, William Rogers	IX	Teusler, Rudolf Bolling	IX
Taylor, William Vigneron	IX	Tevis, Lloyd	IX
Taylor, Zachary	IX	Thacher, Edwin	IX
Tazewell, Henry	IX	Thacher, George	IX
Tazewell, Littleton Waller	IX	Thacher, James	IX
Tchelitchew, Pavel	6	Thacher, John Boyd	IX
Teagarden, Weldon Leo		Thacher, Peter (d. 1727)	IX
("Jack")	7	Thacher, Peter (d. 1802)	IX
Teall, Francis Augustus	IX	Thacher, Samuel Cooper	IX
Teasdale, Sara	IX	Thacher, Thomas Anthony	IX
Tecumseh	IX	Thacher, Thomas Day	4
Tedyuskung	IX	Thalberg, Irving Grant	2
Teeple, John Edgar	1	Thanet, Octave	
Teggert, Frederick John	4	See French, Alice	
Telfair, Edward	IX	Thatcher, Benjamin Bussey	IX
Teller, Henry Moore	IX	Thatcher, George	
Temple, Oliver Perry	IX	See Thacher, George	
Temple, William Grenville	IX	Thatcher, Henry Knox	IX
Templeton, Alec Andrew	7	Thatcher, Mahlon Daniel	IX
Ten Broeck, Abraham	IX	Thatcher, Roscoe Wilfred	IX
Ten Broeck, Richard	IX	Thaw, Harry Kendall	4
Tené-Angpóte		Thaw, William	IX
See Kicking Bird		Thaxter, Celia Laighton	IX
Tennent, Gilbert	IX	Thaxter, Roland	IX
Tennent, John	IX	Thayer, Abbott Handerson	IX
Tennent, William (d. 1745)	IX	Thayer, Alexander Wheelock	IX
Tennent, William (d. 1777)	IX	Thayer, Amos Madden	IX
Tenney, Charles Daniel	IX	Thayer, Eli	IX
Tenney, Edward Payson	IX	Thayer, Ezra Ripley	IX
Tenney, Tabitha Gilman	IX	Thayer, Gideon French	IX

Complete Index Guide

Name	Vol./Supp.	Name	Vol./Supp.
Thayer, James Bradley	IX	Thomas, John William Elmer	7
Thayer, John	IX	Thomas, John Wilson	IX
Thayer, John Milton	IX	Thomas, Joseph	IX
Thayer, Joseph Henry	IX	Thomas, Lorenzo	IX
Thayer, Nathaniel	IX	Thomas, Martha Carey	1
Thayer, Sylvanus	IX	Thomas, Philip Evan	IX
Thayer, Thomas Baldwin	IX	Thomas, Philip Francis	IX
Thayer, Tiffany Ellsworth	6	Thomas, Richard Henry	IX
Thayer, Whitney Eugene	IX	Thomas, Robert Bailey	IX
Thayer, William Makepeace	IX	Thomas, Seth	IX
Thayer, William Roscoe	IX	Thomas, Theodore	
Thayer, William Sydney	IX	See Thomas, Christian	
Thébaud, Augustus J.	IX	Friedrich Theodore	
Theobald, Robert Alfred	6	Thomas, Theodore Gaillard	IX
Theobald, Samuel	IX	Thomas, William Isaac	4
Theus, Jeremiah	IX	Thomas, William Widgery	IX
Thierry, Camille	IX	Thomes, William Henry	IX
Thilly, Frank	1	Thompson, Alfred Wordsworth	IX
Thoburn, Isabella	IX	Thompson, Arthur Webster	IX
Thoburn, James Mills	IX	Thompson, Benjamin	IX
Thomas, Allen	IX	Thompson, Cephas Giovanni	IX
Thomas, Amos Russell	IX	Thompson, Charles Oliver	IX
Thomas, Augustus	IX	Thompson, Daniel Pierce	IX
Thomas, Calvin	IX	Thompson, David	IX
Thomas, Charles Spalding	IX	Thompson, David P.	IX
Thomas, Christian Friedrich		Thompson, Denman	IX
Theodore	IX	Thompson, Dorothy	7
Thomas, Cyrus	IX	Thompson, Edward Herbert	1
Thomas, David (d. 1831)	IX	Thompson, Egbert	IX
Thomas, David (d. 1882)	IX	Thompson, Hugh Miller	IX
Thomas, Edith Matilda	IX	Thompson, Hugh Smith	IX
Thomas, Elbert Duncan	5	Thompson, Jacob	IX
Thomas, Francis	IX	Thompson, James Maurice	IX
Thomas, Frederick William	IX	Thompson, Jeremiah	IX
Thomas, George	IX	Thompson, Jerome B.	IX
Thomas, George Clifford	IX	Thompson, John (d. 1799)	
Thomas, George Henry	IX	See Thomson, John	
Thomas, Isaiah	IX	Thompson, John (d. 1891)	IX
Thomas, Jesse Burgess		Thompson, John Bodine	IX
(d. 1853)	IX	Thompson, John Reuben	IX
Thomas, Jesse Burgess		Thompson, Joseph Parrish	IX
(d. 1915)	IX	Thompson, Josiah Van Kirk	IX
Thomas, John	IX	Thompson, Launt	IX
Thomas, John Charles	6	Thompson, Malvina Cynthia	5
Thomas, John Jacobs	IX	Thompson, Martin E.	IX

Complete Index Guide

Name	Vol./Supp.	Name	Vol./Supp.
Thompson, Maurice		Thornton, Henry Worth	IX
See Thompson, James		Thornton, Jessy Quinn	IX
Maurice		Thornton, John Wingate	IX
Thompson, Oscar Lee	3	Thornton, Matthew	IX
Thompson, Richard Wigginton	IX	Thornton, William	IX
Thompson, Robert Ellis	IX	Thornwell, James Henley	IX
Thompson, Robert Means	1	Thorp, John	IX
Thompson, Samuel Rankin	IX	Thorpe, James Francis	5
Thompson, Seymour Dwight	IX	Thorpe, Rose Alnora Hartwick	2
Thompson, Slason	1	Thorpe, Thomas Bangs	IX
Thompson, Smith	IX	Thrasher, John Sidney	IX
Thompson, Thomas Larkin	IX	Throop, Enos Thompson	IX
Thompson, Waddy	IX	Throop, Montgomery Hunt	IX
Thompson, Wiley	IX	Thulstrup, Bror Thure	IX
Thompson, William	IX	Thumb, Tom	
Thompson, William Boyce	IX	See Stratton, Charles	
Thompson, William Gilman	IX	Sherwood	
Thompson, William Hale	3	Thurber, Charles	IX
Thompson, William Oxley	IX	Thurber, Christopher Carson	IX
Thompson, William Tappan	IX	Thurber, George	IX
Thompson, Will Lamartine	IX	Thurber, James Grover	7
Thompson, Zadock	IX	Thurber, Jeannette Meyer	4
Thomson, Charles	IX	Thurman, Allen Granberry	IX
Thomson, Edward	IX	Thursby, Emma Cecilia	IX
Thomson, Edward William	IX	Thurston, Howard	2
Thomson, Elihu	2	Thurston, Lorrin Andrews	IX
Thomson, Frank	IX	Thurston, Robert Henry	IX
Thomson, John (d. 1799)	IX	Thurston, Robert Lawton	IX
Thomson, John (d. 1926)	IX	Thurstone, Louis Leon	5
Thomson, John Edgar	IX	Thwaites, Reuben Gold	IX
Thomson, Mortimer Neal	IX	Thwing, Charles Franklin	2
Thomson, Samuel	IX	Tibbett, Lawrence Mervil	6
Thomson, William	IX	Tibbles, Susette La Flesche	
Thomson, William McClure	IX	See Bright Eyes	
Thorburn, Grant	IX	Tibbles, Thomas Henry	IX
Thoreau, Henry David	IX	Tichenor, Isaac	IX
Thorek, Max	6	Tichenor, Isaac Taylor	IX
Thorndike, Ashley Horace	IX	Ticknor, Elisha	IX
Thorndike, Edward Lee	4	Ticknor, Francis Orray	IX
Thorndike, Israel	IX	Ticknor, George	IX
Thorndike, Lynn	7	Ticknor, William Davis	IX
Thorne, Charles Robert		Tidball, John Caldwell	IX
(b. c. 1814)	IX	Tiebout, Cornelius	IX
Thorne, Charles Robert		Tiedeman, Christopher	
(b. 1840)	IX	Gustavus	IX

Complete Index Guide

Name	Vol./Supp.	Name	Vol./Supp.
Tiernan, Frances Christine Fisher	IX	Tinkham, George Holden	6
Tierney, Richard Henry	IX	Tipton, John (*d. 1813*)	IX
Tiffany, Charles Lewis	IX	Tipton, John (*d. 1839*)	IX
Tiffany, Katrina Brandes Ely	IX	Tisquantum	
Tiffany, Louis Comfort	IX	See Squanto	
Tiffany, Louis McLane	IX	Titchener, Edward Bradford	IX
Tiffin, Edward	IX	Titcomb, John Wheelock	IX
Tigert, John James	IX	Tittle, Ernest Fremont	4
Tigert, John James, IV	7	Tobani, Theodore Moses	IX
Tikamthi		Tobey, Charles William	5
See Tecumseh		Tobey, Edward Silas	IX
Tilden, Samuel Jones	IX	Tobias, Channing H.	7
Tilden, William Tatem ("Big Bill"), II	5	Tobin, Daniel Joseph	5
Tileston, Thomas	IX	Tobin, Maurice Joseph	5
Tilghman, Edward	IX	Tod, David	IX
Tilghman, Matthew	IX	Tod, George	IX
Tilghman, Richard Albert	IX	Tod, John	IX
Tilghman, Tench	IX	Todd, Charles Stewart	IX
Tilghman, William	IX	Todd, Eli	IX
Tilghman, William Matthew	IX	Todd, Henry Alfred	IX
Tillich, Paul	7	Todd, John	IX
Tillman, Benjamin Ryan	IX	Todd, Mabel Loomis	IX
Tilney, Frederick	2	Todd, Mike	6
Tilson, John Quillin	6	Todd, Sereno Edwards	IX
Tilton, Edward Lippincott	IX	Todd, Thomas	IX
Tilton, James	IX	Todd, Thomas Wingate	2
Tilton, John Rollin	IX	Toland, Hugh Huger	IX
Tilton, Theodore	IX	Tolley, Howard Ross	6
Tilyou, George Cornelius	IX	Tolman, Edward Chace	6
Tilzer, Harry von	4	Tolman, Herbert Cushing	IX
Timberlake, Gideon	5	Tolman, Richard Chace	4
Timberlake, Henry	IX	Tome, Jacob	IX
Timby, Theodore Ruggles	IX	Tomkins, Floyd Williams	IX
Timken, Henry	IX	Tomlin, Bradley Walker	5
Timm, Henry Christian	IX	Tomlins, William Lawrence	IX
Timme, Walter	6	Tomlinson, Everett Titsworth	IX
Timon, John	IX	Tomochichi	IX
Timothy, Lewis	IX	Tompkins, Arnold	IX
Timrod, Henry	IX	Tompkins, Daniel Augustus	IX
Tincker, Mary Agnes	IX	Tompkins, Daniel D.	IX
Tingey, Thomas	IX	Tompkins, Sally Louisa	IX
Tingley, Katherine Augusta Westcott	IX	Tompson, Benjamin	IX
		Tondorf, Francis Anthony	IX
		Toner, Joseph Meredith	IX
		Tonty, Henry de	IX

Complete Index Guide

Name	Vol./Supp.	Name	Vol./Supp.
Toole, Edwin Warren	IX	Townsend, Robert	IX
Toole, Joseph Kemp	IX	Townsend, Virginia Frances	IX
Toombs, Robert Augustus	IX	Townsend, Willard Saxby, Jr.	6
Topliff, Samuel	IX	Toy, Crawford Howell	IX
Torbert, Alfred Thomas		Tracy, Benjamin Franklin	IX
Archimedes	IX	Tracy, Joseph	IX
Torrence, Frederick Ridgley	4	Tracy, Nathaniel	IX
Torrence, Joseph Thatcher	IX	Tracy, Uriah	IX
Torrey, Bradford	IX	Traetta Filippo	
Torrey, Charles Cutler	6	See Trajetta, Philip	
Torrey, Charles Turner	IX	Train, Arthur Cheney	3
Torrey, John	IX	Train, Enoch	IX
Toscanini, Arturo	6	Train, George Francis	IX
Totten, George Muirson	IX	Trajetta, Philip	IX
Totten, Joseph Gilbert	IX	Trask, James Dowling	3
Tou, Erik Hansen	IX	Traubel, Horace L.	IX
Toucey, Isaac	IX	Trautwine, John Cresson	IX
Toulmin, Harry	IX	Travers, Jerome Dunstan	5
Toulmin, Harry Theophilus	IX	Travis, Walter John	IX
Toumey, James William	IX	Travis, William Barret	IX
Tourgée, Albion Winegar	IX	Traylor, Melvin Alvah	IX
Tourjée, Eben	IX	Treadwell, Daniel	IX
Tousard, Anne Louis de	IX	Treat, Robert	IX
Tousey, Sinclair	IX	Treat, Samuel	IX
Tower, Charlemagne	IX	Treat, Samuel Hubbel	IX
Tower, Zealous Bates	IX	Tree, Lambert	IX
Towers, John Henry	5	Trelease, William	3
Towle, George Makepeace	IX	Tremain, Henry Edwin	IX
Towler, John	IX	Tremaine, Henry Barnes	IX
Town, Ithiel	IX	Trenchard, Stephen Decatur	IX
Towne, Benjamin	IX	Trenholm, George Alfred	1
Towne, Charles Arnette	IX	Trent, William	IX
Towne, Charles Hanson	4	Trent, William Peterfield	2
Towne, Henry Robinson	IX	Tresca, Carlo	3
Towne, John Henry	IX	Trescot, William Henry	IX
Townley, Arthur Charles	6	Trevellick, Richard F.	IX
Towns, George Washington		Trimble, Allen	IX
Bonaparte	IX	Trimble, Isaac Ridgeway	IX
Townsend, Edward Davis	IX	Trimble, Robert	IX
Townsend, Francis Everett	6	Tripp, Bartlett	IX
Townsend, George Alfred	IX	Tripp, Guy Eastman	IX
Townsend, John Kirk	IX	Trippe, John	IX
Townsend, Luther Tracy	IX	Trist, Nicholas Philip	IX
Townsend, Mary Ashley	IX	Troland, Leonard Thompson	IX
Townsend, Mira Sharpless	IX	Troost, Gerard	IX

Complete Index Guide

Name	Vol./Supp.	Name	Vol./Supp.
Name	*Vol./Supp.*	*Name*	*Vol./Supp.*
Trott, Benjamin	IX	Tucker, Henry St. George	
Trott, Nicholas	IX	(*d. 1848*)	X
Troup, George Michael	IX	Tucker, Henry St. George	
Troup, Robert	IX	(*d. 1932*)	X
Trow, John Fowler	IX	Tucker, John Randolph	
Trowbridge, Augustus	IX	(*d. 1883*)	X
Trowbridge, Edmund	IX	Tucker, John Randolph	
Trowbridge, John	IX	(*d. 1897*)	X
Trowbridge, John Townsend	IX	Tucker, Luther	X
Trowbridge, William Petit	IX	Tucker, Nathaniel Beverley	
Troye, Edward	X	(*d. 1851*)	X
Trude, Alfred Samuel	X	Tucker, Nathaniel Beverley	
Trudeau, Edward Livingston	X	(*d. 1890*)	X
Trudeau, Jean Baptiste		Tucker, St. George	X
See Truteau, Jean Baptiste		Tucker, Samuel	X
True, Alfred Charles	X	Tucker, Stephen Davis	X
True, Frederick William	X	Tucker, William Jewett	X
Trueblood, Benjamin Franklin	X	Tuckerman, Bayard	X
Truett, George Washington	3	Tuckerman, Edward	X
Truman, Benjamin Cummings	X	Tuckerman, Frederick	X
Trumbauer, Horace	2	Tuckerman, Frederick Goddard	X
Trumbull, Benjamin	X	Tuckerman, Henry Theodore	X
Trumbull, Henry Clay	X	Tuckerman, Joseph	X
Trumbull, James Hammond	X	Tuckey, William	X
Trumbull, John (*d. 1831*)	X	Tudor, Frederic	X
Trumbull, John (*d. 1843*)	X	Tudor, William	X
Trumbull, Jonathan (*d. 1785*)	X	Tufts, Charles	X
Trumbull, Jonathan (*d. 1809*)	X	Tufts, Cotton	X
Trumbull, Joseph	X	Tufts, James Hayden	3
Trumbull, Lyman	X	Tufts, John	X
Truteau, Jean Baptiste	X	Tulane, Paul	X
Truxtun, Thomas	X	Tully, William	X
Truxtun, William Talbot	X	Tumulty, Joseph Patrick	5
Tryon, Dwight William	X	Tupper, Benjamin	X
Tryon, George Washington	X	Tupper, Henry Allen	X
Tryon, William	X	Turell, Jane	X
Tubman, Harriet	X	Turkevich, Leonid	
Tuck, Amos	X	Ieronimovich	
Tucker, Allen	2	See Leonty, Metropolitan	
Tucker, Benjamin Ricketson	2	Turnbull, Andrew	X
Tucker, George	X	Turnbull, Robert James	X
Tucker, Gilbert Milligan	X	Turnbull, William	X
Tucker, Henry Holcombe	X	Turner, Asa	X
Tucker, Henry St. George		Turner, Charles Yardley	X
(*d. 1959*)	6	Turner, Daniel	X

Complete Index Guide

Name	Vol./Supp.	Name	Vol./Supp.
Turner, Edward	X	Tyler, Ransom Hubert	X
Turner, Edward Raymond	X	Tyler, Robert	X
Turner, Fennell Parrish	X	Tyler, Robert Ogden	X
Turner, Frederick Jackson	X	Tyler, Royall (d. 1826)	X
Turner, George	X	Tyler, Royall (d. 1953)	5
Turner, George Kibbe	5	Tyler, Samuel	X
Turner, Henry McNeal	X	Tyler, William	X
Turner, James Milton	X	Tyler, William Seymour	X
Turner, John Wesley	X	Tyndale, Hector	X
Turner, Jonathan Baldwin	X	Tyng, Edward	X
Turner, Josiah	X	Tyng, Stephen Higginson	X
Turner, Nat	X	Tyson, George Emory	X
Turner, Richmond Kelly	7	Tyson, James	X
Turner, Ross Sterling	X	Tyson, Job Roberts	X
Turner, Samuel Hulbeart	X	Tyson, Lawrence Davis	X
Turner, Walter Victor	X	Tyson, Stuart Lawrence	X
Turner, William	2	Tytus, John Butler	3
Turney, Peter	X		
Turpin, Ben	2	Udden, Johan August	X
Tuthill, William Burnet	X	Uhler, Philip Reese	X
Tuttle, Charles Wesley	X	Ulloa, Antonio de	X
Tuttle, Daniel Sylvester	X	Ulrich, Edward Oscar	3
Tuttle, Herbert	X	Unangst, Erias	X
Tutwiler, Henry	X	Uncas	X
Tutwiler, Julia Strudwick	X	Underhill, Frank Pell	X
Twachtman, John Henry	X	Underhill, John	X
Twain, Mark		Underwood, Benjamin Franklin	X
See Clemens, Samuel		Underwood, Francis Henry	X
Langhorne		Underwood, Frederick Douglas	3
Tweed, Blanche Oelrichs		Underwood, Horace Grant	X
See Strange, Michael		Underwood, John Curtiss	X
Tweed, William Marcy	X	Underwood, John Thomas	2
Twichell, Joseph Hopkins	X	Underwood, Joseph Rogers	X
Twiggs, David Emanuel	X	Underwood, Loring	X
Twining, Alexander Catlin	X	Underwood, Lucien Marcus	X
Twitchell, Amos	X	Underwood, Oscar Wilder	X
Tydings, Millard Evelyn	7	Untermyer, Samuel	2
Tyler, Bennet	X	Upchurch, John Jordan	X
Tyler, Charles Mellen	X	Updegraff, David Brainard	X
Tyler, Daniel	X	Updike, Daniel	X
Tyler, George Crouse	4	Updike, Daniel Berkeley	3
Tyler, John (d. 1813)	X	Upham, Charles Wentworth	X
Tyler, John (d. 1862)	X	Upham, Samuel Foster	X
Tyler, Lyon Gardiner	1	Upham, Thomas Cogswell	X
Tyler, Moses Coit	X	Upham, Warren	X

Complete Index Guide

Name	Vol./Supp.	Name	Vol./Supp.
Upjohn, Richard	X	Vance, Harold Sines	6
Upjohn, Richard Michell	X	Vance, Louis Joseph	1
Upshaw, William David	5	Vance, Zebulon Baird	X
Upshur, Abel Parker	X	Van Cortlandt, Oloff	
Upshur, John Henry	X	Stevenszen	X
Upton, Emory	X	Van Cortlandt, Philip	X
Upton, George Bruce	X	Van Cortlandt, Pierre	X
Upton, George Putnam	X	Van Cortlandt, Stephanus	X
Upton, Winslow	X	Van Curler, Arent	X
Urban, Joseph	X	Van Dam, Rip	X
U'Ren, William Simon	4	Van Deman, Esther Boise	2
Urso, Camilla	X	Vandenberg, Arthur Hendrick	5
Usher, John Palmer	X	Vandenberg, Hoyt Sanford	5
Usher, Nathaniel Reilly	X	Vandenhoff, George	X
Utley, George Burwell	4	Van Depoele, Charles Joseph	X
		Vanderbilt, Arthur T.	6
Vaca, Alvar Núñez Cabeza de		Vanderbilt, Cornelius (d. 1877)	X
See Núñez Cabeza de		Vanderbilt, Cornelius (d. 1899)	X
Vaca, Alvar		Vanderbilt, George	
Vail, Aaron	X	Washington	X
Vail, Alfred	X	Vanderbilt, Gloria Morgan	7
Vail, Stephen Montfort	X	Vanderbilt, Grace Graham	
Vail, Theodore Newton	X	Wilson	5
Vaillant, George Clapp	3	Vanderbilt, William Henry	X
Valentine, David Thomas	X	Vanderbilt, William Kissam	X
Valentine, Edward Virginius	X	Vanderburgh, William Henry	X
Valentine, Milton	X	Van der Donck, Adriaen	X
Valentine, Robert Grosvenor	X	Vandergrift, Jacob Jay	X
Vallandigham, Clement Laird	X	Vandergrift, Margaret	
Vallejo, Mariano Guadalupe	X	See Janvier, Margaret	
Vallentine, Benjamin Bennaton	X	Thomson	
Valliant, Leroy Branch	X	Van der Kemp, Francis Adrian	X
Van Allen, Frank	X	Vanderlip, Frank Arthur	2
Van Alstyne, Fanny Crosby		Vanderlyn, John	X
See Crosby, Fanny		Van der Stucken, Frank	
Van Amringe, John Howard	X	Valentin	X
Van Anda, Carr Vattel	3	Vander Veer, Albert	X
Van Beuren, Johannes	X	Vander Wee, John Baptist	X
Van Brunt, Henry	X	Van Devanter, Willis	3
Van Buren, John	X	Van de Velde, James Oliver	X
Van Buren, Martin	X	Van de Warker, Edward Ely	X
Van Buren, William Holme	X	Van Dine, S. S.	
Vance, Ap Morgan	X	See Wright, Willard	
Vance, Arthur Charles		Huntington	
("Dazzy")	7	Van Doren, Carl	4

Complete Index Guide

Name	Vol./Supp.	Name	Vol./Supp.
Van Dorn, Earl	X	Van Vechten, Carl	7
Van Druten, John William	6	Van Vleck, Edward Burr	3
Van Dyck, Cornelius van Alen	X	Van Winkle, Peter Godwin	X
Van Dyke, Henry	X	Van Wyck, Charles Henry	X
Van Dyke, John Charles	X	Vanzetti, Bartolomeo	
Van Dyke, John Wesley	2	See Sacco, Nicola	
Van Dyke, Nicholas (d. 1789)	X	Vardaman, James Kimble	X
Van Dyke, Nicholas (d. 1826)	X	Vardill, John	X
Van Dyke, Paul	X	Vare, William Scott	X
Vane, Sir Henry	X	Varela y Morales, Félix	
Van Fleet, Walter	X	Francisco José María de la	
Van Hise, Charles Richard	X	Concepción	X
Van Hook, Weller	X	Varèse, Edgard	7
Van Horn, Robert Thompson	X	Varick, James	X
Van Horne, William Cornelius	X	Varick, Richard	X
Van Ilpendam, Jan Jansen	X	Varnum, James Mitchell	X
Van Lennep, Henry John	X	Varnum, Joseph Bradley	X
Van Lennep, William Bird	X	Vasey, George	X
Van Loon, Hendrik Willem	3	Vasiliev, Alexander	
Van Meter, John Blackford	X	Alexandrovich	5
Van Name, Addison	X	Vassall, John	X
Van Ness, William Peter	X	Vassar, Matthew	X
Van Nest, Abraham Rynier	X	Vattemare, Nicolas Marie	
Van Nostrand, David	X	Alexandre	X
Van Osdel, John Mills	X	Vauclain, Samuel Matthews	2
Van Quickenborne, Charles		Vaudreuil-Cavagnal, Pierre de	
Felix	X	Rigaud, Marquis de	X
Van Raalte, Albertus Christiaan	X	Vaughan, Benjamin	X
Van Rensselaer, Cortlandt	X	Vaughan, Charles	X
Van Rensselaer, Mariana		Vaughan, Daniel	X
Griswold	X	Vaughan, Thomas Wayland	5
Van Rensselaer, Martha	X	Vaughan, Victor Clarence	X
Van Rensselaer, Nicholas	X	Vaux, Calvert	X
Van Rensselaer, Solomon	X	Vaux, Richard	X
Van Rensselaer, Stephen	X	Vaux, Roberts	X
Van Santvoord, George	X	Vawter, Charles Erastus	X
Van Schaack, Henry Cruger	X	Veatch, Arthur Clifford	2
Van Schaack, Peter	X	Veazey, Thomas Ward	X
Van Schaick, Goose	X	Veblen, Oswald	6
Van Slyke, Lucius Lincoln	X	Veblen, Thorstein Bunde	X
Van Sweringen, Mantis James	1	Vedder, Edward Bright	5
Van Twiller, Wouter	X	Vedder, Elihu	X
Van Tyne, Claude Halstead	X	Vedder, Henry Clay	1
Vanuxem, Lardner	X	Veiller, Lawrence Turnure	6
Van Vechten, Abraham	X	Venable, Charles Scott	X

Complete Index Guide

Name	Vol./Supp.	Name	Vol./Supp.
Venable, Francis Preston	X	Vilas, William Freeman	X
Venable, William Henry	X	Villagrá, Gasper Pérez de	X
Verbeck, Guido Herman Fridolin	X	Villard, Fanny Garrison See Villard, Helen Frances Garrison	
Verbeck, William	X		
Verbrugghen, Henri	X	Villard, Helen Frances Garrison	X
Vérendrye, Pierre Gaultier de Varennes, Sieur de la See La Vérendrye, Pierre Gaultier de Varennes, Sieur de		Villard, Henry	X
		Villard, Oswald Garrison	4
		Villeré, Jacques Philippe	X
		Vincennes, François Marie Bissot, Sieur de	X
Verhaegen, Peter Joseph	X	Vincennes, Jean Baptiste Bissot, Sieur de	X
Verity, George Matthew	3		
Vermilye, Kate Jordan See Jordan, Kate		Vincent, Frank	X
		Vincent, George Edgar	3
Vernon, Samuel	X	Vincent, John Heyl	X
Vernon, William	X	Vincent, Marvin Richardson	X
Verot, Jean Marcel Pierre Auguste	X	Vincent, Mary Ann	X
		Vinson, Fred(erick) Moore	5
Verplanck, Gulian Crommelin	X	Vinton, Alexander Hamilton	X
Verrill, Addison Emery	X	Vinton, Francis	X
Verrill, Alpheus Wyatt	5	Vinton, Francis Laurens	X
Verwyst, Chrysostom Adrian	X	Vinton, Frederic	X
Very, Jones	X	Vinton, Frederic Porter	X
Very, Lydia Louisa Ann	X	Vinton, Samuel Finley	X
Vesey, Denmark	X	Visscher, William Lightfoot	X
Vesey, Télémaque See Vesey, Denmark		Vitale, Ferruccio	X
		Vizcaíno, Sebastián	X
Vesey, William	X	Vizetelly, Frank Horace	2
Vest, George Graham	X	Vladeck, Baruch Charney	2
Vetch, Samuel	X	Vogrich, Max Wilhelm Karl	X
Vethake, Henry	X	Volck, Adalbert John	X
Vezin, Hermann	X	Volk, Leonard Wells	X
Vibbard, Chauncey	X	Volstead, Andrew Joseph	4
Vick, James	X	Von Holst, Hermann Eduard See Holst, Hermann Eduard von	
Vickery, Howard Leroy	4		
Victor, Frances Fuller	X		
Victor, Orville James	X	von Kármán, Theodore See Kármán, Theodore (Todor) von	
Viel, François Étienne Bernard Alexandre	X		
Viele, Aernout Cornelissen	X	Von Moschzisker, Robert	2
Viele, Egbert Ludovicus	X	Von Neumann, John	6
Viereck, George Sylvester	7	Vonnoh, Robert William	X
Vignaud, Henry	X	Von Ruck, Karl	X
Vigo, Joseph Maria Francesco	X	Von Stroheim, Erich	6

Complete Index Guide

Name	Vol./Supp.	Name	Vol./Supp.
Von Teuffel, Blanche Willis Howard See Howard, Blanche Willis		Waidner, Charles William	X
		Wailes, Benjamin Leonard Covington	X
		Wainwright, Jonathan Mayhew (d. 1854)	X
Von Wiegand, Karl Henry	7		
Voorhees, Daniel Wolsey	X	Wainwright, Jonathan Mayhew (d. 1863)	X
Voorhees, Edward Burnett	X		
Voorhees, Philip Falkerson	X	Wainwright, Jonathan Mayhew (d. 1953)	5
Voorsanger, Jacob	X		
Vopicka, Charles Joseph	1	Wainwright, Richard (d. 1862)	X
Vose, George Leonard	X	Wainwright, Richard (d. 1926)	X
Vought, Chance Milton	X	Wait, Samuel	X
Vroom, Peter Dumont	X	Wait, William	X
		Wait, William Bell	X
Wabasha	X	Waite, Henry Matson	3
Wachsmuth, Charles	X	Waite, Morrison Remick	X
Wacker, Charles Henry	X	Wakeley, Joseph Burton	X
Waddel, James	X	Walcot, Charles Melton (d. 1868)	X
Waddel, John Newton	X		
Waddel, Moses	X	Walcot, Charles Melton (d. 1921)	X
Waddell, Alfred Moore	X		
Waddell, Hugh	X	Walcott, Charles Doolittle	X
Waddell, James Iredell	X	Walcott, Henry Pickering	X
Waddell, John Alexander Low	2	Wald, Lillian D.	2
Wade, Benjamin Franklin	X	Walden, Jacob Treadwell	X
Wade, Decius Spear	X	Walden, John Morgan	X
Wade, Jeptha Homer	X	Walderne, Richard	X
Wade, Jeptha Homer	1	Waldo, David	X
Wade, Martin Joseph	X	Waldo, Samuel	X
Wadsworth, Eliot	6	Waldo, Samuel Lovett	X
Wadsworth, James	X	Waldo, Samuel Putnam	X
Wadsworth, James Samuel	X	Waldron, Richard See Walderne, Richard	
Wadsworth, James Wolcott, Jr.	5		
Wadsworth, Jeremiah	X	Wales, James Albert	X
Wadsworth, Peleg	X	Wales, Leonard Eugene	X
Waesche, Russell Randolph	4	Walgreen, Charles Rudolph	2
Wagener, John Andreas	1	Walke, Henry	X
Waggaman, Mary Teresa McKee	X	Walker, Alexander	X
		Walker, Amasa	X
Wagner, Clinton	X	Walker, Asa	X
Wagner, John Peter	5	Walker, Madame C. J. See Walker, Sarah Breedlove	
Wagner, Robert Ferdinand	5		
Wagner, Webster	X		
Wagner, William	X	Walker, David (d. 1830)	X
Wahl, William Henry	X	Walker, David (d. 1879)	X

199

Complete Index Guide

Name	Vol./Supp.	Name	Vol./Supp.
Walker, David Shelby	X	Wallace, William Ross	X
Walker, Francis Amasa	X	Wallack, Henry John	X
Walker, Frank Comerford	6	Wallack, James William	
Walker, Gilbert Carlton	X	(d. 1864)	X
Walker, Henry Oliver	X	Wallack, James William	
Walker, James	X	(d. 1873)	X
Walker, James Barr	X	Wallack, John Lester	
Walker, James John	4	See Wallack, Lester	
Walker, John Brisben	X	Wallack, Lester	X
Walker, John Grimes	X	Waller, Emma	X
Walker, Jonathan Hoge	X	Waller, Fats	
Walker, Joseph Reddeford	X	See Waller, Thomas	
Walker, Leroy Pope	X	Wright	
Walker, Mary Edwards	X	Waller, Frederic	5
Walker, Pinkney Houston	X	Waller, John Lightfoot	X
Walker, Reuben Lindsay	X	Waller, Thomas Macdonald	X
Walker, Robert Franklin	X	Waller, Thomas Wright	3
Walker, Robert John	X	Waller, Willard Walter	3
Walker, Sarah Breedlove	X	Wallgren, Monrad Charles	7
Walker, Sears Cook	X	Walling, William English	2
Walker, Stuart Armstrong	3	Wallis, Severn Teackle	X
Walker, Thomas	X	Waln, Nicholas	X
Walker, Thomas Barlow	X	Waln, Robert (b. 1765)	X
Walker, Timothy (d. 1782)	X	Waln, Robert (b. 1794)	X
Walker, Timothy (d. 1856)	X	Walsh, Benjamin Dann	X
Walker, Walton Harris	4	Walsh, Blanche	X
Walker, William	X	Walsh, David Ignatius	4
Walker, William Henry Talbot	X	Walsh, Edmund Aloysius	6
Walker, William Johnson	X	Walsh, Edward Augustine	6
Walker, Williston	X	Walsh, Francis Patrick	2
Wallace, Charles William	X	Walsh, Henry Collins	X
Wallace, David	X	Walsh, James Anthony	2
Wallace, Henry	X	Walsh, Michael	X
Wallace, Henry Agard	7	Walsh, Robert	X
Wallace, Henry Cantwell	X	Walsh, Thomas	X
Wallace, Horace Binney	X	Walsh, Thomas James	X
Wallace, Hugh Campbell	X	Walsh, Thomas Joseph	5
Wallace, John Findley	X	Walter, Albert G.	X
Wallace, John Hankins	X	Walter, Bruno	7
Wallace, John William	X	Walter, Eugene	3
Wallace, Lewis	X	Walter, Francis Eugene	7
Wallace, William	X	Walter, Thomas (d. 1725)	X
Wallace, William Alexander		Walter, Thomas (d. 1789)	X
Anderson	X	Walter, Thomas Ustick	X
Wallace, William James	X	Walters, Alexander	X

Complete Index Guide

Name	Vol./Supp.	Name	Vol./Supp.
Walters, Henry	X	Ward, Lester Frank	X
Walters, William Thompson	X	Ward, Lydia Arms Avery	
Walthall, Edward Cary	X	Coonley	X
Walthall, Henry Brazeal	2	Ward, Marcus Lawrence	X
Walther, Carl Ferdinand		Ward, Montgomery	
Wilhelm	X	See Ward, Aaron	
Walton, George	X	Montgomery	
Walton, Lester Aglar	7	Ward, Nancy	X
Walworth, Clarence Augustus	X	Ward, Nathaniel	X
Walworth, Jeannette Ritchie		Ward, Richard	X
Hadermann	X	Ward, Richard Halsted	X
Walworth, Reuben Hyde	X	Ward, Robert DeCourcy	X
Wambaugh, Sarah	5	Ward, Samuel (d. 1776)	X
Wanamaker, John	X	Ward, Samuel (d. 1832)	X
Wanamaker, Lewis Rodman	X	Ward, Samuel (d. 1839)	X
Wanamaker, Reuben Melville	X	Ward, Samuel (d. 1884)	X
Waner, Paul Glee	7	Ward, Samuel Ringgold	X
Wanless, William James	X	Ward, Thomas	X
Wanton, Joseph	X	Ward, Thomas Wren	X
Warbasse, James Peter	6	Ward, William Hayes	X
Warburg, Felix Moritz	2	Warde, Frederick Barkham	1
Warburg, Paul Moritz	X	Warden, David Bailie	X
Ward, Aaron Montgomery	X	Warden, Robert Bruce	X
Ward, Arch Burdette	5	Warder, John Aston	X
Ward, Artemas	X	Wardman, Ervin	X
Ward, Artemus		Ware, Ashur	X
See Browne, Charles		Ware, Edmund Asa	X
Farrar		Ware, Henry (b. 1764)	X
Ward, Charles Alfred	5	Ware, Henry (b. 1794)	X
Ward, Charles Henshaw	1	Ware, John	X
Ward, Cyrenus Osborne	X	Ware, John Fothergill	
Ward, Elizabeth Stuart Phelps	X	Waterhouse	X
Ward, Frederick Townsend	X	Ware, Nathaniel A.	X
Ward, Genevieve	X	Ware, William	X
Ward, George Gray	X	Ware, William Robert	X
Ward, Henry Augustus	X	Warfield, Benjamin	
Ward, Henry Baldwin	3	Breckinridge	X
Ward, Henry Dana	X	Warfield, Catherine Ann Ware	X
Ward, Herbert Dickinson	X	Warfield, David	5
Ward, James Edward	X	Warfield, Solomon Davies	X
Ward, James Harmon	X	Waring, George Edwin	X
Ward, James Warner	X	Warman, Cy	X
Ward, John Elliott	X	Warmoth, Henry Clay	X
Ward, John Quincy Adams	X	Warner, Adoniram Judson	X
Ward, Joseph	X	Warner, Amos Griswold	X

Complete Index Guide

Name	Vol./Supp.	Name	Vol./Supp.
Warner, Anna Bartlett	X	Warren, William Fairfield	X
Warner, Anne Richmond	X	Warrington, Albert Powell	2
Warner, Charles Dudley	X	Warrington, Lewis	X
Warner, Edward Pearson	6	Warthin, Aldred Scott	X
Warner, Fred Maltby	X	Washakie	X
Warner, Glenn Scobey ("Pop")	5	Washburn, Albert Henry	X
Warner, Harry Morris	6	Washburn, Cadwallader Colden	X
Warner, Hiram	X	Washburn, Charles Grenfill	X
Warner, James Cartwright	X	Washburn, Edward Abiel	X
Warner, Jonathan Trumbull	X	Washburn, Edward Wight	X
Warner, Juan José		Washburn, Elihu Benjamin	
See Warner, Jonathan		See Washburne, Elihu	
Trumbull		Benjamin	
Warner, Langdon	5	Washburn, Emory	X
Warner, Olin Levi	X	Washburn, George	X
Warner, Seth	X	Washburn, Ichabod	X
Warner, Susan Bogert	X	Washburn, Israel	X
Warner, William	X	Washburn, Margaret Floy	2
Warner, Worcester Reed	X	Washburn, Nathan	X
Warren, Charles	5	Washburn, William Drew	X
Warren, Cyrus Moors	X	Washburne, Elihu Benjamin	X
Warren, Francis Emroy	X	Washington, Booker Taliaferro	X
Warren, George Frederick	2	Washington, Bushrod	X
Warren, Gouverneur Kemble	X	Washington, Dinah	7
Warren, Henry Clarke	X	Washington, George	X
Warren, Henry Ellis	6	Washington, Henry Stephens	X
Warren, Henry White	X	Washington, John Macrae	X
Warren, Herbert Langford	1	Waterhouse, Benjamin	X
Warren, Howard Crosby	X	Waterhouse, Frank	X
Warren, Israel Perkins	X	Waterhouse, Sylvester	X
Warren, James	X	Waterman, Lewis Edson	X
Warren, John	X	Waterman, Robert H.	X
Warren, John Collins (d. 1856)	X	Waterman, Thomas Whitney	X
Warren, John Collins (d. 1927)	X	Waters, Daniel	X
Warren, Joseph	X	Waters, William Everett	X
Warren, Josiah	X	Watie, Stand	X
Warren, Leonard	6	Watkins, George Claiborne	X
Warren, Mercy Otis	X	Watkins, John Elfreth	X
Warren, Minton	X	Watson, Andrew	X
Warren, Sir Peter	X	Watson, Charles Roger	4
Warren, Richard Henry	X	Watson, David Thompson	X
Warren, Russell	X	Watson, Elkanah	X
Warren, Samuel Prowse	X	Watson, Henry Clay	X
Warren, William (d. 1832)	X	Watson, Henry Cood	X
Warren, William (d. 1888)	X	Watson, James Craig	X

Complete Index Guide

Name	Vol./Supp.	Name	Vol./Supp.
Watson, James Eli	4	Webb, William Robert	X
Watson, James Madison	X	Webber, Charles Wilkins	X
Watson, John Broadus	6	Webber, Herbert John	4.
Watson, John Crittenden	X	Weber, Albert	X
Watson, John Fanning	X	Weber, Gustav Carl Erich	X
Watson, John William Clark	X	Weber, Henry Adam	X
Watson, Sereno	X	Weber, Joseph Morris	3
Watson, Thomas Augustus	X	Weber, Max	7
Watson, Thomas Edward	X	Webster, Alice Jane Chandler	X
Watson, Thomas John	6	Webster, Arthur Gordon	X
Watson, William	X	Webster, Daniel	X
Watterson, Harvey Magee	X	Webster, Edwin Sibley	
Watterson, Henry	X	See under Stone, Charles	
Watterston, George	X	Augustus	
Watts, Frederick	X	Webster, Harold Tucker	5
Watts, Thomas Hill	X	Webster, Jean	
Wattson, Lewis Thomas		See Webster, Alice Jane	
See Francis, Paul James		Chandler	
Waugh, Beverly	X	Webster, John White	X
Waugh, Frederick Judd	2	Webster, Joseph Dana	X
Wayland, Francis (d. 1865)	X	Webster, Noah	X
Wayland, Francis (d. 1904)	X	Webster, Pelatiah	X
Waymack, William Wesley	6	Webster-Powell, Alma	
Wayman, Alexander Walker	X	See Powell, Alma Webster	
Waymouth, George	X	Weddell, Alexander Wilbourne	4
Wayne, Anthony	X	Weed, Lewis Hill	5
Wayne, Arthur Trezevant	X	Weed, Thurlow	X
Wayne, James Moore	X	Weeden, William Babcock	X
Weare, Meshech	X	Weeks, Edwin Lord	X
Weatherford, William	X	Weeks, John Elmer	4
Weaver, Aaron Ward	X	Weeks, John Wingate	X
Weaver, James Baird	X	Weeks, Joseph Dame	X
Weaver, Philip	X	Weeks, Stephen Beauregard	X
Weaver, William Dixon	X	Weems, Mason Locke	X
Webb, Alexander Stewart	X	Weems, Ted	7
Webb, Charles Henry	X	Wegmann, Edward	1
Webb, Daniel	X	Wehle, Louis Brandeis	6
Webb, George James	X	Weidenmann, Jacob	X
Webb, Harry Howard	2	Weidenreich, Franz	4
Webb, James Watson	X	Weidig, Adolf	X
Webb, John Burkitt	X	Weidner, Revere Franklin	X
Webb, Thomas	X	Weigel, Gustave	7
Webb, Thomas Smith	X	Weightman, William	X
Webb, Walter Prescott	7	Weil, Richard	X
Webb, William Henry	X	Weill, Kurt	4

Complete Index Guide

Name	Vol./Supp.	Name	Vol./Supp.
Weir, Ernest Tener	6	Wells, Samuel Roberts	X
Weir, John Ferguson	X	Wells, William Charles	X
Weir, Julian Alden	X	Wells, William Harvey	X
Weir, Robert Fulton	X	Wells, William Vincent	X
Weir, Robert Walter	X	Welsh, John	X
Weisenburg, Theodore Herman	X	Wemyss, Francis Courtney	X
Weiser, Johann Conrad	X	Wende, Ernest	X
Weiss, Ehrich		Wende, Grover William	X
See Houdini, Harry		Wendell, Barrett	X
Weiss, John	X	Wendte, Charles William	X
Weiss, Sonia	3	Wenley, Robert Mark	X
Weitzel, Godfrey	X	Wenner, George Unangst	X
Welby, Amelia Ball Coppuck	X	Wentworth, Benning	X
Welch, Adonijah Strong	X	Wentworth, Cecile de	X
Welch, Ashbel	X	Wentworth, George Albert	X
Welch, Charles Clark	X	Wentworth, John (d. 1820)	X
Welch, John	X	Wentworth, John (d. 1888)	X
Welch, Joseph Nye	6	Wentworth, Paul	X
Welch, Philip Henry	X	Werden, Reed	X
Welch, William Henry	X	Wergeland, Agnes Mathilde	X
Welch, William Wickham	X	Wernwag, Lewis	X
Weld, Arthur Cyril Gordon	X	Wertenbaker, Charles Christian	5
Weld, Theodore Dwight	X	Wertheimer, Max	3
Weld, Thomas	X	Wesbrook, Frank Fairchild	X
Welker, Herman	6	Wesselhoeft, Conrad	X
Weller, John B.	X	Wesselhoeft, Walter	X
Welles, Benjamin Sumner	7	Wesson, Daniel Baird	X
Welles, Gideon	X	West, Allen Brown	2
Welles, Noah	X	West, Andrew Fleming	3
Welles, Roger	X	West, Benjamin (b. 1728)	X
Welling, James Clarke	X	West, Benjamin (b. 1730)	X
Welling, Richard Ward Greene	4	West, Francis	X
Wellington, Arthur Mellen	X	West, George	X
Wellman, Samuel Thomas	X	West, Henry Sergeant	X
Wellman, Walter	X	West, James Edward	4
Wellons, William Brock	X	West, Joseph	X
Wells, David Ames	X	West, Oswald	6
Wells, Erastus	X	West, Roy Owen	6
Wells, Harriet Sheldon	7	West, Samuel	X
Wells, Harry Gideon	3	West, William Edward	X
Wells, Henry	X	Westcott, Edward Noyes	X
Wells, Horace	X	Westcott, Thompson	X
Wells, James Madison	X	Westergaard, Harold Malcolm	4
Wells, John	X	Westermann, William Linn	5
Wells, Robert William	X	Western, Lucille	X

Complete Index Guide

Name	Vol./Supp.
Westervelt, Jacob Aaron	X
Westinghouse, George	X
Westley, Helen	3
Weston, Edward	2
Weston, Edward Henry	6
Weston, Edward Payson	X
Weston, Nathan Austin	X
Weston, Thomas	X
Weston, William	X
Wetherill, Charles Mayer	X
Wetherill, Samuel (d. 1816)	X
Wetherill, Samuel (d. 1890)	X
Wetzel, Lewis	X
Wexler, Irving	5
Weyerhaeuser, Frederick Edward	3
Weyl, Hermann	5
Weymouth, Frank Elwin	3
Whalen, Grover Aloysius	7
Whalley, Edward	X
Wharton, Anne Hollingsworth	X
Wharton, Charles Henry	X
Wharton, Edith Newbold Jones	2
Wharton, Francis	X
Wharton, Greene Lawrence	X
Wharton, Joseph	X
Wharton, Richard	X
Wharton, Robert	X
Wharton, Samuel	X
Wharton, Thomas	X
Wharton, Thomas Isaac	X
Wharton, William H.	X
Whatcoat, Richard	X
Wheatley, Phillis	X
Wheatley, William	X
Wheaton, Frank	X
Wheaton, Henry	X
Wheaton, Nathaniel Sheldon	X
Whedon, Daniel Denison	X
Wheeler, Andrew Carpenter	X
Wheeler, Arthur Leslie	1
Wheeler, Benjamin Ide	X
Wheeler, Everett Pepperrell	X
Wheeler, George Montague	X
Wheeler, (George) Post	6
Wheeler, George Wakeman	X
Wheeler, James Rignall	X
Wheeler, John Hill	X
Wheeler, John Martin	2
Wheeler, Joseph	X
Wheeler, Nathaniel	X
Wheeler, Royall Tyler	X
Wheeler, Schuyler Skaats	X
Wheeler, Wayne Bidwell	X
Wheeler, William	X
Wheeler, William Adolphus	X
Wheeler, William Almon	X
Wheeler, William Morton	2
Wheelock, Eleazar	X
Wheelock, John	X
Wheelock, Joseph Albert	X
Wheelock, Lucy	4
Wheelwright, Edmund March	X
Wheelwright, John	X
Wheelwright, Mary Cabot	6
Wheelwright, William	X
Wheery, Elwood Morris	X
Whelpley, Henry Milton	X
Wherry, Kenneth Spicer	5
Whetzel, Herbert Hice	3
Whipple, Abraham	X
Whipple, Amiel Weeks	X
Whipple, Edwin Percy	X
Whipple, Frances Harriet See Green, Frances Harriet Whipple	
Whipple, Henry Benjamin	X
Whipple, Sherman Leland	X
Whipple, Squire	X
Whipple, William	X
Whistler, George Washington	X
Whistler, James Abbott McNeill	X
Whitaker, Alexander	X
Whitaker, Charles Harris	2
Whitaker, Daniel Kimball	X
Whitaker, Nathaniel	X
Whitcher, Frances Miriam Berry	X
Whitcomb, James	X

Complete Index Guide

Name	Vol./Supp.	Name	Vol./Supp.
Whitcomb, Seldon Lincoln	X	White, Thomas Willis	X
White, Albert Smith	X	White, Walter Francis	5
White, Alexander (d. 1804)	X	White, William	X
White, Alexander (d. 1872)	X	White, William Alanson	2
White, Alfred Tredway	X	White, William Allen	3
White, Alma Kent	4	White, William Nathaniel	X
White, Andrew	X	White Eyes	X
White, Andrew Dickson	X	Whitefield, George	X
White, Benjamin Franklin	6	Whitehead, Alfred North	4
White, Canvass	X	Whitehead, Wilbur Cherrier	X
White, Charles Abiathar	X	Whitehead, William Adee	X
White, Charles Ignatius	X	Whitehill, Clarence Eugene	X
White, Clarence Cameron	6	Whitehill, Robert	X
White, David	1	Whitehouse, Frederic Cope	X
White, Edward Douglass		Whiteside, Arthur Dare	6
(d. 1847)	X	Whitfield, Henry	X
White, Edward Douglass		Whitfield, Owen	7
(d. 1921)	X	Whitfield, Robert Parr	X
White, Ellen Gould Harmon	X	Whiting, Arthur Battelle	2
White, Emerson Elbridge	X	Whiting, Charles Goodrich	X
White, George	X	Whiting, George Elbridge	X
White, George Leonard	X	Whiting, William	1
White, Henry (d. 1786)	X	Whiting, William Henry Chase	X
White, Henry (d. 1927)	X	Whitlock, Brand	X
White, Henry Clay	X	Whitman, Albery Allson	X
White, Horace	X	Whitman, Charles Otis	X
White, Hugh Lawson	X	Whitman, Charles Seymour	4
White, Israel Charles	X	Whitman, Ezekiel	X
White, James	X	Whitman, Marcus	X
White, James Clarke	X	Whitman, Royal	4
White, James William	X	Whitman, Sarah Helen Power	X
White, John	X	Whitman, Walt	X
White, John Blake	X	Whitmer, David	X
White, John De Haven	X	Whitmore, Frank Clifford	4
White, John Williams	X	Whitmore, William Henry	X
White, Joseph Malachy	6	Whitney, Adeline Dutton	
White, Leonard Dupee	6	Train	X
White, Pearl	2	Whitney, Alexander Fell	4
White, Richard Grant	X	Whitney, Anne	X
White, Samuel	X	Whitney, Asa (b. 1741)	X
White, Samuel Stockton	X	Whitney, Asa (b. 1797)	X
White, Stanford	X	Whitney, Caspar	1
White, Stephen Mallory	X	Whitney, Charlotte Anita	5
White, Stephen Van Culen	X	Whitney, Eli	X
White, Steward Edward	4	Whitney, George	7

Complete Index Guide

Name	Vol./Supp.	Name	Vol./Supp.
Whitney, Gertrude Vanderbilt	3	Wiggins, Carleton	X
Whitney, Harry Payne	X	Wigglesworth, Edward	
Whitney, James Lyman	X	(d. 1765)	X
Whitney, Josiah Dwight	X	Wigglesworth, Edward	
Whitney, Mary Watson	X	(d. 1794)	X
Whitney, Myron William	X	Wigglesworth, Edward	
Whitney, William Collins	X	(d. 1896)	X
Whitney, William Dwight	X	Wigglesworth, Michael	X
Whitney, Willis Rodney	6	Wight, Frederick Coit	X
Whiton, James Morris	X	Wight, Peter Bonnett	X
Whitsitt, William Heth	X	Wigmore, John Henry	3
Whittelsey, Abigail Goodrich	X	Wignell, Thomas	X
Whittemore, Amos	X	Wikoff, Henry	X
Whittemore, Thomas	X	Wilbur, Cressy Livingston	X
Whittemore, Thomas	4	Wilbur, Curtis Dwight	5
Whittier, John Greenleaf	X	Wilbur, Hervey Backus	X
Whittingham, William		Wilbur, John	X
Rollinson	X	Wilbur, Ray Lyman	4
Whittredge, Worthington	X	Wilbur, Samuel	X
Whitworth, George Frederic	X	Wilcox, Cadmus Marcellus	X
Whorf, Benjamin Lee	3	Wilcox, Delos Franklin	X
Whyte, William Pinkney	X	Wilcox, Ella Wheeler	X
Wickersham, George		Wilcox, Reynold Webb	X
Woodward	2	Wilcox, Stephen	X
Wickersham, James Pyle	X	Wilczynski, Ernest Julius	X
Wickes, Lambert	X	Wilde, George Francis Faxon	X
Wickes, Stephen	X	Wilde, Richard Henry	X
Wickham, John	X	Wilder, Alexander	X
Wickliffe, Charles Anderson	X	Wilder, Harris Hawthorne	X
Wickliffe, Robert Charles	X	Wilder, John Thomas	X
Wickson, Edward James	X	Wilder, Laura Ingalls	6
Widener, Harry Elkins	X	Wilder, Marshall Pinckney	X
Widener, Peter Arrell Brown	X	Wilder, Russell Morse	6
Widforss, Gunnar Mauritz	X	Wildman, Murray Shipley	X
Widney, Joseph Pomeroy	2	Wildwood, Will	
Wiechmann, Ferdinand		See Pond, Frederick	
Gerhard	X	Eugene	
Wieland, George Reber	5	Wiley, Andrew Jackson	X
Wiener, Leo	2	Wiley, Calvin Henderson	X
Wiener, Norbert	7	Wiley, David	X
Wigfall, Louis Trezevant	X	Wiley, Ephraim Emerson	X
Wigger, Winand Michael	X	Wiley, Harvey Washington	X
Wiggin, Albert Henry	5	Wilkes, Charles	X
Wiggin, James Henry	X	Wilkes, George	X
Wiggin, Kate Douglas	X	Wilkeson, Samuel	X

Complete Index Guide

Name	Vol./Supp.	Name	Vol./Supp.
Wilkie, Franc Bangs	X	Williams, Charles David	X
Wilkins, Ross	X	Williams, Charles Richard	X
Wilkins, William	X	Williams, Daniel Hale	X
Wilkinson, David	X	Williams, David Rogerson	X
Wilkinson, James	X	Williams, Edward Thomas	3
Wilkinson, Jemima	X	Williams, Edwin	X
Wilkinson, Jeremiah	X	Williams, Egbert Austin	
Wilkinson, John	X	See Williams, Bert	
Wilkinson, Robert Shaw	X	Williams, Eleazar	X
Wilkinson, Theodore Stark	4	Williams, Elisha (d. 1755)	X
Will, Allan Sinclair	X	Williams, Elisha (d. 1833)	X
Willard, Daniel	3	Williams, Elkanah	X
Willard, De Forest	X	Williams, Ephraim	X
Willard, Emma Hart	X	Williams, Fannie Barrier	3
Willard, Frances Elizabeth		Williams, Francis Henry	2
Caroline	X	Williams, Frank Martin	X
Willard, Frank Henry	6	Williams, Frederick Wells	X
Willard, James Field	1	Williams, Gaar Campbell	1
Willard, Joseph (d. 1804)	X	Williams, Gardner Fred	X
Willard, Joseph (d. 1865)	X	Williams, George Henry	X
Willard, Joseph Edward	X	Williams, George Huntington	X
Willard, Josiah Flint	1	Williams, George Washington	X
Willard, Mary Hatch	X	Williams, Harrison Charles	5
Willard, Samuel (d. 1707)	X	Williams, Henry Shaler	X
Willard, Samuel (d. 1859)	X	Williams, Henry Willard	X
Willard, Sidney	X	Williams, (Hiram) Hank	5
Willard, Simon (d. 1676)	X	Williams, Israel	X
Willard, Simon (d. 1848)	X	Williams, James	X
Willard, Solomon	X	Williams, James Douglas	X
Willcox, Louise Collier	X	Williams, Jesse Lynch	
Willcox, Orlando Bolivar	X	(d. 1886)	X
Willebrandt, Mabel Walker	7	Williams, Jesse Lynch	
Willet, William	X	(d. 1929)	X
Willett, Herbert Lockwood	3	Williams, John (d. 1729)	X
Willett, Marinus	X	Williams, John (d. 1818)	X
Willey, Samuel Hopkins	X	Williams, John (d. 1837)	X
Willey, Waitman Thomas	X	Williams, John (d. 1899)	X
Williams, Alpheus Starkey	X	Williams, John Elias (d. 1919)	X
Williams, Aubrey Willis	7	Williams, John Elias (d. 1927)	X
Williams, Barney	X	Williams, John Fletcher	X
Williams, Ben Ames	5	Williams, John Foster	X
Williams, Bert	X	Williams, John Joseph	X
Williams, Catharine Read		Williams, John Sharp	X
Arnold	X	Williams, John Skelton	X
Williams, Channing Moore	X	Williams, John Whitridge	X

Complete Index Guide

Name	Vol./Supp.	Name	Vol./Supp.
Williams, Jonathan	X	Wilmarth, Lemuel Everett	X
Williams, Linsly Rudd	X	Wilmer, James Jones	X
Williams, Marshall Jay	X	Wilmer, Joseph Père Bell	X
Williams, Nathaniel	X	Wilmer, Richard Hooker	X
Williams, Otho Holland	X	Wilmer, William Holland	
Williams, Reuel	X	(d. 1827)	X
Williams, Robert	X	Wilmer, William Holland	
Williams, Roger	X	(d. 1936)	2
Williams, Samuel May	X	Wilmot, David	X
Williams, Samuel Wells	X	Wilson, Alexander	X
Williams, Stephen West	X	Wilson, Allen Benjamin	X
Williams, Talcott	X	Wilson, Augusta Jane Evans	
Williams, Thomas Scott	X	See Evans, Augusta Jane	
Williams, Walter	1	Wilson, Bird	X
Williams, William (d. 1811)	X	Wilson, Charles Erwin	7
Williams, William (d. 1850)	X	Wilson, Clarence True	2
Williams, William Carlos	7	Wilson, Edith Bolling	7
Williams, William R.	X	Wilson, Edmund Beecher	2
Williams, William Sherley	X	Wilson, Ernest Henry	X
Williamson, Andrew	X	Wilson, Francis	1
Williamson, Charles	X	Wilson, George Francis	X
Williamson, Hugh	X	Wilson, George Grafton	5
Williamson, Isaac Halsted	X	Wilson, Halsey William	5
Williamson, William Durkee	X	Wilson, Harry Leon	2
Willie, Asa Hoxie	X	Wilson, Henry	X
Willing, Thomas	X	Wilson, Henry Lane	X
Willingham, Robert Josiah	X	Wilson, Henry Parke Custis	X
Willis, Albert Shelby	X	Wilson, Hugh Robert	4
Willis, Bailey	4	Wilson, James (d. 1798)	X
Willis, Henry Parker	2	Wilson, James (d. 1920)	X
Willis, Nathaniel	X	Wilson, James Falconer	X
Willis, Nathaniel Parker	X	Wilson, J(ames) Finley	5
Willis, Olympia Brown		Wilson, James Grant	X
See Brown, Olympia		Wilson, James Harrison	X
Willis, William	X	Wilson, James Southall	7
Williston, Samuel (d. 1874)	X	Wilson, John	X
Williston, Samuel (d. 1963)	7	Wilson, John Fleming	X
Williston, Samuel Wendell	X	Wilson, John Leighton	X
Williston, Seth	X	Wilson, John Lockwood	X
Willkie, Wendell Lewis	3	Wilson, Joseph Miller	X
Willoughby, Westel Woodbury	3	Wilson, Joshua Lacy	X
Wills, Childe Harold	2	Wilson, Louis Blanchard	3
Wills, Harry	6	Wilson, Mortimer	X
Willson, Augustus Everett	X	Wilson, Peter	X
Willys, John North	1	Wilson, Robert Burns	X

Complete Index Guide

Name	Vol./Supp.	Name	Vol./Supp.
Wilson, Samuel	X	Winnemucca, Sarah	X
Wilson, Samuel Graham	X	Winship, Albert Edward	X
Wilson, Samuel Mountford	X	Winship, Blanton	4
Wilson, Samuel Ramsay	X	Winship, George Parker	5
Wilson, Samuel Thomas	X	Winslow, Cameron McRae	X
Wilson, Theodore Delavan	X	Winslow, Charles-Edward	
Wilson, Thomas Woodrow		Amory	6
See Wilson, Woodrow		Winslow, Edward (d. 1655)	X
Wilson, Warren Hugh	2	Winslow, Edward (d. 1753)	X
Wilson, William (d. 1857)	X	Winslow, Edward Francis	X
Wilson, William (d. 1860)	X	Winslow, Hubbard	X
Wilson, William Bauchop	X	Winslow, John	X
Wilson, William Dexter	X	Winslow, John Ancrum	X
Wilson, William Hasell	X	Winslow, John Bradley	X
Wilson, William Lyne	X	Winslow, John Flack	X
Wilson, Woodrow	X	Winslow, Josiah	X
Wiltz, Louis Alfred	X	Winslow, Miron	X
Wimar, Carl	X	Winslow, Sidney Wilmot	X
Wimmer, Boniface	X	Winslow, William Copley	X
Winans, Ross	X	Winsor, Justin	X
Winans, Thomas De Kay	X	Winston, John Anthony	X
Winans, William	X	Winston, Joseph	X
Winant, John Gilbert	4	Winter, William	X
Winchell, Alexander	X	Winthrop, Fitz-John	
Winchell, Horace Vaughn	X	See Winthrop, John	
Winchell, Newton Horace	X	(d. 1707)	
Winchester, Caleb Thomas	X	Winthrop, James	X
Winchester, Elhanan	X	Winthrop, John (d. 1649)	X
Winchester, James	X	Winthrop, John (d. 1676)	X
Winchester, Oliver Fisher	X	Winthrop, John (d. 1707)	X
Winchevsky, Morris	X	Winthrop, John (d. 1779)	X
Winder, John Henry	X	Winthrop, Robert Charles	X
Winder, Levin	X	Winthrop, Theodore	X
Winder, William Henry	X	Winton, Alexander	X
Windom, William	X	Wirt, William	X
Winebrenner, John	X	Wirt, William Albert	2
Wines, Enoch Cobb	X	Wise, Aaron	X
Wines, Frederick Howard	X	Wise, Daniel	X
Wing, Joseph Elwyn	X	Wise, Henry Alexander	X
Wingate, Paine	X	Wise, Henry Augustus	X
Wingfield, Edward Maria	X	Wise, Isaac Mayer	X
Winkler, Edwin Theodore	X	Wise, John (d. 1725)	X
Winlock, Herbert Eustis	4	Wise, John (d. 1879)	X
Winlock, Joseph	X	Wise, John Sergeant	X
Winn, Richard	X	Wise, Stephen Samuel	4

Complete Index Guide

Name	Vol./Supp.	Name	Vol./Supp.
Wise, Thomas Alfred	X	Wood, Edith Elmer	3
Wislizenus, Frederick Adolph	X	Wood, Edward Stickney	X
Wislocki, George Bernays	6	Wood, Fernando	X
Wisner, Henry	X	Wood, Frederick Hill	3
Wissler, Clark	4	Wood, George	X
Wistar, Caspar (d. 1752)	X	Wood, George Bacon	X
Wistar, Caspar (d. 1818)	X	Wood, Grant	3
Wister, Owen	2	Wood, Henry Alexander Wise	2
Wister, Sarah	X	Wood, Horatio Charles	X
Withers, Frederick Clarke	X	Wood, James (d. 1867)	X
Witherspoon, Alexander		Wood, James (d. 1925)	X
Maclaren	7	Wood, James Frederick	X
Witherspoon, Herbert	1	Wood, James J.	X
Witherspoon, John	X	Wood, James Rushmore	X
Witherspoon, John Alexander	X	Wood, Jethro	X
Witmark, Isidore	3	Wood, John	X
Witte, Edwin Emil	6	Wood, John Taylor	X
Witthaus, Rudolph August	X	Wood, Joseph	X
Woerner, John Gabriel	X	Wood, Leonard	X
Wofford, William Tatum	X	Wood, Mary Elizabeth	X
Wolcott, Edward Oliver	X	Wood, Reuben	X
Wolcott, Oliver (d. 1797)	X	Wood, Samuel	X
Wolcott, Oliver (d. 1833)	X	Wood, Sarah Sayward Barrell	
Wolcott, Roger	X	Keating	X
Wolf, George	X	Wood, Thomas	X
Wolf, Henry	X	Wood, Thomas Bond	X
Wolf, Innocent William	X	Wood, Thomas John	X
Wolf, Simon	X	Wood, Walter Abbott	X
Wolfe, Catharine Lorillard	X	Wood, William	X
Wolfe, Harry Kirke	X	Wood, William Burke	X
Wolfe, John David	X	Wood, William Robert	X
Wolfe, Thomas Clayton	2	Woodberry, George Edward	X
Wolff, Kurt August Paul	7	Woodbridge, Frederick James	
Wolfskill, William	X	Eugene	2
Wolfsohn, Carl	X	Woodbridge, John	X
Wolfson, Erwin Service	7	Woodbridge, Samuel Merrill	X
Wolheim, Louis Robert	1	Woodbridge, William	X
Woll, Matthew	6	Woodbridge, William	
Wolle, John Frederick	X	Channing	X
Wolman, Leo	7	Woodbury, Charles Jeptha Hill	X
Wong, Anna May	7	Woodbury, Daniel Phineas	X
Wood, Abraham	X	Woodbury, Helen Laura	
Wood, Casey Albert	3	Sumner	X
Wood, Charles Erskine Scott	3	Woodbury, Isaac Baker	X
Wood, David Duffle	X	Woodbury, Levi	X

Complete Index Guide

Name	Vol./Supp.	Name	Vol./Supp.
Woodford, Stewart Lyndon	X	Woolsey, Theodore Dwight	X
Woodford, William	X	Woolsey, Theodore Salisbury	X
Woodhouse, James	X	Woolson, Abba Louisa Goold	X
Woodhull, Alfred Alexander	X	Woolson, Constance Fenimore	X
Woodhull, Nathaniel	X	Woolworth, Frank Winfield	X
Woodhull, Victoria Claflin	X	Wooster, Charles Whiting	X
Woodin, William Hartman	X	Wooster, David	X
Woodrow, James	X	Wootassite	
Woodruff, Charles Edward	X	See Outacity	
Woodruff, Lorande Loss	4	Wootton, Richens Lacy	X
Woodruff, Theodore Tuttle	X	Worcester, Edwin Dean	X
Woodruff, Timothy Lester	X	Worcester, Elwood	2
Woodruff, Wilford	X	Worcester, Joseph Emerson	X
Woodruff, William Edward	X	Worcester, Noah	X
Woods, Alva	X	Worcester, Samuel	X
Woods, Charles Robert	X	Worcester, Samuel Austin	X
Woods, James Haughton	4	Worden, John Lorimer	X
Woods, Leonard (d. 1854)	X	Work, Henry Clay	X
Woods, Leonard (d. 1878)	X	Work, Hubert	3
Woods, Robert Archey	X	Work, Milton Cooper	X
Woods, William Allen	X	Workman, Fanny Bullock	X
Woods, William Burnham	X	Wormeley, Katharine Prescott	X
Woodson, Carter Godwin	4	Wormeley, Mary Elizabeth	
Woodward, Augustus Brevoort	X	See Latimer, Mary	
Woodward, Calvin Milton	X	Elizabeth Wormeley	
Woodward, Henry	X	Wormley, James	X
Woodward, Joseph Janvier	X	Wormley, Theodore George	X
Woodward, Robert Simpson	X	Worth, Jonathan	X
Woodward, Samuel Bayard	X	Worth, William Jenkins	X
Woodward, William	5	Worthen, Amos Henry	X
Woodworth, Jay Backus	X	Worthen, William Ezra	X
Woodworth, Samuel	X	Worthington, Henry Rossiter	X
Wool, Jolin Ellis	X	Worthington, John	X
Woolf, Benjamin Edward	X	Worthington, Thomas	X
Woollcott, Alexander		Wovoka	X
Humphreys	3	Woytinsky, Wladimir	
Woolley, Celia Parker	X	Savelievich	6
Woolley, Edgar Montillion		Wragg, William	X
("Monty")	7	Wrather, William Embry	7
Woolley, John Granville	X	Wraxall, Peter	X
Woolley, Mary Emma	4	Wright, Benjamin	X
Woolman, John	X	Wright, Carroll Davidson	X
Woolsey, John Munro	3	Wright, Charles	X
Woolsey, Melancthon Taylor	X	Wright, Charles Barstow	X
Woolsey, Sarah Chauncy	X	Wright, Chauncey	X

Complete Index Guide

Name	Vol./Supp.	Name	Vol./Supp.
Wright, Elizur	X	Wyeth, John Allan	X
Wright, Fielding Lewis	6	Wyeth, Nathaniel Jarvis	X
Wright, Frances	X	Wyeth, Newell Convers	3
Wright, Frank Lloyd	6	Wylie, Andrew	X
Wright, George Frederick	X	Wylie, Elinor Morton Hoyt	X
Wright, George Grover	X	Wylie, Robert	X
Wright, Hamilton Kemp	X	Wylie, Samuel Brown	X
Wright, Harold Bell	3	Wyllys, George	X
Wright, Hendrick Bradley	X	Wyman, Horace	X
Wright, Henry (d. 1895)	X	Wyman, Jeffries	X
Wright, Henry (d. 1936)	2	Wyman, Morrill	X
Wright, Horatio Gouverneur	X	Wyman, Robert Harris	X
Wright, James Lendrew	X	Wyman, Seth	X
Wright, John Henry	X	Wythe, George	X
Wright, John Stephen	X		
Wright, Jonathan Jasper	X	Xántus, János	X
Wright, Joseph	X		
Wright, Joseph Albert	X	Yale, Caroline Ardelia	X
Wright, Joseph Jefferson Burr	X	Yale, Elihu	X
Wright, Luke Edward	X	Yale, Linus	X
Wright, Marcus Joseph	X	Yancey, James Edward	5
Wright, Orville	4	Yancey, William Lowndes	X
Wright, Patience Lovell	X	Yandell, David Wendell	X
Wright, Philip Green	X	Yandell, Lunsford Pitts	X
Wright, Richard Nathaniel	6	Yates, Abraham	X
Wright, Richard Robert	4	Yates, John Van Ness	X
Wright, Robert	X	Yates, Matthew Tyson	X
Wright, Robert William	X	Yates, Richard	X
Wright, Silas	X	Yates, Robert	X
Wright, Theodore Lyman	X	Yeadon, Richard	X
Wright, Wilbur	X	Yeager, Joseph	X
Wright, Willard Huntington	2	Yeaman, William Pope	X
Wright, William	X	Yeamans, Sir John	X
Wright, William	1	Yeardley, Sir George	X
Wrigley, William	1	Yeates, Jasper	X
Wrosetasatow		Yeatman, James Erwin	X
See Outacity		Yell, Archibald	X
Wu P'an-Chao		Yellin, Samuel	2
See Ng Poon Chew		Yellowley, Edward Clements	7
Wurtz, Henry	X	Yeomans, John William	X
Wyant, Alexander Helwig	X	Yerger, William	X
Wyatt, Sir Francis	X	Yerkes, Charles Tyson	X
Wyckoff, John Henry	2	Yerkes, Robert Mearns	6
Wyckoff, Walter Augustus	X	Yoakum, Benjamin Franklin	X
Wyeth, John	X	Yoakum, Henderson	X

Complete Index Guide

Name	Vol./Supp.	Name	Vol./Supp.
Yohn, Frederick Coffay	X	Yulee, David Levy	X
Yon, Pietro Alessandro	3	Yung Wing	X
York, Alvin Cullum	7		
Yorke, Peter Christopher	X		
Yost, Casper Salathiel	3	Zach, Max Wilhelm	X
Yost, Fielding Harris	4	Zacharias, Ellis Mark	7
You, Dominique	X	Zachos, John Celivergos	X
Youmans, Edward Livingston	X	Zaharias, Mildred ("Babe")	
Youmans, Vincent	4	Didrikson	6
Youmans, William Jay	X	Zahm, John Augustine	X
Young, Aaron	X	Zahniser, Howard Clinton	7
Young, Alexander	X	Zakrzewska, Marie Elizabeth	X
Young, Alfred	X	Zamorano, Agustin Juan	
Young, Allyn Abbott	X	Vicente	X
Young, Ammi Burnham	1	Zane, Charles Shuster	X
Young, Art	3	Zane, Ebenezer	X
Young, Brigham	X	Zeilin, Jacob	X
Young, Charles Augustus	X	Zeisberger, David	X
Young, Clark Montgomery	X	Zeisler, Fannie Bloomfield	X
Young, David	X	Zeisler, Sigmund	X
Young, Denton True	5	Zellerbach, James David	7
Young, Ella Flagg	X	Zenger, John Peter	X
Young, Ewing	X	Zentmayer, Joseph	X
Young, George	1	Zerrahn, Carl	X
Young, Hugh Hampton	3	Zeuner, Charles	X
Young, Jesse Bowman	X	Zevin, Israel Joseph	X
Young, John	X	Ziegemeier, Henry Joseph	X
Young, John Clarke	X	Ziegfeld, Florenz	X
Young, John Richardson	X	Ziegler, David	X
Young, John Russell	X	Ziegler, William	X
Young, John Wesley	X	Ziehn, Bernhard	X
Young, Josue Maria	X	Ziff, William Bernard	5
Young, Karl	3	Zilboorg, Gregory	6
Young, Lafayette	X	Zimmerman, Eugene (d. 1914)	X
Young, Mahonri Mackintosh	6	Zimmerman, Eugene (d. 1935)	1
Young, Owen D.	7	Zinsser, Hans	2
Young, Pierce Manning Butler	X	Zinzendorf, Nicolaus Ludwig	X
Young, Robert Ralph	6	Znaniecki, Florian Witold	6
Young, Samuel Hall	X	Zogbaum, Rufus Fairchild	X
Young, Stark	7	Zollars, Ely Vaughan	X
Young, Thomas	X	Zollicoffer, Felix Kirk	X
Younger, Maud	2	Zook, George Frederick	5
Younger, Thomas Coleman	X	Zubly, John Joachim	X
Youngs, John	X	Zunser, Eliakum	X
Yount, George Concepcíon	X	Zuppke, Robert Carl	6